Travels in Time

RECENT TITLES IN
STUDIES IN COLLECTIVE MEMORY

Astrid Erll and Jeffrey K. Olick, General Editors

Travels in Time
Essays on Collective Memory in Motion
Astrid Erll

Travels in Time

Essays on Collective Memory in Motion

ASTRID ERLL

OXFORD
UNIVERSITY PRESS

Oxford University Press is a department of the University of Oxford.
It furthers the University's objective of excellence in research, scholarship,
and education by publishing worldwide. Oxford is a registered trade mark of
Oxford University Press in the UK and in certain other countries.

Published in the United States of America by Oxford University Press
198 Madison Avenue, New York, NY 10016, United States of America.

© Oxford University Press 2025

All rights reserved. No part of this publication may be reproduced, stored in a retrieval system, transmitted, used for text and data mining, or used for training artificial intelligence, in any form or by any means, without the prior permission in writing of Oxford University Press, or as expressly permitted by law, by licence or under terms agreed with the appropriate reprographics rights organization. Inquiries concerning reproduction outside the scope of the above should be sent to the Rights Department, Oxford University Press, at the address above

You must not circulate this work in any other form
and you must impose this same condition on any acquirer

CIP data is on file at the Library of Congress

ISBN 9780197767733
ISBN 9780197767740 (pbk.)

DOI: 10.1093/oso/9780197767740.001.0001

Printed by Sheridan Books, Inc., United States of America
Cover image: Johanna Bühler

For Johanna and Jochen

Contents

Introduction: Traveling in Time   1

PART I TRAVELING AND TRANSCULTURAL MEMORY

1. Traveling Memory   15
2. Traveling Memory in European Film   34
3. Homer—A Relational Mnemohistory   52
4. Memory Worlds in Times of Corona   70

PART II MEMORY IN FAMILIES AND GENERATIONS

5. Locating Family in Memory Studies   91
6. Generation in Literary History: Genealogy, Generationality, Memory   113
7. Fictions of Generational Memory: Caryl Phillips's *In the Falling Snow* (2009)   140

PART III MEMORY AND MEDIATION

8. Literature, Film, and the Mediality of Cultural Memory   157
9. Remediation across Time, Space, and Cultures: The Indian Rebellion of 1857–1858   172
10. Plurimediality and Traveling Schemata: "District Six"   203
11. The Ethics of Premediation in James Joyce's *Ulysses*   235

PART IV DIALOGUES WITH PSYCHOLOGY

12. The Hidden Power of Implicit Collective Memory   263

13. Ecologies of Trauma   283

14. Flashbulb Memories: An Interdisciplinary Research Program (with William Hirst)   305

    Afterword: Traveling On   323

Acknowledgments   326
Bibliography   330
Filmography   371
Index   372

Introduction

Traveling in Time

I.1 Collective Memory

In 1985, psychologist Endel Tulving famously defined "remembering" as a form of "mental time travel," which involves projecting ourselves into the past as well as into the future. Collective memory research asks how travel in time is performed not only through neuronal and mental operations, but also through social and mediated ones. This book explores such time traveling in an expanded field.

"Collective memory" has become a household term in the humanities and the social sciences. This was not always the case. After the sociologist Maurice Halbwachs (1925, 1950) coined the term and theorized collective memory in the 1920s, the concept was largely forgotten, only to re-emerge in the 1980s. Critics dismissed the notion of collective memory as a misleading "myth" or a fashionable "boom."[1] But over the past three decades, intensive research worldwide has compellingly demonstrated that collective memory functions as a vital connective tissue—between past, present, and future, between minds and mediations, within and between mnemonic communities.

Collective memory is not so much "a thing" as a tool to think with. It is a tool that helps us understand what it is that makes us remember (or forget) our first day at school, what we learn from our grandmothers, why different nations can entertain vastly different versions of the past, and what kinds of futures we can and cannot envision. It opens a perspective on our world. Collective memory has thus advanced from a promising "sensitizing" term (Olick and Robbins 1998, 112) to a highly generative concept at the heart

---

[1] On collective memory as a "myth," see Gedi and Elam (1996); on the "memory boom," see Huyssen (1995). The full story is in a chapter by Olick (2025), felicitously titled, "Who is afraid of collective memory?"

Travels in Time. Astrid Erll, Oxford University Press. © Oxford University Press (2025).
DOI: 10.1093/oso/9780197767733.003.0001

of a field called memory studies, one that enables and fuels collaborative research across disciplines and continents.[2]

Collective memory is memory. Contrary to popular belief, there is no pre-social or pre-medial pristine "memory in the brain," at least not for the higher cognitive processes such as mental time travel.[3] This is what Halbwachs meant when, in his *Cadres sociaux de la mémoire* (1925), he emphasized that "social frameworks" first make individual memories possible and then shape them deeply. But neither is there a hypostasized "memory of the collectivity," which could be abstracted from the bodies and minds involved in the emergence of representations of the past. Memory is a biological, mental, social, cultural, medial, material, human and nonhuman phenomenon. How to model the co-constructive multidimensionality of collective memory thus remains a fascinating conundrum, occupying multiple scholars in the field of memory studies—from cognitive psychologists to literary historians.[4]

The present book is based on the assumption that the many dimensions of collective memory *cannot* be envisioned as neatly stacked Russian dolls, where we can expect to find similar phenomena reappearing on different scales. The neuronal process of forgetting, for instance, is vastly different from the social dynamics of forgetting in authoritarian regimes. To give another example, the role of language in official national memory is not just a larger version of the role of language in family memory. And last but not least, the memory-identity link does not function for transnational remembering in the same way it does for individual remembering.[5] The dimensions of collective memory, that is, are not built on top of each other as a "great chain of mnemonic being." Instead, they interact and are networked with each other, in uneven and non-analogous ways. What emerges as collective memory is not one unified representation of the past, but rather certain tendencies of bringing past, present, and future in relation, which

---

[2] For handbooks on memory studies, see Erll and Nünning (2010); Kattago (2015); Tota and Hagen (2016); for an introduction to the field, see Erll (2011a). Leading journals include *Memory Studies* (SAGE, since 2008), *Memory, Mind & Media* (Cambridge University Press, since 2022), and the *Memory Studies Review* (Brill, 2024). The international Memory Studies Association was founded in 2016 (https://www.memorystudiesassociation.org/).

[3] For a taxonomy of collective memory that not only includes episodic memory (according to Tulving characterized by a conscious form of time travel), but also semantic and implicit systems, see Chapter 12, "The Hidden Power of Implicit Collective Memory."

[4] Major recent modellations of collective memory were undertaken in sociology (Olick and Robbins 1998), cultural history (J. Assmann 2011 [1992]; A. Assmann 2011 [1999]), literary and media studies (Erll and Rigney 2009), social psychology (Pennebaker et al. 1997), and cognitive psychology (Hirst et al. 2018).

[5] For these arguments, see Chapter 13, "Ecologies of Trauma."

can be identified in individual subjects as well as in mediations or in social interactions.

The essays in this book trace some of these memory-making dynamics. They address the role of cultural, medial, and mental dimensions in the emergence of memories related to the First and Second World Wars, the Holocaust, 9/11, British colonialism in India, and histories of migration, as well as the mythical narrative of the *Odyssey*.

I.2 Travels in Time

Travels

Memory is a capacity and a continuous process. It never stands still, is always becoming, or "in the works" (Rigney 2010a, 345). Memory is characterized by ongoing motion: neuronal activity, emergent mental representations, their externalization and transcription from medium to medium, and the travels of narratives within and across social groups. Memory also moves across time and space. It is because of collective memory that we still know today about Egyptian kings, or that people in Pakistan might remember the fall of the German Wall. This is the logic of traveling memory.[6]

Time

Memory is not only about the past. As current psychological research argues, remembered pasts, perceptions of the present, and imagined futures appear to emerge from one underlying neural and cognitive system, the "simulation system," which is also responsible (uncomfortably perhaps for some) for entirely fictional simulations.[7] This is what medieval philosopher Augustine suggested when he wrote that all we have is "a present of things past, a present of things present and a present of things future."[8] Memory can thus be thought of as a "remembering-imagining system" (RIS, Conway et al.

---

[6] See Erll 2011b and Chapter 1, "Traveling Memory."

[7] Schacter and Addis (2007); Addis (2020). On "mnemicity attribution" to distinguish between remembering and imagining, see Mahr et al. (2023). On collective mental time travel, see Szpunar and Szpunar (2016); Topcu and Hirst (2022); critically, Sutton and Michaelian (2019).

[8] St. Augustine, *The Confessions* (Book 11, Chapter 20). For a theory of history-perspective on the relation between "space of experience" and "horizon of expectation," see Koselleck (2004 [1979]).

2016), and the collective remembering-imagining system relates personal, familial, national, and transnational pasts, presents, and futures.

History

"History" is the elephant in the room of memory studies. Reinhart Koselleck's (2004 [1979]) caveat that history is in fact a "collective singular" is a key premise for all memory research. At least three levels of "history "need to be distinguished: First, there is history as the totality of *past happenings* (the raw, in its entirety unintelligible past); second, there are *historical events* and processes, which are constructed retrospectively through operations of selection, combination, narrativization, and meaning-making,[9] that is, through the active work of humans (and increasingly algorithms); third, there is history as *academic discipline*, and its medium historiography. There is no fundamental opposition between "memory" and "history" once we leave the first level (history-as-the-past) and move to the second (history-as-a-construct-of-the-past). Here, history is memory.[10] Modern academic history is just one particular *mode* of making the past meaningful in the present. Other modes include family memory, religious memory, or aesthetically mediated memory. Nonetheless, academic history remains indispensable. Biases of nationalist historiographies aside and granted the increasing necessity to include various other mnemonic modes and their mediations as historical sources (from oral traditions to social media posts), academic history's commitment to source-criticism and method-driven approaches to the past also characterizes memory studies—especially when it tackles, as many chapters of this book do, "mnemohistories."

Mnemohistory

Jan Assmann famously stated in *Moses the Egyptian* (1997, 9): "Unlike history proper, mnemohistory is concerned not with the past as such, but only with the past as it is remembered." Today, many memory scholars

---

[9] On the narrativization of the past, see White (1973) and Ricœur (1984 [1983]).
[10] On history as a form, or art, of memory, see Burke (1989) and Hutton (1993); on historical consciousness as orientation in time, see Rüsen (2017). See also the *Oxford Handbook of History and Memory* (Kansteiner and Morina, 2025).

would agree, but some might want to delete the "only." The (re)emergences, forgettings, and (ab)uses of the past are not an ancillary, but a vital part of—well—"the past." Memory is history, and it is history that matters enormously.[11]

I.3 Mediation

Mediation is a key factor in the memory process. Collective memory emerges from the ongoing translation of information between minds and mediations. I use the term "mediation of memory" in the broadest possible sense: A gesture or an anecdote can convey the past as much as a monument, an artwork, or a landscape (think of the White Cliffs of Dover), as do media in the more classical sense, such as newspaper articles, TV broadcasts, or social media posts.[12]

But whether eyewitness account, war photography, or historical novel—mediations of memory will remain fruitless, fall through the net of the collective remembering-imagining system without even a plop, if there is nobody to hear, see, or read them. Mediations require *reception* in the minds of individuals in order to become active as collective memory. This process can be utterly delayed in time. Letters may be found thousands of years later; or ethically problematic statues can suddenly be seen anew, after they had appeared invisible to most for decades.[13] This is why the field of memory research necessarily spans communication studies to ancient history.

The memory-making motion between minds and mediations is always situated within a particular media culture. Media cultures are made up of available media technologies and their social uses. The mediation of memory in a preliterate culture will work differently than in societies shaped by broadcast media, or by digital and social media. This is a question not only of media history, but also of specific sociopolitical constellations that impact

---

[11] On mnemohistory, see also Tamm (2015). In this book, Chapter 9 ("Remediation across Time, Space, and Cultures: The Indian Rebellion of 1857–1858") in particular shows how historical sources are usually no more than mnemohistorical sources temporally close to the event (emerging, e.g., from the collective memory of administrators or eyewitnesses). All history is mnemohistory.
[12] See Chapter 8, "Literature, Film, and the Mediality of Cultural Memory."
[13] For current research on de-commemoration, see Gensburger and Wüstenberg (2023); Rigney (2023).

education, censorship, or accessibility. Collective memory made on TikTok unfolds a different dynamic in Great Britain and China.

A media culture perspective on collective memory, moreover, brings its own logic to travels in time: Memory mediations—from letters carved in stone to Netflix series—are never singular events, but always part of diachronic processes of remediation and premediation (Erll and Rigney 2009).[14]

I.4 Terminology

The focus of this book is on the role of media culture in the making of collective memory. The simple reason for this accentuation is competence. Its author works in literary, cultural, and media studies. But this also raises an important point for collective memory research: Each memory scholar will have their particular "entry portal" to the complex process of collective memory, as far as materials and methodologies are concerned. No one can "do it all." This is why memory studies is constitutionally an interdisciplinary field. We all need to bring our pieces to the multidimensional puzzle, and ideally engage in the work of translation and connection.

One outcome of the prodigious multidisciplinary endeavor of memory studies is a multiplicity of terminology. In this book, "collective memory" is used as a cover term for the overall memory process. However, sociologists tend to speak about "social memory," and in many of the following essays, the term "cultural memory" will feature strongly. These designators do not so much characterize a *type of* memory; rather, they describe a particular *approach to* memory. They do not provide an answer to the question of what memory "really is," but show from what angle it is temporarily seen. Thus, "cultural memory" is a shorthand for an interest in the cultural and media aspects of collective memory. Similarly, "transcultural memory" flags an approach that ventures beyond memories shared within sociocultural groups. "Digital memory" indicates a curiosity about dimensions of remembering and forgetting brought about by digital technologies. A simple way to deal with the terminological maze of memory studies is to feel comfortable with this fuzziness. After all, even "collective memory" is no more than a

---

[14] On the dynamics of remediation and premediation, see the chapters in Part II, "Memory and Mediation."

designator of a standpoint. It shows that research is interested in the more-than-neuronal-and-mental dimensions of memory. At the end of the day, it is all "memory."

I.5 Violence

Memory studies today has a pronounced emphasis on the violent aspects of pasts that continue to haunt.[15] This book, too, addresses colonial warfare, the First and Second World Wars, the Holocaust, South African apartheid, 9/11, and the Russian War in Ukraine. It studies not only memory *after* violence (the commemoration and remediation of violent histories), but also memory *before* violence (narratives and images of the past that pre-shape the next act of violence).

Yet at the same time, it needs to be emphasized that collective memory is not a violence-recording-and-making machine, but it is—more fundamentally—the very capacity to orient ourselves in time and within our sociocultural environments. Moreover, collective memory does not necessarily remain transfixed by violent pasts, but as a remembering-imagining system it provides the very resources to envisage different futures and thus change the path of history.[16]

I.6 Odyssey

This collection has several leitmotifs woven through its essays. One is the World Wars and how they were remembered in novels and films across the past century. Another is colonial and postcolonial memories, in particular of the Indian rebellion of 1857–1858. A third leitmotif is—surprisingly perhaps—the *Odyssey*.

The Homeric epics are not about historically verifiable events and existents (as Plato already complained in *The State*). Thinking with the *Odyssey* confirms that elements of collective memory can be strictly "historical" in

---

[15] This at least is the research lens of humanities and social science quarters of memory studies, not so much that of the psychology of collective memory. On commonalities and differences between research on collective memory in psychology, on the one hand, and in the humanities and social sciences, on the other, see Erll and Hirst (2025).

[16] This vital futurity of collective memory is particularly relevant in the recent "turns" of the field of memory studies: the "transcultural," "activist," and "environmental" turns (see also Chapter 1, "Traveling Memory").

the modern sense, but also mythical, or purely imaginary. No matter what their provenance, memory narratives fulfill similar functions for collective identities, values and norms, and orientation in time (see J. Assmann 2011 [1992]). The Homeric epics have proven to be particularly powerful memory narratives, standing today (however erroneously) for the "fundaments of Western civilization."[17] What makes them media of memory is the impact they had over millennia as narratives that people both remembered and "remembered with" (i.e., using their patterns to craft new memories, as Virgil did in his *Aeneid* to construct a narrative about the Roman past).

The mnemohistory of the *Odyssey* exemplifies travels in time par excellence. The *Odyssey* is an epic about movement and the passing of time (only after twenty years can Odysseus return to his Penelope). And it has traveled widely, over circa 3,000 years, passing through ancient, medieval, and modern memory regimes, as well as virtually across the globe—often as a transformative power.[18] The "Odysseys" that we see today (in translation, in Caribbean literature, on Instagram, or in the discourse about refugees in the Mediterranean) are the result of a *longue durée* mnemohistory, that is, a history of remembering and forgetting stretching over centuries and millennia. This is also a history of mediation and remediation, from an oral-performative tradition across ancient Greek city-states to Egyptian papyri, Byzantine handwritten manuscripts, Irish rewritings (such as Joyce's *Ulysses*), and to today's digital remediations.[19]

Longue durée mnemohistories such as the *Odyssey*'s reveal the double logic of collective memory as an operation that proceeds from a present moment, yet is at the same time shaped by multiple pasts. As Halbwachs already stated:

> A remembrance is in very large measure a reconstruction of the past achieved with data borrowed from the present, a reconstruction prepared, furthermore, by reconstructions of earlier periods wherein past images had already been altered. (Halbwachs 1980 [1950], 68)

---

[17] For a critique of this simplified genealogy, see Chapter 3, "Homer—A Relational Mnemohistory."

[18] On the "game-changing energy" of Homeric memory, see Erll (2024a).

[19] Some glimpses at this Odyssean mnemohistory are provided in Chapter 3, "Homer—A Relational Mnemohistory"; Chapter 11, "The Ethics of Premediation in James Joyce's *Ulysses*"; and in Chapter 13, "Ecologies of Trauma."

The study of collective memory therefore requires both a *presentist* lens (as each act of memory takes place in a particular present and is influenced by current knowledges, interests, and concerns) and a *historicist* lens, attuned to memory's path-dependencies (Olick 2016, 60), jumps and breaks in the mnemonic process across time and space. The travels of collective memory are not a simple one-way trip. They are more like Odyssean travels.

I.7 This Book

The chapters in this book are organized in four parts. Part I ("Traveling and Transcultural Memory") showcases memory research after the so-called transcultural turn around 2010. Moving away from nation-centered memory research (exemplified by the "sites of memory" approach championed by Pierre Nora), new memory studies looked at mnemonic processes unfolding across different nations, ethnicities, religions, or languages. The globalizing memory of the Holocaust is the best-researched instance of traveling memory. But South African apartheid, the Argentinian "Nunca Mas!," "#MeToo," and memories of the transatlantic slave trade also have left their mnemonic locations and have become active elsewhere. Part I theorizes "Traveling Memory" (Chapter 1). It shows how traveling memory in Europe is reflected and constructed in films (Chapter 2). It discusses the *Odyssey* as a *longue durée* traveling memory and reveals its constitutively relational dynamics (Chapter 3). And it considers the logics of global collective memory before, during, and after the Coronavirus pandemic (Chapter 4).

Part II ("Memory in Families and Generations") zooms in on the family as a framework of collective memory. After a theoretical introduction to the place of "family" in memory studies, which also features an in-depth discussion of Maurice Halbwachs (Chapter 5), the attention turns towards questions of "generation." Chapter 6 discusses "generation" and "genealogy" as both biological and cultural phenomena. It uses media representations of the First World War's "lost generation" (in the novel and film *All Quiet on the Western Front*), post-memories of the Holocaust, and problems of genealogy in British and American migratory settings as examples to think through the nexus of generation and collective memory. In Chapter 7, the interest in generation and genealogy after slavery, migration, and in light of continued racism in European societies informs the close reading of Caryl Phillips's novel *In the Falling Snow* (2009).

Part III ("Memory and Mediation") addresses the logics of mediation in the memory process. Chapter 8 is an important node of the book in that it introduces the key concepts of a mediation-oriented "cultural memory studies." It discusses "remediation," "premediation," and "plurimedial constellations" as methodological tools of memory research, which provide insight into the circulation, strength, and work of memory mediations at particular times and places. Using the Indian rebellion of 1857–1858 against British rule as an example, Chapter 9 shows how a focus on the mediations and remediations of violence (from witness accounts to imperial historiography, the Indian novel, and Bollywood) can throw light on the dynamics of colonial and postcolonial memory cultures. Chapter 10 turns to South Africa and asks how Cape Town's "District Six" became a transnational schema of remembering apartheid in urban space and the loss of multicultural communities. Again, the methodology consists in analyzing the logic of plurimedial constellations, which range, in this case, from literary and life writings to iconic photography and to alien movies. Chapter 11 offers the book's second close reading. It shows how James Joyce's modernist classic *Ulysses* (1922) stages and problematizes the ethics of premediation, that is, the preformation of experience and action by racist and anti-Semitic schemata derived from mediated collective memory. It also asks how the novel can be understood as premediated by the *Odyssey*.

Part IV ("Dialogues with Psychology") comes back to the basic idea that collective memory means travels in time and emerges from the interaction between minds and mediations. Studying such phenomena requires interdisciplinarity. While memory studies can look back on intensive and productive interdisciplinary collaboration between sociology, history, and literary, cultural, and media studies, the dialogue with psychology remains one of the field's most underdeveloped arenas of exchange—yet arguably should be one of its most pressing concerns. Part IV makes three forays into such a dialogical space: Chapter 12 traces "The Hidden Power of Implicit Collective Memory" by bringing together research on priming derived from cognitive psychology with concepts of framing and priming in communication studies and a mnemohistorical perspective on premediation. Chapter 13 addresses "Ecologies of Trauma." It critically discusses the sociological constructivist theory of "cultural trauma." To avoid the "analogical trap" that lurks in attempts in memory research to link the mental and the social, it draws on cognitive philosophy's "extended mind" and new materialist concepts of "assemblage." The *Odyssey* makes a third and last appearance in this chapter—as a powerful transtemporal trauma narrative. The final chapter (Chapter 14) starts from the realization that interdisciplinary memory research is best practiced in joint projects. Together with William Hirst, professor of cognitive psychology at the New School in New York and one of the most prominent proponents of collective memory research from the field of psychology, I lay out a research program for the study of flashbulb memories (that is, the seemingly highly accurate memories we retain of emotionally charged public events, such as 9/11), from both cognitive and cultural perspectives. It is from such dialogues that I hope collective memory research will continue to travel in the future.

PART I
TRAVELING AND TRANSCULTURAL MEMORY

Chapter 1
Traveling Memory

1.1 Whither Memory Studies?

Es wurde schon alles gesagt, nur noch nicht von jedem—"everything has already been said, just not yet by everyone." It is in the spirit of this famous saying by the comedian Karl Valentin that observers and critics of memory studies today tend to sum up the state of the field.[1]

And indeed, after a two-decade frenzy of research, we have charted the sites of memory of not only France, but also Germany, Italy, the Netherlands, Belgium, and the United States, as well as Okinawa, Cape Town, and Latin America. We have been given insight into forms of remembrance in ancient Egypt, in medieval Europe, and into the memory of the modern. We know how the invention of tradition leads to the creation of identities and to political legitimation. And we have certainly gained deeper insight into issues of war, genocide, trauma, and reconciliation with a specific focus on memory.

With the methodology at hand, memory studies will easily be able to keep generations of scholars busy, charting the mnemomic practices of all ages and places. However, the question arises whether "memory" is thus turning into a mere "stencil," and memory studies into an additive project: we add yet another site of memory, we address yet another historical injustice. While such memory work is for many historical, political, and ethical reasons an important activity, memory research finds itself faced with the decisive question of how it envisages its future. Since its beginnings in the early twentieth century, memory studies has developed into a vital and vigorous interdisciplinary and international research field, which stretches across the

---

[1] "Traveling Memory" was originally published in 2011—at a time when critical observers assumed that the preoccupation with collective memory had reached a point of saturation. This essay contended that the opposite was the case. In retrospect, "Traveling Memory" (Erll 2011b) was part of a significant "turn" in memory studies, which led to new collaborative and international research on transcultural, transnational, and globalizing memory. See also Bond and Rapson (2014); Crownshaw (2011a); De Cesari and Rigney (2014).

Travels in Time. Astrid Erll, Oxford University Press. © Oxford University Press (2025).
DOI: 10.1093/oso/9780197767733.003.0002

humanities and the social sciences all the way to the natural sciences.[2] As a long-standing academic polylogue, and with the degree of exchange and synergy already gained between different disciplines and across methodological and linguistic borders, memory studies seems ideally suited to address new questions emerging from new developments and challenges—questions, for example, about the relation of nature and culture, about globalization and its discontents, and about the futures that we envision.

In short, after a first phase of research on cultural memory, which took place in the early twentieth century (with Maurice Halbwachs, Aby Warburg, Walter Benjamin, and Frederic Bartlett as some key protagonists), and a second phase roughly starting with Pierre Nora's (1984–1992) publication of *Les lieux de mémoire*—will there be a third phase of memory studies? Or will the field continue in the mode established since the mid-1980s?

The question now seems to be "whither memory studies?" In his article entitled "A Looming Crash or a Soft Landing?," Gavriel D. Rosenfeld (2009) articulates one now rather common idea among memory studies' critics about the future prospects of the field, namely that after more than two decades of intensive work done on the Holocaust and the unearthing of historical injustices all across the globe, from the Aboriginals' "stolen generation" to apartheid—we have now arrived at a point of saturation with memory. Instead of continuing to deal with the past, such critics argue, we should start looking at the present and future. Rosenfeld (2009, 147) considers 9/11 as the tipping point and the beginning of the demise of memory studies, summarizing: "In such a world, the study of memory . . . may increasingly appear to be a luxury that a new era of crisis can ill afford."

I would rather claim the opposite: today (and whether this is more an era of crisis than any other age is also open to debate) we cannot afford the luxury of not studying memory. If we want to understand 9/11, the actions of Islamic terrorists, or the reactions of the West, we must naturally look at certain mental, discursive, and habitual paradigms that were formed in long historical processes—via cultural memory, as it were. We must try to understand the different ways in which people handle time, and this not only refers to their "working through the past," but also includes their understanding of the present and visions for the future. If we want to get our heads around, as Rosenfeld suggests, current wars in Afghanistan,

---

[2] For an overview of the history and disciplines of memory studies, see Erll (2011a). For a reader of key texts, see Olick et al. (2010).

Iraq, and on the African continent, the rise of China and India, global warming—and especially around the ways that people make sense of these experiences and from there begin to deal with them (or fail to do so)—then we have to acknowledge that many of the "hard facts" of what we encounter as economy, power politics, or environmental issues are at least partly the result of "soft factors," of cultural processes grounded in cultural memory.

However, I would also claim that it is rather difficult to address these issues with the methodological tools that memory studies has at hand now. One reason for this lies in a choice that scholars of the "second phase" made, namely, conceiving of the field essentially as *cultural* memory studies (see Erll and Nünning 2010).

In using the term "cultural memory studies," we need to be aware of the fact that there are conspicuous national and disciplinary differences in the current debate: in Germany, for example, there is a rather rigorous definition of the term (*das kulturelle Gedächtnis*), which was introduced by Aleida and Jan Assmann and in which concepts of anthropology and media history play a significant role (see Assmann 2010). In the United States, there seems to be no unified theory, but a trend toward looking at aesthetic media, popular and mass culture, when the adjective "cultural" is applied to "memory" (as testified, for example, by Marita Sturken's definition in *Tangled Memories*, 1997). In Britain, memory studies emerged out of, and is institutionally still part of, British cultural studies in the tradition of the Birmingham school. Its scholarship is characterized by Marxist and psychoanalytical approaches (see, e.g., Radstone and Hodkin 2003).

Rather than address such specific, and conceptually often quite elaborate, notions of cultural memory, I will, in the following, challenge some of the implicit ideas of culture that have slipped into the now virtually worldwide preoccupation with memory, especially in the wake of Pierre Nora's influential model of *lieux de mémoire*.

1.2 From "Memory in Culture" to the "Memories of Cultures"

What, then, is the problem with culture? While ever since the inception of memory studies in the 1920s, "culture" in the singular has proved a leading, and in many different ways illuminating, concept for the field, more recently an oversimplifying notion of "cultures" in the plural has crept into the discourse on memory and has acted as an often misleading and obfuscating category.

The emergence of the new memory studies in the 1980s and 1990s can be seen as part of the larger movement of refashioning the humanities as the study of culture. "Culture" was then understood in a broad sense. Symbolic anthropology described it as a way of life which is based on shared knowledge and beliefs that become manifest in social organization, habits, and the material world (Geertz 1973). Even more fundamentally, in the early twentieth century, cultural philosophers such as Ernst Cassirer had defined the human being as an *animal symbolicum*, whose universal symbol-making capacity and activity find expression in a range of "symbolic forms" (Cassirer 1944), such as art, religion, law, politics, and economy. In such a perspective, "culture" exists in the singular; its opposite term is "nature." Culture thus defined constitutes the principal research object of the humanities and social sciences.

Studying "memory in culture" may therefore simply mean looking at remembering and forgetting through the lens of the humanities and social sciences, rather than the natural sciences (see Erll 2011a). More specifically, it means turning our attention to the fact that all forms of human remembering (from neuronal processes to media representations) take place within sociocultural contexts, within frameworks made by the *animal symbolicum*. This definition is the one I want to adhere to, because it avoids tying culture—and by extension, cultural memory—to clear-cut territories and social formations.

But what happened then? In much of culture studies in general, and in particular in the field of memory studies, culture became slowly but persistently reified. What was studied was the culture, and the memory, of a social formation: a religious group, a social class, an ethnicity. The focus thus shifted from the dynamics of memory in culture to the specific memories of (allegedly stable and clearly demarcated) cultures, the most popular social unit being the nation-state, which was then swiftly seen as isomorphic with national culture and a national cultural memory. Memory studies thus entered the stage of "national memory studies," which characterized much of the work done in the 1990s.

Pierre Nora's admittedly groundbreaking French *lieux de mémoire* were the catalyst for this phase of national memory studies. In the wake of Nora's project, which was quickly adopted virtually across the globe, cultural memory was reincarnated as, and became synonymous with, national remembrance. The sites-of-memory approach was used as a tool to reconstruct—and at the same time, wittingly or unwittingly, to actively construct—national memory.

There is of course nothing wrong with looking at the nation-state as a social framework of remembrance. In fact, even in today's age of accelerated globalization it is the nation-state that plays a major role in the creation of memory culture: initiating rituals of public commemoration, setting up memorials, financing museums, conceiving of educational agendas. Also within unifying Europe, it is still the nation-states which provide the occasions and structures for public remembrance. Work done by sociologists and oral historians has shown that these national frameworks impinge on personal memories, even if they are further refracted according to additional frames, such as familial, generational, or religious ones (Welzer 2007).

However, it is also clear that Pierre Nora bequeathed an entire chain of conceptual flaws to the study of memory and the nation. His declared aim to represent an "inventory of the house of France" reveals an antiquated idea of French culture.[3] It is imagined as a formation situated within the boundaries of the *hexagone* and carried by an ethnically homogeneous society. Nora's approach binds memory, ethnicity, territory, and the nation-state together, in the sense of what could call "a (mnemonic) space for each race." His old-fashioned concept of national culture and its puristic memory drew criticism from many quarters. Hue-Tam Ho Tai (2001), for example, professor of Vietnamese history, pointed out that Nora's *lieux* neglected the history of colonialism, *la France d'outre mer*, and the large immigrant communities of today's France, which is, after all, a multiethnic and multicultural formation.

This short, and no doubt oversimplified, history of memory studies and its shifting focus from "memory in culture" to the "memories of (national) cultures" did not take into account various attempts to break away from a strict nation-focus, for example in the comparative work done by Jay Winter (1995) on European memories of the First World War or by Jan Assmann (2011 [1992]) on memory in ancient civilizations. However, cultures here, too, remain relatively clear-cut social formations, usually coinciding with the contours of regions, kingdoms, and nation-states. Even sophisticated approaches, which allow for difference and exchange between mnemonic communities, therefore tend to operate with distinct "containers." And this is what cultures constructed upon the assumption of an isomorphy

---

[3] Nora (1990, 8) in his preface to a shortened German edition of *Lieux de mémoire*.

between territory, social formation, mentalities, and memories are called in transcultural studies: "container-culture."[4]

1.3 Transcultural Studies—Transcultural Memory Studies

In his writings on transculturality, the German philosopher Wolfgang Welsch (1999, 194) has sharply criticized notions of container-culture, the origin of which he traces back to Johann Gottfried Herder. He identifies three determinants of the "traditional concept of single cultures." First, "social homogenization" refers to the idea that culture "moulds the whole way of life," so that "every act and every object is an unmistakable instance of precisely *this* culture." An understanding of culture as socially homogeneous does not take into account the inner complexity of cultural formations, their vertical and horizontal divisions. The second false credo, according to Welsch, is that of "ethnic consolidation," the idea that culture is always folkbound. This incorrect assumption is a legacy of the nineteenth-century racialization of culture. Third, "intercultural delimitation" means that concepts of single cultures tend to be "separatory." Cultures are seen as monads, as remaining distinguished from one another. It is such delimiting thinking that generates racism and other forms of tension between local, ethnic, and religious groups. As an alternative way of thinking about culture, Welsch proposes the concept of transculturality. The "transcultural" has a twofold meaning. According to Welsch, it describes phenomena which reach across and—eventually, as a result of the contemporary process of globalization—also beyond what is constructed as cultures.

For memory studies, the old-fashioned container-culture approach is not only somewhat ideologically suspect. It is also epistemologically flawed, because there are too many mnemonic phenomena that do not come into our field of vision with the "default" combination of territorial, ethnic, and national collectivity as the main framework of cultural memory—but which may be seen with the transcultural lens. There are the many fuzzy edges of national memory, for example, the sheer plethora of shared *lieux de mémoire* that have emerged through travel, trade, war, and colonialism. There is the great internal heterogeneity of cultural remembering within the nation-state. Different social classes, generations, ethnicities, religious

---

[4] See Hannerz (1996, 8): "As people move with their meanings and meanings find ways of traveling even when people stay put, territories cannot really contain cultures."

communities, and subcultures all generate their own, but in many ways intersecting, frameworks of memory. And there is the increasing relevance that formations beyond the nation-state have for cultural remembering: the world religions, global diasporas, the European Left, but also football, music culture, and consumer culture generate transnational networks of memory.

The nation-state may have proved a useful grid when addressing nineteenth- and twentieth-century constellations of memory. In view of both earlier historical periods and the current age of global media cultures and diasporic public spheres, the nation, however, appears less and less as the key arbiter of cultural memory. "Methodological nationalism" (Beck 2007) in memory research therefore means an unnecessary restriction to the field. But a transcultural perspective also implies questioning those other grids (territorial, social, temporal), which we tend to superimpose upon the complex realities of remembering in culture. It therefore seems that the overall aim of transcultural memory studies must consist in complicating the notion of "single memory cultures."

The growing interest in transcultural memory can be seen as part of a larger movement currently taking place in academia: that toward transcultural studies. While intercultural studies and the theories and policies of multiculturalism were still governed by ideas of single cultures, a look at recent research conducted in various disciplines reveals an almost ubiquitous curiosity about dynamics which challenge and transcend prevalent ideas of self-contained (usually Western) culture. In departments of history, concepts of "cultural transactions," "cultural exchange," "entangled," "braided history," and "global history" are used to take a fresh look at constellations from the ancient times all the way to contemporary history. Sociology, ethnology, and political philosophy are interested in "diaspora," "globalization," and "cosmopolitanism," in "global multiculture" and "world culture." Comparative literature theorizes "world literature," and art history "global art." In departments of English, the term "transcultural studies" is strategically used to move beyond postcolonial theory when studying contemporary writing in the former colonies. All these are of course the very disciplines which were involved in the "cultural turn" of the 1980s. They now seem to be taking a "transcultural turn."

Within memory studies, too, concepts of the transcultural are currently being developed in many different quarters—even if this is not always the term of choice. Daniel Levy's and Natan Sznaider's groundbreaking study *The Holocaust and Memory in the Global Age* (2006 [2001]) paved the way for research on "cosmopolitan memory." Andreas Huyssen (2003) provided insights into the logic of the "Holocaust" as a transnational mnemonic symbol, and Michael Rothberg's *Multidirectional Memory* (2009) shows how Holocaust discourses enabled the remembering of violent pasts in an age of decolonization. New work on *lieux de mémoire* has started to tackle shared, multicultural, and transnational sites of memory, thus combining memory studies with postcolonial and diaspora studies (Baronian et al. 2007; Sengupta Frey 2009). And finally, research on mediated memory can boast a comparatively long record of thinking about how media disseminate versions of the past across time, space, and mnemonic communities. The transgenerational mnemonic power of photography is, for example, addressed in Marianne Hirsch's *Family Frames* (1997). Alison Landsberg's *Prosthetic Memory* (2004) studies the transcultural impact of cinema in an age of global media cultures. And with a view to digitization and the new media, Joanne Garde-Hansen, Andrew Hoskins, and Anna Reading (2009) are working on "new media ecologies" and the "globital memory."

In light of all these different approaches, what is meant by "transcultural memory"? I would propose using "transcultural" as an umbrella term for what in other academic contexts might be described with concepts of the transnational, diasporic, hybrid, syncretistic, postcolonial, translocal, creolized, global, or cosmopolitan. But what, then, is the common denominator of work on transcultural memory, which is probably as varied as this list of terms suggests? It is certainly not the research objects, because as in memory studies in general—and this is one of the fascinations of the field—there is an infinity of objects and topics that can be studied. Neither is it the research methods. The multidisciplinarity of memory studies has generated great methodological richness and virtually unparalleled possibilities of probing new combinations between seemingly distant approaches. Therefore, "transcultural memory" seems to me rather a certain research perspective, a focus of attention, which is directed toward mnemonic processes unfolding across and beyond cultures. It means transcending the borders of traditional cultural memory studies by looking beyond established research assumptions, objects, and methodologies.

1.4 Conceiving Transcultural Memory

Does "the transcultural" as a research perspective imply a difference in quality, or merely a difference in degree to mainstream memory research?

This is a crucial question, because even if memory studies does take into account the great variety and different social levels of mnemonic frameworks, and even if it does consider that these intersect and can become entangled, it is complicating, but still operating within, the model of relatively clear-cut social formations as containers of cultural memory.

It seems that this problem is a legacy of one of the field's founding fathers, Maurice Halbwachs. In his writings on *mémoire collective*, Halbwachs (1994 [1925]) introduced the concept of *cadres sociaux de la mémoire*, social frameworks of memory—a notion which implies a certain "framed-ness" connected with all memory, and may thus connote boundaries and a certain stability. To avoid these conceptual pitfalls lurking behind the leading paradigm of mnemonic frameworks, let us assume for a moment that memory is first and foremost *not* bound to the frame of a place, a region, a social group, a religious community, or a nation, but is truly transcultural, continually moving across and beyond such territorial and social borders.

How can such truly transcultural memory be conceived? First of all, transculturality is part of everybody's individual everyday experience. It is grounded in what intercultural communication studies calls our "multiple memberships." For example, a German Protestant football fan or a Buddhist Englishwoman playing jazz combine already three different memberships: national, religious, and subcultural ones, with their respective forms, contents, media, and practices of remembering. Interestingly, it is the very concept of *cadres sociaux de la mémoire* which provides a model to understand the workings of such multiple mnemonic memberships. According to Halbwachs, different *cadres sociaux* overlap and intersect in individual minds. People draw on different frameworks when they remember. As Halbwachs showed in many examples, memories will differ significantly according to the frames that are selected and mixed.[5] It is the specific transcultural makeup of each mind—and of the memories produced by it—which makes each person unique.

Evidently, the idea of an inherent transculturality of memory was present in memory studies from its very beginning. But the question, and the methodological problem, is how to conceive of mnemonic transculturality as soon as we move on from the level of the individual to the level of the collective. (I employ here the twofold model proposed by Jeffrey Olick 1999.[6]) In Halbwachs's work, the transcultural disappears as soon as the

---

[5] See Halbwachs's (1997 [1950]) second chapter on individual and collective memory.
[6] For the distinction between cognitive (or: individual) and social and medial (or: collective) levels of cultural memory, see also Erll (2011a).

sociologist turns his attention from individual minds to group memories. Halbwachs (1997 [1950]) sets his *mémoire collective* in a strict opposition to "historical memory" and explains that the collective memory of social communities is self-centered and above all interested in similarity and identity.[7] It is essentially non-transcultural.

Conceiving of cultural memory in such a way means making use of, and in fact adopting, an actors' category. But actors' ideas about their lifeworlds should not necessarily be turned into analytical, or observers', categories. For the European nation-state, it was of course vital to make people believe in a homogeneous national memory. For a family, it may be just as important to rehearse familial memories over the dinner table and act as if their neighbors' opinions about the past were of no interest. This logic of closing-in is what Halbwachs described in detail. The question is, however, whether we should follow Halbwachs in turning into our own ideas those usable fictions which the groups we study like to believe in.

Halbwachs seems undecided: when he writes about the individual, he provides a good model of the transculturality of memory. But when he looks at the production of collective memory in social settings, he appears to imagine a "containered" memory.

To understand the workings of transcultural memory on the level of the social and the medial, we have to turn to that other founding father of memory studies, Aby Warburg. Warburg drew attention to transcultural processes as early as the 1920s, when he reconstructed the "afterlife of classical antiquity" in European art and prepared the exhibition of his *Mnemosyne*-atlas (1924–1929; see Warburg 2000). What Warburg focuses on is the movement, the migration or travel, of symbols across time and space. And this is in fact how I would like to conceive of transcultural memory: as the incessant wandering of carriers, media, contents, forms, and practices of memory, their continual travels and ongoing transformations through time and space, across social, linguistic, and political borders.

Such an understanding of memory as fundamentally "traveling memory" can certainly be backed by the sheer evidence of mnemohistory. The current age of accelerated globalization has brought forth global media cultures, in which historical novels are quickly translated, movies dealing with the past are screened simultaneously in different corners of the

---

[7] See Halbwachs's (1997 [1950]) third chapter on collective memory and historical memory. The unfruitful opposition of "memory versus history" is Halbwachs's legacy, which, via Pierre Nora, became part of contemporary memory studies and has hindered research more than it has helped.

globe, and worldwide TV audiences can have mass-mediated experience in real time (as, for example, in the case of 9/11 or the 2009 inauguration of the U.S. president Barack Obama). But as Warburg's work reminds us, it is actually since ancient times that memory lives in and through its movements, and that mnemonic forms and contents are filled with new life and new meaning in changing social, temporal, and local contexts.

To describe such processes, I draw on James Clifford's metaphor of "traveling culture." The anthropologist famously said that "cultures do not hold still for their portraits" (Clifford 1986, 10). The same is true for memory: Memories do not hold still. On the contrary, they seem to be constituted first of all through movement. What we are dealing with, therefore, is not so much (and perhaps not even metaphorically) "sites" of memory, *lieux de mémoire*, but rather the "travels" of memory, *les voyages* or *les mouvements de mémoire*. Possible contexts of such movement range from everyday interaction among different social groups to transnational media reception and from trade, migration, and diaspora to war and colonialism. In fact, the very fundaments of what we assume to be Western cultural memory are the product of transcultural movements. There is the Persian influence on the Old Testament; there is the share that Islam had in the European Renaissance; and there are the French origins of what the Grimm brothers popularized as "German" fairy tales. Even the "first memories" of a civilization, a nation, or a religious community are often more likely the effect of mnemonic movement than of pure indigenous origin. With Paul Gilroy (1993), one could say that memory can be studied through the reconstruction of its "routes" (the paths which certain stories, rituals, and images have taken) and not so much by echoing what social groups may claim as their "roots" (the alleged origins of a cultural memory).

1.5 How Memory "Travels"

I am using the term "travel" not to reify memory and assign it an agency that it does not possess. The term "traveling memory" is a metaphorical shorthand, an abbreviation for the fact that in the production of cultural memory, people, media, mnemonic forms, contents, and practices are in constant, unceasing motion. My concept of traveling memory is at once less literal and more radical than Clifford's (1992) "traveling cultures." I claim that *all* cultural memory must travel, must be kept in motion, in order to "stay alive," to have an impact both on individual minds and social formations.[8] Such travel consists only partly in movement across and beyond territorial and social boundaries. On a more fundamental level, it is the ongoing exchange of information between individuals and the motion between minds and media which first of all generates what Halbwachs termed "collective memory."[9] "Travel" is therefore an expression of the principal logic of memory: its genesis and existence through movement.

How does memory "travel"? In *Modernity at Large*, Arjun Appadurai identifies media and migration as the two major diacritics of global movement. These created a "new order of instability" with transformative effects on the "work of the imagination" (Appadurai 1996, 3). In the production of transcultural "mnemoscapes," too, media and carriers of memory appear to be key factors. To address the specific dynamics of traveling memory, I will distinguish among five dimensions of movement: carriers, media, contents, practices, and forms. I do so decidedly in a *longue durée* perspective, because it seems that today's "global memories" intensify, and are connected with a heightened reflexivity of, what is in fact a fundamental mnemonic process.

Carriers of memory are the individuals who share in collective images and narratives of the past, who practice mnemonic rituals, display an inherited habitus, and can draw on repertoires of explicit and implicit knowledge. Travel, migration and transmigration, flight and expulsion, and various forms of diaspora lead to the diffusion of mnemonic media, contents, forms, and practices across the globe. Examples range from the development of Jewish memory in exile and the Black Atlantic as a mnemonic configuration to the practices of remembrance in today's labor diasporas (e.g., Turkish people in Germany) and trade diasporas (e.g., the Chinese in Africa). There are also less conspicuous, or long-range, ways in which memory's carriers travel across space: consider go-betweens among villages, or mnemonic osmoses between country and city.

Media constitute in many respects a key dimension of memory's travels. First, there is the question of how mnemonic contents (for example, founding myths, such as the Homeric stories) travel through media history: from orality to writing to print, film, and the internet. Such travel

---

[8] This idea has been aptly expressed by Ann Rigney (2010, 345) in the image of a swimmer: "collective memory is constantly 'in the works' and, like a swimmer, has to keep moving even just to stay afloat."
[9] Although insights about the brain cannot be simply transferred to social and medial dimensions, it is interesting to note that in the brain, too, it is movement, the continual (re-)activation and modification of neuronal connections (rather than stable patterns), which enables remembering.

through time and technologies, the transcription of information from one medium to the next, has been studied using the concept of "remediation" (Erll and Rigney 2009). Second, media technologies move across borders and are appropriated and localized as technologies of memory. The introduction of film and photography throughout the British Empire and their uses as media of vernacular remembrance is one example. Third, the deterritorialization of memory is effected through media of circulation. Books, movies, and TV disseminate versions of the past across space. Mnemonic mediascapes are the condition for Landsberg's "prosthetic memory" (i.e., the taking on of other people's pasts). Digital media, finally, imply movement on the very level of their underlying technology: what we call a computer's or the internet's "memory" is in fact the result of ongoing algorithmic processes.

Contents of cultural memory largely consist in shared images and narratives. The "Holocaust" and "apartheid" are prime example of mnemonic contents with a virtually global reach—and an equally broad range of localized appropriations. The event of 9/11 shows a global dimension both as mediated real-time experience and in the translocal forms of its remembrance. From the consequences of the French Revolution in Haiti to the repercussions that the "Indian Mutiny" of 1857–1858 had all across Europe, it is especially the memories of political "impact events" (Fuchs 2010) which seem to develop a great centrifugal force. But bodies of knowledge and fictional stories travel, too. Aby Warburg's research shows how astrological knowledge migrated from ancient Greek to Arabic, Ptolemaic, and Indian contexts, and from there to medieval Italy. Stories of Odysseus and Aeneas have traveled through many centuries and across vast spaces. More fundamentally, contents of cultural memory must be kept in motion, because they do not possess any materiality and meaning in themselves. They do not exist outside individual minds, which have to actualize and re-actualize those contents continually to keep them alive. In this sense, it is the constant travel of mnemonic contents between media and minds, their ongoing interpretation and renewal, as well as their incessant contestation among different constituencies, which "make the memory."

A good example of how *mnemonic practices* travel is the development of cults of the war dead after the First World War, when the Tomb of the Unknown Soldier and the Two Minutes of Silence were adopted across Europe and in the colonies. Languages of memory and commemoration seem to travel faster and faster in the current globalizing age. Theme parks and experiential museums are obvious instances of how modes of conveying knowledge about the past have become globalized. As Levy and Sznaider (2006 [2001]) show, certain practices of Holocaust remembrance (such as the sounding of sirens throughout Israel on Yom HaShoah, the Holocaust Memorial Day) have gained worldwide currency. They are drawn upon to commemorate victims of other genocides (e.g., in Rwanda) and even to express anti-Israeli memory (e.g., the Palestinian Nakba-remembrance, which adopts rituals of Holocaust remembrance). Yet again, the travel of mnemonic practices is not a purely modern phenomenon, but has a long history. It goes back to the migration of Greek cults to Rome, the diffusion of Buddhist practices along the Silk Road, and to the spread of medieval *memoria*, the liturgical cult of the dead, across Europe.

Mnemonic forms are the condensed "figures" (symbols, icons, or schemata) of remembering that enable repetition and are often themselves powerful carriers of meaning. In fact, much of traveling memory is first of all enabled through the condensation of complex and confusing traces of the past into succinct mnemonic forms. "Exodus," "the Somme," or "the fall of the Berlin Wall" are such "memory figures" (Assmann 2011 [1992])—shorthands that are eminently transportable.[10]

"Old" mnemonic forms can thus be used to make sense of "new" and different experiences. In their displacement, memory figures tend to be stripped of their complexity, detached from the details and contextual meanings they originally referred to. This can lead to distortion, even perversion, of memories. But Andreas Huyssen (2003, 99) also emphasizes the enabling potential of such "floating signifiers," for example when he describes the role of the "Holocaust" for the work of the Truth and Reconciliation Commission in South Africa as a "motor energizing the discourses of memory elsewhere." Some mnemonic forms display a powerful transgenerational tenacity. They are often handed down unwittingly, via non-conscious ways of speaking and acting. In this vein, discursive patterns such as "East and West" can predetermine the ways in which we experience and interpret reality. I have called this phenomenon "premediation."[11]

---

[10] Cognitive psychology studies such memory figures as "schemata" and "scripts," which contain rudimentary plot structures and provide slots to be filled. Their cultural significance has been addressed from many angles, for example, as the "metaphors we live by" (Lakoff and Johnson 1980) or as the "protonarratives of possible lives" (Appadurai 1996).

[11] On "remediation" and "premediation," see Chapter 8, "Literature, Film, and the Mediality of Cultural Memory."

What should have become clear from this short outline of memory's multidimensional movements is that "memory in culture" implies far more than remembrance, let alone national remembrance. It involves knowledge, repertoires of stories and scripts, implicit memory, bodily aspects such as habitus, and—next to remembering—also that other basic operation of memory: forgetting. In the transcultural travels of memory, elements may get lost, become repressed, silenced, and censored, and remain unfulfilled. This is a consequence of the existence and variable permeability of borders. Movement across boundaries is always contingent on specific possibilities and restrictions, which can be of a medial, social, political, or semantic nature.

Is everything on the move, then? Are memories never stable, bound to clear-cut social groups and territories? Mnemonic constellations may look static and bounded when scholars select for their research, as they tend to do, manageable sections of reality (temporal, spatial, or social ones), but they become fuzzy as soon as the perspective is widened. And likewise, ostensible indicators of permanence—the canon, heritage, homelands—are quickly revealed as having been constructed by specific constituencies in order to stabilize the unstable, to hold off inevitable flux, and to create ordered, and politically "usable," pasts from a messy state of mnemonic affairs. Stability of memory may thus be an actor's (and scholar's) desire, but it is not necessarily the logic of memory. And as soon as we look at the field from a broader angle (e.g., do rigorously historical work and not confine the study of memory to the age of the nation-states), we find ourselves confronted with dynamic, multilinear, and often fuzzy trajectories of cultural remembering and forgetting—a research field, that is, which calls for a transcultural approach.

In view of all these considerations, memory studies should develop an interest in mnemonic itineraries, follow the non-isomorphic trajectories of media, contents, and carriers, the paths, and path-dependencies, of remembering and forgetting. It should also pay close attention to the various ways in which traveling memory is localized (and local contexts are not sufficiently described as "another culture," but must be reconstructed as complex constellations of intersecting group allegiances, mnemonic practices, and knowledge systems). It should ask how translocal mnemonic forms and practices are translated and integrated into local repertoires; how media technologies of memory become vernacularized; and how contents of memory are continually hybridized and recombined in often surprising ways. Through its ongoing hybridization, traveling memory engenders complex temporal phenomena, such as time-space compressions[12] and anachronies (*tiempos mixtos, Ungleichzeitigkeit des Gleichzeitigen*[13]), which have been diagnosed as conditions of the modern and postmodern age, but actually seem to belong to the deep history of memory and transculturality.

1.6 What Is, and to What End do We Study, Transcultural Memory?

Traveling memory is a process that scholars can describe; but its outcomes cannot be predicted. There is no inherent connection to good or bad, positive or negative, reconciliatory or destructive, enabling or banalizing uses of the past. The idea that (as Levy and Sznaider seem to suggest with a view to Holocaust memory) there is a "de-territorialized, transnational and globalizing *and therefore* cosmopolitan memory" (2006, 9; my emphasis) is thus only partly correct. Not each "memory around the globe" will automatically become a veritable "global memory." Not every worldwide available object of remembrance will be turned into a cosmopolitan, an ethical, or an empathetic memory. Although we can discern a functional potential that comes with specific media and contents (the internet works differently than stone carvings; the *Odyssey* lends itself to other meaning-making than the *Iliad*), much of the actual semantic shape that traveling memory takes on will be the result of the routes it takes in specific contexts and of the uses made by specific people with specific agendas. It is this localizing aspect of traveling memory which requires a close reading of our material. This is meant as a caveat with a view to the otherwise groundbreaking work done on "cosmopolitan memory" and "prosthetic memory." The global circulation of mnemonic media, such as movies, may indeed effect a change of perspective in viewers from other parts of the world and may lead to empathy and trans-ethnic solidarity. But there is of course also the option of misuses, the hijacking, or distortion, of transcultural memory—and, perhaps more often than we think, its idle running: travel without effect.

To sum up, I would like to come back to my initial question: by what means, and to what end, should scholars of a "third phase" turn their attention to transcultural memory? As I hope to have shown, I conceive

---

[12] The concept was introduced by David Harvey. See May and Thrift (2001).
[13] For *tiempos mixtos*, see Pieterse (2003). The term *Ungleichzeitigkeit des Gleichzeitigen* (the non-simultaneity of the simultaneous) was coined by Wilhelm Pinder and Ernst Bloch; see also Koselleck (2004).

of transcultural memory as an approach which is based on the insight that memory fundamentally means movement: traffic between individual and collective levels of remembering, circulation among social, medial, and semantic dimensions. Such an approach means moving away from site-bound, nation-bound, and in a naïve sense, cultures-bound research and displaying an interest in the mnemonic dynamics unfolding across and beyond boundaries. Transcultural memory studies would then imply a specific curiosity—an attentiveness to the border-transcending dimensions of remembering and forgetting. I am fully aware of the fact that there are other ways of looking at memory and that by absolutizing one approach our findings will become predictable. In the same way that memories can be said to be "always transcultural," they are also "always constructed," and "always contested." Much fruitful work has been done applying these former two "lenses."

Transcultural memory studies, however, with its strong focus on worldwide mnemonic processes, opens up the possibility to go one step further and question the field's basic assumptions, which are derived from Western thought on memory: above all from ancient *ars memoriae* and from modern philosophies of identity-through-memory. It invites the question of how, from non-Western perspectives, we might challenge and reconsider our categories, "provincialize cultural memory," as it were, and conceive of memory in its multiplicity and discrepancy.[14]

The "transcultural lens" promises a better understanding of our own globalizing age, in which memory travels at high speed across, and increasingly beyond, boundaries. But it is also a tool to tackle the "deep history" of cultural memory which goes back hundreds and thousands of years. And eventually, it is a means to understand how from this history we derive certain patterns of thought that shape the way we see things in the present and envisage the future.

1.7 Coda

In or around 2010, research on collective memory changed. My "Traveling Memory" was part of a movement that has come to be called "the transcultural turn" (Bond and Rapson 2014). The essay appeared in a special issue of the journal *Parallax* (Crownshaw 2011a), each single article

---

[14] For the "provincialization" of Western concepts, see Chakrabarty (2000).

of which proved generative, and some indeed prophetic, for new understandings of collective memory—all the way from Michael Rothberg's and Yasemin Yildiz's (2011) piece on "memory citizenship" and Holocaust memory in multicultural Germany to Andrew Hoskins (2011) on the "connective turn," Rick Cronshaw (2011b) on "perpetrator memory," Dirk Moses (2011) on the "catastrophization" of Israeli and Palestinian history, and Susannah Radstone's (2011) *caveat* not to forget the "locatedness" of memory.[15]

"Traveling memory" emerged together with a range of similar terms, such as "transnational memory" (De Cesari and Rigney 2014) emphasizing the different scales of collective memory, "multidirectional memory" (Rothberg 2009) interested in the logic of comparisons, "moving memory" (McIvor and Pine 2017) focusing on affect, migration, and mobilization, and so on.[16] Despite their different accentuations, all were conceived in the wake of cultural globalization, and all were in agreement about the need to overcome methodological nationalism as well as overly homogenizing concepts of collective identity that tend to be connected with collective memory.[17]

A decade later, memory studies have "turned" once again.[18] A "fourth wave" of environmental memory research was announced first by Stef Craps (Craps et al. 2018) and then in the first issue of the new journal *Memory Studies Review* (Gülüm et al. 2024). And rightly so: The challenge of remembering (in) the Anthropocene—in the face of climate change, species extinction, and toxic waste—is to find new ways of traveling in time. This requires developing ecological perspectives on past, present, and future that decenter the human; dealing with the enormous scales of geological time; and identifying forms of remembering that enable acts of productive collective future thinking.[19] Together with research on what Rigney (2018) calls the "memory-activism nexus" (see also Gutman and Wüstenberg 2023) and

---

[15] On the dynamics of remembering between travel *and* locatedness, see Dorr et al. (2019).

[16] For transcultural memory in film, see Brunow (2015); for "migrant and diasporic memory," see Creet and Kitzmann (2014) and Butt (2015); for "transcultural trauma," see Craps (2013); for "connective postmemory," see Hirsch (2012); for transcultural memory in Europe, see Sindbæk Andersen and Törnquist Plewa (2017) and Erll and Rigney (2017); for "cosmopolitan memory" in Latin America and Europe, see Baer and Sznaider (2018); on "co-memoration," see Henke and Vanassche (2019). For inventories of memory research after the transcultural turn, see Bond et al. (2016) and Erll and Rigney (2018).

[17] For a critique of collective identity, see Chapter 13, "Ecologies of Trauma."

[18] For a definition of a "turn" in the humanities and social sciences, see Bachmann-Medick (2016); on the "mnemonic turn," see Olick (2025).

[19] On "slow memory," see Wüstenberg (2023); on "ecologies of violence," see Knittel (2023); on "ecological mourning," see Craps (2023); on collective future thinking, see Szpunar and Szpunar (2016).

on digital ecologies (Hoskins 2017; Mandolessi 2023), the "environmental turn" makes it possible to address today's global crises through the lens of collective memory.

But waves flow into each other. Memory continues to travel, and in our age of environmental crisis, transcultural perspectives have not disappeared[20] (just like the "national" as a key framework of collective memory never fully disappeared from the horizon of memory studies after the transcultural turn and is currently re-emerging as a pressing concern in times of populism and authoritarianism[21]). Some of the most exciting new research on traveling memory is conducted in an interdisciplinary and increasingly empirical way.[22] Translation, both interlingual and cultural, is justly highlighted and studied as a key mode of how memory travels.[23] Moreover, research on frictions of traveling memory in non-European contexts has not only shown that memory never travels seamlessly, but also provided deeper insight into its postcolonial dynamics.[24] With the new wars in Ukraine and Israel, the question of which memories are shareable, or "good travelers," and which are not, and what histories can or cannot be compared, is re-emerging with new urgency.[25]

---

[20] For the connection between transcultural memory and "eco-logical memory," see Erll (2024b).
[21] For recent research on national memory, see Wertsch and Roediger (2021).
[22] See Ortner et al. (2022) on "mnemonic migration" (i.e., the question of how distant empirical readers understand literary mediations of war memories).
[23] For major interventions, see Brems (2019); Laanes (2021); Deane-Cox, and Spiessens (2022); Jünke (2023); Jünke and Schyns (2024). For a thorough overview of research on translation and memory, see Hou (2023). For a wealth of new perspectives on translation and traveling memory, see Laanes et al. (2025).
[24] Teichler (2021); Adebayo (2023); Mwambari (2023).
[25] See, for example, Wertsch (2021) on "mnemonic standoffs," and Rothberg (2022b) on the "German historians' debate 2.0."

Chapter 2
Traveling Memory in European Film

2.1 Traveling Memory and Mnemonic Relationality

When memory travels, it meets other memories. But what happens when different mnemonic repertoires come together? And how can film document, imagine, and intervene in this convergence? This chapter identifies three types of mnemonic relationality in European films devoted to traveling memory: Robert Thalheim's German *Am Ende kommen Touristen* (*And Along Come Tourists*, 2007) stages dialogic memory of the Holocaust; Bulgarian filmmaker Adela Peeva's documentary *Chia e tazi pesen?* (*Whose is This Song?* 2003) is a cautionary tale exposing unreflexive transcultural memory across the Balkans; and Marc Isaacs's *Calais: The Last Border* (2003) is a British documentary about refugees in a French port city which uses montage to produce multidirectional memory. Emphasizing the power of aesthetic forms in memory culture, this chapter will demonstrate how plot structures, the distribution of information, and editing techniques both represent and produce mnemonic relationality.

Film is a medium of memory that holds the potential to be at once popular, pervasive, and powerful. More than other media, film arguably has the capacity to convey images and stories not only about Europe's entangled histories, but also about the present experience of "Europe" and of being European vis-à-vis conflicting and disputed, yet also resonant and converging, memories.[1] This chapter deals with a loose cluster of productions brought together under the umbrella term of the "traveling memory-film": road movies and travel films, quest documentaries, anthology films, episodic films, and essay films[2]—all of which address Europe and its transcultural memories through the depiction or performance of movement, involving travel at various levels.

---

[1] On the complex issue of European memory, see Leggewie and Lang (2011); Rigney (2012b); Sindbæk-Andersen and Törnquist-Plewa (2016).

[2] On the essay film as a medium of transcultural memory, see Brunow (2016).

Travels in Time. Astrid Erll, Oxford University Press. © Oxford University Press (2025).
DOI: 10.1093/oso/9780197767733.003.0003

"Travel" is the basic process of memory (see Erll 2011b, 2015). Transcultural memory results from literal and not-so-literal travels through dimensions of culture, from the movement not only of people, but also of materials and media, forms and practices, and the contents they carry. The "transcultural turn"[3] in memory studies heralded a move away from the "methodological culturalisms"[4] that characterized the re-emergence of collective memory in the framework of cultural studies (in Germany: *Kulturwissenschaft*) during the 1980s and 1990s. Memory research at that time often was—and sometimes still remains—shaped by a perspective on cultures as distinct, bounded entities, or discrete containers. Memory cultures were identified as residing in diverse social, institutional, regional, linguistic, or ethnic dimensions. Research addressed *the* memory of *a* family, of *a* nation, *an* ethnic community, *a* social class, *a* city, *a* region. And while it may be true that members of a family, residents of a city, or citizens of a nation can establish a memory culture and will usually conceive of it as pure, holistic, and discrete (this is the actors' perspective), an analytical observer's point of view on the people, contents, media, forms, and practices of such memory cultures will always reveal their inherent transcultural nature. All memories produced in culture are transcultural. They are borrowed from elsewhere, inspired by neighbors, stolen from strangers. They are co-constructed and amalgamated.

According to Monica Juneja, art historian and theorist of the transcultural, a perspective on travel or circulation "challenges us to take our enquiry to another register so as to find a precise language to theorize the morphology of the many possible relationalities that are engendered by mobility and encounter" (Juneja 2015, 61). It is in this sense that I propose that memory studies need to develop a more precise language to theorize the morphology of the many possible *mnemonic* relationalities that are engendered by traveling memory. Thus, if travel, or movement, is the fundamental dynamic of all memory, and transcultural memory (the variable mixtures of mnemo-cultural repertoires) its outcome, then "mnemonic relationality" directs our attention to a structuring process: toward acts of connecting[5] and

---

[3] Crownshaw (2011a); Bond and Rapson (2014).
[4] On methodological nationalism, see Beck (2007).
[5] In fact, memory studies across the disciplines tend to emphasize the *connectivity* of memory. Memory thus emerges as a process that connects neurons, people, time periods, spaces, experiences, and histories. Jan Assmann (2011 [1992]) speaks of the "connective structure" of cultural memory that creates linkages in the dimensions of time and the social. From a neuroscientific perspective, a similar argument was made by Schacter and Welker (2016). With a view to transnational memory,

blending, co-constructions and negotiations that are necessary for bringing heterogeneous mnemonic elements into meaningful relations with one another.

The concept of relationality plays a role in the theorizing of both memory and transculturality. In the neurosciences, relationality describes a basic process of the brain, "most generally, the linking (or binding) of two or more memory items," which produces, at higher levels, a "network of meaning" (Anastasio et al. 2012, 108f.). Psychoanalytically inspired approaches to memory emphasize the relational character of human personhood and memory. Individual memory is seen not merely as "socially framed" (in Halbwachs's sense[6]), but more emphatically as shaped by specific interpersonal relations (Mitchell 2000, Campbell 2003). Last but not least, new materialism has enabled memory scholars to articulate the fundamentally relational dynamics between materiality and memory (Munteán et al. 2016).

Memory can therefore be seen as a relational process that encompasses biological, mental, social, and material dimensions, thus creating changeable mnemonic assemblages. The term "mnemonic relationality" emphasizes that memory is a co-constructive and transformative process: elements (such as images and narratives of the past) are not only connected, linked to each other, but in this process all the elements involved are transformed. They become related to one another in a way that creates new meaning and—once this has happened—makes it hard or impossible to disentangle the individual elements again.

But to what extent are relational memories transcultural? The Caribbean writer and philosopher Édouard Glissant claims that the cultural process consists of ongoing acts of relating. He highlights the transformative potential of a form of thinking and imagining that he calls the "Poetics of Relation, in which each and every identity is extended through a relationship with the Other" (Glissant 1997, 11). Rather than reserving such insights into relationality for the study of memory in (post-)colonial contexts, we should keep

---

De Cesari and Rigney (2014) define "articulation" as the process that both connects and expresses memories across borders. Michael Rothberg's (2009) "multidirectional memory" is a specific type of such connections, which enables the articulation of violent histories and produces solidarities. "Connective postmemory," according to Marianne Hirsch (2012), combines transgenerational memories with transnational ones. Andrew Hoskins (2011) uses the term "connective memory" to describe memory in the digital age.

[6] See Halbwachs (1994 [1925]) on the "social frameworks of memory."

in mind that this is a fundamental cultural dynamic that also shapes memories in Europe—which is, after all, a postcolonial Europe, and has always been a transcultural Europe.[7] How, then, are memories brought into relation with each other, and how do new memories emerge from relations across Europe?

This chapter discusses three examples of traveling memory and mnemonic relationality in European film. Juneja's notion (in the quote above) of "morphology" as method suggests turning our attention to different processes of formation and the resultant shapes of transcultural memory. With film under scrutiny here as an aesthetic medium of memory, the analysis will address not only discursive patterns (more commonly the focus of analysis in memory studies), but also aesthetic forms of filmic narration, which play an important role for meaning-making in the memory film.

2.2 The Traveling Memory-Film

The three European films discussed here all deal with travel and memory. Robert Thalheim's *Am Ende kommen Touristen* (*And Along Come Tourists*, 2007) is a fictional feature film about a young man from Berlin who travels to Poland in order to work for a year at the Auschwitz-Birkenau memorial and museum. *Chia e tazi pesen?* (*Whose is This Song?*, 2003), a documentary by the Bulgarian filmmaker Adela Peeva, stages a quest across the Balkans, in search of a shared musical tradition. And Marc Isaacs's documentary *Calais: The Last Border* (2003) screens illegal immigrants in Calais, who want to make it to Great Britain.

This is a corpus of highly diverse filmic genres, modes of production, and ways of distribution, from the fictional feature film screened in major European cinemas to the musical documentary whose public appearance remains restricted to the festival circuit.[8] For the purposes of this chapter, the variety is productive. My concept of the traveling memory-film cuts

---

[7] Max Silverman (2013, 71) notes: "Ironically, the newly valued terms of hybridity, diaspora, méttisage, créolisation, relationality and the mosaic (originally associated predominantly with the critical work of Homi Bhabha and the writing of Édouard Glissant), which should provide the vocabulary to realize a genuinely 'travelling' model, rarely go beyond the space demarcated by colonial histories." How postcolonial thinking and the idea of Europe keep "irritating" each other is shown by Schulze-Engler (2013).

[8] Thalheim's film was screened in German, Austrian, and French cinemas, and aired on Finnish TV. Isaacs's and Peeva's films have gone through the international film festival circuit. These channels of distribution of course influence where and among whom such films travel.

across genres and other categories. It enables scholars to collect different materials, view these together, and assess their potential to represent and produce mnemonic relationality.

Traveling memory-films display, are the result of, or engender mnemonic movement. Three major manifestations of the traveling memory-film can be distinguished. First, in a literal sense, the *representation of physical travel* characterizes road movies and other films where movement and border-crossing are an essential part of the plot structure. But since road movies, travel films, adventure films, and migration films appear to be rather presentist genres, not much attention has been paid thus far to memories that are carried along "on the road" and that may merge with or transform ideas of the past encountered en route.[9] However, upon closer scrutiny, transcultural memory often proves to be deeply imbedded in films dealing with movement. Migrant, diasporic, or "accented" cinema, for example, frequently features films about returns to the "homeland."[10] Just as in Atom Egoyan's much-discussed and highly memory-reflexive *Ararat* (2002), the story of a young Canadian's quest for his family history in Armenia, such travels in search of roots tend to turn into encounters with transcultural memory.[11] Memories of and actual returns to the homeland also play a role in the tragicomic migrant and diasporic cinema that has developed in Great Britain (e.g., *West Is West*, 2010, dir. Andy DeEmmony) and later in Germany (e.g., *Almanya*, 2011, dir. Yasemin Safındereli). A different approach is taken in documentaries like *Donau, Duna, Dunaj, Dunav, Dunarea* (2003, dir. Goran Rebic), which substitutes the river for the road and explores the flow of memories across Europe. Jean Luc Godard's *Film Socialisme* (2011) combines present-day tourism and European long-term memory by having passengers on a cruise recall figures of classical antiquity as their ship crosses the Mediterranean. Increasingly, fictional films and documentaries

---

[9] Mazierska and Rascaroli's (2006) book on the European road movie does not systematically include aspects of history. The same applies to research on border-crossing in European cinema (Barriales-Bouche and Salvodon, 2007) as well as to most studies of the migration film in mainstream cinema (Korte and Sternberg 2004), with the exception of Berghahn (2013). In Loshitzky's important *Screening Strangers* (2010), the preoccupation with memory remains marginal. A systematic connection between Francophone films about illegal immigration and the transculturality of memory is made by Fevry (2014, 2017).

[10] On "accented cinema," see Naficy (2011); on "intercultural cinema," see Marks (2000); on diasporic memory and "rites of return," see Hirsch and Miller (2011).

[11] This Canadian example indicates that the traveling memory-film is a global phenomenon, likely to be encountered in filmmaking across the world. The focus of this chapter, however, rests on films about and produced in Europe.

about refugees address memories that are carried to Europe and then enter a transcultural dynamic (e.g., *Le Havre*, 2011, dir. Aki Kaurismäki; *Welcome Europa*, 2006, dir. Bruno Ulmer). All these productions, diverse as they may be, are examples of traveling memory in film. Their representation of movement across space leads to a kind of filmic multi-sited ethnography of European memory.

Second, mnemonic movement can also be detected in anthology films, episodic films, or films that rely heavily on montage, in which the editing of materials sourced from different archives can be understood as travel between and across different European memories. This second type of "travel" in the film's structure often informs documentary films. John Akomfrah's films about migration—such as his essay film *The Nine Muses* (2010), his three-screen film installations *Vertigo Sea* (2015) and *The Airport* (2016), and his short film *Auto Da Fé* (2016)—are characterized by his strategy of reassembling archival materials in order to create transcultural filmic memories.[12] Moreover, mnemonic relationality can emerge from the sum, or juxtaposition, of individual short films collected in anthology productions such as *Visions of Europe* (2004, dir. Fatih Akin et al.). While all three examples discussed in this chapter belong to the first type of traveling memory-film—films depicting border-crossings in the literal sense—*Calais: The Last Border* is additionally an example of the second type. It shows how a sense of mnemonic relationality can be produced by montage, by the movement and arrangement of footage that deals with memories.

Third, the industrial and social dimensions of film can engender mnemonic movement. Many films today are European co-productions, sponsored by different national funding bodies and produced by international teams whose members are often far-traveled themselves. All of these individuals and institutions may bring their own mnemonic repertoires to the film. Last but not least, we can also speak of mnemonic movement whenever a film becomes so popular that it is screened in different European countries and finds transnational audiences, thus traveling across Europe. Arguably, it is in a film's transcultural reception that the social life of memory across Europe becomes palpable.[13] As it is the aim of this

---

[12] For more on Akomfrah's method, see Brunow (2015).
[13] For the social life of the memory film, see also Erll and Wodianka (2008); Erll (2012); and Chapter 8 of this volume, "Literature, Film, and the Mediality of Cultural Memory." For theoretical perspectives on memory and reception, see Sindbæk Andersen and Törnquist-Plewa (2017).

chapter to compare the internal logic of memory travel in different films, however, I touch on this third type of *travel as social circulation* only in passing.

What the films discussed here all have in common is their depiction of acts of journeying: fictional characters, people interviewed in the documentaries, or filmmakers are on the move across Europe. All three films display a primary orientation toward the present. Journeys are made in a "Europe now." The films avoid flashbacks, the inclusion of documentary footage, and other typical strategies of the memory film, but they all find ways to convey a sense of the "presence of European pasts." What emerges in all three films, through different acts of movement, is mnemonic relationality.

2.3 *And Along Come Tourists:* Travel and Dialogic Memory

Literally translated, *Am Ende kommen Touristen* (2007, dir. Robert Thalheim) means "in the end come tourists." This is an apt general statement about what frequently happens to sites of violent history in today's culture of memory. Turned into objects of a "memory industry," the sites become magnets of "dark tourism."[14]

"Travel" appears in this film in a literal, a physical sense. The young German Sven Lehnert (Alexander Fehling) moves from Berlin to Poland, in order to fulfill his year of alternative civilian service at the Auschwitz-Birkenau memorial and museum.[15] He is assigned the task of assisting the elderly concentration camp survivor Stanislaw Krzeminski (Ryszard Ronczewski), whose resentment toward the young German, however, is unmistakable. Slowly and carefully, the film develops their difficult relationship.[16] Sven falls in love with the young Polish woman Ania (Barbara Wysocka), who works as a museum guide at Auschwitz and is fluent in German. Ironically, in the end Ania will leave Sven and go to Brussels to become a simultaneous interpreter for the European Union. More ironically still, Sven had originally planned to go to Amsterdam (symbolic of a youthful, hedonistic western Europe despite existing Holocaust-related sites such as the Anne

---

[14] Lennon and Foley (2000); on *Am Ende kommen Touristen*, see Emonds (2011).
[15] Until the suspension of conscription in 2011, civilian service was the obligatory alternative to military service in Germany.
[16] On this key aspect of the film, which combines the issue of perpetrator/victim memories with intergenerational memory, see Bayer (2010) and Ebbrecht (2011).

Frank House), but Auschwitz was the place he was offered; so, without giving much thought to the matter, he moves to Oświęcim, the Polish town located next to the former Nazi camps Auschwitz, Auschwitz-Birkenau, and Monowitz.

It is this clash between the protagonist's naivety, on the one hand, and the weight of history to which he is inevitably bound as a German citizen, on the other, that creates much of the plot dynamics. The film is about a young man who has to find his role and a sense of responsibility in the face of both genocidal history and the new Europe. Sven's increasing understanding of Krzeminski's obsession with the former inmates' suitcases, as well as his courageous intervention on behalf of the old man at a commemoration ceremony that turns into an empty, cynical ritual, are important steps in Sven's development.[17] *And Along Come Tourists* thus draws on the plot of the *Bildungsroman* (the novel of formation), which typically revolves around a young hero, often naive in the beginning, who moves toward greater understanding and his place in society. The external journey is matched by an internal one. At the end of the film, when Sven, heartbroken and disappointed with Ania, wants to leave Oświęcim and go back to Berlin, a group of German tourists appears (as the title literally suggests) and Sven responsibly helps them find their way to the memorial site. Whether or not he will stay on remains unclear in the movie's open ending.

By moving to Oświęcim, Sven travels into the past of the Nazi-Holocaust, but also into the present of a young Polish democracy, a recent member of the European Union.[18] For Sven, Oświęcim is an ambiguous chronotope. This clash is visualized in the scene of a bike tour that Sven and Ania, as they become closer, take through the area of Auschwitz (see Figure 2.1). Sven realizes that Monowice ("Auschwitz III"), the site where thousands of mainly Jewish slave laborers had to work in the Buna-factories for the chemical syndicate I. G. Farben (with a life expectancy of just a few months), is now a small picturesque Polish village, showing almost no visible traces that would indicate its violent past. It is summer time. In the midst of lush nature, Sven and Ania find a lake where they take a rest. Sven asks Ania how it feels to live in a place where the "biggest crime against humanity" was committed.

---

[17] See specifically Ebbrecht-Hartmann (2011).
[18] O'Dea (2013, 40) argues that *And Along Come Tourists* is a "'third wave' Holocaust film that distances itself from cinematic, historical reconstruction on a visual and narrative level by focusing attention on the pieces of the past that continue to affect contemporary German-Polish relationships."

Figure 2.1 *Am Ende kommen Touristen* (2007, dir. Robert Thalheim).

Ania is irritated and retorts that she doesn't understand the question: "I was born here, I live here. . . . And you, what do *you* feel—as a German?" (my translation).[19] At that moment, the two young characters do not find an easy answer to these difficult questions.

However, this brief conversation is an exchange about the positionality vis-à-vis the Holocaust of those belonging to the third, or even fourth, generation of Europeans since World War II—Europeans who in different ways are "implicated" (*sensu* Rothberg 2019) in an entangled history. In a transcultural setting—the result of travel—this is an *attempt* at what Aleida Assmann (2014) calls "dialogic memory," at an understanding of the past as shared history and at recognizing the other's perspective on it: mnemonic relationality as conscious effort and work-in-progress. Sven's interest in the other's memory is surely also motivated by his love for Ania and thus an element of the film's open-ended subplot of intercultural romance, a variation on the theme of "Europe in love," as Passerini (1999) has studied it. Rather than focusing on large-scale political dialogues among EU member states, *And Along Come Tourists* chooses the scale of the intimate.[20] In a miniature about two individuals belonging to the third generation of Europeans

---

[19] *Am Ende kommen Touristen*, 46:55 to 48:30.
[20] For different "scales" of transnational remembering, see De Cesari and Rigney (2014). Tellingly, in an interview the director Thalheim mentions Alain Resnais's *Hiroshima mon amour* as an influence on his film (Gansera 2007).

since the Holocaust and World War II, the film shows how an awareness of mnemonic relationality emerges, and how dialogue can begin.

2.4 *Whose is This Song?* Traveling Melodies and Unreflexive Transculturality

Adela Peeva's *Chia e tazi pesen?* (*Whose is This Song?*, 2003) is also a film about movement and memory in Europe. But it works in a very different way. First of all, this is a documentary film, made in what Bill Nichols (2010, 31f.) defines as "participatory" and "performative" modes. The Bulgarian documentary filmmaker Adela Peeva is present on the scene. She visibly interacts with the people she interviews, and she is deeply involved with the documentary's topic: the idea of a transcultural musical heritage in southeastern Europe.

The documentary starts with a scene that re-enacts an experience Peeva professes to have had in Istanbul. Sitting in a pub with an international cast of friends—a Greek, a Macedonian, a Turk, and a Serb—she hears a singer perform a song. Everybody at the table recognizes it, knows its lyrics in their mother tongue, and everybody claims the song as their own national heritage. "Whose is This Song?" is thus the question that stands at the beginning of Peeva's journey through the Balkans in search of a "traveling melody."[21] Adela Peeva sets out on a long voyage that takes her to Turkey, Greece, Macedonia, Albania, Bosnia, Serbia, and Bulgaria. She soon discovers that the melody is found all over the region. But in each country, the lyrics to the melody are different (see Figures 2.2 and 2.3). Some traditions have turned the melody into a love song, others into a religious hymn, a revolutionary anthem, or a military march. All musicians interviewed by Peeva claim passionately that theirs is the original version, that the song is *their own*. Peeva is almost drawn into a brawl in a restaurant for playing it with what locals perceive as the wrong lyrics. All "owners" of the song come up with elaborate histories to prove its local or national origins. Childhood memories, films, and photographs are produced as evidence.

Whose is This Song? belongs to a genre that Nevena Daković (2007) has called the "Balkan road movie." The filmmaker searches for transcultural memory in a European border-region that encompasses the Balkans and

---

[21] For the term "traveling melodies" (*wandernde Melodien*), see Tappert (1889).

Figure 2.2 *Whose is This Song?* (2003, dir. Adela Peeva). Performance of the Turkish version of the song.

parts of Turkey, a region whose history is characterized by formative processes of cultural exchange—an interesting example of memory processes that "irritate" (and "are irritated by") concepts of Europe (Schulze-Engler 2013). However, what Peeva finds is an embittered national, linguistic, and ethnic boundary-maintenance. While obviously a shared heritage, the melody does not bring people together in an acknowledgment of cultural contact, common roots, and common tastes. Instead, in each location the song will trigger outbursts of nationalism and hatred.

This film, too, depicts the act of physical traveling, but in this case, viewers follow the filmmaker's quest. Through Peeva's authoritative voice-over, her film thematizes the transculturality of memory more explicitly than Thalheim's. It showcases a memory that connects Turkey and the Balkans and is based on a shared musical heritage—with the melody as a traveling medium of memory. However, this documentary clearly has a double structure when it comes to the experience of transcultural memory and the negotiation of mnemonic relationality. For the filmmaker and the viewers, the melody

Figure 2.3 *Whose is This Song?* (2003, dir. Adela Peeva). Performance of the Greek version of the song.

is a sign of a shared heritage, but for the people filmed and interviewed, the song is a medium of ethno-national memory and identity. The latter's stubborn nationalism contrasts with the filmmaker's and viewers' insight into the melody's transnational life and points to the difference between actors' and observers' perspectives on memory (what anthropologists call emic and etic perspectives).

This also creates the film's bitter dramatic irony: the unequal distribution of information about, or insight into, transcultural memory. The spectators and the filmmaker know more (or better) than the filmed people on the ground. *Whose is This Song?* reminds us that traveling memory need not necessarily go hand in hand with a consciousness about (or emphatic approval of) resultant transculturality. Using dramatic irony, the film demonstrates what is arguably (if regrettably) the state of mnemonic relationality most frequently encountered in Europe and across the world: a transculturality of memory that remains unreflexive and is even vehemently denied.

2.5 *Calais: The Last Border*—Multidirectional Montage

The third case discussed here is also a documentary, and although the camera stays in one location—Calais—it is also a film about movement. Marc Isaacs's *Calais: The Last Border* (2003) observes people who travel through the French port city. *Calais* is one of the many documentaries about illegal immigration, a type of film that Yosefa Loshitzky (2010) has described as "screening strangers." Michael Winterbottom's *In This World* (2002) is one of the best-known examples of such European cross-border films. Marc Isaacs, arguably, adds a few more layers of complexity to this existing form.[22]

Calais focuses on a port city in decline and on its notorious refugee camps, which have come to be called the "Calais jungle." After Sangatte, a reception facility opened by the Red Cross in 1998, was closed due to overcrowding in 2002, illegal camps sprang up in the woods and beaches around the port. Most migrants dwelling in these makeshift camps hoped to illegally enter the United Kingdom, by boat or via the Eurotunnel. Since Isaacs's filming in 2002, the "Calais jungle" has come to public attention again and again, with repeated, but often ineffectual, attempts by French authorities at clearing the camps and providing alternative shelter.[23]

Marc Isaacs interviews different groups of people who are on the move. First, there is a group of English day-trippers who have come over by ferry in search of cheap alcohol and whose comments on the illegal immigrants in Calais verge on the fascistic. Second, the focus rests on a group of migrants—from Afghanistan, eastern Europe, and the Caribbean—who stayed on the beach and in the streets of Calais after the official refugee camp Sangatte was closed. They will try desperately, again and again, to illegally cross the channel to England. The central figure is Ijaz, a refugee from war-torn Afghanistan. He was granted asylum in France, but to Isaacs's question of why he should take the risk of a dangerous journey to Britain, he answers that he does not like the French (thus providing some comic relief—for the most part, presumably, in English cinemas). Third, we encounter Steve, a young Englishman, with his French girlfriend and their child. Disillusioned with the lack of opportunities in Britain, Steve has opened up an English

---

[22] I would like to acknowledge here my collaboration with Sébastien Fevry, who brought Isaacs's films to my attention in a co-teaching project in the summer of 2014. As Fevry (2015) argues, Isaacs's film turns the *non-lieu* of Calais into a *lieu d'entre-mémoire*.

[23] In October 2016, a clearing of the Calais camps was undertaken by the French government. An estimated 10,000 migrants were moved to "reception centers" across France, but many have returned to Calais.

pub in Calais, which, however, does not yield much profit. Later in the documentary, he will leave his debts behind and escape with his family to Spain. Fourth, there is the extravagant Tulia, seemingly an Englishwoman, who has settled in Calais with her husband Les. The older couple are running an unsuccessful advertising agency, and their debts are rising, so bankruptcy and even homelessness loom large.

Marc Isaacs's documentary relies on an intricate way of editing that can usefully be called "multidirectional montage."[24] The trajectories and life histories of different people are presented and then crosscut in such a way as to make them resonate with each other. In a key scene with the two main characters of the film, viewers learn that Ijaz has lost all his family in a rocket attack on Kabul, and that Tulia—this becomes clear only at this point in the documentary—has a history as a refugee, too.[25] Six decades ago, as a nine-year-old during World War II, she was interned in a political camp in Franco's Spain and was separated from her mother, whom she would never see again. Her story is brought into dialogue with Ijaz's story by means of montage: images of Tulia sitting at her kitchen table, remembering and narrating her story, are crosscut with images of Ijaz standing at the beach of Calais, facing England (while Tulia's narration continues as voice-over). Tulia's narrative starts with her comment that seeing the "white cliffs of Dover" always brings back to her "good memories, but also very sad ones"— the very cliffs, that is, which Ijaz is facing while on the beach (see Figures 2.4, 2.5, and 2.6).

In film theory, crosscutting is defined as an "an editing technique that interweaves segments of two or more sequences, usually to show simultaneous action or to illuminate related themes" (Kroon 2010, 184). The scene that reveals Tulia's history as a refugee is an example of parallel editing, which is a type of crosscutting that remains vague about the temporal order of its sequences, while clearly suggesting a related theme. This sense that the issues dealt with in both interviews are connected is emphasized by related questions. After Tulia has ended her story with the statement that she never found her mother again, the film switches back to Ijaz, who is now lying on the beach, facing the sky. Isaacs's question ("What did your mother look like?") creates a continuity of themes. Ijaz answers that he has lost her photograph on his dangerous journey, and so the audience hears of another mother

---

[24] I refer to Michael Rothberg's (2009) concept of "multidirectionality" (i.e., a cross-referencing of different memories that helps articulate histories of suffering).

[25] *Calais*, 30:22 to 33:25.

48 TRAVELS IN TIME

Figure 2.4 *Calais* (2003, dir. Marc Isaacs). A photograph of Tulia as a child.

Figure 2.5 *Calais* (2003, dir. Marc Isaacs). Tulia in her kitchen in Calais.

TRAVELING MEMORY IN EUROPEAN FILM 49

Figure 2.6 *Calais* (2003, dir. Marc Isaacs). Ijaz at the beach of Calais, facing Dover (with Tulia's refugee-story as voice-over).

whose image will be retained only in the memory of a border-crossing child. By means of parallel editing, both life histories are "articulated" in the sense of Stuart Hall: they are connected *and* expressed.[26]

Through montage, two individual life trajectories, as well as a European past and present, are brought into relation with one another: the history of fascism in Europe and the refugees it produced, and the current histories of illegal immigration to "fortress Europe." Such an echo chamber emerges precisely through the film's focus on *one* single site. Calais is presented as a "migratory setting,"[27] a contact zone of different people and their memories. Isaacs's film furthers an understanding of the plight of today's illegal

---

[26] For this usage of "articulation" in the field of transnational memory studies, see De Cesari and Rigney (2014).

[27] This useful term was coined by Aydemir and Rotas (2008, 7) who describe it as follows: "'migratory' alludes to movement, 'settings' to emplacement; the former indicates the 'real' political, social, and economic world, the latter an assembled scenery: fictional, staged, imagined, perceived, or aesthetic in some other way." For the traveling memory film, too, it implies "a shift in perspective from migration as movement from place to place to migration as installing movement *within* place" with "effects on place," which is "'thickened' as it becomes the setting of the variegated memories, imaginations, dreams, fantasies, nightmares, anticipations, and idealizations that experiences of migration, of both migrants and native inhabitants, bring into contact with each other." See also

immigrants through the lens of older European memories. It is in this sense that *Calais* is a multidirectional montage.

Much as in *Whose is This Song?*—and in contrast to *And Along Come Tourists* the filmed characters do not consciously engage themselves in relational remembering. Ijaz and Tulia do not even know each other as residents of Calais. Only the effects of the documentary's editing evoke multidirectional memory. It remains up to the viewer to actualize the film's potential of conveying an image of transcultural memory in a migratory setting such as Calais.

2.6 Toward a Morphology of Mnemonic Relationality

This chapter cannot offer more than a first step on the way toward a morphology of mnemonic relationality. But some of its elements can be gleaned from my discussion of three traveling memory-films: there is the dialogic effort of thematizing a shared history, the phenomenon of unreflexive memory that implies a denial of transcultural processes, and the multidirectional strategy of cross-referencing different, historically possibly unrelated, but resonant histories. These mnemo-cultural forms are represented, evoked, and actively created through a range of filmic forms.

The films studied here represent and produce mnemonic relationality on different levels—characters, filmmakers, audiences, filmic structure—and by means of different formal strategies. *And Along Come Tourists* draws on a specific plot structure, which is then adapted to the agenda of the traveling memory-film. The traditional plot of the *Bildungsroman* re-emerges in Thalheim's film to represent an individual's development into a citizen of Europe, capable of initiating dialogic memory. *Whose is This Song?* is part of a body of films that seem to be forming a distinct genre, one that might be called the "transnational memory-quest-documentary." Such films draw on elements of the road movie and the quest-narrative, and they often trace a transcultural musical heritage, which is arguably one of the most evident instances of traveling memory.[28] Fatih Akin's *Crossing the Bridge: The Sound of Istanbul*

---

the discussion of *Calais* in Dasgupta (2008). On "memory citizenship" in migratory settings, see Rothberg and Yildiz (2011).

[28] Fevry (2015) has shown that "traveling photographs" are also a significant media form in contemporary memory-quest-documentaries (for example, in *No Pasarán, Album Souvenir*, 2003, dir.

(2005) belongs to this group of films, as does, for example, *The Pied Piper of Hützovina* (2007, dir. Pavla Fleischer). While *And Along Come Tourists* deals with questions of mnemonic relationality in a mode of soft, reconciliatory irony, the critical form in Peeva's film is an often bitter dramatic irony. It exposes the false rationalizations underlying nationalist memories in what actually is a transcultural mnemonic space.

Calais: The Last Border evokes mnemonic relationality through a form of crosscutting, which—ever since the early twentieth century—has been used to convey the simultaneity or relatedness of events, usually in order to create suspense. With the critical vocabulary developed by memory studies today, we can describe the technique of *Calais* and its functions as multidirectional montage. As in the case of the *Bildungsroman* plot and the structure of dramatic irony, a time-tested aesthetic feature is turned into a vehicle of the traveling memory-film. More than the other filmic forms discussed here (which are forms of *representing* processes of transcultural memory), multidirectional montage actively creates a sense of mnemonic relationality, thus *producing* transcultural memory. With its action taking place in a migratory setting, the film moreover highlights that traveling memory requires a "stop on the road." The movement of mnemonic repertoires needs to come to a (however preliminary) halt so that the process of mnemonic relationality can begin.

In the traveling memory-films presented in this chapter, the ineluctable transculturality of memory in Europe emerges in different ways. Europe is represented as a site of shared histories, in which attempts at dialogic memory are made. It is exposed as a space in which traveling memory remains unacknowledged, and transculturality is resentfully denied. It is, eventually, seen as a contact zone, in which multidirectional memory could create a broadened space of experience that is shared by both citizens and illegal immigrants, by "old" and "new" Europeans.

Henri-François Imbert). The sheer extent of the transcultural circulation of melodies was pointed out as early as the nineteenth century by Wilhelm Tappert. As Tappert (1889, 5) asserts: "Melodies travel. They are the most indefatigable tourists on earth." (My translation; I owe this reference to Jarula Wegner.)

Chapter 3
Homer—A Relational Mnemohistory

3.1 Odysseus, the Refugee

In his much acclaimed book *The New Odyssey: The Story of Europe's Refugee Crisis*, Patrick Kingsley (2016, 10), then migration reporter for *The Guardian*, writes about today's refugees:

> Their voyages through the Sahara, the Balkans, or across the Mediterranean—on foot, in the holds of wooden fishing boats, on the backs of land cruisers—are almost as epic as that of classical heroes such as Aeneas and Odysseus.

It was in the eventful year of 2015 that Kingsley traveled with refugees from places like Syria, Afghanistan, and Eritrea, all of them on what he calls a "latterday Homeric odyssey" (Kingsley 2016, 251).

Refugees from Asia and Africa as new Odysseus figures? This is cultural memory at work. One of memory's fundamental dynamics consists in the actualization of (sometimes age-old) narrative schemata in order to capture new challenges. Seen in this way, the *Odyssey* is a powerful source for premediation (see Erll 2017). Clearly, there are cues in the present situation that elicit memories of the *Odyssey*, most obviously the refugees' dangerous sea journeys across the Mediterranean. One major, perilous, and much-covered refugee route is that via inflatable boat from the west coast of Anatolia—the likely location of Troy (from where Odysseus set out on his ten-year journey home to Ithaca after the Trojan War)—across the Aegean Sea to Greek islands such as Lesbos, and thus to an aspired-to new "home" in the European Union. Of course, there is also the fact that the word "odyssey" has crept into everyday speech as a term for a proverbially long, errant, and adventurous journey. (The *Oxford English Dictionary* registers this use since the late nineteenth century.)

Yet strictly speaking, Homer's Odysseus is no refugee figure at all. He is a war hero on his way home, inventor of the Trojan horse, and thus responsible for the destruction of Troy. Using him as a paradigm for today's refugees fleeing from war in the Near East and dismal living conditions elsewhere is a highly selective actualization of *one* epithet that the Homeric epic associates with Odysseus: *polytlas*, "much-enduring." This adjective is repeatedly used in Kingsley's *New Odyssey* to refer to its protagonists. Homer's hero, however, is characterized by a few more and rather different epithets. He is also a "much-traveled" (*polytropos*) and a "cunning" (*polymetis*) man—for Dante, in his *Divina Commedia* (1321), a good reason to imagine him as a sinner, a fraudulent counselor, and also as someone who wants to know too much and therefore travels too far.

The mnemohistory of the *Odyssey* is rich in selective actualization as we see it in Kingsley (and for other reasons also in Dante).[1] Banal memory, this Homeric framing of the refugee crisis, one might say, but when unpacked, such references to the *Odyssey*, and to Homer in general, reveal much about present European self-images and narrative capabilities in the face of crisis. They prove to be loaded with crucial assumptions about Europe, its history and heritage, its present, and its future.

Understanding histories of exile and migration in terms of an odyssey is not entirely new. It was a major form of Homeric memory in the twentieth century. Ever since the early 1900s, memories of the *Odyssey* have been used to address the displacements brought about by modernization, colonialism, wars, and the Holocaust—from James Joyce's modernist errancy in Dublin (*Ulysses*, 1922) to Primo Levi's testimony of Auschwitz (*Se questo è un uomo*, 1947) to Derek Walcott's new world epic *Omeros* (1990) and to Jonathan Shay's psychological study *Odysseus in America: Combat Trauma and the Trials of Homecoming* (2010).[2] What is new is the cast. We have seen Irish, Jewish, African American, and Caribbean Odysseus figures, but the articulation of histories experienced by refugees from sub-Saharan Africa and the Near and Middle East in Homeric terms is new—at least within the Anglophone media cultures within which Kingsley operates.

What are the implications of a British, a European (and then-still European Union) reporter framing the journeys of the refugees he has followed as Odyssean? What is the explanatory value of re-actualizing this archaic memory when it comes to the entangled histories that are currently in the making

---

[1] On the concept of "memohistory" as the history of cultural remembering, see Assmann (1997).
[2] Hall (2008) provides an excellent account of the myriad reuses of the *Odyssey*. Standard works on *Odyssey* rewritings are Stanford (1954) and Boitani (1994). On the reception of Homer in the twentieth century, see Graziosi and Greenwood (2010).

between Europe, Africa, and Asia in the so-called refugee crisis? These are questions that call not only for transnational and transcultural approaches to memory but also for a focus on memory's *longue durée*—for a transtemporal perspective on the histories of remembering that may (as in the case of Homer) extend over millennia.[3]

3.2 Reconsidering Mnemohistory from a Transcultural Perspective

Over the past decade, and in the wake of its preoccupation with transcultural dynamics, research in memory studies has greatly widened its field of inquiry in the category of space. Yet at the same time, it has converged around a somewhat restricting canon of *remembered times*. The entangled histories addressed tend to be the violent events of the twentieth century, with offshoots into nineteenth-century colonialism and into twenty-first-century terrorism. The *time of remembering* (i.e., of mnemonic practices) studied is usually the "now" of contemporary globalizing society, media, and arts. As a result of these choices, the field has narrowly focused on certain *modes of remembering*, first and foremost that of the traumatic, a mode of addressing the past that seems to travel particularly well in today's media cultures.

What the field tends to overlook in its current constellation is, first, long-term developments of transcultural memory beyond the span of three or four generations; second, ecologies of media and traveling memory (e.g., manuscript cultures) that are distinctly different from those of the past century, which centered around print, broadcast, and the digital; and third, the production of memory across knowledge and belief systems, spatial imaginaries, temporal and emotional regimes other than those in our globalizing present. In short, what we miss is mnemohistory in a transcultural perspective.[4] Such mnemohistorical approaches would provide the opportunity to throw into relief the detailed knowledge that memory studies has gained

---

[3] The *Annales* historians' use of *longue durée* with its emphasis on permanence does not quite catch the long-term dynamics of memory. Memories like that of Homer are both enduring and highly versatile. A more fitting concept is Armitage's (2012, 498) "transtemporal history," modeled on "transnational history to stress elements of linkage and comparison across time, much as transnational history deals with such connections across space."

[4] Jan Assmann's (2011 [1992]) groundbreaking work on "cultural memory in early civilizations" is a synchronic comparative history of memory; but his *Moses the Egyptian* (1997) unfolds a transtemporal mnemohistory.

about transcultural and transnational remembering in the present, and even enable the possibility of finding unexpected solutions for some of the conundrums generated by (or at least difficult to solve within) its predominantly presentist approach.

How can we study transcultural memory in a transtemporal perspective? As the current discourse around refugees on their way to Europe shows, Homer is one of the striking examples of memory contents that have "come a long way" and still reverberate today.[5] We can look back on more than two and a half millennia of remembering Homer (virtually across the globe), accompanied by ever-changing forms of temporal consciousness, ideas of identity, and normativity. The conundrum dealt with in this chapter is the problematic idea of "Homer as heritage" in an age of globalization, transnational theory, and transcultural memory studies, in view of the European project and the current refugee crisis.

3.3 Homer: A Genea-Logic

Cultural memory has a history, and in some cases a very long history. Homer marks the advent of writing in archaic Greece. The Homeric epics (the *Iliad* and the *Odyssey*) are among the first extant poetic texts in ancient Greek script (Graziosi 2016). This is why they are often cast as Europe's "first memory." A hazy memory—even today, the "Homeric question" is not solved. Virtually nothing is known about the author(s). Most scholars assume that the epics are *not* the product of one "original genius," but have emerged from a long-standing oral tradition and were transcoded into writing during the late eighth or seventh century BCE, in all probability by more than one person.[6]

Memories of Homer span more than 2,500 years. This mnemohistory reaches a first peak in Athens of the fifth and fourth centuries BCE, when Homeric texts had become institutionalized and canonized literature, sung at Panhellenic festivals and taught to schoolboys. Jan Assmann (2011 [1992]) has shown how, during the period of classical Greece, Homer was used to effect "Greek ethnogenesis." Remembering the *Iliad* had the integrative

---

[5] Other obvious choices would be the Bible, other sacred and mythological texts (from the Vedas and Mahabharata to the Qur'an), and texts by canonical authors (e.g., Virgil and Shakespeare).

[6] Oral-formulaic theory was developed by Milman Parry in the early twentieth century and was anticipated by Friedrich August Wolf in the late eighteenth century. With its distinction between oral and written forms of transmission, it is also a cornerstone of both media and memory studies.

power to unite many different political units under a Panhellenic awareness, specifically in the face of the Greco-Persian wars. In classical Greece, Homer was thus cast as a cultural "forefather," and the stories he was supposed to have sung were seen as crucial for the cohesion of a "transnational" formation of Hellenes living in different *poleis* as well as in various settlements across the Mediterranean. Homer's epics "became a 'great tradition' that ... kept the consciousness of belonging to a wider, 'interlocational' community alive" (Assmann, 2011 [1992], 251).

Today Homer is remembered along surprisingly similar lines in many parts of the world. The dominant memory is that of Homer as origin, founding father, and cornerstone—not so much of Hellas, but of European (or "Western") civilization. This becomes obvious (to give just one example from the thick texture of classical memory in Europe and beyond) in Dublin's Trinity College Library. Since 1743, its Long Room has been adorned with a line of marble busts of what the college's webpage calls "the great philosophers and writers of the western world." It features heads of Aristotle, Shakespeare, Cicero, Francis Bacon, John Locke, and Jonathan Swift. And it starts with: "Homerus."[7]

Such a spatial arrangement expresses a genealogical imagination, a line that runs from Greece via Rome to early modern England, Ireland, and to present-day Dublin. This is an instantiation of a modern Homeric "genea-logic" (to adapt a term coined by Sigrid Weigel, 2006), the idea of an uninterrupted teleological and generative movement, starting in archaic Greece and ending up wherever the rememberer may be positioned—usually somewhere in Europe, or "the West."

Parts of this logic were already in place in antiquity, during the Middle Ages and the Renaissance. But it was Romantic Hellenism of the eighteenth and nineteenth centuries that vigorously posited the Homeric epics as the foundational texts of Europe—an appropriation of the cultural memory of Greek antiquity whose consequences are still palpable today. In the words of literary critic Harold Bloom (1975, 33), "Everyone who now reads and writes in the West, of whatever racial background, sex or ideological camp, is still a son or daughter of Homer." This is the acknowledgment of a debt,[8] but when turned around, it raises some delicate questions. What about those who write in the East? Or the Global South? The modern Homeric genea-logic suggests that Homer is the rightful "inheritance" of the West, one that has

---

[7] https://www.tcd.ie/library/old-library/long-room/ (accessed September 7, 2023).
[8] On the history of the idea of "classical debt" and its role in the Eurozone crisis, see Hanink (2017).

come through the "bloodline" of Europe's history—Homer as European heritage.

Even for those who are less sure of the blessings of the West, Homer's foundational position remains a given. In the *Dialectic of Enlightenment*, a seminal work of the Frankfurt School written shortly after the Holocaust and World War II, Adorno and Horkheimer (2009 [1948], 37) position the Homeric epics as "the basic text of European civilization." In their reading, the *Odyssey* already enacts the dialectic between myth and enlightenment that would come to characterize modern Europe and culminate in the "fraudulent myth of fascism." Odysseus emerges as the "prototype of the bourgeois individual" (Adorno and Horkheimer 2009 [1948], 25), a figure whose instrumental rationality will bring him home to Ithaca in the end, but only at the expense of his crew and most of the creatures he meets. Thus, even in critical theory, the Homeric genea-logic is inescapable, a tenacious and seemingly natural given—a fact that reveals the path-dependency of cultural memory, the longevity of patterns of recall that are established and re-established in the course of long mnemohistories. While Adorno and Horkheimer question the *normative* implications of this heritage, its *formative* dimension (its connection to the identity of Europe) is still taken for granted. Homer is turned into a "dark genealogy," but it remains European genealogy.

If we consult recent scholarship on Homer that is produced within the interesting new field of "classical reception studies,"[9] then the verdict about such ideas of Homer as heritage of Europe or the West is unmistakable. In *Afro-Greeks*, a study of the presence of Greco-Roman antiquity in Anglophone Caribbean literature, Emily Greenwood (2010, 2) states with sufficient clarity, "Through false genealogies and cultural traditions masked as historical continuities, ancient Greece is often carelessly and erroneously linked with modern Europe, as though they shared a single, continuous history."

The concept of Homer as heritage, in the sense of "property"[10] passed on by an ancestor, inherited through a genealogical line, to which present-day Europeans (whoever *they* might be in an age of postcolonialism and

---

[9] In her editorial to the first issue of the *Classical Receptions Journal* (founded in 2009), classicist Lorna Hardwick (2009, 1) states that the field of classical reception studies covers "all aspects of the reception of the texts and material culture of ancient Greece and Rome, both within antiquity and subsequently." Classical receptions are essentially a form of cultural memory. There is a great and as yet largely untapped potential for a dialogue between the two fields (see Scherer 2021).

[10] One of the problems of the term "heritage" is that it "invariably implies ownership," as heritage scholar Sharon Macdonald (2013, 18) emphasizes.

migration) would have a "right," even an exclusive right—this Homer does not exist. There is no single historical, continuous line that would lead from archaic Greece to Ireland, Britain, or Germany, to any other European nation, to Europe as we envision it today, or to the much-maligned "West."

The reasons for this are many, and they are well researched: Near and Middle Eastern, and possibly Egyptian influences on Homer's epics (on the levels of language, mythology, and literary forms); the strong likelihood that the *Iliad* was created and is set in Asia Minor, today's Anatolia; or the fact that manuscripts of the Homeric epics were all but lost to western Europe during the Middle Ages and could only be brought back with help from Byzantine scholars. Today, Homer, if anything, seems to have become a kind of global heritage, appropriated and remediated in Hollywood as well as in Indigenous poetry from New Zealand.[11] Some of the aesthetically most convincing claims to Homeric memory have been made in twentieth-century Caribbean literature. When we search the internet for a modern-day Odysseus, it is very likely that it will refer us to the current refugee crisis or to films like Samir's *Iraqi Odyssey* (2014), a documentary about new diasporas from the Middle East.

And last but not least, our present conception of Europe (part and parcel of the modern Homeric genea-logic) emerged only millennia after Homer. In the *Iliad*, "Europe" is still evoked as a Phoenician princess, abducted by Zeus and brought to the island of Crete. In light of all this, how can we address the conspicuous presence of Homer today, the significant cultural work that memories of the *Iliad* and the *Odyssey* are doing across the globe—in the face of a tenacious discourse that continues to turn Homer into European heritage? How can we speak about Homer and Europe in a way that is both critical of false genealogies and still meaningful for Europe's present and future?

3.4 Homer as Heritage? Toward a Relational Mnemohistory

One way of dealing with the question of Homer as European heritage would be to deconstruct the whole idea and forget about Homer. Another way would be to universalize and treat Homer as the heritage of humankind,

---

[11] For example, the Coen Brothers' movie *O Brother, Where Art Thou* (2000) and Robert Sullivan's collection of poems *Star Waka* (1999).

a world heritage. But while the strategy of deconstruction might lead to a denial of those links between Homer and Europe that *do* exist (most of all, its strong reception or mnemohistory), the strategy of universalization, the claim that Homer is "everybody's heritage," implies the risk of unspecific, ahistorical generalization, foreclosing engagement with the specific, sometimes uneven, histories of what Homer has meant to whom at different times.

There is a third way of addressing the conundrum of Homer as heritage after the transcultural turn in memory studies, a way of making the memory of Homer meaningful for today's Europeans and non-Europeans alike. This entails conceiving Homeric memory through the lens of relationality: as the result of ongoing interactions between individuals and groups, among partners, neighbors, strangers, or even enemies, in the texts' creation as well as in their transmission and reuse—within transregions as well as across time. Understanding Homer as relational memory means more than just reiterating the truism of our postcolonial and globalizing age that much of what is cast as "European heritage" has its roots and uses elsewhere. Starting with the idea that the processes of memory that make and unmake heritage are fundamentally relational, this chapter tries to tease out the potential of the relationality concept for research interested in the transtemporal dynamics of transcultural memory.

"Relationality" is a term discussed in philosophy, psychoanalysis, feminist theory, autobiography research, sociology, family studies, the neurosciences, postcolonial studies, and new materialism. Across these various fields, it tends to describe an ongoing connectivity among diverse elements, which creates meaningful structures and at the same time transforms all elements involved. In the words of sociologist Powell (2013, 187), a radically relational perspective means "understanding all phenomena as constituted through relations, and treating relations themselves as processes or transformations." Bringing together the concepts of memory and relationality, it can be claimed (with a nod to psychoanalysis) that the Other is co-constitutive when it comes to the making of our own memory and identity,[12] and (with a nod to sociology) that memory *is* relation and does not *have* relations.[13]

---

[12] See also Eakin (1999, 43) in his seminal study on life writing: "All identity is relational." For a memory studies approach, see Campbell (2003).

[13] A phrase adapted from relational sociologist Pierpaolo Donati (2011, xv): "society does not host relations, it is not a space-time where relations happen, *it is* relations." See also Crossley (2012).

There is no entity called "memory" prior to relationality—this was basically Maurice Halbwachs's insight.[14] And there is no heritage prior to often long histories of relational remembering. Writing mnemohistory through the lens of relationality promises to provide a sense of how all remembering is grounded in diverse forms of interrelation, across the diverse scales and dimensions of memory: between individuals and groups; different cultural formations; neuronal, social, and material dimensions; the human and the nonhuman. Seen through the lens of relationality, memory emerges as a co-constructive and transformative process, one in which images and narratives about the past become related to one another in a way that creates new meaning and—once this has happened—makes it hard or impossible to disentangle the individual elements again.

To put this theoretical idea into practice, I will outline a relational mnemohistory of Homer by highlighting three decisive moments. The first moment is the beginning of Homer translations in the western European Middle Ages, the second leads us back to archaic Greece, and the third propels us forward to modernist and postcolonial writing of the twentieth century.

3.5 *Aide-mémoire*: Finding Homer in the Middle Ages

> Believe me, I could receive no more valuable nor acceptable merchandise either from the Chinese, or the Arabs, or from the shores of the Red Sea.[15]

This is Francesco Petrarch in the year 1360. What the man who significantly prepared Renaissance Humanism (he is often called the "first modern poet") writes about in this letter to his friend Boccaccio, and what emerges here as an exotic, precious good from the East, is a manuscript of Homer's epics.

The example of Petrarch shows that what we understand today without much further thought as the foundation of European literature and culture, ubiquitous and easily accessible, appeared to medieval scholars in western Europe as all but lost. The few surviving manuscripts of the Homeric epics were scattered across the Byzantine Empire. The world around

---

[14] Halbwachs emphasized how social interaction shapes the way we remember, even in most personal situations—to the extent that "we are in fact never alone" ("C'est qu'en réalité nous ne sommes jamais seuls" (Halbwachs 1997 [1950], 52).

[15] Milan, August 18, 1360 (quoted in Cosenza 1910, 179).

Constantinople (today's Istanbul), the eastern Roman Empire, is the region where schoolboys had to memorize lines from the Homeric epics and where scholars continued to copy, edit, interpret, and comment on Homer, within shifting contact zones of Greece, the Balkans, and the Arabic-Islamic world (Browning 1975).

In 1353–1354, a few years before Petrarch wrote his letter to Boccaccio, Nicola Sigero, the ambassador of the Byzantine emperor, had already sent him from Constantinople a copy of the *Iliad*. But ancient Greek was utterly unreadable to the medieval poet (Sowerby 1997). In a thank-you letter to Sigero, Petrarch's famous words are: "Your Homer remains silent to me, or rather I am dumb to him."[16] All reliable Latin translations from earlier centuries had been lost or forgotten. And worse still, translators with a grasp of both Latin and ancient Greek were rare to nonexistent in fourteenth-century Italy. Petrarch could lay his hands on two go-betweens from the Byzantine Empire, Calabrians of Greek ancestry, and about the second one, Leonzio Pilato, he writes: "With the help of God may he restore to us Homer, who, as far as we are concerned, is a lost author."[17] In Florence, Boccaccio made Leonzio the first professor of Greek in western Europe.

Petrarch and his friends were instrumental in recovering what they saw as a lost treasure. In the end, it would take Petrarch thirteen years to eventually read the Latin translation of the Homeric epics he had commissioned. But he was not happy with Leonzio's result, a verbatim prose translation in vulgar Latin. For Petrarch, his difficult transactions with Leonzio had produced a warped memory of Homer.

Petrarch's search and eventual finding of Homer is a key moment in modern European mnemohistory. There is a sense in Petrarch's letters that Homer is "inaccessible heritage"—the paradox of something that appears to be a rightful inheritance and at the same time remains illegible. Four hundred years later, a similar desire to claim an unsighted or unrevealed heritage can be sensed in Johann Joachim Winckelmann's approach to classical Greece, in the young Goethe teaching himself Homeric Greek (and later ironizing the emotional attachment to "my Homer" in *Werther*, 1774), as well as in John Keats's praise of George Chapman's early modern English translations of the epics ("On First Looking into Chapman's Homer," 1816).

---

[16] Milan, January 10, 1354 (Petrarch 1985, 46–47). Despite several attempts, Petrarch would never be able to learn ancient Greek during his life.

[17] Petrarch's letter to Boccaccio from August 18, 1360 (quoted in Cosenza 1910, 180).

Even today, it can be felt in the ongoing and highly emotionalized controversies about the location of Troy and the identity of Homer.

But more importantly, Petrarch's case also shows how the modern European memory of Homer was first of all enabled by a history of relational memory-making: the travel of manuscripts from eastern Roman to western Roman spheres, the renewed relationality of Latin and Greek through the activity of translation, as well as the (often difficult) relations between a group of wealthy Italian artists, full of prejudice toward the Byzantine Greek world but eager to recover ancient Greek cultural memory, and two rather reluctant (and as it seems, at least in the case of Leonzio, charlatanesque) *emigré*-translators from the Byzantine Empire.

In fact, many players involved in the making of Homer as heritage were *not* what is commonly understood as "European" today. Without the significant eastern Roman legacies of the modern West, but also—going further back in time—without Mesopotamia and Phoenicia as sources of stories and script for the Homeric epics, without Hellenistic Egypt and its library of Alexandria (since the third century BCE), where manuscripts were copied and edited, and where the groundwork for Homer as material heritage was laid, there would be no "Homer" today, and certainly no "Homer as European heritage." In Petrarch's age, it needed a little *aide-mémoire*, a little help from, not a friend, but rather a rivaling and mistrusted co-inheritor of Greco-Roman antiquity, to set Homer as heritage on the road to western Europe. But before that road and its ramifications are further explored, a glance back toward the beginnings of what is cast now as "Homer" may be in place.

3.6 Archaic Constellations: Transculturality and Tellability

Homer marks the introduction of Greek script in the archaic world. This is the very script in which the foundational texts by Herodotus, Plato, Aristotle, Sophocles, and Euripides would be written, texts that would become models for Latin writing in the Roman Empire and would "travel" from there (as we have seen, not always in straightforward ways) to the Middle Ages, in order to end up (among other places) in modern western Europe.

But of course, the Greek alphabet was adapted from the Phoenicians in the mid-eighth century BCE, during a phase of close cultural contact that resulted, as Walter Burkert has emphasized, in the "orientalizing period" in Greek art.[18] Thus, we encounter relationality, connectedness, and co-construction already on the level of the very medium that encoded "Europe's first memory." The Phoenicians were a Semitic civilization, with origins in what is now Lebanon, Israel, Gaza, Syria, and southwest Turkey. They were traders, and trade brought them all over the Mediterranean. At the same time, Ionians and other Greek tribes had colonized the coast of Asia Minor. Islands like Euboea, Cyprus, Crete, and Rhodes were what we might call today Iron Age contact zones. The Hellenic world was a transregion whose range of communications reached far beyond present-day maps of Greece or Europe. All this calls into question what Burkert (1992, 3) criticizes as "the image of pure self-contained Hellenism which makes its miraculous appearance with Homer."

In their production, the Homeric epics are a prime example of an object of memory that resulted from the mix of cultural repertoires, confirming the idea that once we move from the remembering actors' to the analytical perspective, we see that all memory is always already transcultural (see Erll 2011b). There is a long history of scholarship investigating the non-European influences on Greek antiquity. Books like Victor Bérard's *Les Phéniciens et l'Odyssée* (1902) come to mind, a book that James Joyce read while he was writing his *Ulysses* (1922). Martin Bernal's popular *Black Athena* (1987) puts strong emphasis on the alleged African roots of Greek antiquity. Walter Burkert's *The Orientalizing Revolution* (1992) studies Near Eastern influence on Greece in the archaic age. In *The East Face of Helicon*, Martin L. West (1997) details, among other aspects, the parallels between the Mesopotamian Gilgamesh-epic and Homer's *Odyssey*. And Johannes Haubold (2013) has pointed to the cultural dialogues of Greece and Mesopotamia across time.

All these authors have grappled with and intervened in mnemohistory. They tell critical histories of how dominant memories of Greek antiquity were produced, in order to question, deconstruct, or recast them. Seen in this way, Bernal's controversial *Black Athena* (1987) and its discussion of the history of German classical studies (*Altertumswissenschaften*) during the nineteenth century as a history of the vigorous "purging" of classical antiquity of Egyptian and Semitic influences is a mnemohistorical treatise in its

---

[18] Burkert (1992). See also West (1997, 624–625): "The Greek poets' debts to Near Eastern traditions . . . presuppose situations in which Greeks and peoples of the East lived side by side for extended periods and communicated fluently in a shared language."

own right—albeit one that is strongly contested in classics departments.[19] This line of research (from popular, even populist, examples to serious scholarship) constitutes in itself an interesting history of the shifting grounds of transcultural memory, of imagining and coming to terms with the relational nature of European heritage, a process complicated by often scanty linguistic, literary, and archaeological evidence, "the scattered and difficult cultural data that have come down to us," in the words of classicists Lefkowitz and Rogers (1996, xii).

It also testifies to the recurring problems of making histories of relationality heard. As much as the contributions by Bernal, West, Burkert, and many others are visible and much read (Bernal in fact continues to appeal to a wide non-academic readership, including Afrocentric activist circles), the dominant memory of what the German classicist Joachim Latacz (1989) calls "Homer as the first poet of the occident" springs back again and again. Memory studies has worked with different concepts to make sense of such paradoxes: "frameworks" and "framing," for example, "aphasia," and "tellability."[20]

The concept of tellability was originally developed in conversational storytelling analysis. It is connected to the notion of relevance and refers to

> features that make a story worth telling, its "noteworthiness." Tellability ... is dependent on the nature of specific incidents judged by storytellers to be significant or surprising and worthy of being reported in specific contexts, thus conferring a "point" on the story. (Baroni 2014, 836)

A good story, a tellable story—however surprising it may be—needs to be in accordance with the basic cognitive schemata and frames of its listeners. In mainstream memory cultures across Europe (and possibly beyond), the cognitive frame of "interrelation" tends to clash with the frame of "classical heritage." The story of the interrelatedness of Homer within Iron Age transregions (or that of transcultural memories leading up to Bronze Age Mesopotamia or Egypt) does not reach the threshold of tellability in many contexts—a problem resulting largely from the fact that modern memory

---

[19] Most of Bernal's claims about Egyptian influences that he racializes as "black" are refuted by classicists. For critical discussions of Bernal's work, see Lefkowitz and Rogers (1996) and Berlinerblau (1999); for a reappraisal, see Orrells et al. (2011).
[20] On "social frameworks of memory," see Halbwachs (1994 [1925]); on "colonial aphasia," see Stoler (2008); on memory and "tellability," see Savolainen (2017).

lacks an idea of relationality. How can an epic be "Hellenic" (and thus, as the genealogical story goes, foundational for Europe) and at the same time have ancestors elsewhere? How can a heritage be European but also related to Near and Middle Eastern, possibly even African worlds? These recurrent frame-clashes give rise to the question of how the historical relationalities at the basis of cultural memory in and about Europe can be adequately remembered today.

3.7 Relationality in Reception: Modernist and Postcolonial Remediations of Homer

Relationality operates not only across space but also in the dimension of time, as transtemporal relationality. Translation, rewriting, remediation, transformation, or classical receptions—these are some of the terms used to describe the ever-renewed Homeric memories created over the centuries. Traveling memory is never a one-way road. Each author, each epoch will "return" a transformed Homer. This is a dynamics addressed in postcolonial studies as well as in research on world literature and classical reception studies. Remediations (my cover term of choice) are acts of cultural memory. They are ineluctably relational processes, bringing into relation authors of different times, old and new media forms and technologies, the ancient and the modern. In the case of Homer, remediations go back at least as far as Virgil and—as the example of his Roman epic, the *Aeneid*, shows—they have often been instrumental in producing (purely imaginary) genealogies, connecting empires and nations to what in the Middle Ages was called the "matter of Troy," or creating "genealogies of poetic spirit," such as when Goethe in his elegy "Hermann und Dorothea" (1796) understands himself as a "Homeride."[21]

A glance at twentieth-century literary history reveals that remediations of Homer flourished most in colonial and postcolonial situations. With the Irishman James Joyce (*Ulysses*, 1922) and the St. Lucian Derek Walcott (*Omeros*, 1990), two hypercanonical authors have produced striking memories of Homer—and both hail from countries with histories of British colonialism. Paradoxically, however, as Emily Greenwood (2010, 3) points out, modern postcolonial studies tends to unwittingly perpetuate the

---

[21] *Homeridae* (Greek for "children of Homer") were professional rhapsodes (first mentioned by Pindar in the early fifth century BCE), who sang poems attributed to Homer.

erroneous conception of ancient Greece as exclusive heritage and property of Europe:

> [I]nsofar as "Greece" makes it into contemporary postcolonial theory at all, it tends to be carelessly subsumed in loose, totalizing descriptors such as: "the west," "European cultural heritage," "European history," "European *imperium*," "western history," "western culture," "western *imperium*," "western episteme," "occidental knowledge," or, even more loosely, phrases such as "the imperial tradition" or "the colonial archive."

How could it have come to that? In the nineteenth and early twentieth centuries, Homer had become an integral part of the imperial project. After the revival of Greek antiquity in the eighteenth century (the second emphatic turn to Homer after Renaissance Humanism), the study of ancient Greek, and particularly of Homer's *Iliad* and *Odyssey*, became the kernel of education in many European nation-states. Homer was cast as the heritage—not *of* Europe, but rather of many individual nations within Europe.[22] In Britain, Romantic Hellenism turned into colonial Hellenism, Greco-Roman antiquity was used to legitimize the imperial project, to link Britain with ancient imperial powers, and to justify her civilizing mission. This also included bringing colonial education to places like the Caribbean. The roots of the modern equation of Homer, with, first, authority and civilization, then, European nations, and eventually, the imperial center and "the West"— the roots, that is, of the very genea-logic discussed at the outset of this chapter—lie in the eighteenth and nineteenth centuries.

It is one of the ironies of the history of the British Empire that, after the thorough exposure of colonized people to Greek and Latin, it is now Caribbean authors like Derek Walcott and Wilson Harris who can lay the strongest claim to Homer as their heritage. But they don't. Derek Walcott rejects the modern European genea-logic, and he advances in his seminal essay "The Muse of History" (1974) the alternative idea of a simultaneity with the Old. Homer is thus not cast as a literary ancestor, to be retrieved through the construction of a line, but as a co-presence, with whom the Caribbean author can enter into a relation on par.

Both Joyce's *Ulysses* and Walcott's *Omeros* are literary texts that use their fictional space to create new, imaginative forms of relationality. In a

---

[22] Nation-building and the translation of Homer went hand in hand; by the early twentieth century, Homer was available in almost all European vernaculars (see Young 2003, 127–136).

self-reflexive mode, both have titles that already point to a relational mnemohistory and to the texts' own position in a chain of remediations: "Ulysses" is the Latinized version of the name Odysseus, as it can be found, for example, in Virgil's rewriting of the Homeric epics, the *Aeneid*. "Omeros" is a transcription of the modern Greek spelling of Homer. It thus evokes texts like Nikos Kazantzakis's *The Odyssey: A Modern Sequel* (1938), and it seems to ask what the remediation of an *ancient* text means in an age of *modernity*.

In *Omeros*, references to Homer, Virgil, and Dante are interwoven with histories of colonialism and slavery in the Caribbean. *Omeros* thus navigates across incommensurable histories and discrepant memories. Such literary relationalities do not support the assumption that histories of European colonialism and slavery may simply be mapped onto histories of colonialism and slavery in the Hellenic world. Such "analogical commensuration" (Melas 2007, 17) would mean falling back into the Homeric genea-logic of nineteenth-century imperialism.

What these relationalities do show only becomes visible once text and mnemonic context are combined in the analysis: Homer is a transcultural schema. In the twentieth century, it became available to (middle-class) Caribbean authors who used it to premediate new and different stories. In *Omeros*, literary relationalities are therefore a reminder of historical relationalities: of colonial education in the Caribbean, and of the transatlantic slave trade. Such acts of imaginative relational remembering make sure that the memory of Homer becomes and remains related to the memory of slavery—not because of aspects intrinsic to the Homeric epics or to the history of ancient Greece, but because of a mnemohistory that went hand in hand with colonial history.

In the modernist novel *Ulysses*, the protagonist Leopold Bloom, an Irish Jew, is a latter-day Odysseus, who crisscrosses Dublin on the single day of June 16, 1904. With Bloom's Semitic heritage, Joyce seems to nod toward the theories of his contemporary Victor Bérard about the Phoenician influence on the *Odyssey*. Irishness, Jewishness, and Greekness are reflexively interrelated in the novel as repertoires of modernist cultural memory. The novel thus displays an ironic fusion of cultures and memories that were, during Joyce's time, largely understood as separate and distinct. This is a comment on the impossibility of remembering Homer as a "thread that may have remained pure and virgin without having undergone the influence of a neighbouring thread"—to put it in Joyce's own words of his Trieste Lecture (Joyce 1959 [1907], 165). *Ulysses* and *Omeros* are literary

68   TRAVELS IN TIME

laboratories of mnemonic relationality. They explore new connections of available histories and memories, thus rendering relationality tellable.

3.8 New Relationalities

Three different perspectives on memory and relationality have emerged from my study of Homer as mnemohistory. First, *relationality of the remembered* describes a dynamics at the basis of the very historical events that will later be turned into objects of cultural memory. In the case of Homer in the archaic age, transcultural processes created and shaped what would soon be cast as exclusive heritage.

Second, *relational remembering* refers to forms of interaction and co-construction in the memory process. An investigation of the search for and arrival of Homer in the western European Middle Ages reveals relational dynamics among rivaling contemporaries in the archiving, passing on, and curating of memory. When practiced across time, relational remembering turns into a thoroughly mediated process. The neighboring field of classical reception studies draws attention to the histories of remediation that relate authors and readers, mediations and remediations over millennia.

A third dimension is *mnemonic relationality*, the relationalities that are consciously (and imaginatively) produced in (creative) acts of memory, as we find them in modernist and postcolonial remediations of Homer. This is a reflexive form of relational remembering, one that is often, but not exclusively, found in literature and the arts. In memory studies, the diverse forms of mnemonic relationality have been theorized, for example, as "dialogic" (A. Assmann 2014), "multidirectional" (Rothberg 2009), or "agonistic" (Bull and Hansen 2016). Mnemonic relationality describes acts of memory that bring into relation diverse (mnemo-)histories, thus enabling new or transformed memories to emerge.

Homer's epics, their creation, and passing-on are clearly *not* pure European history, and neither are they pure European memory. At the same time, there is no denying that Homer has been a strong, productive, and emotionally charged mnemonic presence in Europe across many centuries. Is Homer, then, European heritage? Taking mnemohistory into account, I would argue that Homer is a *relational* heritage (not *of*, but) *in* Europe.

Dealing with authors like Walcott in particular keeps the memory of relationality alive. It reminds readers in Europe that you cannot get your Homer cozily today without the memory of colonialism and slavery. But reading Petrarch's letters will also remind them that it was cultural exchanges across western and eastern empires that once made possible the idea of Homer as heritage.

All this is more complex than a neat chain of busts in a library, but it also offers a chance both to those who understand themselves as European or "Western" and those who do not: namely, the chance to develop a non-naïve sense of Homer (as well as any other object of cultural memory) as a heritage with a history—a history in which selves and others have been deeply entangled. Homer as heritage makes us aware that Europe and the West are "relational selves" (for better and worse), continually co-constructed and transformed, impossible to disentangle from its shifting "Other."

In *The New Odyssey*, Patrick Kingsley repeatedly resorts to framing his story on an epic scale, evoking not only Homer but also Virgil and Dante. Such references are not only a rhetorical strategy, the creation of a monumentalizing, larger-than-life mode, and thus a means of emphasis in a media culture vying for audiences' attention. They are also a hint at the idea of European heritage. Epic references are doing relational work here. They relate what is perceived (wrongly, as we have seen, but tenaciously so) as the heritage of Europe to what is perceived as "Europe's Others." Cultural schemata are turned into transcultural schemata and are used to create mnemonic relationality—on an epic scale indeed: across the *longue durée* of millennia and the transregions of Europe, Asia, and Africa. Kingsley (2016, 10) states: "Three millennia after their classical fore-bears created the founding myths of the European continent, today's voyagers are writing a new narrative that will influence Europe, for better or worse, for years to come." In light of the refugee crisis, Odysseus is both the forefather of a Syrian or Eritrean refugee *and* a foundational figure for Europe. Engaging the Homeric genea-logic in order to complicate it turns today's refugees into a constitutive part of Europe. It builds relationality through cultural memory and thus prepares readers for the new relationalities that the future will bring.

Chapter 4
Memory Worlds in Times of Corona

4.1 COVID-19 and Collective Memory

This essay, "Memory Worlds in Times of Corona," was written in the spring of 2020. It was an attempt at "thinking with memory studies" at the very onset of the pandemic. The voices from across the globe collected and analyzed in this essay all belong to the very first reactions to the pandemic. They each engaged collective memory in their efforts to achieve meaning in times of crisis.

COVID-19 was quickly understood as a global and near-simultaneous occurrence. It nevertheless played out very differently in different parts of the world. The coronavirus pandemic was an instance of what Ulrich Beck (2009) called our "world risk society," yet at the same time it revealed the fundamental situatedness of all experience. When the virus struck, people across the globe were "all in the same boat," but in vastly different ways.

This is also true for collective memory. Experiencing, remembering, forgetting, and memorializing are—even when humanity grapples with a more or less identical string of RNA—situated phenomena. They are part of particular "worlds of memory." Cultures and traditions of memory, knowledges of the past, are variable. "*The* collective memory" of COVID-19 therefore doesn't exist. Corona-memory must be thought of in the plural.

In the case of the coronavirus pandemic, it remains difficult to answer even the basic questions that arise in the social construction of a recent past: Was COVID-19 a singular, unprecedented event or part of a continuous history, a surprise or a foreseeable calamity? The answer depends on how pandemics have been collectively remembered (or forgotten) in a given world of memory.

Who is responsible for the pandemic? Who are its heroes? Who are the villains? Who are the victims? These anthropocentric questions, part and parcel of the modern memory regime, need to be rethought from a posthuman perspective, in light of an event with a viral mutation as the major agent of change. Moreover, responsibility is not easily locatable in a world shaped

Travels in Time. Astrid Erll, Oxford University Press. © Oxford University Press (2025).
DOI: 10.1093/oso/9780197767733.003.0005

by the coronavirus pandemic, which implicated individuals in complex ways (Rothberg 2019), sometimes as bystander, victim, hero, and beneficiary, all at the same time.

Last but not least, how can we imagine and build a future after the pandemic? This, too, depends on collective memory—on commemorative practices and on various other forms of remembering and forgetting (in science, the public, or education) that always take place *in* the present and *for* the future.

This chapter begins by considering some of the new social rhythms that emerged in the wake of COVID-19 in early 2020 around the world. It then turns to the role of collective memory *before*, *during*, and *after* the corona pandemic, thus providing a basic—but in terms of temporalities, highly permeable—grid for how the COVID-19 pandemic could be addressed using memory studies expertise. A "Coda" reconsiders the linkages of corona and collective memory from the vantage point of 2024.

4.2 New Rhythms: What COVID-19 Has Done to Time

Frankfurt, March 2020: After the lockdown, the order of time as we knew it is shaken. Clear temporal separations between time at work and time at home are suddenly obsolete. A variety of tasks, private and professional, have become embedded in and distributed across what appears like boundless days, unordered weeks, and indistinguishable months. The modern everyday experience of time and space—while moving in space, we realize how time passes—does not hold any longer. Everyone stays put. All that seems to be moving is the sun. Repetitive, cyclical patterns of temporal experience are emerging.

The corona crisis has subjected people around the world to new rhythms. Work, childcare, homeschooling, family visits, leisure, even eating, sleeping, and taking showers are—temporally—not what they used to be. What would a "rhythmanalysis" (Lefebvre 2017) look like, given the profound temporal changes in everyday life that the corona crisis brought about? The pandemic and resultant curfews and lockdowns across the world have shown how seemingly "natural patterns" of social time can break down and be thoroughly repatterned.

These new rhythms of everyday life may almost seem medieval, pointing back to a time when workplace (the bakery, the pottery, the blacksmith's forge) was part of the home, and working rhythms were woven together with domestic rhythms. Modernity, industrial revolution, and the more recent "great acceleration" of the globalizing age have, successively and ever-increasingly, done away with such older spatiotemporal patterns. For those caught up in the spiraling cycle of social acceleration, the lockdowns may even have come as "something akin to the relief one feels when one falls sick with exhaustion after a long period of hyperactivity," as the Indian novelist Amitav Ghosh notes.[1] According to the German sociologist of acceleration Hartmut Rosa, the collective forced deceleration is an opportunity to experience a new "resonance" with our immediate surroundings.[2]

But of course, all these observations are made from the relatively comfortable positions of middle-class authors, whether in Frankfurt, Calcutta, or Jena. Corona-rhythms look different in other worlds of temporal experience, and these worlds can be both far away and close to home, nested in otherwise leisurely paralyzed villages and cities. People in densely populated slum areas, from South Africa to Brazil, have to develop new routines when, under lockdown, everyone is forced to stay in tiny huts that were never designed to keep a great number of people inside all day. Workers without social security, from the United States to Kenya, keep following their daily routines, because they just cannot afford to do otherwise.[3] Outbreaks of COVID-19 among migrant workers in Germany's meat industry and in Singapore's building sector show that for some people, even in affluent countries, neither slowing down nor social distancing is possible. In this perspective, the new rhythms associated with the corona pandemic emerge as a marker of privilege.

The stasis of many middle-class lives also stands in stark contrast to the vortex of acceleration into which all those working in the critical infrastructures are drawn: truck drivers, police, and cashiers see their working hours extended in unprecedented ways. Medical personnel and politicians are

---

[1] Amitav Ghosh, "What We Have to Think about, Above All, Is to Slow Down," *The Hindu*, April 26, 2020. https://www.thehindu.com/books/what-we-have-to-think-about-above-all-is-how-to-slow-down-ami-tav-ghosh/article31414696.ece (unless stated otherwise, all websites were accessed in spring 2020 and reconfirmed and, if necessary, updated on December 1, 2023).

[2] Hartmut Rosa, "Es war nicht das Virus, das uns angehalten hat," *Zeit Magazin*, April 3, 2020, https://www.zeit.de/zeit-magazin/2020-04/hartmut-rosa-coronavirus-gesellschaft-wirtschaftssystem. See also Rosa (2017).

[3] Julian C. Jamieson, "Lockdowns Will Starve People in Low-Income Countries," *Washington Post*, April 20, 2020, https://www.washingtonpost.com/outlook/2020/04/20/lockdown-developing-world-coronavirus-poverty/.

having 24/7 rhythms and need to make fundamental, sometimes existential decisions in a formerly unheard of brevity of time.

This parallel world of ever-increasing speed—rising case numbers across the globe, ad hoc political measures, new scientific insights about the virus—is brought to those locked at home via media in real time. Digital media and methods make it possible to track the global spread of a virus with unprecedented precision. But interestingly, at the same time, we can observe the return of an older, almost forgotten regime of mass media: In addition to the now common forms of asynchronous information (via digital news and social media), people are returning to their radios and television sets (or their digital equivalents) in order to receive information about COVID-19 simultaneously. This is the return of a media-cultural practice last seen in the 1980s and 1990s. Nations assemble again before the 8 o'clock (or 9 o'clock) news in a way they haven't done in decades.[4] Is this a practice of coming together in a world where physical closeness is prohibited, a practice of experiencing and performing community?

Other practices of creating synchronicity in times of radical spatial separation are noticeable across the globe: Italians singing together from balconies, Spaniards clapping to applaud to their medical staff every evening, rainbows painted by children on windows worldwide. It seems that a new aesthetics of synchronicity as "social eurythmy" is emerging.[5]

The coronavirus pandemic engenders a sense of global simultaneity, produced by the mediation of minute statistics about infections and deaths around the world. This undeniably leads to a sense of the planetariness of our condition. But it does not necessarily lead to greater solidarity. With its rapid spread, COVID-19 paradoxically leaves the world in both a paralyzed and frenzied "now," with little time for future-thinking or attention paid to those outside the narrow emergency-frames of collective (usually national) identity—for example, the refugees on Europe's borders.[6]

---

[4] Television news such as the German *Tagesschau* have seen soaring viewing figures: https://www.ndr.de/fernsehen/sendungen/zapp/Mit-Corona-schlaegt-die-Stunde-der-Qualitaetsmedien.coronavirus620.html. In the United Kingdom, Boris Johnson's COVID-19 address is one of most-watched TV programs ever: https://www.theguardian.com/tv-and-radio/2020/mar/24/boris-johnsons-covid-19-address-is-one-of-most-watched-tv-programmes-ever.

[5] One example is a choreography for dancers of the Berlin State Ballet, who move to Beethoven's Symphony No. 7 (this is another anniversary thwarted by corona), each individually, from their home offices, and cross-cut into one collective stream. Staatsballett Berlin, "From Berlin with Love: Creating in Times of Corona," 2020, https://www.youtube.com/watch?v=h7Vt2MVJk4o.

[6] Emran Feroz, "In Europe, the Lives of Refugees Are on Hold," *Foreign Policy*, April 20, 2020, https://foreignpolicy.com/2020/04/20/europe-refugees-coronavirus-deportations-health-care/.

If COVID-19 is another moment of what Ulrich Beck (2009) has termed the "world risk society," then the pandemic seems to expose the world's unevenness, rather than bringing about a "cosmopolitan moment."[7] What happens at the same time around the globe is not the same everywhere. The synchronous experience of the viral process does not lead to a planetary eurythmy.

4.3 Memory *before* Corona: Forgetting Pandemics

What was remembered before the onset of the coronavirus pandemic? We could have seen it coming: Ebola, 2014–2016; Zika virus, 2015–2016; MERS, 2015; swine flu, 2009–2010; avian flu, 2004; SARS (i.e., SARS-CoV, the first SARS coronavirus), 2002–2003; AIDS (HIV), since 1980; Russian flu, 1977–1978; Hong Kong flu, 1968–1970; Asian flu, 1957–1958.

Pandemics are no surprises coming out of the blue, but rather are recurring events. But not so in European consciousness: For most Europeans, the idea of the pandemic was either projected on the premodern self (the plague) or the cultural and geographical Other: Ebola as a problem of West Africa, and recent influenzas, as their names falsely suggest, a concern of Asia.

If all these more recent pandemics were not memorable enough, the sheer casualty numbers of the Spanish flu of 1918–1919 should have guaranteed it a firm place in collective memory. The Spanish flu came in three waves, from spring 1918 to early 1919. According to recent estimations by medical historians, it killed between 50 and 100 million people worldwide, that is, between 2.5% and 5% of the global population.[8] According to Laura Spinney, author of the compelling *Pale Rider* (2018), a global history of the Spanish flu, which is full of food for thought for mnemonologists, this influenza pandemic was "the greatest demographic disaster of the 20th century, possibly of any century" (Spinney 2018, 171), with a death toll "surpassing the First World War (17 million dead), the Second World War (60 million dead) and possibly both put together" (Spinney 2018, 4). The Spanish flu is "the mother of all pandemics," also because it led, through viral mutations, to many of the smaller influenza and respiratory illness pandemics in the

---

[7] Beck (2009, 55–56) defines the "cosmopolitan moment" as a combination of "enforced enlightenment, communication across all divides and boundaries, the political power of catharsis, enforced cosmopolitanism, risks as a wake-up call in the face of the failure of governments, and the possibility of alternative forms of governance in a globalized world."

[8] See Johnson and Müller (2002); Spinney (2018, 4, 309, fn. 2).

following hundred years. But in everyday historical consciousness it seemed utterly forgotten.

In early 2020, pandemics such as the Spanish flu were, for most Europeans, just not part of what Reinhart Koselleck (2004) has called the "space of experience." In what could be termed a "collective remembering-imagining system,"[9] what is remembered in culture constitutes the space of experience, which in turn shapes what can be imagined as possible futures, the "horizon of expectation." But the Spanish flu was not a major item of the commemorative cycle or of school education, even after the recent "reawakening" of its memory in the context of the flu's centenary (see Beiner 2021). Perhaps most importantly, it was nowhere impressively mediated—while its mnemonic competitors, the world wars, were all this, and in all respects.

And this is precisely why the onset of the COVID-19 pandemic could thoroughly jumble up the relationship between space of experience and horizon of expectation: What Europeans thought or knew yesterday (about the dangers of a respiratory illness, about the possibilities of curfews or ad hoc legislation in their democratic societies, about compulsory school attendance, or economic stability) was blown away today—and would again be thoroughly transformed tomorrow. With surprising, and ever more surprising, virological and political news coming in each day, the new corona experience just did not match up with usual expectations. The corona pandemic quickly turned into an "imposition," as chancellor Angela Merkel said in her governmental statement on April 23, 2020, not only "on democracy," but also on many people's everyday sense of time and rhythms of change.[10]

All this has been different in different places of the world. South Korea showed a greater preparedness, because of their recent experience of severe SARS (2002) and MERS (2015) epidemics. People in Guinea, Sierra Leone, and Liberia appear little surprised by the COVID-19 pandemic, as they vividly remember the devastating Ebola epidemic of 2014. And then there are differences in habit memory (Connerton 1989) and differing situated knowledges (Haraway 1988), such as the ready usage of face masks

---

[9] On the psychological concept of the remembering-imagining system (RIS), see Conway et al. (2016).
[10] Angela Merkel, "Regierungserklärung von Bundeskanzlerin Dr. Angela Merkel zur Bewältigung der Covid-19-Pandemie in Deutschland und Europa vor dem Deutschen Bundestag am 23. April 2020 in Berlin," https://www.bundesregierung.de/breg-de/suche/regierungserklaerung-von-bundeskanzlerin-dr-angela-merkel-1746978.

across Asia (a habit which seems to go back in Japan and China to the Spanish flu) compared to arduous controversies over their relative usefulness in Europe.[11]

The anticipation of, preparedness for, and coping with future events on the basis of remembered experience has been discussed in the field of memory studies with a series of concepts holding "pre-" prefixes, such as "preforgetting" and "prememory" by Guy Beiner (2018), and "pretrauma" by Ann Kaplan (2016). I use the term "mnemonic premediation" (Erll 2017), because collective memory is essentially a matter of mediation, from oral conversation to films and social media. As all collective memory is mediated memory, all collective anticipation (or lack thereof) is therefore a matter of premediation. And in Europe, pandemics just have not been sufficiently mediated and remediated in the past—no famous paintings, novels, film, rarely very exciting lore of oral family history—so that they could then turn into a premediating force in the present. Such is the temporal dynamics of mediated memory.

The memory of the Spanish flu therefore remains, as Spinney (2018, 1) puts it, the "elephant in the room." But why are some elephants more visible than others in the commemorative room? Ann Rigney (2016) has thought about this question with the concept of "(differential) memorability." Considering the Spanish flu, several aspects emerge as playing into its failure to be memorable, and to mnemonically premediate the corona pandemic.

First, there is the question of the discreteness of historical events and the possibility of gaining a (however patchy) overview of them.[12] The Spanish flu virus was incredibly quick. It killed people often within no more than three days, and it was not diagnosable at the time, as viruses had not yet been made visible under the electron microscope. Therefore, the flu became entangled with other rampant sickness and epidemics, like tuberculosis and venereal disease. As an event, the Spanish flu therefore lacked discreteness, at least at the time of its experience.

What follows from this, second, is a lack of narrativity, the possibility to evoke a story in people's minds.[13] How can a story about an event emerge,

---

[11] Norimitsu Onishi and Constant Méheut, "Mask-Wearing Is a Very New Fashion in Paris (and a Lot of Other Places)," *New York Times*, published April 9, 2020 (updated May 7, 2020), https://www.nytimes.com/2020/04/09/world/europe/virus-mask-wearing.html.

[12] On the narrative logic of the historical event, see Ricœur (1984, 96–111); for a new memory studies approach to "restless events," see Wagner-Pacifici (2017).

[13] For a narratological definition of narrativity, see Ryan (2004).

if people don't know what the event is, where it started, and how it evolved?[14] Third, in its historical context, the flu lacked tellability: Harrowing as they were, flu deaths were less tellable (i.e., less noteworthy, they had less of a "point") than stories of heroic deaths on the battlefields of the First World War.[15] Fourth, memory culture verges toward the evaluative. And evaluations are easier to make when remembering human-made catastrophes, like war, genocide, or terror, where agency and responsibility are more clearly discernible than in what appears as natural catastrophes.[16]

Fifth, there is the question of archives: If an event like the Spanish flu pandemic cannot clearly be discerned by contemporaries, there will be a lack of sources which encode experience and memory for future reference. To be sure, in recent decades, historians have brought together global traces of the Spanish flu. But there are no major contemporaneous (or later) memoirs, paintings, novels, or films dedicated to the Spanish flu.[17] (Edvard Munch's self-portrait *After Spanish Influenza*, 1919, and Egon Schiele's *The Family*, 1918, are impressive, but not the artists' central works.) No strong visual icon seems to have survived. Arguably, collective memories of the medieval plague are still strong due to impressive long-living artworks, such as the painted *Dances of Death* still found in many churches all over Europe or Giovanni Boccaccio's *Decameron* (ca. 1349–1353).[18] In 1918, however, as Spinney argues, "people didn't know how to think about it; they still don't" (2018, 291). Adapting a concept by cultural historian Samuel Hynes (1990), the Spanish flu was "not sufficiently imagined." As it was not a pandemic imagined, it did not turn into a pandemic remembered.

But again, there are different worlds, also of forgetting, and different reasons for forgetting. Spinney argues that in "Australia, the Spanish flu became telescoped into people's minds with a 1900 outbreak of bubonic plague, in part because newspapers referred to both as 'plague,'" while "in Japan it was

---

[14] These are the key questions for any emplotment of historical events into a meaningful narrative; see Ricœur (1984) and White (1973).

[15] See Baroni (2014); for an application to memory studies, see Savolainen (2017).

[16] This has to be qualified in two respects: Instead of clearly demarcated groups of victims and perpetrators, human-made catastrophes are generated and suffered by a range of "implicated" subject-positions (see Rothberg 2019). The human factor in the COVID-19 pandemic has repeatedly been pointed out through the destruction of wildlife and the world's ecosystems.

[17] A reassessment of the role of the Spanish flu in literary modernism is provided by Outka (2019, 5), who teases out the "subtle but significant presence of the viral tragedy within iconic modernist texts" by Virginia Woolf, T. S. Eliot, and W. B. Yeats.

[18] On the importance of mediation and remediation for memory (Erll and Rigney 2009), on the longevity and afterlives of art, see Rigney (2012a).

eclipsed by another natural disaster, the great Kanto earthquake of 1923, which destroyed Tokyo" (Spinney 2018, 293).

There was and is, however, one strong and detailed form of memory of the Spanish flu. It is not found in state commemoration, textbooks, art and literature, or family history, but in scientific memory systems. In the emergence of epidemiology and virology as modern scientific disciplines since the 1950s, the flu attained foundational status. Other academic fields such as the social history of medicine, too, reconstruct, retain, and transmit memories of the Spanish flu (see Phillips and Killingray 2001). Such specialized systems are also memory worlds. These worlds do not operate with commemoration but with archives, knowledge retention (Bowker 2005), and in the case of "reverse genetics" also with the reconstruction of flu RNA (Tumpey et al. 2005). In times of crisis, such specialized forms of memory can come to the fore and feed into more mainstream interdiscursive collective memory. Importantly, scientific worlds of memory verge more toward the abstract "knowledge-pole" than toward the time-bound, identity-related, experiential, and emotional "remembering-pole" of collective memory (see Erll 2011a, 107–108). But both systems are part of collective memory, and memories can migrate between them. I will come back to this point at the end of the chapter.

4.4 Memory *during* the Corona Pandemic: Triggered, Used, and Abused

What is remembered during corona times? What memories are triggered by the experience of a pandemic? Again, there are manifold memory worlds. In different contexts, different memories are activated when people are confronted with COVID-19.

Paradoxically, a transnationally operative virus has engendered a re-nationalization, also in terms of memory. Patriotism and national repertoires are ransacked for historical analogies to understand the present and legitimate political action. Vocabularies of past wars have been tried out, as by Boris Johnson,[19] who invoked the British effort during the Second World

---

[19] Kevin Rawlinson, "'This Enemy Can Be Deadly': Boris Johnson Invokes Wartime Language," *The Guardian*, March 27, 2020, https://www.theguardian.com/world/2020/mar/17/enemy-deadly-boris-johnson-invokes-wartime-language-coronavirus.

War, and Donald Trump,[20] who compared the corona pandemic to Pearl Harbor (by implication, another devious attack by "Asians").

The British Queen's address is an interesting case. Her appeals to English national character ("self-discipline," "quiet, good-humored resolve") and the idea of a "strong generation" are all core elements of British collective memory of the Second World War. These are mixed with what is staged as a spontaneous personal memory: "It reminds me of the very first broadcast I made, in 1940, helped by my sister. We, as children, spoke from here at Windsor to children who had been evacuated from their homes and sent away for their own safety." What apparently cues this episodic memory is the similar situation of people in the United Kingdom today facing "separation from their loved ones."[21]

Memories of the Second World War are always quick at hand when framing great crises. But corona also seems to bring back memories of colonialism. Cameroonians have been reported attacking white people as bearers of the virus (an ethnologist's report has made it into a German debate).[22] Memories of influenza and other diseases brought by European colonizers are emerging again in countries with Indigenous populations (from the Amazonas region to Australia), who—from Columbus's times onward—had been decimated, often to the brink of extinction, by illnesses brought by white people, against which they had no immunity (Spinney, 2018: 20).

How pretrauma and crises-related memory-cues work together becomes clear in the case of the Philippines where, as Jocelyn Martin explains, people are not only reminded of devastating typhoons such as "Ondoy" in 2009, when many were forced to stay indoors, but with the lockdown and "the enforcement of military personnel on the streets . . . citizens are starting to see shadows of Ferdinand Marcos' terrifying Martial Law."[23]

---

[20] "Trump Says Coronavirus Worse 'Attack' than Pearl Harbor," *BBC News*, May 7, 2020, https://www.bbc.com/news/world-us-canada-52568405.

[21] "'We will Succeed': The Queen's Coronavirus Broadcast," *BBC*, April 5, 2020, https://www.youtube.com/watch?v=2klmuggOElE. In the televised address, a black and white photograph is cut into the Queen's speech, showing herself and her sister Margaret as ten- and thirteen-year-old girls in front of a radio microphone. Such remediations, which stage royal memory as personal, familial, medialized, and of national import *at the same time* are a typical mnemonic device of the royal family's public relations (see Jordan 2019), now activated in times of crisis.

[22] Susan Arndt, "Privilegien in der Corona Krise," *TAZ*, April 21, 2020, https://taz.de/Privilegien-in-Corona-Krise/!5677150;moby/.

[23] Jocelyn Martin, personal communication, May 19, 2020. See also Rebecca Ratfliffe, "Philippines' Main Channel Forced Off-Air Amid Coronavirus Lockdown," *The Guardian*,

The corona pandemic also triggers racial stereotypes, which belong to the (often non-conscious) standard repertoire of collective memory. There is a long history of coding fear of others into a language of infection, disease, and decay. Nineteenth-century Sinophobia among Europeans and Americans found expression in the phrase "yellow peril" (Tchen and Yeats 2014). The sheer extent and detrimental power of such re-emerging stereotypes is evidenced by the fact that as of May 2020, Wikipedia featured a "List of incidents of xenophobia and racism related to the COVID-19 pandemic" with more than 350 entries, ranging all the way from Sinophobia in Nigeria to anti-Semitism in the United States.[24] Deep-seated, sometimes millennia-old practices of negative stereotyping are popping up again that many thought were no longer part of societies' working memory—implicit cultural patterns, which James Wertsch (2019) calls "habits of thought."

Meanwhile, among those who can afford to be more bookish, in their attempts to make sense of the current situation, COVID-19 triggered a renewed interest in the history of pandemics. Laura Spinney's *Pale Rider* is sold out. The outbreak of AIDS in the 1980s is revisited.[25] New books about the medieval plague are published. Albert Camus's *La Peste* (1947) and Daniel Defoe's *A Journal of the Plague Year* (1772) are reread. And Boccaccio's *Decamerone* shows how social distancing (during the plague in Florence, a group of young people flee to a villa in the countryside) leads to a suspension in time, which can give rise to narration. Once more, the power of literary stories as both a form of framing harrowing experience and a manner of archiving cultural memory comes to the fore.

All these disparate examples (and there are myriad more) show that current crises tend to work like retrieval cues for collective memory, from consciously drawn historical analogies all the way to non-consciously emerging stereotypes.[26] Politicians, journalists, and other professional

May 5, 2020, https://www.theguardian.com/world/2020/may/05/philippines-main-channel-abs-cbn-forced-off-air-amid-coronavirus-lockdown.

[24] https://en.wikipedia.org/wiki/Xenophobia_and_racism_related_to_the_COVID-19_pandemic.

[25] *Social Research* republished in summer 2020 their 1988 issue entitled *In Time of Plague: The History and Social Consequences of Lethal Epidemic Diseases*, which was a response to the hysteria surrounding the AIDS epidemic at the time. It features a comment by Bill Hirst (2020, 251) on the future of the memory of COVID-19, where the psychologist confesses to being "not very sanguine about the long-term prospect of this endeavor, for all the evidence suggests that we will forget."

[26] Commemorative memory is another important aspect of memory during the corona pandemic. Commemorative events related to the end of the Second World War have been affected in unprecedented ways. Tobias Ebbrecht-Hartman (2020) shows in the Austrian IWM blog how the "restrictions posed by the COVID-19 pandemic on Holocaust commemoration intensified the

"meaning-makers" are groping for earlier, comparable, analogous situations. But future-oriented "lessons of history" are difficult to draw in the case of natural disasters. Or what could a "corona—never again!" look like?

4.5 Memory after Corona: The Open Horizon

What will be remembered after the corona pandemic has passed? In terms of sheer sources, one is tempted to say: everything. Instant history-making abounds. Every second of pandemic time seems to be recorded on digital media, distributed, and shared via social networks. What the Spanish flu lacked (a consciously created archive in the first place) is exactly what COVID-19 is characterized by: It is the first worldwide digitally witnessed pandemic, a test case for the making of global memory in the new media ecology.[27] But the question is: Which mediated experiences, beliefs, and narratives will make it into the dominant memory discourses that shape the global future?

The game of naming is part of a conscious effort to encode certain narratives about the pandemic into future memory. When Trump calls COVID-19 the "Chinese virus," and the Chinese government counters by suggesting that it is more likely an "American virus," we are in the middle of the age-old game of attributing sources—and with that, responsibilities— for pandemics.[28] In the Middle Ages, Jews and prostitutes were identified as origins of, and thus scapegoats for, the bubonic plague. The Spanish flu got its name because in 1918 Spain was the first European country to acknowledge its influenza epidemic, while other European powers were covering up their casualties as part of wartime censorship (Spinney 2018, 63). Wrong as it was, the term stuck. To stop such practice of "blaming the obvious other,"[29]

development of distinct modes of social media memory." Tobias Ebbrecht-Hartman (2020) Transformation of Holocaust Memory in Times of COVID-19, 06.05.2020, https://www.iwm.at/blog/transformation-of-holocaust-memory-in-times-of-covid-19 (See also Ebbrecht-Hartmann 2021).

[27] See Hoskins (2017) for approaches to understanding the digital dynamics of global crises like COVID-19. As forms of active archiving, dozens of initiatives building digital corona archives have sprung up across the globe. See, for example, the German "coronarchiv" (https://coronarchiv.blogs.uni-hamburg.de/) or the NYC COVID-19 Oral History, Narrative and Memory Archive (https://wp.nyu.edu/covid19histories/2020/04/25/nyc-covid-19-oral-history-narrative-and-memory-archive/).

[28] See, for example, Yukteshwar Kumar in *Outlook India* on May 1, 2020: "Only Independent Probe Can Settle US-China 'Conspiracy Theories' around COVID-19 Origins," https://www.outlookindia.com/website/story/opinion-as-us-and-china-peddle-conspiracy-theories-about-covid-19s-origins-only-independent-probe-way-forward/351874.

[29] For Spinney (2018, 64), the "time-honoured rules of epidemic nomenclature" imply the blaming "of the obvious other. In Senegal it was the Brazilian flu and in Brazil the German flu, while

and in an act of what one could call prospective memory politics, in 2015, the World Health Organization (WHO) issued guidelines for naming new infectious diseases in ways that are not stigmatizing or misleading, stipulating the avoidance of reference to (alleged) origins in geographical locations, peoples, animals, or food.

The production of antagonistic collective identities and of counterfactual narratives vying for entrance into collective memory are the last things needed in a global pandemic. But the process of narrativization itself is inevitable. Any historical event begs the questions of "where did it begin," "what course did it take," and "how did it end." It calls for an "explanation by emplotment," which, according to Hayden White (1973, 7), is at the basis of all historical accounts. It is the active, recklessly simplifying and falsifying intervention, the attempt at creating false memories—prospective "memory abuse" (McConnell 2019)—that is shameful.[30]

The power of narrative in the construction of these memory worlds cannot be underestimated. Literary and cognitive scientist Fritz Breithaupt has addressed the narrative possibilities emerging from the corona crisis. He distinguishes five narrative patterns, among them the "rise of total control," "failure of egomaniac leadership," and the narrative of "depression."[31] In memory studies, scholars increasingly point out the necessity of finding alternatives to the pervasive narrative pattern of "cultural trauma" (Alexander 2012). With regard to the corona epidemic in particular, patterns of "tragedy" (Simko and Olick 2020) or narratives of "outrage" and collective action (Rigney 2020) could be more enabling to build resilient futures.

For careful observers, the difficulties inherent in all pandemics of making sense and remembering remain. Contrary to what populists and conspiracists may suggest, there are no easy normative equations. Pandemics are not brought about by evil people, but by genetic accident. Pandemics are not entirely just—or entirely unjust—in whom they hit (affluent skiing parties were affected first in Europe, but so were residents of nursing homes and migrant workers), although the social dimension of pandemics usually leads to the poor being hit harder (Spinney 2018, 203).

---

the Danes thought it 'came from the south'. The Poles called it the Bolshevik disease, the Persians blamed the British."

[30] On agenda setting and "mediated prospective memory," see Tenenboim-Weinblatt (2013).

[31] Fritz Breithaupt, "Erzählt die Zukunft! Was kommt nach der Corona-Krise? Das hängt auch davon ab, wie Studierende und Professoren davon sprechen," *Die Zeit*, April 27, 2020, https://www.zeit.de/2020/18/corona-krise-studierende-professoren-narrative?page=2#comments.

Running counter to such conscious attempts at framing and narrating the pandemic for future memory is the fact that COVID-19 has posed great challenges to ways of "being with the dead" (see Ruin 2018). Too many people died too quickly—in Wuhan, in northern Italy, in New York—and could not be buried with the usual public funeral rites. As political philosopher Magdalena Zolkos points out, with the "collective inability to process this in the present," the dead "might return to haunt, but belatedly."[32]

What emerges as a more general pattern of meaning-making is the relationality between humans, animals, and microbes. One of the ironies of the past century's pandemics is that the "swine flu" of 2006 was not a flu coming from swine, but the Spanish flu returning to its original host a century later, after humans had given it to their domestic pigs (Spinney 2018, 186). What might play a role in the future is a greater awareness of the deep time of human-animal-microbe interactions (Barad 2007, ix, would possibly call it "entangled intra-relating") in the making of influenza and other pandemics, a process whose origins go back some 12,000 years to human settlement, the agricultural revolution, and ensuing "crowd diseases" (Spinney 2018, 16). Human-viral temporality is thus roughly equal to Anthropocene time, and current pandemics seem to share many causes with climate change and mass extinction.[33]

Collective memory depends on top-down commemorative investment: Will nations launch corona commemoration days? Some countries, like Spain and Italy, which were hit so hard will perhaps do so. Sweden, which seems to navigate through the crisis with minimal adjustments, is less likely.

But there are other pathways of collective memory: bottom-up ones based on shared, deeply felt experience. Generational memory might be one significant path. Corona will most likely have brought forth a "generation."[34] The experience of the pandemic, at least in countries under lockdown, has all the ingredients of a generation-defining experience. It is a fundamental and extended[35] change of life for young people, who, in what Karl Mannheim (1952 [1928], 300) has called their "formative period," no longer go to school,

---

[32] Magdalena Zolkos, personal communication, June 4, 2020.
[33] See Cazzolla Gatti (2020). For an overview on memory studies research on the Anthropocene and its temporalities, see Craps et al. (2018).
[34] See Mannheim (1952 [1928]). On generation and collective memory, see Schuman and Scott (1989); on the transnational dynamics of generational memory, see Chapter 6, "Generation in Literary History."
[35] See Draaisma (2012) for the different perceptions of time in younger and older people.

remain locked at home, and realize through an almost uncanny global simultaneity the connectedness of the planet. They witness and become aware of a historical moment. And historicizing the lived present and severing it from the past (here: the pre-COVID-19 world) is one condition of historical thinking. With the "reminiscence bump" in autobiographical memories,[36] the fact that events from late adolescence and early adult life seem to be remembered best, this generation will likely retain a focus on the COVID-19 pandemic.

How long is the mnemonic half-life period of the corona crisis likely to be? How long and how strongly will this global memory carry into the future? And how differently across the world? All this is difficult to gauge and depends largely on the memory's interaction with other experiences and memories. Corona may be blocked out or overwritten by other events that may happen in the near future, by economic and political crises in particular.

One thing is clear: Memory after corona will play out in different modes. There may be active commemorative memory. There will be a sense of common experience in generational memory, possibly transnationally. There will be legacies of the pandemic (financial, ecological, educational, digital). There may be effects on social habit memory: new modes of interaction shaped by corona (politeness, education, work, play). There will be memories of the sensual, rhythmic, and affective specificity of this time. There will be new scientific knowledge, about the virus, and about the social, political, cultural, and medial dimensions of pandemics in the twenty-first century.

What this suggests is that memory analysis needs to differentiate between different systems and modes, such as explicit forms of collective memory (institutionalized commemoration, storytelling as intergenerational transmission within families, scientific knowledge) and implicit forms (legacies, aftereffects on mentalities, emotions, affects, behaviors, ways of speaking).[37]

Here is an optimistic scenario: If the experience of an unprecedented, global slow-down and all its positive side effects—from clear water (if not dolphins) in the canals of Venice,[38] to what Monika Büscher (2020, 58) sums up as "less air pollution, an increase in cycling and walking in some areas

---

[36] See Rubin and Schulkind (1997). For an up-to-date overview of psychological approaches to collective memory, see Hirst and Merck (2024).
[37] On the dynamics of implicit collective memory, see Chapter 12, "The Hidden Power of Implicit Collective Memory."
[38] https://www.theguardian.com/environment/2020/mar/20/nature-is-taking-back-venice-wildlife-returns-to-tourist-free-city (accessed May 24, 2020).

and an upsurge in birds singing in the trees"[39]—is connected in collective memory with what had been formative for many young people in the year before—the Fridays for Future movement—then the COVID-19 pandemic might turn into a memory that engenders ecological thinking and transnational solidarity. But admittedly, this scenario is based on more than a pinch of wishful thinking on the author's side, and as in all other respects, there will be different ways forward, different "worlds" of corona memory, depending on whether the pandemic was experienced in autocratic regimes, in failing or succeeding democracies, from the top or the bottom of global society.

Frankfurt, June 2020: While the George Floyd protests are gaining momentum, and their entanglements with the coronavirus pandemic will have to be illuminated in the future, we are gazing at the open horizon of COVID-19 as a global occurrence, long before it has fully unfolded into a historical event. Narrative closure or retrospective teleologies are a sheer impossibility. While this situation makes any account of the pandemic—like all analysis of the contemporary—a "desperately uncertain" (Gadamer 1960, 271) affair, it forcefully brings home the temporal dynamic that Barad (2017, 68) describes as "different times bleeding through one another": Images of the plague of 700 years ago jump time and unfold affective agency in the present moment. Current experiences of lockdowns activate memories of totalitarian regimes in Poland and the Philippines, and of the legacies of slavery and racism in the United States. Our ever-accelerating present is challenged by processes that started in deep Anthropocene time. And all the while, there are many futures—many worlds—that are now still possible.

4.6 Coda

Frankfurt am Main, March 2024: The program for memory research that this essay laid out in early 2020 has since been redeemed and extended in many quarters. In 2021, Guy Beiner's edited collection on the "unforgotten flu of 1918–1919" appeared as a comprehensive historians' account of the global experience of the Spanish flu. Collective memory research

---

[39] Büscher (2020, 58) notes that these facts are comparatively little covered in the media. Such "collateral benefits" of the corona pandemic are sometimes noted (for example, by the South Asia Network of Dams, Rivers and People: https://sandrp.in/2020/04/22/earth-day-2020-can-we-sustain-the-collateral-benefits-of-covid-lockdown/). But they seem more of a prenarrative experience than a full-fledged narrative pattern. Pointing these out should not be misunderstood as cynical in the face of a devastating virus, but as a way of gesturing toward potentialities in the midst of crisis.

addressed corona temporalities (Kattago 2021; Parui and Simi Raj 2021), compared the public memory of COVID-19 with other pandemics such as HIV/AIDS (Catlin 2021), studied practices of mourning (Simko 2021), patterns of global and national memories of the pandemic (Öner et al. 2022), the logics of the emerging COVID-19 commemoration (Mazzucchelli and Panico 2022), the politics of memory (Honigsbaum 2023), the digital transformation of Holocaust memory (Ebbrecht-Hartmann 2021), and the differences between remembrance and knowledge in pandemic memory (Vinitzky-Seroussi and Maraschin 2021).

The practices of "memory during corona" witnessed a decisive shift after the spring of 2020. At the pandemic's onset, using collective memory meant primarily groping after historical analogies, in order to understand a new phenomenon and locate it in history. But the event soon came into its own. After a short time, mnemonic activity started to center around the coronavirus pandemic itself as a stand-alone event, and a veritable boom of collecting, archiving, and commemorating COVID-19 set in.

A major stock-taking of such memory practices is offered by Sarah Gensburger's and Orli Fridman's edited collection *The COVID-19 Pandemic and Memory* (2023). Gensburger and Fridman diagnose a "COVID-19 memory boom." This refers, first, to the memorialization of the pandemic itself, with countless initiatives of collecting, archiving, and curating; and second, to the (re-)emergence and transformation of other objects of collective memory during the pandemic, such as the Holocaust, the Yugoslav wars, and colonialism.

The coronavirus pandemic appears to have acted as a catalyst for two major changes in collective memory: first, for the digitalization of memory culture, with the emergence of new forms of online commemoration; second, for a new phase of memory activism addressing the social injustices that were particularly strongly felt (like under a magnifying glass) in times of corona.[40] The global reaction to the murder of George Floyd, the Black Lives Matter movement, the toppling of the Edward Colston statue in Bristol—in 2020, the uneven experience of the pandemic rekindled memories of colonialism and slavery, and linked these histories to the continuities of injustice today.

Both transformations (the digitalization of memory and a new phase of remembering colonialism and racism) had already been palpable and

---

[40] See Gensburger and Fridman (2023). For memory activism, see Gutman and Wüstenberg (2023).

prepared before the pandemic, in the intensified digitization of archives, museums, and heritage, and in major acts of "de-commemoration" (Gensburger and Wüstenberg 2023), such as the "Rhodes Must Fall" movement that started in Cape Town in 2015. But these processes were amplified by the digital necessities and potentialities, as well as by the combined and uneven social experience that the COVID-19 pandemic brought about.

As far as "memory after corona" is concerned, what has arguably *not* happened is that corona engendered a new kind of memory that combines ecological thinking and transnational solidarity. The forced standstill was not used as the productive "moratorium" that Aleida Assmann called for in 2020.[41] By 2024, air travel had almost returned to pre-pandemic proportions. While the year 2023 will go down in history as the warmest year on record, the 2023 climate summit (again) did not bring about the advances needed to limit global warming to 1.5 degrees. Meanwhile, the wars in Ukraine (since 2022) and Israel/Gaza (since 2023) bind the cognitive capacities needed for shaping a relational and ecological collective memory and force thinking back into national and ethnic boundaries, and binary friend/enemy categories.

Generational memory has emerged from the pandemic, but less in an explicit, identity-forming sense of a shared past than as an implicit legacy of affliction. Mental health problems can be observed globally among younger people, with significant rises in symptoms of depression and anxiety (Racine et al. 2021), a veritable "mental health pandemic" (Lloyd et al. 2023), as it were.

The questions that memory scholars were asked again and again during the pandemic—"(how) will we remember COVID-19?"—cannot be conclusively answered. But there are certain indicators. First, in some countries, there is a significant investment in national commemorative memory, which tends to bolster the continued awareness of the history and legacies of the COVID-19 pandemic. For example, in Italy, Mario Draghi initiated a "national day of remembrance of the victims of the COVID-19 pandemic" on March 18, 2021, and this remembrance day has been observed annually since. In the United Kingdom, a Commission on COVID Commemoration was set up, whose final report, published in September 2023, recommends the preservation of existing grassroots memorials (such as the National

---

[41] Aleida Assmann, "Wir brauchen Helden. Aber die Heldenbilder wandeln sich," *Die Zeit*, December 17, 2020, https://www.zeit.de/kultur/2020-12/aleida-assmann-corona-kollektives-gedaechtnis-erinnern (accessed December 28, 2023).

COVID Memorial Wall in central London, the famous "Wall of Hearts"), holding a national "day of reflection" every year, the collection of oral histories, as well as investment in education and research.[42] All these measures are typical strategies of (Western) commemorative culture, signaling the strong will to turn the memory of COVID-19 into a long-term "cultural memory" (*sensu* J. Assmann 2011 [1992]).

Second, the "durable arts" have dedicated themselves to the experience of COVID-19. Short forms such as comics and poems emerged early in the pandemic. Quite surprisingly, there is also already a large corpus of pandemic novels available—including works by famous authors such as Louise Erdrich or Juli Zeh. This pace of processing experience in long literary forms is unusual. This becomes clear when compared with the production of novels about the First World War, which began only ten years after its end (Erll 2003), or when considering how long Germany waited for its "Wenderoman" (Novel of Reunification).

Third, the coronavirus pandemic is indeed by now the best-recorded and archived health crisis. But what future generations will make of this global mega archive is another question. Collective memory depends on activity. Available materials must be used in order to become accessible to mnemonic communities. Whether memories of the "corona years" will cross the generational threshold will depend on whether the pandemic is perceived in retrospect as a transformative event—not just an incisive one, but one that fundamentally changed the family, the urban community, the nation, or global society.

---

[42] *The UK Commission on COVID Commemoration: Final Report*, September 18, 2023, https://www.gov.uk/government/publications/the-uk-commission-on-covid-commemorations-final-report (accessed December 28, 2023).

PART II
MEMORY IN FAMILIES AND GENERATIONS

Chapter 5
Locating Family in Memory Studies

5.1 Family and Memory

What is the place of "family"[1]—and of family memories—in the field of memory studies? And how can the concept of collective memory be used as a tool in comparative family research?[2] This chapter presents, first, the main concepts of Maurice Halbwachs's theory of *mémoire collective* and asks how the sociologist places family within collective memory. Second, it discusses the "new memory studies" of the 1980s and 1990s (in particular, the works of Pierre Nora, and Aleida and Jan Assmann), which clearly showed a bias toward large-scale, often national memories. How can these approaches be refocused through the lens of small-scale family memories? Third, the chapter provides an overview of research on the dynamics of remembering within families. It discusses how studies that are based mostly on qualitative interviewing have adopted innovative transgenerational, transnational, and media culture perspectives. Fourth, the chapter widens the perspective toward non-Western, non-heteronormative, and posthuman forms of "making kin" and memory.

5.2 Maurice Halbwachs: *Mémoire collective*—Locating the Family within Collective Memory

The French sociologist Maurice Halbwachs (1877–1945), a student of Henri Bergson and Emile Durkheim, developed his concept of *mémoire collective*

---

[1] I am aware of the complexity of the notion of "family" and the multitude of different "world families" (see Adam and Trost 2004). Much of the research presented here has the European nuclear middle-class family as its mental model, whether this is acknowledged or not. (On different research traditions in family studies from Germany, France, and the United States, see Gollac and Oeser 2011.) How existing approaches to family memory can be challenged and refined by more sophisticated notions of "family" and "kin" is one of the most interesting questions of current research. I will come back to these questions at the end of the chapter.

[2] For memory studies perspectives on family, see Levin et al. (2011) and Švaříčková Slabáková (2020). For family historians' perspectives on family memory, see Barclay and Koefoed (2021). For a communication studies perspective on family memory, see Lohmeier and Böhling (2017); for a cultural psychology perspective on family memory, see Shore and Kauko (2017).

Travels in Time. Astrid Erll, Oxford University Press. © Oxford University Press (2025).
DOI: 10.1093/oso/9780197767733.003.0006

in three books that still occupy a central place in memory studies today.[3] In 1925 he published his study *Les cadres sociaux de la mémoire* (1994 [1925]; "The Social Frameworks of Memory," partially translated in *On Collective Memory*, 1992), in which he attempted to establish that memory is dependent on social structures. Halbwachs opposed the theories of memory put forward by his contemporaries such as Henri Bergson and Sigmund Freud, who emphasized the individual dimension of memory. Halbwachs's theory, which sees even the most personal memory as a *mémoire collective*, a collective phenomenon, provoked significant protest, not least from his colleagues at the University of Strasbourg, Charles Blondel and Marc Bloch. The latter accused Halbwachs, and the Durkheim School in general, of an unacceptable collectivization of individual psychological phenomena (Bloch 1925).

Stirred by the criticism, Halbwachs began elaborating his concept of collective memory in a second book. For more than fifteen years he worked on the text of *La mémoire collective* (1997 [1950]; *The Collective Memory*, 1980 [1950]), but it did not appear until 1950, posthumously and incomplete. Before that, Halbwachs published a third book, in which he illustrated the forms and functions of memory sites using a specific example: *La topographie légendaire des évangiles en terre sainte* (1941; "The Legendary Topography of the Gospels in the Holy Land"; partially translated in *On Collective Memory*, 1992). In August 1944, the Nazis deported Halbwachs, whose wife was Jewish, to Buchenwald, where he was killed on March 16, 1945.[4]

Halbwachs's writings on collective memory were largely forgotten in the postwar period. Today, however, there are virtually no theoretical models of collective memory that do not refer to his work. Three areas of analysis in Halbwachs's studies on *mémoire collective* can be distinguished, and they point to three main directions of research on families and memories: first, Halbwachs's theory of the dependence of individual memory on social frameworks; second, his reflections on different mnemonic communities (the family among them); and third, his expansion of the term *mémoire collective* to include cultural transmission and the creation of tradition.

---

[3] An English translation of Halbwachs's works on collective memory will appear with Oxford University Press in 2025.

[4] For more on Halbwachs, see Vromen (1975); Namer (2000); Echerhoff and Saar (2002); Becker (2003); Olick (2007, 2010), and Gensburger (2016).

In his theory, Halbwachs unites two fundamental and distinct aspects of *mémoire collective*, which Jeffrey Olick (1999) later distinguished as "collected memory" and "collective memory":

- *mémoire collective* as the cognitive apparatus of individual people, which operates within the frameworks of a sociocultural environment. This is what Olick terms "collected memory." It refers to the individual, or cognitive, level of collective memory;
- *mémoire collective* as the creation of shared versions of the past, which comes into being through interaction, communication, (symbolic) mediation, and institutionalization—within small social groups as well as large cultural communities. This is Olick's more narrowly defined "collective memory." It refers to the social and media levels of collective memory.

Memory in this second sense is often seen as a mere metaphor. But in fact, these two options of looking at collective memory constitute two *perspectives* on a complex process, emphasizing either its mental or its socio-medial dimensions.

5.3 Families as *cadres sociaux de la mémoire*

The starting point of Halbwachs's theory of collective memory is his concept of *cadres sociaux de la mémoire*, social frameworks of memory. In the first part of *Les cadres sociaux de la mémoire*, Halbwachs illustrates in detail the collective elements of individual memory using his reflections on dreams and language. He comes to the conclusion that the recourse to *cadres sociaux* is an indispensable prerequisite for every act of remembering.

Social frameworks of memory are, for Halbwachs, primarily the people around us. Without contact with other humans, individuals are not only denied access to such obviously collective phenomena as language and customs, but also, he argues, to their own memories. This is, first of all, because we often experience things in the company of other people who can later help us to recall these events.

From *cadres sociaux* in the literal sense (i.e., social environments) derive *cadres sociaux* in the metaphorical sense: It is through interaction and communication with our fellow humans that we acquire knowledge about dates and facts, collective concepts of time and space, and ways of thinking and experiencing. Because we participate in a collective symbolic order, we can discern, interpret, and remember past events. Metaphorically speaking, therefore, social frameworks are thought patterns, cognitive schemata that steer our perception and memory in particular directions.[5]

Families play a major role as *cadres sociaux* in both the literal and the metaphorical sense. Family members are the people who usually constitute the first, and often most important, social frameworks for a child. And family life is arguably one of the main sites where sociocultural schemata are acquired. Halbwachs (1992, 61) accordingly notes: "Our kin communicate to us our first notions about people and things."

This insight has been taken up in today's psychological research. The most significant contribution from narrative psychology on the relation between family memory and autobiographical memory is the work of Robyn Fivush (2019), who shows the fundamental significance of families and their memory practices for the development of autobiographical memory in children.

How does Halbwachs conceive of the relationship between individual and collective memory? He maintains that "there exists a collective memory and social frameworks for memory; it is to the degree that our individual thought places itself in these frameworks and participates in this memory that it is capable of the act of recollection" (Halbwachs 1992, 38). Our perception is group specific, our individual memories are socially formed, and both are unthinkable without the existence of collective memory—which can be that of a circle of friends, of a religious group, or of a family. However, collective memory is not a supra-individual entity separate from individual memories. Instead, social and cognitive levels are mutually dependent: "One may say that the individual remembers by placing himself in the perspective of the group, but one may also affirm that the memory of the group realizes and manifests itself in individual memories." (Halbwachs 1992, 40) It is only through individual acts of remembering that collective memory is performed, and can be observed. For Halbwachs, "each memory is a viewpoint on the collective memory" (Halbwachs 1980, 48). This viewpoint (*point de vue*) is the position or standpoint that people assume based on their socialization and cultural influences.

Every individual memory is related to several collective memories because every person belongs to several social groups—not only to a family,

---

[5] The psychologist Frederic Bartlett took up this idea in his 1932 study *Remembering* and identified culture-specific schemata which guide the understanding of stories.

but also, say, to a village community, a political movement, a group of football fans, or a class of students. Each person, therefore, has at his or her disposal a supply of different, group-specific experiences and thought systems. What Halbwachs seems to suggest is that, on the one hand, memory must be seen in its fundamentally social dimension. Yet, on the other hand, there *is* a certain individuality of individual memory: It rests in a person's specific group allegiances and in the resultant, always unique combination of social frameworks of memory that the individual draws on.

Halbwachs's approach is particularly interesting for the study of cross-cultural families whose members may refer to different, perhaps conflicting, frameworks; but it also helps to understand the mnemonic dynamics resulting from the interaction of various generations or professions within a family. Family memory is not a monolithic, stable entity, but an ongoing process shaped by the multidimensional *cadres sociaux* of family members. This produces a variety of "viewpoints" on mnemonic contents and meanings which, depending on the particular family structure, can lead to a continual renegotiation of the past.

5.4 Family Memory as a Type of Collective Memory

In the second part of *Les cadres sociaux de la mémoire*, Halbwachs considers family memory as a specific type of collective memory, alongside other types, such as religious community and social class. He notes that "the family has its own peculiar memory, just as do other kinds of communities. Foremost in this memory are relations of kinship" (Halbwachs 1992, 63). Halbwachs is aware of the many different ways in which the concept of family can play out in culture. He considers the anthropological and historical literature of his day and sets family memory in perspective to religious communities, the cult of the dead, and the "modern" phenomenon of separated families. But he also makes some general assumptions. For example, he states that there is a certain inescapability of family memory: "No matter how we enter a family—by birth, marriage or some other way—we find ourselves to be part of a group, where our position is determined ... by rules and customs independent of us that existed before us" (Halbwachs 1992, 55). Moreover, he stresses the power of family ties and family feelings and finds it quite "extraordinary that families generally succeed in motivating their members to love each other" (Halbwachs 1992, 57). To Halbwachs, family memory is a type of collective memory which is characterized by the strength of its group allegiances and its powerful emotional dimension. Another characteristic of family memory is that it is highly personalizing, or individualizing:

> [T]here is ... no other milieu in which the personality of each individual stands out so clearly. There is no other institution, moreover, in which each member of the group is considered as a being that is "unique in its kind" ... [A] family is not so much a group with specialized functions as a group with differentiated persons ... [I]n the memory of each [there is] a singularly precise and rich image of all the other members of the family. (Halbwachs 1992, 70)

Family memory is a typical intergenerational memory: a kind of collective memory that is constituted through ongoing social interaction and communication between children, parents, and grandparents. Through the repeated recall of the family's past—usually via oral stories that are told at family get-togethers—those who did not experience past events firsthand can also share in the memory. In this way, an exchange of "living memory" takes place between eyewitnesses and descendants. Intergenerational memory thus goes back as far as the oldest members of the social group can remember either their own experiences or stories that they heard from their elders.

Another important feature of collective memory is its ability to construct and reconstruct. Halbwachs argues that because collective memory is oriented toward the needs and interests of the group in the present, it proceeds in an extremely selective and reconstructive manner. Along the way, what is remembered can become distorted and shifted to such an extent that the result is closer to fiction than to a past reality. Memory thus does not provide a faithful reproduction of the past—indeed, quite the opposite is true:

> [A] remembrance is in very large measure a reconstruction of the past achieved with data borrowed from the present, a reconstruction prepared, furthermore, by reconstructions of earlier periods wherein past images had already been altered. (Halbwachs 1980, 68)

Family memories, just like any other individual and collective memory, are constructs. They may ring true, but they are never an accurate "re-presentation" of past events. Family memories amalgamate what are taken to be elements from the past with perspectives, knowledge, and desires of the present. They are—to adapt a concept from cognitive psychology—"collective ecphories."[6]

Family memories often take the shape of condensed images, which sum up long processes, repetitive actions, customs, and detailed events into a "gripping abbreviation, the idea of a family." One function of such condensation is representation. It "projects a singularly vivid image on the screen of an obscure and unclear past" (Halbwachs 1992, 66).

However, memories are rarely rehearsed for their own sake; they also tend to serve as models for future conduct and as a way of self-description. Halbwachs stresses the fact that:

> each family has its proper mentality, its memories which it alone commemorates, and its secrets that are revealed only to its members. But these memories ... consist not only of a series of individual images of the past. They are at the same time models, examples, and elements of teaching. They express the general attitude of the group. (Halbwachs 1992, 59)

Thus, family memories clearly fulfill normative and formative, value-related and identity-related, functions.[7] In *La mémoire collective*, Halbwachs considers the construction of identity through collective memory in greater detail and emphasizes that families and other social groups tend to remember that which corresponds to the self-image and the interests of the group. Particular emphasis is placed on similarities and continuities that demonstrate that the group has remained the same (Halbwachs 1997 [1950], 131f.).

5.5 Family Memory and Cultural Traditions

In his work *Les cadres sociaux de la mémoire* (in the chapters on aristocracy and the memories of religious communities; 1994 [1925]), and even more so in his later study on the Christian mnemonic topography of the

---

[6] The psychology of memory posits the existence of "engrams," or memory traces. At least as important for remembering, however, are retrieval cues. These can be external stimuli, but also internal cues—emotional, cognitive, or motivational, for example. "Ecphory" means that each memory is the result of a synthesis of engram and cue, of stored information regarding past experience and the conditions at the time of recall: "The cue combines with the engram to yield a new, emergent entity—the recollective experience of the remember—that differs from either of its constituents" (Schacter 1996, 70).

[7] Jan and Aleida Assmann have studied the "normative and formative dimension" of the cultural memory (J. Assmann 2011 [1992]).

Gospels, *La topographie légendaire* (1941), Halbwachs breaks through the barriers that had restricted his study of intergenerational memory, whose medium is everyday communication and whose contents are for the most part autobiographical experience.

In *La topographie légendaire*, he turns his attention to collective memories, whose temporal horizons reach back thousands of years beyond the horizons of living memory and which, therefore, need objects and topographical sites to provide structure. Material phenomena, such as architecture, pilgrimage routes, and graves, take on a primary meaning. At this point, Halbwachs leaves the realm of socially shared memories of recent events and enters the area of culturally constructed knowledge about a distant past and its transmission through the creation of traditions.

With his interest in mnemonic space and objects, Halbwachs paved the way for subsequent historical research that would deal with the transmission of cultural knowledge (Jan and Aleida Assmann) and with national sites of memory (Pierre Nora). Clearly, family as a community of collective memory is removed from center stage here. Nevertheless, it is important to ask how families function as "mnemonic intersections" that can mediate, transmit, and transform cultural traditions. Halbwachs (1992, 83) already hints at these questions when he maintains that family "tends to interpret in its own manner the conceptions it borrows from society." Such questions are increasingly raised in current social research on family memory.

We can reconstruct three important ways in which Halbwachs uses the concept of the family in his groundbreaking work on *mémoire collective*:

1. The family as a fundamental component of the individual's *cadres sociaux de la mémoire*, in both the literal and the metaphorical sense: Family members constitute the first social framework for most human beings, the people in whose company we have and remember life experience. Moreover, family interactions convey the cognitive schemata and exemplary stories that help us to encode and recall events.
2. Family memory as a type of collective memory: The family is a mnemonic community with specific mnemonic practices (face-to-face interaction, conversations at family get-togethers), contents of memory (kinship patterns, family-related past events), characteristics (emotional, allegiance-based, individualizing memory), and functions (normative and formative).
3. The family as an important link between the individual memory and larger formations of collective memory, such as religious traditions.

5.6 The "New Memory Studies": Refocusing National Remembrance through Family Memory

The interest that the work by Halbwachs and others had sparked in a small community of scholars in the 1920s and 1930s dwindled away after the Second World War. It was only in the mid-1980s (after the "death of history," the narrative turn, and the anthropological turn) that "collective," "social," or "cultural" memory, first slowly and then at breathtaking speed, developed into buzzwords not only in the academic world, but also in the political arena, mass media, and the arts.

The "new memory studies" were very much an emergent phenomenon that took hold more or less concurrently in many disciplines and countries. In the 1980s we saw the work of the French historian Pierre Nora on national *lieux de mémoire* and the publications by a German group of researchers around Aleida and Jan Assmann, who focused on media and memory in ancient societies. Oral history flourished. And in psychology, behavioral and purely cognitive paradigms were supplemented with ecological approaches to human memory and the study of conversational and narrative remembering.

Historical and political changes became a catalyst for the new memory studies. First, forty years after the Holocaust, the generation that had witnessed the Shoah began to fade away. This effected a major change in the forms of collective remembering. Without autobiographic memories of individual people, societies are solely dependent on media (such as books, movies, and monuments) to transmit experience. Second, issues of trauma and witnessing were not only discussed in the context of Holocaust studies, but more and more also in gender studies and postcolonial studies. Third, major transformations in global politics, such as the breakdown of the communist states and other authoritarian regimes, brought to the fore new ways of dealing with the past, among them "transitional justice" and "reconciliation." Fourth, and more generally, the shape of late twentieth-century media societies (with the regime of mass media and the emergence of digital media) raised questions of how collective memory is shaped by available media technologies and depends on the circulation of media products.

The two most prominent bodies of scholarly work to have emerged from the new memory studies—by Pierre Nora and the Assmanns—are characterized by their focus on large mnemonic formations, such as nations and ethnic and religious groups. But some of their insights are also useful for the study of family memories. Moreover, refocusing their ideas through the lens of family memory may give rise to new perspectives on collective memory; while some of the shortcomings, especially of the *lieux de mémoire* approach, can be remedied with a consideration of familial dynamics.

5.7 Pierre Nora: *Lieux de mémoire*

Between 1984 and 1992, Nora edited his multi-volume *Les lieux de mémoire*. Its three main parts—*La République, La Nation,* and *Les France*—feature 130 essays on French "sites of memory." Nora introduces the collection with an essay entitled "Entre mémoire et histoire" ("Between Memory and History," 1989, 8) in which he closely follows Halbwachs in emphasizing that "[m]emory and history, far from being synonymous, appear now to be in fundamental opposition."

Yet unlike Halbwachs, who starts from the premise of the existence of collective memories, Nora summarizes our current time by saying: "We speak so much of memory because there is so little of it left" (Nora 1989, 7). As premodern *milieux de mémoire* seem to have disappeared, and the *nation mémoire* that originated in the nineteenth century has lost its binding quality, what is left now are merely *lieux de mémoire*, sites of memory. In the tradition of ancient mnemotechnics, Nora understands these as *loci* in the broadest sense, which call up *imagines*, the images of a French past. *Lieux de mémoire* include geographical locations, buildings, monuments, and works of art, as well as historical persons, memorial days, philosophical and scientific texts, and symbolic actions. Thus, Paris, Versailles, and the Eiffel Tower are sites of memory, but so are Joan of Arc, the French flag, July 14, the Marseillaise, and Proust's *A la recherche du temps perdu*. Many critics have posed the question of just what exactly can become a *lieu de mémoire*. The answer is probably: any cultural phenomenon (whether material, social, or mental) that a society connects to the past and to national identity, and which thus can be made into an object of mnemohistorical research.

Nora's *lieux de mémoire* became an international key concept, a central paradigm, for the study of national remembrance.[8] However, there are some

---

[8] Nora's project of charting national sites of memory has been favorably received and imitated in many other countries. There are publications on Italian *luoghi della memoria* (Isnenghi 1987ff.); German *Erinnerungsorte* (François and Schulze 2001); Dutch *Plaatsen van Herinnering* (Wesseling 2005/2006); a Belgian *parcours van herinnering* (Tollebeek and Buelens 2008); and *Lieux de mémoire au Luxembourg/Erinnerungsorte in Luxembourg* (Kmec et al. 2008).

aspects of his work which need to be reconsidered—and might productively be tackled from the perspective of family memory. First of all, as critics Hue Tam Ho Tai (2001) and Tony Judt (1998) convincingly showed, Nora actively constructs (rather than merely records) French national memory. What Nora ignores (or forgets), however, is "la *France d'outre-mer*," the French colonies, as well as the memories of immigrants. In the light of the history of cultural contact, exchange, and colonialism, and with a view to today's complex global migration patterns and multicultural societies, the sites of memory-approach must be fundamentally re-examined through a "transcultural lens" (see Crownshaw 2011a). It is through the study of family memory (especially of cross-cultural, transnational, and immigrant families, cf. Bryceson and Vuorela, 2002; Grillo 2008) that the actual, multivoiced processes of remembering the nation become discernible.[9] The study of family memory can thus serve as an important corrective to the top-down approach taken by those who chart "purist" sites of national memory.

Second, Nora's contradistinction between *milieux de mémoire* and *lieux de mémoire* is questionable. According to Nora, "there are *lieux de mémoire*, sites of memory, because there are no longer *milieux de mémoire*, real environments of memory" (Nora 1989, 7). Sites of memory thus seem to function as artificial substitutes for the no longer existent, "natural" collective memory (see Carrier 2000). One might be tempted to regard family memory as a typical *milieu de mémoire*, a kind of memory, which is authentic, neither constructed nor "invented," and which may even be a site of "counter-memories" to the official narrative of the past. But whereas family memory is clearly less official and institutionalized than national *lieux de mémoire*, it does not follow that such "memories from below" are necessarily more precise, "true," or even morally good. It seems more useful to ask how different frameworks of memory function, how *milieux* and *lieux de mémoire* interact, how national memory feeds into family memory, and, in turn, how family memory contributes to, questions, or disregards national sites of memory.

In his work on the sites of memory that emerged after the world wars all across Europe, Jay Winter has repeatedly addressed this complex interplay between family memory and national memory (Winter 1995; Winter and Sivan 1999). Remembrance of the war dead, he argues, is the result

---

[9] This has of course been the focus of oral historians. See, e.g., Thompson (1978), Passerini (1992). For anthropological approaches to the study of familial memory, see Carsten (2007).

of a complex dynamics unfolding between family frameworks and public commemoration:

> [The] framework of family transmission of narratives about the past is an essential part of public commemoration. It also helps us understand why some commemorative forms are changed or simply fade away. When the link between family life and public commemoration is broken, a powerful prop of remembrance is removed. Then, in a short time, remembrance atrophies and fades away. Public reinforcements may help keep alive the ritual and practice of commemoration. But the event becomes hollow when removed from the myriad small-scale social units that breathed life into it in the first place. (Winter 2010, 72)

Winter (2010, 71) comes to the conclusion that "[c]ommemorative ritual survives when it is inscribed within the rhythms of community and, in particular, family life. Public commemoration lasts when it draws about overlaps between national history and family history." Family memory, to sum up, is an indispensable framework, which mediates between national sites of memory and the actual people who do the remembering within social groups. It keeps *lieux de mémoire* alive. But it can also lead to their decay.

5.8 Jan and Aleida Assmann: Cultural Memory and Communicative Memory

The theory of "cultural memory" (*das kulturelle Gedächtnis*) was introduced by Aleida and Jan Assmann in the late 1980s (J. Assmann 1995 [1988]). Its starting point is the distinction between two registers of collective memory. The Assmanns' concept, which is in many aspects indebted to Halbwachs's findings, is grounded in the fundamental insight that there is a qualitative difference between a collective memory that is based on forms of everyday communication (such as we would find in families) and a collective memory that is more institutionalized and rests on symbolic objectivations (such as we usually find at the national level). In response, they differentiate between two "memory frameworks": communicative memory on the one hand, and the cultural memory on the other. The contents, forms, media, temporal structure, and carriers of these two memory frameworks are fundamentally different from one another (J. Assmann 2011 [1992], 34–41; J. Assmann 2010).

Communicative memory comes into being through everyday interaction. Its contents consist of the historical experiences of contemporaries, and it thus refers to a limited, shifting temporal horizon of about eighty to a hundred years. The contents of communicative memory are changeable and are not ascribed a determined meaning. Within this framework, everyone is considered equally competent in remembering and interpreting the common past. Communicative memory, according to Jan Assmann, belongs to the field of oral history.

Cultural memory, on the other hand, is a memory that is tied to material objectivations. It is consciously established, media-based, and ceremonialized. Remembering within the framework of cultural memory takes place in what Jan Assmann calls the "temporal dimension of the festival" (while communicative memory is tied to the "temporal dimension of everyday life") (J. Assmann 2011 [1992], 40). Cultural memory transports a fixed set of contents and meanings. Its media are maintained and interpreted by trained specialists (for example, priests, shamans, or archivists). Its objects are mythical events from a distant past, which are interpreted as foundational to the community (for example, the exodus from Egypt or the battle for Troy). Between the time remembered in the framework of the communicative memory and that remembered in the cultural memory, thus, there is a gaping hole—or, using the ethnologist Jan Vansina's (1985) term, a shifting "floating gap" that moves along with the passage of time.

It is clear that family memories belong primarily to the field of communicative memory, with its focus on everyday life, face-to-face interaction, oral communication, and its restricted time span of about three to four generations. However, communicative memory is linked to cultural memory and cannot be separated from the latter's myths. One striking example is how the Bible and other "cultural texts" (J. Assmann 2006) shape family memory and provide "cultural paradigms" (see Erll 2017) to interpret events that occur in small communities.

Family memory is a framework of communicative remembering, which intersects with, feeds into and draws on, and may be congruent, overlapping, or at odds with, the cultural memory. One of the most interesting questions in studying family memory is how culturally available narratives and images shape or are refracted by family remembrance—as well as vice versa, how family memories are translated into cultural memory (as can be seen in case of royal families or the families of famous artists). Such dynamic and multimodal processes, which include different forms of mediation as well as the transnational circulation of memory, are what recent approaches to the study of family memory are increasingly paying attention to.

5.9 Transnational, Transgenerational, and Media Culture Perspectives on Family Memory

National memory lay at the heart of the new memory studies. However, important mnemonic processes unfold on levels *above* and *below* the nation. We are dealing with "multiple mnemonic memberships" (Erll 2011b) in migrant, diasporic, and transnational families (Leydesdorff and Chamberlain 2004; Assmann 2018). At the same time, sociologists and oral historians have shown that official, national, and even transnational memory is continually refracted through acts of remembrance taking place within small communities, such as families.

Studying family memory is increasingly seen as an interdisciplinary effort, which combines transgenerational research (focusing on the transmission of memory across the genealogical chain of grandparents, parents, and children) with comparative and transnational perspectives. Moreover, scholars have become more sensitive to how mediations—photography, literature, mass media, and digital media—function as powerful agents in the production of family memory (Lohmeier and Böhling 2017).

A significant body of research on family memory was produced by a German group of scholars led by Harald Welzer. They were interested in how historical experience is handed down from eyewitnesses to children and grandchildren. Welzer (2010a, 2010b) uses the terms *Vergleichende Tradierungsforschung* (comparative research on the transmission of memory between generations) and *Weitererzählforschung* (research on re-narrating) for a specific method of family-as-memory studies. The approach combines interview-based qualitative social research with a broad interdisciplinary perspective on collective memory. The question is how memories of Nazism, the Holocaust, and the Second World War are "re-narrated," from generation to generation.

The Welzer group introduced several key concepts for the study of family and memory: The "social memory" (Welzer 2001) describes the non-intentional fabrication of the past, *en passant*, as it occurs in everyday communication, especially within the family. Welzer emphasizes the important role that various media play in this process, such as photographs, which can initiate conversations about the past. Welzer's (2002, 2010a) use of "communicative memory" (which differs considerably from the Assmanns' term) updates Halbwachs's *cadres sociaux de la mémoire* in the light of modern memory studies. By combining concepts from sociology, psychology, and the neurosciences, Welzer shows that individual memory is indeed inherently a "communicative" memory in that it develops and works in conjunction with social interaction and communication. An important neuroscientific concept on which he draws is the "plasticity of the brain," which refers to the fact that neuronal networks are constantly changing and reorganizing themselves to adapt to new experience. Experience is usually had within social contexts. But it can also be gathered from media. Accordingly, Welzer looks at the influence of media representations on our memory. In interviews with Second World War veterans, for example, he discovered how war movies had shaped their personal memories (Welzer 2002; similarly, Bourke 1999). In their collaborative publications, Welzer and the members of his research group have repeatedly drawn attention to the ways in which family memories are shaped by media (movies, TV, books, etc.) and how culturally available plot structures, logics of dramaturgy, topoi, and metaphors—often widely circulated in media culture—influence the ways in which families narrate their past (Moller, Tschugnall, and Welzer 2001; see also Figes 2007).

Such an insistence on the relevance of media for family memory can also be observed in American memory research. Marianne Hirsch, in her work *Family Frames* (1997), emphasizes that family photos depend on "a narrative act of adoption that transforms rectangular images of cardboard into telling details connecting lives and stories across continents and generations" (Hirsch 1997, xii; see also Kuhn 1995). Indeed, an old family portrait that we find at a flea market "tells us" little or nothing. At most, it has a function as a vague medium of memory. For example, the stance and clothing might be interpreted as typical expressions of a past era. In contrast, for a great-granddaughter who knows her family's history, the photograph is a media cue that taps a far richer vein of memories from the past. For Hirsch, photographs are "the medium connecting first- and second-generation remembrance, memory and postmemory" (Hirsch 1997, 23).

Marianne Hirsch introduced the concept of "postmemory" in order to explain how traumatic experiences of parents and grandparents can be mediated to children and grandchildren and adopted by them as "memory," even if they did not experience the events themselves. In *The Generation of Postmemory* (2012, 5f.), Hirsch defines the term as follows:

"Postmemory" describes the relationship that the "generation after" bears to the personal, collective, and cultural trauma of those who came before—to experiences they "remember" only by means of the stories, images, and behaviors among which they grew up. Postmemory's connection to the past is thus actually mediated not by recall but by imaginative investment, projection, and creation.

The postmemorial work analyzed by Hirsch includes Art Spiegelman's graphic novel *Maus* (1986) and W. G. Sebald's novel *Austerlitz* (2001). But while postmemories of the Holocaust remain her primary example, Hirsch also studies postmemorial dynamics in survivor families of other catastrophes, such as the Armenian genocide, the Vietnam War, and South African Apartheid. With the notion of "connective postmemory," Hirsch introduces a perspective that connects postmemories of different violent histories, such as Jewish and Palestinian stories of return. Similar to the thrust of Michael Rothberg's *Multidirectional Memory* (2009), Hirsch uses her studies on family memory for "capacious, nonessentialist approaches to memory as practices of 'reparative reading'" (Hirsch 2012, 24).

What these different strands of research emphasize unanimously is that family memory is not simply "there"—it is not a mnemonic content stored in a family archive—but that, instead, versions of the familial past are fabricated collectively, again and again, in situ, through concrete acts of communication and interaction. Angela Keppler (1994), for example, has shown through conversational analysis that the unity of family memory rests not so much on the consistency of the stories that are being told, but more on the continuity of the opportunities for and acts of shared remembering. Family memory is, thus, a dynamic, context-dependent construction that can change considerably over time, as well as according to different settings and audiences.

In their interviews with individual members of German families, the Welzer group found that stories about the past were subject to continual transformation during their transmission across generations. Interestingly, stories about a grandparent's role during the Nazi regime tended to become more positive as the interviewers spoke to successively younger generations:

Moving through the generations, stories can become so altered that in the end they have undergone a complete change of meaning. This reconfiguration generally functions to turn grandparents into people who always possessed moral integrity, according to today's standards and normative appraisal. This reformulation of stories is undertaken precisely because, in interviews, most members of the children's and grandchildren's generations exhibit no doubt at all that Nazism was a criminal system and the Holocaust an unparalleled crime. This assessment of the Nazi past—the standard fare of history lessons, the media and the official German culture of commemoration—breaks down under the resulting questioning of the role played by one's own grandparents during the period; it even evokes the subjective need to assign one's grandfather or grandmother the role of the "good" German in everyday life under the Nazis. Thus emerges the paradoxical result of successful education about the Nazi past: the more comprehensive the knowledge about war crimes, persecution, and extermination, the stronger is the need to develop stories to reconcile the crimes of "the Nazis" or "the Germans" and the moral integrity of parents or grandparents. (Welzer 2020b, 7)

This astonishing insight into the sheer extent of the "re-formatting of heard and narrated stories" (Welzer 2010b, 7) on the part of children and grandchildren led the research group to coin the term "cumulative heroization." The result of this remarkable practice of intergenerational memory-making in German families is concisely, if cheekily, summed up in the study's title *Opa war kein Nazi* [Granddad wasn't a Nazi] (Moller, Tschugnall, and Welzer 2001). The phenomenon of "cumulative heroization" shows that there is obviously a gap between official and private memories, between cultural and communicative memory, between institutionalized commemoration and the dynamics of everyday remembering in social contexts—and that this gap is filled in most surprising ways by those who do the remembering.

The family is not only an interesting framework for the study of "memory *after* violence," as the prime channel through which trauma as well as exculpatory stories are transmitted, especially in situations where histories of violence or certain versions of the past remain tabooed or silenced in broader society. It is also a key site for "memory *before* violence," practices of collective memory that prepare for future violence by providing it with narrative and emotional underpinnings.[10]

In his work on Rwandan family narratives that *preceded* the genocide of 1994, historian Philippe Denis (2021) realized that the mass violence was

---

[10] On "memory *before* and *after* violence," see Buckley-Zistel et al. (2024).

preformed by Hutu family narratives that reached back to the 1950s: "Family memories transmitted from parents to children from a young age played a critical role in the development of the ideology that led to the genocide against the Tutsi" (Denis 2021, 159). Postmemories of Hutu humiliation and Tutsi arrogance had rested inactive for decades, but were cued and became active again in the 1990s: "People who had almost forgotten the stories told by their parents when they were small suddenly remembered them under the pressure of the more and more vociferous Hutu extremist media" (Denis 2021, 160). To sum up, for every act of mass violence, there "is a before as much as there is an after" (Denis 2021, 160), and family memories seem to play a considerable role in the making of the "before."

Around 2010, the field of memory studies saw a move toward comparative and transnational perspectives, a trend which has also had repercussions for the study of family memory. The defining contribution of transnational memory studies has been provided by Daniel Levy and Natan Sznaider in *The Holocaust and Memory in the Global Age* (2006 [2001]). It is perhaps no wonder that this first full-length study on globalization and memory was on the Holocaust, which is, in fact, the very paradigm of a global object of remembrance. As a historical event, it affected many different nations, ethnicities, and families; today, it is commemorated in many places around the world. As a result of mass-mediation, the Holocaust has become a global site of memory, an example of a "de-territorialized, transnational, and globalizing memory." The Holocaust has become the founding myth of global justice, and, in this sense, has effected the emergence of "cosmopolitan memory cultures" (Levy and Sznaider 2006 [2001], 2). The worldwide remembrance of the extermination of the Jews led to the international establishment, legitimization, and adherence to a set of normative rules concerning democracy, tolerance, and humanism, most notably in the form of the Universal Declaration of Human Rights in 1948. The Holocaust functions as a "transnational symbol" for the violation of human rights. According to Levy and Sznaider, the cosmopolitan memory of the Holocaust could only take shape in a "dual process of particularization and universalization" (Levy and Sznaider 2006 [2001], 3), through the interaction between local relevance and global reference.

The family is an arena where the particularizing and universalizing dynamics of cosmopolitan memory play out in situ. Again, it was Welzer and his group who focused on family memory in a comparative and transnational perspective. *Der Krieg der Erinnerung* [The war of memory]

(Welzer 2007) studies the ways in which European Holocaust memories are produced by and between different generations in Germany, Norway, Denmark, the Netherlands, Switzerland, Serbia, and Croatia. Claudia Lenz and Harald Welzer (2007) identified the "national basic narratives"[11] of the Holocaust. They investigated how their interviewees in different European nations related to those basic narratives. They explored whether official national stories about the Holocaust did or did not serve as a matrix or framework in guiding the interpretation of family history and endowing it with meaning. It turned out that the contents and meanings of institutionalized, official memory (Lenz and Welzer call this the "lexicon") and the communicative practice of everyday familial remembering (the "album") can differ to a great degree (Lenz and Welzer 2008, 8). Family loyalties and emotional ties (as already highlighted by Halbwachs) play a great role in the interpretation of the past (Lenz and Welzer 2008, 18).

Families serve as a kind of switchboard between individual memory and larger frameworks of collective memory. Lenz and Welzer see the "family as a relay between personal, autobiographical remembering on the one hand and public remembrance and official images of history on the other" (2008, 15). This intermediary function of family memory is further complicated when one takes the increasingly transnational dimension of collective memory into account. In the case of the Holocaust, it is the younger generations, in particular, who seem to remember according to "cosmopolitan memory," which is grounded in universalist narratives about human rights, democracy, tolerance, and anti-racism, and is disseminated via globalizing media cultures. At the same time, elements of such globalizing memory are set in relation to national basic narratives and further refracted according to family memories.[12]

Researchers of family memory are faced with the complex interaction of various mnemonic levels: the individual-autobiographical, the interactive-familial, the institutionalized-national, and the mass mediated–transnational. To complicate matters, the relationships between these various levels are not continuous. There are always "gaps" between different mnemonic practices and the social frameworks under consideration.

---

[11] Lenz and Welzer draw on the concept of "national basic narratives" as it was developed by Eriksen (1995) and Bryld and Warring (1998).
[12] On the different scales of transnational memory—intimate, familial, urban, national, transnational, etc.—and their intersections, see De Cesari and Rigney (2014).

In Claudia Lenz's (2006) words, research on family memory therefore must always "mind the gap."

5.10 "Making Kin," Making Memory: Slavery, Queer Postmemory, and the Anthropocene

Research on family memory is a vibrant field with, as Švaříčková Slabáková (2020) rightly notes, a potential which is largely untapped. An orientation toward memory studies enables family studies to consider questions about the relation between family memory and memory activism (Smaoui 2023), how gender, class, and race figure in the familial memory archive (Hemmings 2022), and how digital modes of communication serve to facilitate family relations across generations (Grønning 2021).

Donna Haraway's (2016, 103) exhortation to "make kin, not babies" in our age of the Anthropocene is a challenge for memory studies to think far beyond the nuclear family. How are kin made and (re-)made through memory in different groups, around the world, in history, and between humans and nonhumans?

As Corinna Assmann (2018) has pointed out, "doing family"—just like doing memory—depends on the "social construction of relatedness." How familial relationalities are constructed around the world using the resources of collective memory is addressed in Švaříčková Slabáková's (2020) collection of essays, which provides a truly transnational overview of family memory on five different continents. In-depth research on non-Western family memories provides important insights for memory studies. For example, Lentz and Lobnibe's (2022) book on one extended African family with more than five hundred members in Northern Ghana and Burkina Faso shows that what binds these family members together is shared memories, which show a strong futural dimension.

Family historians Barclay and Koefoed (2021, 4) note that there are not only historical differences in family memory (e.g., in ancient and premodern settings) to account for, but that:

> [f]ollowing a concern with how the family is defined, histories of family memory are also increasingly interested in groups whose family inheritances are less available or more contested. Attention has turned to how orphans, care-leavers, members of Stolen Generations communities (First

Nations children removed from their families and often institutionalized), illegitimate children, fictive kin, and similar groups have made sense of who they are, where they came from, and how family history and memories can be deployed to construct family.

What needs to be added here is the difficult question of memory in families descended from former slaves. It makes clear that the possibility of constructing family history is in fact a "privilege" not shared by everyone (Field 2022).

Saidiya Hartman shows how slavery—and the "social death" it produces (Patterson 1982)—leads to massive gaps in family memory. In *Lose Your Mother* (2008), Hartman writes about her grandfather's "sadness and anger of not knowing his people," and about herself starting to wonder about all the "relatives whose only proof of existence was fragments of stories and names that repeated themselves across generations. . . . The gaps and silences of my family were not unusual: slavery made the past a mystery, unknown and unspeakable." Hartman's own research on family history therefore becomes an endeavor "in search of people who left behind no traces" (Hartman 2008, 13).

Attempts at creating memory for families whose histories are shaped by slavery, forced removal, or genocide draw frequently (and given the gaps in more traditional historical sources, do so necessarily) on imaginative investment. This is the reason why "fictions of family memory"—in novels, poems, plays, film, and other aesthetic media with degrees of poetic license—are important mediations of such family memories. As in the case of the miniseries *Roots* (1977) or *Holocaust* (1979), they assume a memory-unlocking and path-opening agency for other families, and larger society. For the understanding of how slavery impacts family memory, Toni Morrison's *Beloved* (1987) remains the "paradigmatic" and "hypercanonical" case of such fictional investment (Rothberg 2022a; see also de Souza Sutter 2019).

One of the most exciting recent developments in family memory research is the study of "queer postmemory." The term was coined by Dilara Çalışkan (2019). Drawing on Hirsch's (2012) work on "postmemory" and connecting it with queer studies' research on "chrononormativity" and "queer temporalities,"[13] Çalışkan questions the "unmarked temporal and familial dimensions

---

[13] Freeman (2010, 3–4) understands chrononormativity as "temporal regulation" according to heteronormative standards, the prescription of seemingly natural rhythms and concepts centering

in the study of collective and personal memory." She draws on fieldwork with trans women in Istanbul and focuses on "mutually formed mother and daughter relationships" between these trans women. Such practices of doing family call for "alternative understandings of inter-generational transmission of memory," where, for example, a trans mother can be much younger (though more experienced) than the trans daughter. Çalışkan's work invites us to consider "other types of time, other types of relationalities and other types of inheritability" (2019, 261).

The greatest challenge to our understanding of family and memory is Donna Haraway's exhortation in *Staying with the Trouble* (2016) to "make kin, not babies!" and to understand "kin" to "mean something other/more than entities tied by ancestry or genealogy." For Haraway, "all earthlings are kin in the deepest sense" (Haraway 2016, 102–103).

> *Kin* is a wild category that all sorts of people do their best to domesticate. Making kin as oddkin rather than, or at least in addition to, godkin and genealogical and biogenetic family troubles important matters, like to whom is one actually responsible. . . . What must be cut and what must be tried if multispecies flourishing on earth, including human and other-than-human beings in kinship, are to have a chance? (Haraway 2016, 2)

The survival of humankind may depend on "making kin" with animals, plants, and even the atmosphere. The challenge is to think new relationalities and to find ways to encode these into collective memory—to give them a past, a present, and a future. Such a new posthuman family memory may be the greatest challenge for the human "memory-making animal"[14] as well as for memory studies.

---

around the heteronormative idea of family (marriage, childbirth, inheritance, etc.) For Freeman, these are "institutionally and culturally enforced rhythms, or timings."

[14] I use this term with a nod to Ernst Cassirer (1944) who called humans the "symbol making animal," the *animal symbolicum*.

Chapter 6
Generation in Literary History
Genealogy, Generationality, Memory

6.1 Generation, Generationality, Genealogy

The concept of generation is like the air that we breathe—essential and largely unnoticed. It is constitutive of our understanding of family and society, of biological and historical processes; and at the same time, it tends to remain invisible, a cluster of tacit assumptions underlying a ubiquitous formula.

"Generation" is a twofold term. Understood as generational identity ("generationality"), the history of generation can be traced back to its foundational moment during the First World War. In its second meaning, as "genealogy," the idea of generation is age-old. While sociological and historical research tends to focus on generationality, literary and cultural studies have reinvigorated the study of generation as genealogy. Both concepts are steeped in ideas of cultural memory, a fact which memory studies has not yet acknowledged in all its complexity. A closer look reveals, moreover, how deeply generationality and ideas of genealogy are enmeshed with literature and other representational media. Such entanglements point well beyond literary studies' traditional practice of using the notion of generation as a means of writing literary history (from the "First Generation Romantics" to the "Angry Young Men"). What is at stake, rather, is the development of comprehensive and conceptually rigorous approaches to the many-layered interrelationships between generation, memory, and literature.

This chapter proposes an integrative literary and memory studies perspective on generation, combining classic and more recent theories of generation with historical case studies. It reconstructs three discursive constellations around "generation" that have shaped the past century: the First World War and the "lost generation," the Holocaust and the "generation of postmemory," and the nexus between immigration and generation. Literary works have unfolded co-constructive agency in all three constellations.

There is a rich, and still largely untapped, potential of studying generationality and genealogy as part of (literary) mnemohistory.

6.2 The First World War and the Birth of Generationality

Talk about generations is everywhere today. We count generations of immigrants and educational strivers, of survivors of war and other catastrophes. The media weld their stories of human interest, economic cycles, or cultural styles around generational entities such as the baby boomers, the generation of 1968, and, as more recent phenomena, the generations X, Y (Millennials), and Z. Such labels, of course, never capture the entirety of an age cohort. As a rule, they are attached to small circles of middle-class white male Western people. However tenuous as a description of society these generation labels may therefore be, they have proven powerful and tenacious in the past century.

What can be found in popular discourse today has its roots in the early twentieth century. It may not be exaggerated to position the so-called Great War of 1914–1918 as the starting point for the emergence of concepts of generations as we know them today. One of the reasons is that the First World War engendered a strong idea of the "war generation" or, in the title of Robert Wohl's (1979) influential book, of "the generation of 1914." After the war, veterans in various European countries claimed the label "lost generation" for themselves. They referred not only to the great number of young soldiers who had died in an unprecedented mechanized mass slaughter, but also to their own disillusioning war experience, and to their inability to regain hold in civil society after having spent much of their early adulthood at the front.[1]

Interestingly, what was heatedly debated in the social arena in the late 1920s—the "war generation" and what it really was: lost or heroic, dutiful or deluded—also became the center of scholarly attention. Thinkers as different as Walter Benjamin, Martin Heidegger, Edmund Husserl, Wilhelm Pinder, and Julius Petersen wrote about generations in the 1920s and 1930s, either apparently under the impression of, or with direct reference, to the First World War. Still today, Karl Mannheim's sociological essay *The Problem of Generations* (1928), with its key concepts of *Generationslagerung* (similarity of location), *Generationszusammenhang* (generation as actuality),

---

[1] On the myth of the lost generation, see Wohl (1979), Hynes (1990), and Winter (1995). A thorough attempt at debunking the myth from the perspective of military history is Bond (2014).

and *Generationseinheit* (generation unit), is the main reference for studies of generational identities.[2] Therefore, in terms of intensity, or discursive density, "generation" belongs to the aftermath of the Great War.

Seen from the vantage point of the late 1920s, a then middle-aged generation looked back at the years 1914 to 1918 as its formative years, and at experiences of war, violence, hunger, and death as generation-defining events. Formed by these early impressions, the war generation is, in Mannheim's words, a "generation as actuality,"[3] which falls into different, in fact often highly antagonistic, "generation units." In the German case, this spectrum unfolds from the pacifist "lost generation" all the way to the war enthusiasts of the "Conservative Revolution" (Ernst Jünger being the most notorious among these). Such units are, according to Mannheim, "polar forms of the intellectual and social response to an historical stimulus experienced by all in common."[4]

Translated into the terms of today's research, the unit of the "lost generation" is a typical case of "generationality," that is, the conscious identification of a group of people, either by itself or by others, *as* a generation. The term *Generationalität* (which I translate as "generationality") was introduced by German social historians, who started in the early 2000s to reflect again upon generation-history. Ute Daniel (2001, 331) defines generationality as "an ensemble of age-specific attributions, by means of which people locate themselves within their respective historical period" (my translation). We could also say with Samuel Hynes (1990, 383), "A generation exists when it thinks it does." Or with Robert Wohl (1979, 5), "Historical Generations are not born; they are made." Jürgen Reulecke (2010, 119), one of Germany's most prolific historians of generations, explains:

> The term "generationality" ... has a twofold meaning. On the one hand, it refers to characteristics resulting from shared experiences that either individuals or larger "generational units" collectively claim for themselves. On the other hand, it can also mean the bundle of characteristics resulting from shared experiences that are ascribed to such units from the outside,

---

[2] See Mannheim (1952 [1928]). For sociological research on generations, see Schuman and Scott (1989), Eyerman and Turner (1998).

[3] According to Mannheim (1952 [1928], 306), "a generation as an actuality is constituted when similarly 'located' contemporaries participate in a common destiny and in the ideas and concepts which are in some way bound up with its unfolding."

[4] Mannheim (1952 [1928], 304). What characterizes each generation unit is the "identity of responses [to the generation-defining events], a certain affinity in the way in which they all move with and are formed by their common experiences" (Mannheim 1952 [1928], 306).

with which members of other age groups—and often also public opinion as expressed in the media—attempt, in the interest of establishing demarcations and reducing complexity, to identify presumed generations as well as the progression of generations.

Generationality is an effect of auto- or hetero-identification. Interestingly, such conscious attribution is something that Karl Mannheim only mentions in passing. The sociologist seems more interested in generation *an sich* (in itself) than *für sich* (for itself), to use Karl Marx's distinction. Mannheim emphatically privileges generation as an unconscious structure, and he dismisses generation as a reflexive self-image.[5] The term "generationality," on the other hand, is clearly a term of our age in that it draws attention precisely to identities—either self-made or fabricated by others—and to their fundamental constructedness. This is in fact one of the main points of this chapter: The ways in which "generation" has (re)appeared in popular and academic discourses across the past century are highly dependent on different historical experiences and changing cultural practices, on intellectual developments and social challenges.

6.3 Generation and Collective Memory: Karl Mannheim

When Mannheim developed his sociological theory in the 1920s, he could draw on an existent body of thinking about generation—and on an existent set of problems connected with it. From the eighteenth century onward, proponents of the philosophy of history, for example David Hume and Auguste Comte, had used the idea of generation in order to understand historical change. Toward the end of the nineteenth century, such theorizing was increasingly flawed by biologistic and mechanistic designs. Historian and statisticians like Ottokar Lorenz and Gustav Rümelin connected the "chain of generations" in overly simplistic ways to changes in mentalities and political systems, which would occur as regularly as a pendulum swings back and forth or waves crash on a beach. Biological rhythms were equated with sociohistorical processes.[6]

---

[5] Mannheim dismisses "consciously developed" generationalities of his age, such as the German Youth Movement, as "mere cliques" (Mannheim (1952 [1928], 288).

[6] See Mannheim's critique, "How the Problem Stands at the Moment" (Mannheim (1952 [1928], 276–286). For the most comprehensive overview to date of thinking about generations, see Parnes et al. (2008).

This is in fact one of the key problems of thinking about generation, even in its most sophisticated manifestations. What sits together here—sometimes inspiringly, more often uneasily—is a fundamentally biological concept of *generatio* (as procreation) with the wish to make sense of socio-historical developments: the natural and the cultural.

It was only in the late nineteenth century, with Wilhelm Dilthey, that the focus in generation theory shifted from biological factors such as the time of birth, which in empirical sociology defines an age cohort, toward cultural factors, such as a shared "space of experience," to use Reinhart Koselleck's (2004 [1985]) term. This space is defined by historical events and processes that occurred during the generation's "impressionable time."[7] The shift from the natural to the cultural implies also a shift in conceptions of time. Qualitative, experienced time is what holds a generation together, not quantitatively measurable time.

In the 1920s, Karl Mannheim drew on Dilthey's work and developed hitherto scattered thoughts about sociocultural generations into a full-fledged sociological theory. Just like Dilthey, Mannheim claimed that there is a formative period for the emergence of a generation, and that this period ranges approximately from age 17 to 25.[8] The intellectual, social, and political events taking place during the time of early adulthood are generation-defining events. This is the so-called imprint or critical period theory, which present-day sociology has been able to substantiate, albeit with modifications (Schuman and Corning 2012).

It is also with Mannheim that generations become mnemonic communities. They are defined by their common reference to certain past events, by their shared anchorage in a specific historical period.[9] Generations center around a "temporal home," a *Zeitheimat* (to use Sebald's evocative term[10])—a certain period of time that was formative for the group, in which its members feel rooted, which has shaped them, to which they travel back in their memories. However, Karl Mannheim insists on a strict separation between memories based on personal experience and what he calls "appropriated memories":

---

[7] This is Wilhelm Dilthey's term: *Zeitalter der Empfänglichkeit* (Dilthey 1957 [1875], 37).
[8] Mannheim (1952 [1928]), 300.
[9] The kind of collective memory involved here is what sociologists call "public memory." Generations are defined by their common reference to events of regional, national, and transnational history. Mannheim's examples of generation-defining events are the French Revolution and the Napoleonic wars.
[10] Sebald (2003, 261) in an interview with Volker Hage.

Here we must make a fundamental distinction between appropriated memories and personally acquired memories (a distinction applicable both to reflective and unreflective elements). It makes a great difference whether I acquire memories for myself in the process of personal development, or whether I simply take them over from someone else. I only really possess those "memories" that I have created directly for myself, only that "knowledge" I have personally gained in real situations. This is the only sort of knowledge, which really "sticks," and it alone has real binding power. (Mannheim 1952 [1928], 296)

Memory studies today has complicated this view. It has recognized the permeability between our own and other people's memories—the fact that our memories are "mediated," in that all kinds of representations preform as well as retrospectively shape our autobiographical memories.[11] But Mannheim's insistence on firsthand experience indicates the extent to which his theory resonates with discussions of his time, with the controversies about the "true" memory of the First World War—although Mannheim never explicitly mentions the war in his essay. At the time he was writing, much of the discourse on the "war generation" was already out in the social field, in Germany as well as elsewhere (see Wohl 1979). Mannheim's theory seems to echo the clear, often brutally clear, demarcations that veterans of the First World War maintained, irrespective of their ideological provenance. What counted as a sign of participation in the war generation was the bodily experience of war (the German language even possesses a specific term for this kind of experience: *Kriegserlebnis*[12]). This alone was the entrance ticket to and marker of the generational mnemonic community. The ironic twist to this is that the most important representations of the war would soon be written and screened by people who had not been (or hardly had been) at the front and who relied heavily on "appropriated memories."

What Mannheim's conception of generational memory appears to rule out is the possibility of secondhand, mediated experience in the formation of identities. In his reflections on "what produces a generational unit," however, Mannheim does realize that works of art can become "vehicles of formative tendencies" and that they possess a "group forming potency."[13] He even states

---

[11] See Erll (2011a); Landsberg (2004); van Dijck (2007).

[12] As opposed to *Kriegserfahrung*, which translates into the more general "war experience." See Mosse (1990); Vondung (1980).

[13] Mannheim (1952 [1928], 304–305). Although scattered throughout his writings, Mannheim makes assumptions about literature and art which resonate surprisingly well with today's literary

that *ideas* can have a "recruiting power" well beyond the contexts of their origin, appealing to wider, spatially scattered groups and thus integrating people who have no direct contact with one another into a generation.[14]

But Mannheim's writings betray no strong sense of *media* as catalysts and "travel agents" of generational identity. And certainly, he does not include transnational dynamics into his reflections.[15] This may appear curious in the light of what was happening at the very time of his writing: In the late 1920s, media such as newspaper articles, political essays, and novels were busy discussing, defining, and eventually producing the "war generation"—in an increasingly transnational field. I will exemplify these processes by drawing on Erich Maria Remarque's novel *All Quiet on the Western Front* (1929), which is arguably the best-known representation of the war generation as a "lost generation."

6.4 Traveling Generationality: Remarque's *All Quiet on the Western Front*

That the war generation was a "lost" generation was, first of all, a very British way of thinking about the First World War.[16] This idea is prefigured in the soldier poets' works, such as Wilfred Owen's "Anthem for Doomed Youth" (1917) and Siegfried Sassoon's "The Parable of the Old Man and the Young" (1920), as well as the literature of high modernism, such as Ezra Pound's poem "Maulberley V" (1919).[17] The lost generation is an integral component of the British "myth of the war," which Samuel Hynes sums up as follows:

> A generation of innocent young men, their heads full of high abstractions like Honour, Glory, and England, went off to war to make the world safe

and memory studies, for instance his assertion that "productive misunderstanding [the result of the ambiguousness of art works] is often a condition of continuing life" (Mannheim (1952 [1928], 305). For a similar notion of the "life" and "agency" of literary works, see Rigney (2012a, 2021).

[14] Mannheim (1952 [1928], 307). This is an early formulation of the idea of "imagined communities" in Anderson's (1991) sense.

[15] This is a key focus of today's research on generations: See, for example, Edmunds and Turner (2005). They discuss the 1960s generation as the first global generation. This essay argues that the "lost generation" of the late 1920s already showed transnational patterns of generationality.

[16] It seems that the "lost generation" was a truly an emergent transnational memory topos. Wohl's *The Generation of 1914* (1979) shows how the discourse about the war generation took hold and developed in different forms in France, Germany, England, Spain, and Italy. In the United States, the idea was popularized by Ernest Hemingway, who quoted Gertrude Stein, "You are all a lost generation," in an epigraph to his novel *The Sun Also Rises* (1926).

[17] "There died a myriad,/And of the best, among them,/For an old bitch gone in the teeth,/For a botched civilization"; in Pound (1977 [1975]), 101.

for democracy. They were slaughtered in stupid battles planned by stupid generals. Those who survived were shocked, disillusioned and embittered by their war experiences, and saw that their real enemies were not the Germans, but the old men at home who had lied to them. They rejected the values of the society that had sent them to war, and in doing so separated their own generation from the past and from their cultural inheritance. (Hynes 1990, x)

In Hynes's tongue-in-cheek summary, the British memory of the First World War emerges as tightly bound up with ideas about generation: It features generational identity, a typically all-male ("a generation of young men"), intergenerational conflict (young men vs. old men), and the question of the transmission of "cultural inheritance" between generations, that is, cultural genealogy.[18]

In Germany, the ground for the label "lost generation" was much less well prepared. There was instead a strong, vociferous strand of heroic sense-making of the war, later called *soldatischer Nationalismus* ("soldierly nationalism").[19] Many ex-soldiers joined military associations and continued war-like attitudes and actions well into the postwar period of the 1920s. But in Weimar Germany, the memory of the war was never nearly as unified as it appeared—comparatively—in Great Britain. Well into the early 1930s, the German debate was characterized by a cacophony of voices quarrelling about the meaning of the First World War and the significance of the "war generation." Ironically perhaps, it is eventually in Germany where we find, with Erich Maria Remarque's novel *Im Westen Nichts Neues* (1929; transl. *All Quiet on the Western Front*), *the* transnationally effective defining representation of the "lost generation."[20]

Im Westen Nichts Neues is a striking example of how generationality is produced in the act of representation and how the transnational travel and

---

[18] See also Todman (2005). After having been a major force throughout the twentieth century, this myth was deeply transformed during the First World War centenary in Britain, 2014–2018. On the one hand, scholarship and commemoration expanded the war memory for the first time to include the significant contribution of colonial troops—from Australia to India to Kenya (see Das 2018; Meredith 2021; Das et al. 2022). On the other hand, in a climate of Brexit, the centenary commemorations also effected a re-nationalization of the transnational memory of a "war generation."

[19] The definitive study is Prümm (1974).

[20] *Im Westen nichts Neues* appeared first in 1928 as a serial in the *Vossische Zeitung* and was issued as a book in early 1929 by Ullstein publishers (Berlin). Partly responsible for its great success was Ullstein's unprecedented marketing campaign. The first English translation by Arthur Wesley Wheen appeared in 1929. With his free translation of the novel's German title, Wheen coined the term "all quiet on the Western front." See Schneider (2004).

translation of memory texts actually occur. Remarque's *Im Westen Nichts Neues* is a combat novel, dedicated in its epigraph to "a generation of men who, even though they may have escaped shells, were destroyed by the war."[21] The image of a lost generation pervades the novel. It finds repeated expression in comments like this: "We are forlorn like children, and experienced like old men ... —I believe we are lost" (Remarque 1929, 123).

The novel features a distinct rhetoric as its most powerful shaping force (Mannheim would say: its vehicle) of generational identity: The combat experience at the Western front is mediated by a first-person narrator, the young volunteer Karl Bäumer, who speaks not only for himself, but for "his generation." Bäumer articulates much of his war experience and critical reflections in the first-person plural. What we are dealing with here is a generation-defining "we-narration," a communal voice of the lost generation.[22] Most famous is the following passage, in which Bäumer reflects on the common fate of his generation:

> I am young, I am twenty years old; yet I know nothing of life but despair, death, fear, and fatuous superficiality cast over an abyss of sorrow. I see how peoples are set against one another, and in silence, unknowingly, foolishly, obediently, innocently slay one another. I see that the keenest brains of the world invent weapons and words to make it yet more refined and enduring. And all men of my age, here and over there, throughout the whole world see these things; all my generation is experiencing these things with me. What would our fathers do if we suddenly stood up and came before them and proffered our account? What do they expect of us if a time ever comes when the war is over? Through the years our business has been killing;—it was our first calling in life. Our knowledge of life is limited to death. What will happen afterwards? And what shall come out of us? (Remarque 1929, 263)

The transition from personal to communal voice occurs with the explicit mention of "my generation," which interestingly (and importantly for the reception of the novel) is framed as an inclusive, transnational lost generation ("all men[23] of my age, here and over there, throughout the

---

[21] In German it says: "Dieses Buch soll weder eine Anklage noch ein Bekenntnis sein. Es soll nur den Versuch machen, über eine Generation zu berichten, die vom Kriege zerstört wurde— auch wenn sie seinen Granaten entkam." Interestingly, the German original speaks broadly of "a generation," whereas the English translation genders it as "a generation of men."

[22] For the narratological concept of "communal voice," see Lanser (1992).

[23] Again, the German original is "Menschen," humans (Remarque 1929, 177).

whole world"). The articulation of intergenerational conflict ("what would our fathers do if we suddenly stood up") is tied up with a notion of the significance of the war as the key experience in their formative period ("killing ... was our first calling in life") and its impact on the future development of a generation ("what shall come out of us?"). In short, *Im Westen Nichts Neues* performs rhetorically and in the medium of fiction much of what Mannheim theorizes about at the very same time. What is more, the novel's rhetorical production of a lost generation had an enormous influence—in a way that Mannheim possibly did not even dream about when he wrote about the potential of artworks as "vehicles of formative tendencies." With Remarque, generationality virtually went global.

When *Im Westen Nichts Neues* was published in early 1929, it sold six hundred thousand copies within the first three months (Kelly 2002). This was the beginning of the war writing boom in Germany—the "war books boom" (Jirgal 1931).[24] The novel seems to have had an enormous identificatory power for many readers. It appeared to convey the "truth" about the war. And this desire for truth sums up much of the expectations and reading practices connected with combat novels in the late 1920s. Readers were looking for authentic and meaningful war narratives, for books that could serve as media of collective memory.[25] This may sound to literary theorists like a fallacious approach, but is arguably a major reading practice in memory culture in general, and particularly for generation-defining texts. At the same time (and in fact for the same reasons), the novel was highly contested in Germany, not least by military, nationalist, and growing fascist circles, who accused the author of "pacifist propaganda" and tried to prove that Remarque had only spent an infinitesimal amount of time at the front and was therefore unfit as a spokesperson of the war generation (Kelly 2002, 49).

---

[24] A quantitative study (Frayn and Houston 2022) has confirmed that there was indeed a "boom" of war books (i.e., a literary memory boom) in Britain during late 1920s that peaked in 1930.

[25] The most important intervention into these international debates was Jean Norton Cru's *Témoins* (1929). The book offers an analysis of 300 French combatant testimonies of the First World War (diaries, memoirs, novels) published between 1915 and 1928. Cru tried to figure out "objectively" which testimonies conveyed the "truth" about the war. Cru relies on painstaking fact-checking and dismisses literariness, as well as what Paul Fussell (1975) would call "cultural paradigms" in war writing. (For a more productive approach to "the soldiers' tale," see Hynes 1997.) What may strike today's memory scholars as an inappropriate approach to testimony was in fact a landmark: the first sustained inquiry into the relation between witnesses' testimony and histories of mass violence. However, after the Second World War, Holocaust denier Paul Rassinier referred to Cru as his role model when he disavowed survivors' testimonies of the concentration camps (in *Le mensonge d'Ulysse*, 1955). In the aftermath of the Holocaust, new approaches to witnessing had to be developed (Winter 2007; Aubert 2015; Wievorka 2017).

The idea of generationality articulated in *Im Westen Nichts Neues* had an enormous "recruiting power" internationally. The novel is a model case of a medium of "traveling memory" (Erll 2011b). It transcended national frames and propelled the idea of the lost generation into the transnational field. This effect is prefigured in its very rhetoric. But the actual transnational travels of Remarque's "lost generation" were only made possible by forms of transcultural remediation: by translation into many different languages, by rewritings, and by adaptation into the then most far-reaching media format: the Hollywood movie.

In 1930, only one year after the German original had been published, there were thirty translations of *Im Westen Nichts Neues* in print. The sales figures imply that it must have been one of the most widely read novels not only in Europe and the United States, but also in Russia and in Japan (Kelly 2002, 43).

In the same year, Lewis Milestone adapted Remarque's novel into the Hollywood movie *All Quiet on the Western Front*.[26] This meant the translation of a novel not only into the medium of film, but also into the specific production logic of Hollywood and for international audiences. Milestone did not attempt to incorporate Bäumer's personal-communal voice into the movie (for instance, as a voice-over), but translated the novel's generation-rhetoric into dialogues and, more strikingly, into visual style. The still (see Figure 6.1) shows how cinematic images convey the sense of a lost generation: The film ends by showing Bäumer with his company on the way to the frontline. Bäumer is looking back at the viewer in a disillusioned gaze while marching forward toward death, as is implied by the technique of crossfading the marching scene with the image of a war cemetery and its endless lines of white crosses.[27]

The movie attracted massive audiences internationally. In no country, however, was the movie screened in its original form. We find different kinds of censorship and reception in different national cinemas: In the United States the erotic scenes with French women were cut, as they were in France,

---

[26] See Kelly (2002) for a comprehensive discussion of the movie; see also Winter (2011).

[27] The translations and Milestone's film adaptation were the first acts of remediation (Erll and Rigney 2009) that would keep the memory of Remarque's novel and its version of the "lost generation" alive over a century. In the wake of the First World War centenary, a new cycle of remediations emerged, such as the graphic novels (*All Quiet on the Western Front*) by Peter Eickmeyers (2014) and Wayne Vansant (2019) and the Academy Award–winning new German film adaptation (2022, dir. Edward Berger). Its movie poster, interestingly, remediates the very still of Milestone's film discussed here (see Figure 6.1).

Figure 6.1 *All Quiet on the Western Front* (1930, dir. Lewis Milestone).

albeit presumably for different reasons. In Britain, the movie was very well received and was acclaimed as an authentic representation of war. In Germany, the Nazis interrupted screenings and denounced the film as a "Jewish movie" (Kelly 2002, 102–132). While these diverse practices of reception point to particular, local ways of actualizing Milestone's representation of the lost generation, the movie also set in motion a surprisingly strong universalizing dynamic. It seems to have expressed a general feeling of the futility of war and of pity with the many young men who had been sacrificed. The fact that most of the war victims represented in *All Quiet* were the still much-mistrusted German soldiers was apparently forgotten by many viewers in the act of reception. *All Quiet on the Western Front* thus managed to detach the "lost generation" from nation-specific meanings and turned it into a transnational figure of memory.[28]

---

[28] Robert Wohl, whose classic comparative study of 1979 on *The Generation on 1914* is still the single most important source on concepts of generationality in postwar Europe, fails to look at such cases of a transnational, connective generationality, which were brought about by traveling media. Wohl (1979, 3) describes his study as "European in scope, comparative in method, though national in structure . . . the secret to the study of European history is '*Eadem sed aliter*: the same things but in another way.'" Interestingly, Wohl discusses Remarque's novel very briefly, in the section

Another, less well known, example of the "lost generation's" transnational travels and translations is the fictional memoir *Not So Quiet... Stepdaughters of War* (1930), a histrionic rewriting of Remarque's novel by the English journalist Evadne Price under the pseudonym Helen Zenna Smith. The fictional war memoir revolves around the experiences of female nurses at the Western Front. Price not only echoes the title of Remarque's book in its English translation but takes over much of its plot structure and character constellation. *Not so Quiet...* is clearly a "deep rewriting" in that it draws on technical details such as the narrator's shifts between personal and communal voice as well as the structure and wording of its generation-rhetoric.[29] All these strategies serve one end: to inscribe *women* into the "lost generation," which by 1930 may have transcended national borders, but was still tacitly assumed to be an all-male formation.

The following excerpt shows how the first-person narrator Helen echoes Bäumer's indictment of the lost generation, as quoted above, and translates it into a speech of a "lost generation of young women":

> I am twenty-one years of age, yet I know nothing of life but death, fear, blood, and the sentimentality that glorifies these things in the name of patriotism. I watch my own mother stupidly, deliberately, though unthinkingly—for she is a kind woman—encourage the sons of other women to kill their brothers. I see my own father—a gentle creature who would not willingly kill a fly—applaud the latest scientist to invent a mechanical device guaranteed to crush his fellow-beings into pulp in their thousands. And my generation watches these things and marvels at the blind foolishness of it... helpless to make its immature voice heard above the insensate clamour of the old ones who cry "Kill, Kill, Kill!" unceasingly. What is to happen to women like me when the killing is done and peace comes... if it ever comes. What will they expect of us, these elders who have sent us to fight? (Smith 1930, 164)

---

about English (!) literature. For the distinction between comparative and connective approaches to memory, see Hirsch (2012).

[29] Interestingly, Price also incorporates Remarque's shift of perspective at the ending of the novel, albeit in an oddly unmotivated manner: Whereas in Remarque the death of young Bäumer can of course not be narrated by himself and must be reported by an anonymous third-person voice, in *Not So Quiet...*, the heroine survives. Only "her soul died" (*Not So Quiet...*, 239). This unnecessary shift from first- to third-person voice indicates that even Remarque's very formal choices had become powerful figures of memory around 1930. Price seems to tap the melodramatic potential of the pretext.

The representation of women at war in *Not So Quiet . . .* may appear to today's readers as often shrill and overdone. But it seems to have struck a chord with the contemporary readership in Britain, where the book quickly became a bestseller. This may be explained by the conspicuous absence of women in the British war memoirs by Edmund Blunden, Siegfried Sassoon, Robert Graves, and the outright misogynist representations in war novels like Richard Aldington's *Death of a Hero* (1929).

Price's feminist "writing back,"[30] moreover, brings to light a promise inherent in discourses about generationality, namely its potential inclusiveness across all strata of society. In his discussion of Mannheim, Wohl emphasizes that "the generational mode of interpreting and organizing social reality" was in the 1920s an important "alternative" to the concept of "class" with its rigid boundaries. Wohl associates this potential of generationality with the romantic "longing after the whole" in interwar Germany (Wohl 1979, 82). But the case of Price shows that we find attempts at turning generationality into a broad all-encompassing category also in very different contexts, and across the lines not of class but of gender. In fact, as the following discussion of Holocaust memories and of immigration will show, the desire for "generational wholeness" seems to be tightly bound up with generation-discourses of the past century.

All Quiet on the Western Front, to sum up, functioned as a kind of node around which transnational and transmedial discourses about the "lost generation" emerged, were amplified, and were streamlined. It shows how literary versions of generational identity can travel through translation, adaptation, and rewriting—not only across media and nations, but eventually also across time: Still today, Remarque's novel stands as *the* definitive representation of the First World War and carries on the idea of a "lost generation."

6.5 Contemporaneity and Transmission: The Double Logic of *Generatio*

Over the past decade, it has been German literary historian Sigrid Weigel's project to write genealogy back into the notion of generation.[31] Weigel reminds us of what had largely been forgotten in the humanities since what

---

[30] On women's rewriting, see Rich (1972); for a memory studies perspective, see Plate 2010.
[31] See Weigel (2002a, 2002b, 2006).

she portrays as Mannheim's horizontal, that is, synchronic or presentist, theory. The term "generation," she maintains, implies not only the synchronicity of a group of people, but also diachronicity, genealogy. Derived from Greek *genesis* and Latin *generatio* ("origin," "arise," "[pro]creation"), the term "generation" has traditionally meant both: vertically, the production and reproduction of a species from one generation to the next, and, horizontally, members of the species who have the same age.

While synchronic generations are meant to capture the experience of contemporaneity, diachronic genealogy is essentially about transmission across time. This is the double logic of *generatio*. It unfolds in the ways that intra- and intergenerational aspects—contemporaneity and transmission—are connected and intersect. Speaking about one dimension always implies (often tacit) assumptions about the other. In the case of the First World War, generationality and the rhetoric of genealogy appear as flipsides of social identification. The "lost generation" inhabits a twofold location: Its identification as a community of victims is inextricably linked to its rejection of and dissociation from the older generation of parents, teachers, and politicians. This double logic can be found in Remarque's rhetoric as well as in Hynes's concise summary of the English "myth of the war." The "lost generation," in short, is unthinkable without "the old men"—no generationality without its "genealogical Other."

As is the case with horizontal generations, vertical genealogy is a matter of nature *and* of culture, and it can be related to familial as well as broader societal frames. According to Weigel, generation as a genealogical term revolves around the "bodily, material, and cultural continuum of a species."[32] It points to inheritance as well as to heritage. With the transition from (familial) inheritance to (societal) heritage, the preoccupation with genealogy enters the area of cultural memory.

Mannheim briefly mentions this link between genealogy and cultural memory when he asks how cultural transmission takes place given the fact of ever-changing generations.[33] In fact, alongside the presentist question of "generationality," the conundrum of transgenerational memory and the reproduction of culture is a veritable obsession of the interwar period, holding in its grip thinkers like Walter Benjamin, Sigmund Freud, and

---

[32] Weigel (2002a, 175) (my translation). Michel Foucault maintained already in "Nietzsche, Genealogy, History" (1971) that "[g]enealogy, as an analysis of descent is . . . situated within the articulation of the body and history" Rabinow (1984, 83).
[33] Mannheim (1952 [1928], 295).

Maurice Halbwachs.[34] At a time that was perceived as a caesura in history, a time of vehement rejection of tradition by self-identified generations, there was also a pressing concern about what had made the continuity of culture possible in the first place. Sigmund Freud addresses this problem in *Moses and Monotheism* (1939), where he brings into play the vexed question of implicit, unconscious forms of cultural transmission. Freud claims that there is "an inheritance of memory—traces of what our forefathers experienced, quite independently of direct communication and of the influence of education by example."[35] Freud's treatise is a remarkable instance of the oscillation between the biological and the social in attempts to understand the transmission of culture across generations.

Today, with the advent of DNA testing, the conceptual entanglements between genealogy and cultural transmission (and the transitions between the natural and the cultural, the familial and the societal) have become even more complicated. Genealogy and genetics have long been linked in the study of biological ancestry, from paternity tests to family tree services. Originally flourishing in the United States, either for religious reasons or as a way of dealing with histories of slavery and migration, genetic testing has become a powerful new vehicle for cultural remembering in postcolonial, diasporic, and multicultural societies.[36] Genealogy emerges in such contexts as an identity-affirming cultural practice, in which DNA testing is used alongside older methods of historical research into familial genealogies.[37] Even more intricate than explorations of kinship along the genealogical line are questions about the inheritance of experience, such as the epigenetic transmission of trauma from parents to children. The cultural afterlife of the Holocaust offers a pertinent example of such complexities.

6.6 The Holocaust, Familial Genealogy, and the "Generation of Postmemory"

While in the aftermath of the First World War, generationality and genealogy were usually discussed in the broader horizon of society, after the Second

---

[34] On Benjanim's and Freud's concepts of genealogy, see Weigel (2006); on Halbwachs's theory of collective memory, see Chapter 5, "Locating Family in Memory Studies." On Halbwachs's generational identity, see Becker (2003).

[35] Freud (1939, 127). For a discussion from a memory studies perspective, see J. Assmann (1997) and Olick (2008).

[36] On the genetic tracing of the African diaspora via DNA tests, see Hirsch and Miller (2011).

[37] See, for example, Hart (2003); Kampourakis (2023).

World War the familial frame emerged as a central focus of interest. Most pressingly, genealogy arose as a concern in the face of family histories disrupted or destroyed by the Holocaust. It was in the mid-1960s that Canadian psychoanalysts Vivian Rakoff and John Sigal (1966) first identified the problem of the transgenerational transmission of traumatic memories in children of Holocaust survivors.[38] The American psychoanalysts Harvey and Carol Barocas noted:

> The children of survivors show symptoms, which would be expected if they actually lived through the Holocaust.... They seem to share an anguished collective memory of the Holocaust in both their dreams and fantasies reflective of recurrent references to their parents' traumatic experiences. These children wake up at night with terrifying nightmares of Nazi persecution.... The children come to feel that the Holocaust is the single most critical event that has affected their lives although it occurred before they were born. (Barocas and Barocas 1979, 331)

What started in Canada was soon also studied in Israel and the United States. The phenomenon of transgenerational trauma, mostly in the children of Holocaust survivors, became a transnational object of study. The terminology which emerged around this phenomenon was that of a "second generation." How deeply the understanding of trauma in Holocaust survivors' families was steeped in genealogical thinking—with its cyclical model of time, and the co-presence of the living and the dead, all reminiscent of premodern concepts of genealogy[39]—is revealed by the choice of metaphors in the *International Handbook of Multigenerational Legacies of Trauma* (1998), where the genealogical tree is evoked: "Each survivor's family tree is steeped in murder, death, and losses, yet its offspring are expected to reroot that tree and reestablish the extended family, and start anew a healthy generational cycle" (Danieli 1998, 5).

As a traveling figure for thinking about the long-term effects of extreme violence, which intertwines biological and social forms of inheritance in ways that are not always quite clear, "second generations" of trauma were identified across the world. *The International Handbook* refers to:

> the second generation of Hibakusha, the Japanese survivors of the atomic bomb, children of collaborators, offspring of both the Turkish genocide

---

[38] See also Bergmann and Jucovy (1982).
[39] See Parnes et al. (2008, 309).

of the Armenians and the Khmer Rouge genocide in Cambodia; those revealed after the fall of communism, such as in the former Yugoslavia, unified Germany, and Hungary; indigenous peoples such as the Australian aborigines, Native Americans, and Africans; and those following repressive regimes including Stalin's purge, the dictatorship in Chile and Argentina, South Africa under apartheid, and the Baha'is in Iran. (Danieli 1998, 4)

What had at first been a specialized discourse of psychoanalysts, family therapists, and oral historians—and a clinical phenomenon at that—gradually entered interdiscursive spaces and transnational mediascapes. Transgenerational trauma and the "second generation" of Holocaust survivors were explored in literature, film, and other art forms as well as in historical scholarship and literary and cultural studies.[40] It is interesting to see how concepts of genealogy and generationality are working together in these discourses. In its initial psychoanalytical use, the term "second generation" described familial genealogy. In its uses today, it has become a powerful signifier of a broad societal, even transnational, generationality.

It seems that medialization and fictionalization engendered a strong sense of generationality among members of the "second generation" of Holocaust survivors. From the *Holocaust* miniseries (1979) and Helen Epstein's series of interviews, *Children of the Holocaust* (1979), to Art Spiegelman's graphic memoir *Maus* (1986) and the large field of "second-generation" Holocaust literature and art that emerged afterward, representations of trauma and its legacies appear to have triggered a sense of shared generationality in affected recipients. To give a rather prominent example, in the autobiographical introduction to *The Generation of Postmemory* (2012, 9), Marianne Hirsch, herself the child of Holocaust survivors, highlights the importance that Spiegelman's *Maus* had for her: "I identified with him ['Artie'] profoundly, without fully realizing what that meant." Here, the sense of a fraught transgenerational memory (in real life) finds expression through and appears intertwined with an identification along intragenerational lines (triggered by an aesthetic representation). Hirsch writes: "As I was reading and viewing the work of second-generation writers and artists, and as I was talking to fellow-children of survivors, I came to see that all of us share certain qualities and symptoms that make us a *postgeneration*" (Hirsch 2012, 4).[41]

---

[40] For literary studies perspectives, see McGlothlin (2006); Schwab (2010).
[41] Hirsch attributes the term "postgeneration" to Eva Hoffman's *After Such Knowledge* (2004).

This statement in fact describes the move from genealogy to generationality, the transition from the recognition of disruptions along the axis of familial genealogy to an emphatic sense of societal, potentially transnational, generationality.

Marianne Hirsch's work on "postmemory" involves one of the most elaborate and productive concepts of generation developed in the field of literary studies. This concept is decidedly horizontal-vertical in its design and pays attention to the intergenerational transmission of memory as much as to the identity-forming significance of contemporaneity for the "postgeneration." It is, moreover, a concept which brings out the complexity of *generatio*. While in her *Family Frames* (1998), Hirsch had circumvented the pitfalls of a potentially essentializing discourse about the "second generation" and introduced "postmemory" as an alternative term, with *The Generation of Postmemory* (2012, 35) she playfully reintroduces the idea of "generation." Postmemory in Hirsch's understanding is "*not* an *identity* position, but a generational *structure* of transmission embedded in multiple forms of mediation." She thus highlights the mediated quality of transgenerational memory and rules out not only biologistic concepts of genealogy and the inheritance of trauma, but also a rigid social positioning of subjects as members of this or that generation.

However, in the (no doubt deliberately) highly ambiguous title of *The Generation of Postmemory*, we find resonances of biological and mediatized transmission, familial and societal memory, generational and genealogical dimensions of *generatio*. Postmemory is generated, *made*, usually with the help of media. It is a memory transmitted along the lines of familial genealogy to "the generation after." And it characterizes the broad, in fact transnational, generational formations of those who identify themselves as children of parents who went through histories of violence and trauma (the "postgeneration" as generationality).

With the concept of "affiliative postmemory," Hirsch brings about an enormous extension of the "postgeneration" to include all those members of a generation who are ready to engage with representations of traumatic histories:

> Eva Hoffmann draws a line, however tenuous and permeable, between "The postgeneration as a whole and the literal second generation in particular." To delineate the border between these respective structures of transmission—between to what I would like to refer to as *familial* and

"*affiliative*" postmemory—we would have to account for the difference between an intergenerational vertical identification of child and parent occurring within the family, and the intragenerational horizontal identification that makes that child's position more broadly available to other contemporaries. (Hirsch 2012, 36)

In this crucial distinction, Hirsch locates familial postmemory firmly on the genealogical axis, whereas she assigns to forms of affiliative postmemory the horizontal axis of generationality.[42] The desire for wholeness that could already be sensed in interwar negotiations of generationality reappears in Hirsch's writing on affiliative postmemory:

Affiliative postmemory is thus no more than an extension of the loosened familial structured [sic!] occasioned by war and persecution. It is the result of contemporaneity and generational connection with the literal second generation, combined with a set of structures of mediation that would be broadly available, appropriable and, indeed, compelling enough to encompass a larger collective in an organic web of transmission. (Hirsch 2012, 36)

The generation of affiliative postmemory can thus encompass the children of both victim and perpetrator communities—Art Spiegelman as well as W. G. Sebald.

Affiliation is thus conceived of by Hirsch as a horizontal, intragenerational dynamics. However, "traveling media" such as literature and photography (Hirsch's main examples) move not only across space and social formations, but also across time and generations. Postmemory as a structure of mediation is therefore potentially producible by and available to members of very different generational locations. Simply put, affiliative postmemories of the Holocaust need not be restricted to people of the age cohorts around the 1940s or, in Mannheimian terms, to members of a generational location who share the Second World War as a space of their family histories. Art and imaginative literature transcend generations. The past century's legacy of violence and trauma may continue to haunt generations to come. To account for such dynamics, we must turn from generationality back to genealogy again, albeit now in a non-familial and *longue-durée* perspective,

---

[42] This echoes Said's (1983) distinction between "vertical filiation" and "horizontal affiliation."

and consider "genealogies of mnemonic affiliation." Such genealogies will reach beyond the limits of the temporal horizon of lived history and generational identities, in which Hirsch's familial and affiliative postmemory as phenomena of the second generation are grounded—but which literature and art will continue to challenge.[43]

6.7 Immigration and Generation

As a negative foundational event (Dan Diner 2007), the Holocaust engendered a new counting of generations: the first generation of victims and survivors, the "1.5 generation" (Suleiman 2002) of children in the Holocaust, and the second generation of postmemory. From the Holocaust emerged, it seems, a new genealogical and temporal order, with its origin in the catastrophe.[44] Such counting of genealogical generations carries biblical overtones, and the fresh start of a genealogy implies either a preceding apocalypse (as is the case with the Holocaust) or the creation of a new people and the entrance into a new world. This is where generation meets immigration.

In many Western countries, the term "first generation" will immediately be associated with migrants, usually meaning those who originally came into the country. Their children who are born in the country are called "second generation," their grandchildren "third generation." The sociology of migration uses such genealogical concepts to describe processes of acculturation. In this vein, the acculturation gap hypothesis stipulates that acculturation discrepancies between (first-generation) parents and (second-generation) children create conflicts in families. Members of the second generation are usually conceived of as "between two cultures," some of the evidence being that they engage in daily forms of code switching and draw on different cultural repertoires.[45] Although the counting of immigrant generations is the standard procedure in sociology as well as an integral part of popular discourse about migration, critics from different quarters have noted that this is not unproblematic, not only because thinking in immigrant generations means assigning to the descendants of immigrants an everlasting immigrant status, but also because, given the actual complexity of immigration

---

[43] For work on postmemory that includes also the "third and fourth generations," see, for example, Alfandari and Baumel-Schwartz (2023); Meyer and Gvelesiani (2024).
[44] See also Weigel (2002b, 264–265).
[45] For a critical perspective, see Bornstein and Cote (2013).

histories, it is an oversimplification to fit these histories "into the Procrustean bed of three generations" (Sollors 1986, 213).

Much of the discourse on immigrant generations seems to be indebted to a genealogical model, which understands the first generation as culturally pure and the second generation as culturally mixed. Biologist notions easily slip into talk about the second generation's "hybridity" (a term derived from nineteenth-century genetics) and may imply an equation of biological offspring with the passing on of sociocultural patterns.[46] This discourse is arguably one of the most striking examples of the uneasy oscillations between nature and culture that can be encountered when dealing with generation. Mixed culture seems to be the function of a certain position in the natural chain of genealogy. What is more, the practice of counting immigrant generations rests entirely on notions of familial genealogy, implying (with its focus on hybridity) a biological determinism in a way that the discourse on the inheritance of traumatic memories (with its interest in symbolic interaction) does not.

Where do we find ways out of these discursive deadlocks? After having focused on literature and media as catalysts and travel agents of ideas about generationality and genealogy, this is the place to point to another major function of literature and art in discourses on generation: the critical reflection of generation-models and the imagination of alternatives. Using the case of South Asian and Caribbean immigration to Great Britain, I will briefly look at three ways of dealing with immigrant generationality and genealogy in the British novel since the turn of the millennium.

From the late 1970s onward, Britain had seen the self-fashioning of a second generation of "Black Britons." Many now-classic British authors, such as Linton Kwesi Johnson, David Dabydeen, and Hanif Kureishi, embraced the rhetoric of a mixed generation and used it positively in order to reconceptualize British identity as encompassing also migrants and their offspring—in Andrea Levy's words, "if Englishness doesn't define me, redefine Englishness."[47]

---

[46] This is not the case in its uses in philosophy and postcolonial theory, for instance in Bhabha's (1994, 162) work, who emphasizes that "colonial hybridity is not a problem of genealogy or identity between two different cultures"; instead, it "is a problematic of colonial representation."

[47] Andrea Levy in Alibhai-Brown (2001, 258). "Black British" is a broad and not uncontested term, used widely in the 1980s and 1990s as an inclusive political term that described people of Caribbean and African as well as South Asian descent; see Hall (1988). In its frequent collocation as "second generation of Black Britons," the term is yet another striking example of the creation of generational wholes.

Not least as a result of the memory work done by this "hybrid" second generation, their parents have emerged as one of the best-known immigrant generationalities: The "Empire Windrush generation" was reinvigorated and publicly commemorated in Great Britain on the occasion of its fiftieth anniversary in 1998. Those Caribbean and South Asian citizens of the British Commonwealth who came to the "motherland" (one of the many colonial metaphors of generation) after the Second World War, some of them on the eponymous decommissioned battleship in 1948, were asked to give testimony in oral history projects, their voices collected in Mike and Trevor Phillips's *Windrush: The Irresistible Rise of Multi-Racial Britain* (1998) and their history visualized in the BBC2 series *Windrush* (1998). The postwar immigrants were thus turned into a broadly identifiable, highly mediatized generation. In the process, the Windrush generation was also reified into a rather typical Mannheimian generational unit: as all-male, all-black, all-Caribbean—a focus which is clearly not corroborated by the evidence of British immigration history.[48]

In her novel *Small Island* (2004), Andrea Levy explores the generational fundaments of multicultural Britain by drawing on the myth of the Empire Windrush. She paints a vivid picture of postwar London in 1948, where newly arrived immigrants from the Caribbean interact with "white Londoners:" Apart from unearthing the entangled histories of people from the metropolis and the colonies who fought together in the Second World War, Levy's novel moreover critically intervenes in popular British constructions of the Empire Windrush generationality and questions its conception as a unit of young male Caribbeans only. In *Small Island*, men and women, immigrants from the Caribbean (Hortense, Gilbert), as well as white Londoners (Queenie) and even English racists (Bernard), appear as variously "implicated subjects" (Rothberg 2019) of the Windrush generation. With the relatively equal distribution of these four voices, the novel creates the image of an entangled generationality.

While *Small Island* is an essential literary intervention into discourses on migration and generationality, Zadie Smith's hugely successful novel *White Teeth* (2000) casts a critical eye on the question of genealogy. In its "root canals" chapters, the novel traces the genealogies of its London-based characters back to the Caribbean and South Asia, to colonialism, the "Indian Mutiny," and the Second World War. Many of these "roots" are

[48] See Mead (2009); Lowe (2018); Donnell (2019).

biological family-genealogies, but more importantly, some are also genealogies of "interracial" friendship, such as that between Samad and Archie. And it is these genealogies of human attachment that are seen to prevail in the end.

White Teeth sets such lineages of friendship and interaction into stark contrast to the other way of establishing "roots": genetics. The "future mouse" subplot about genetic engineering involves a Nazi doctor and thus reminds readers of the very genealogy of genetics, namely its implication in racism and eugenics. With its focus on genetics, *White Teeth* also appears as a prescient comment on genealogical practices in multicultural Britain. TV formats, such as *Empire's Children* (Channel 4, 2007), address the legacies of the British Empire through the family histories of British celebrities. The BBC documentary *Motherland: A Genetic Journey* (2003) uses DNA testing to unravel the African "roots" of British descendants of Caribbean immigrants. It seems that the British Empire itself has become a terrain for genealogical thinking, and DNA testing a major medium to negotiate cultural memory.

White Teeth looks critically and ironically at those emerging discourses and practices by featuring dysfunctional family trees and aligning genetic-genealogical thinking with characters like Marcus Chalfen who are obsessed by their desire for control. However, it is typical of the novel's multi-perspectival mode that genetic thinking is also attributed to the immigrants themselves. The following quotation inverts the genetic anxieties of the host society and imagines the perspective of a Bengali immigrant:

> But it makes an immigrant laugh to hear the fears of the nationalist, scared of infection, penetration, miscegenation, when this is small fry, *peanuts*, compared to what the immigrant fears—dissolution, *disappearance*. Even the unflappable Alsana Iqbal would regularly wake up in a puddle of her own sweat after a night visited by visions of Millat (genetically *BB*, where *B* stands for Bengali-ness) marrying someone called Sarah (aa where 'a' stands for Aryan), resulting in a child called Michael (*Ba*), who in turn marries somebody called Lucy (aa), leaving Alsana with a legacy of unrecognizable great-grandchildren (Aaaaaaa!), their Bengali-ness thoroughly diluted, genotype hidden by phenotype. (Smith 2000, 327)

By spelling out the logic of genetic-genealogical thinking in comic passages like this, Zadie Smith's novel discloses the biologist assumptions and often rather crude ideas about generation underlying many of the present-day negotiations of immigration. Genealogical "purity" is cast aside as an impossible endeavor. Instead, what the young mixed-race protagonist Irie and, by extension, postcolonial Britain have to face is coming to terms with their "chaotic, random flesh" (Smith 2000, 342), with genealogies that are more often than not based on "rumour, folk-tale and myth" (Smith 2000, 338). As Irie thinks about her Caribbean ancestry, *White Teeth* pictures her family tree and, in the novel's typical mock-scientific way, gives this a highly ironic twist by providing the following key to it:

Key
& = copulated with
% = paternity unsure
? = child's name unknown
G = brought up by grandmother (Smith 2000, 338).

The family tree as an age-old metaphor and mode of representing (usually genteel) genealogy is thus adapted to the realities of the ordinary people populating today's multicultural societies—and to the violent histories of colonialism, slavery, and migration that many of them look back on.[49]

A third example, which shows how generationality and genealogy can intersect in surprising ways in contemporary British fiction, is Gautam Malkani's *Londonstani* (2006). In this novel, Jas, the son of a white British family, identifies himself so intensely with the rough boys of his *desi* neighborhood that he speaks, thinks, and acts like a second-generation Hindu or Sikh. Only on the very last pages of the novel is it revealed that Jas is actually not—neither genealogically nor genetically, as it were—"hybrid." His hybridity is instead a chosen identity. It is a cultural performance, which guarantees him membership within a chosen generationality. In this space of literary imagination we find a kind of "generational-genealogical cross dressing," or "generation trouble," as one might be tempted to say, with a nod to

---

[49] An approach to the "chaotic genealogies" that shape postcolonial societies is offered by Rothberg's (2019) concept of the "implicated subject." Using Catherine Hall's and Nicholas Draper's "Legacies of British Slave Ownership" project as an example (see Hall et al. 2014), he discusses complex forms of genealogical implication, when families are descendants of slave-traders and of slaves, of people who made money from colonialism and those who suffered from it. Slavery, Rothberg emphasizes, has "implications for people across racial categories and, in particular, for those who have inherited the cultural capital of whiteness (and non-blackness more generally), if not financial capital itself, from the slave-owners and their heirs" (Rothberg 2019, 67).

Judith Butler. *Londonstani* thus makes a case for generational performativity instead of genetics or familial genealogy.

What these three examples show is how literature in postcolonial and "migratory settings" (Aydemir and Rotas 2008) critically reflects upon the complexities and pitfalls of thinking about immigration and generation today. Literature can carve out alternative spaces for imagining generation, showing that apart from being identified as this or that by sociology or genetics, there is also the option of self-identification in the fields of generationality and genealogy.

6.8 Conclusion

The concept of generation may remain largely unnoticed, but it has shaped the past century, both as an academic term and as a popular figure of thinking about time and identity. In this sense, generation is not a given, but a discursive constellation, or an assemblage, in which politics, different knowledges, technologies, and cultural practices interact—all the way from vociferous generation rhetoric to postmemory work and to DNA testing.

From its very etymological beginnings, "generation" has carried notions of the natural and the cultural, the familial and the societal. Arguably, this conceptual multilayered aspect and the ambiguities that come with it—much as we have to grapple with them still today—are what has ensured the "life" and ongoing attractiveness of the concept. Moreover, all discourses on generation imply generationality *and* genealogy. It is at the intersections of these horizontal and vertical identifications that we can decipher the logic of these discourses.

Generation transcends boundaries of nation and culture. This is true for the genealogies of multicultural societies; and it is also a fundamental dynamics of modern generationality, from the "lost generation" of the 1920s to the protest "generation of 1968" (Hajek 2013) and beyond. In the process of transnationalization, media representations and imaginative literature play an important role as catalysts and travel agents of ideas about generation. Hollywood cinema, TV documentaries, graphic memoirs, and bestselling novels are just some examples. Increasingly, the internet, with its social media sites such Facebook, Instagram, and YouTube, must be taken into account as generation-defining media. Literary works and literary studies, moreover, have provided and continue to provide some of the most nuanced reflections about generationality and genealogy. All this considered, "generation" in its very complexity deserves to become part of the conceptual core of memory studies and (literary) mnemohistory.

Chapter 7
Fictions of Generational Memory

Caryl Phillips's *In the Falling Snow* (2009)

7.1 Generation, Memory, and Black Writing in Britain

In the opening chapter of Caryl Phillips's novel *In the Falling Snow* (2009), we see the Black forty-seven-year-old protagonist Keith riding the London underground, contemplating a group of teenagers sitting opposite him:

> He can see that, like his son Laurie, all three kids are partly white, but it is clear from their baggy dress sense, and from the way they slouch and speak, that they identify themselves as black ... today's teenagers no longer respect any boundaries. Black youths, white youths, mixed race youths, to them all he is just a middle-aged man in a jacket and tie who looks like he doesn't know shit about nothing. He lowers his gaze and tries to figure out the genders of the gang of three, whose faces remain shrouded beneath oversized hoods. (Phillips 2009, 15)

What Keith realizes here is that some of his tried-and-tested concepts of difference in British society have become outdated. Racial divides seem to have been displaced by a generational divide. Keith experiences a gap between himself and the young people he sees, and he understands that he cannot rely any longer on his generation's categories (concerning race as well as gender) in order to make sense of the group of youngsters before him.

To be sure, racism has not disappeared in Phillips's novel, but it is shown to play out very differently along generational lines.[1] One of the questions the novel asks is what "being Black" means to a middle-aged (and middle-class) man in the early 2000s. Another question is how to gain a sense of genealogy in families and cultural formations shaped by experiences of slavery, diaspora, and migration. With these preoccupations, *In the Falling Snow* is

---

[1] See McLeod (2019) for a discussion of the novel as a form of "remembering anti-racism in contemporary Black British writing."

a striking example of the heightened reflexivity on issues of generation and memory that can be found in wide sections of contemporary literature—a feature that defines what I seek to describe in this chapter as "fictions of generational memory."

It is roughly since the turn of the millennium that questions related to "generation"—generationality, genealogy, and genetics[2]—have become an ever-growing concern of Black writing in Britain.[3] Thinking about generation is a way of locating people in time (however difficult that may be in postcolonial and diasporic settings) and thus a practice of memory. A significant portion of Black writing in Britain can in fact be seen as fictions of generational memory.[4] These novels are an integral part of a dynamic memory constellation around questions of postcolonialism, post/imperialism, immigration, and racism in Britain.[5] With their generational stories, they both reflect and actively shape these memory debates.

The problem of "generation" as familial genealogy has traditionally shaped Black writing in Britain. In his study on the "Black British *bildungsroman*," Mark Stein asserts that "the conflict of generations is part and parcel of the novel of transformation, and it is of particular importance in that different generations correspond to different cultural and social affiliations" (Stein 2004, 25). Conflicts between what in Zadie Smith's (2001 [2000], 219)

---

[2] See Chapter 6, "Generation in Literature."
[3] On Black British literature, see Arana and Ramey (2009); Ledent (2009); Dillon and Rosenberg (2015); Osborne (2016); Nasta and Stein (2019a). See also Nasta and Stein (2019b, 9): "In so far as black and Asian British are politically constructed categories, rather than specific references to a narrowly defined race or ethnicity, any critical language employed, any literary or cultural categorisations endorsed are necessarily interventions in acts in history."
[4] On "fictions of memory," see Nünning (2003). On cultural memory in Black British writing, see Eckstein (2006), Rupp (2010), and Pirker (2011). On the dynamics of transcultural memory in postcolonial Britain, see Brunow (2015). On generation in British Asian literature, see Weingarten (2012); and on family and memory in second-generation British migration literature, see Assmann (2018).
[5] The 1990s had seen quite extensive commemoration of the Windrush generation (i.e., the generation of Caribbean and South Asian immigrants, who came to Britain after World War II; see Phillips and Phillips 1998; Korte and Pirker 2011; Donnell 2019). But as the Windrush Scandal of 2018 showed (where members of this generation who had lived for seventy years in Britain were threatened with deportation), this part of the British past remains a "disabled history" (Stoler 2008), and is quickly superseded by the habitual memory of institutional racism (see also Thomas 2018). On memories of empire, see Schwarz (2011). On postcolonial melancholia in Britain, see Gilroy (2004). On how postimperial memory is tied up with Brexit, see Ward and Rasch (2019). In the wake of the Black Lives Matter movement, a renewed concern with Black history and memory (Otele 2022) emphasizes the continuities of structural racism that go back to histories of slavery and its legitimization by ideologies of race (Eddo-Lodge 2017; Mbembe 2017). Black memory practice in Britain today is strongly shaped by memory activist efforts to transform public history and material memory culture, particularly through the "decommissioning" (Rigney 2023) of toxic colonial monuments, such as the Edward Colston statue in Bristol (Otele et al. 2021; on the memory of slavery, see Araujo 2012, 2021).

novel *White Teeth* is called *"fathersons, oldyoung, borntherebornhere"* imply a sense of genealogical transmission disrupted by migration. Many novels of the 1980s and 1990s that operated according to the black *bildungsroman* pattern bore witness to an emerging generationality—the collective identity of a "second generation" of immigrants.

Since the turn of the millennium, a widening of the range of generational concerns has been noticeable in Black writing in Britain. Novels like Zadie Smith's *White Teeth* (2000) and Andrea Levy's *Small Island* (2004) are characterized by their transcultural approaches to generation: English, Caribbean, and South Asian genealogies and generationalities are shown to be inextricably entangled.

Bernadine Evaristo's Booker Prize–winning *Girl, Woman, Other* (2019) presents an intersectional approach to *generatio*. The novel traces *genealogies* of Black queer women in Britain back to the nineteenth century. At the same time, it also highlights the diversity of generational identities (i.e., *generationalities*) in Black Britain today, whose differences crystallize in middle-aged playwright Amma and her nineteen-year-old daughter Yazz.

7.2 Writing in Times of Mnemonic Transition

Caryl Phillips's *In the Falling Snow* (2009) gives literary expression to the fact that at around the turn of the millennium the configuration of immigrant generations in Great Britain had significantly changed. As the "first generation" of Windrushers[6] were getting old, firsthand witnesses of postwar immigration were soon to pass away, and with them the embodied experience, the episodic memories, and the oral stories they could tell in situations of face-to-face interaction. What will remain is mediated representations of the Windrush generation: photographs, documentary footage, videotaped

---

[6] The Windrush generation as a unified "first generation" of Black and Asian immigrants to Britain is of course a myth. First, there was a significant Black and Asian presence before the Second World War (see Fastogi and Renton Stitt 2008; Gilroy 2011; Nasta and Stein 2019a). Second, immigration did not stop after the 1950s, but new "first generations" continue to come to Britain. Despite its many historical shortcomings, the Windrush myth remains a foundational myth for the memory of Britain as a multicultural society (see Mead 2009, Lowe 2018). Donnell (2019, 200) describes the Windrush myth as a "compressed focus." It is a memory figure: "The arrival of SS Empire Windrush at Tilbury Docks in 1948 and the disembarkation of '492' West Indians from that ship has remained a significant and tenacious signifier within black British history. Indeed, just the single word 'Windrush' is now the accepted shorthand for calling into view post-World War II mass migration from the Caribbean to Britain and an attendant narrative of the cultural shift towards a multicultural nation" (Donnell 2019, 195).

oral history interviews, movies, and novels. Such a transition from (mainly) embodied to (exclusively) mediated memory has been theorized by Jan and Aleida Assmann as the change from the register of "communicative memory" to "cultural memory" (J. Assmann 2011 [1992]). In such times of mnemonic transition, which are fundamentally generational—and ultimately biological—transitions, literature tends to become more sensitive to issues of remembering and questions of generation. (This is something that the generational turn in Black British literature shares—surely for very different reasons—with the emergence of the multigenerational memory novel in Germany in the early 2000s, sixty years after the end of Nazism and the Holocaust).

Both Phillips and his fictional protagonist Keith were born in the 1950s as sons of Caribbean immigrants and were raised in Britain. *In the Falling Snow* thus lends itself to being read as a "second-generation novel,"[7] which according to Mark Stein (2004, 5) is produced by "authors who started writing in the 1970s and 1980s, a period ... marked by racial hostility." These second-generation writers are distinct from the writers of the Windrush generation (such as Wilson Harris, Sam Selvon, and George Lamming), who came to Britain after the Second World War, but also from "the third generation who started writing in the 1990s" (Stein 2004, 5). Stein argues that many novels by and about the children of Caribbean and South Asian immigrants tend to draw on patterns of the *bildungsroman*. They are therefore "novels of transformation" in a double sense, as they show the "formation of [their] protagonists as well as the transformation of British society" (Stein 2004, 22).

However, Phillips's novel marks yet another transformation—that of second-generation novel into fiction of generation. This is a development resulting from the simple fact that the second generation has become older.[8] The issues that are negotiated in *In the Falling Snow* are different from those that we find in the mainstays of the Black British *bildungsroman* genre, as in Hani Kureishi's *The Buddha of Suburbia* (1990), in Andrea Levy's *Fruit of the Lemon* (1999), and also in the depiction of intergenerational interaction

---

[7] Phillips was born in St. Kitts in 1958 and came with his parent to Leeds when he was four months old. The fictional Keith, too, was raised in the North of England. Although the novel may thus invite its readership to think about the possibilities and limits of an autobiographical reading, I would argue that its extratextual reference concerns the generational and not so much the individual dimension.

[8] I am indeed making a "biological argument" here, arguing with Karl Mannheim that the "*sociological* problem of generations . . . begins at that point where the sociological relevance of . . . biological factors is discovered" (Mannheim 1952 [1928], 290–291).

in Zadie Smith's *White Teeth* (2000). This is not only because sociopolitical circumstances have changed over time, but also because the concerns that inform these coming-of-age novels of the 1980s and 1990s revolve around "subject formation" (Stein 2004, 22)—that is, around a process closely tied up with what in theories of generation is called the "formative phase." In his classic essay "The Problem of Generations" (1928), Karl Mannheim locates the formative phase of young adults, which will bring forth their generational affiliations and shape their memories, between age 17 and 24.

The second-generation novel has moved on, and in Caryl Phillips's case, this move is connected with a strong and critical reflexivity about the very idea of generation. In *In the Falling Snow*, the fictional protagonist and main focalizer Keith, a middle-aged man in his late forties, grapples with many different aspects of generation: generational transitions, generationality as well as familial and cultural genealogy.

7.3 Three Generational Locations: The Temporal Homes of Laurie, Keith, and Earl

In the Falling Snow features a rather conventional midlife crisis plot: Keith finds himself enmeshed in problems with his wife, his son, and his workplace. Three years ago, his white wife Annabelle turned him out of the house after he had confessed he was cheating on her. He has become estranged from his seventeen-year-old son Laurie, who appears to associate with the wrong crowd. And his boss suspends him from his office, after Yvette, a much younger colleague, makes public the emails he wrote to her during their short-lived affair. All this, however, gives Keith time to embark on a long-planned project of writing a book on soul music. Keith experiences these changes as manifestations of a transitional phase in his life, apparent, for example, in his self-admonishment that he "must now begin to *act his age*" (Phillips 2009, 106; my emphasis).

More crucial are the ways in which the idea of generation is connected to issues of collective memory and identity, thus turning into constructs of generationality. In Keith, we can observe an emphatic identification with "[h]*is generation* of kids, who were born in Britain and who had no memory of any kind of tropical life before England" (Phillips 2009, 41; my emphasis). Keith shows a strong sense of generationality, which shapes his most fundamental decisions in life. As a conscious member of *his* generation, Keith was aware of race riots in the 1970s and 1980s, when he was a young man. He decided to respond to these generation-defining events by choosing not to do postgraduate work, but to leave university with only a bachelor's degree and go into social work, as he realized that Britain needed "people who could help explain black anger to white people, and white liberal do-gooding to disgruntled black people" (Phillips 2009, 45). One of the novel's ironies is that Keith now welcomes the "merging [of] his Race Equality unit with Disability and Women's Affairs," because it means for him "more money, a bigger office, and double the number of staff to manage" (Phillips 2009, 33).[9]

In his family, Keith is the only one to show such a strong, identificatory sense of generationality. Still, the other black male family members are also given their own generational location—their "temporal home" (*Zeitheimat*; Sebald 2003, 261). The reader finds three generations, three different versions of Black experience, three reservoirs of memory, mediated in three different ways.

First, the exploits of Keith's seventeen-year-old son, Laurie, belong to the primary story set in the present of the early 2000s. The worried exchanges between his estranged parents and his teachers suggest the son's preference for American-style gang life. Laurie makes it very clear that despite his own encounters with racism (such as being called a "halfie" as a child; Phillips 2009, 17), Keith and he do not share the same space of experience: "The thing is, Dad, I don't know if things are the same now as they were when you were my age.... It isn't just about discrimination and stuff."[10] Laurie's generational self-description amounts to the belief that "[i]t's got a lot to do with respect"—a concept that Keith, from the viewpoint of his generational location, does not understand: "What have they done to earn respect?" (Phillips 2009, 167).

Second, Keith's internally focalized memories of the 1970s and 1980s paint the picture of the second generation's problematic position in a

---

[9] This, too, is a generational point with a clear extra-fictional reference. In an interview in 2007, Paul Gilroy commented on "some of the things that New Labour has done. A whole generation of activists—my generation—seem to be management consultants! Even the black nationalists are busy managing the health service and the police" (Gilroy qtd. in Richardson 2015, 3) Keith is not only middle-aged, but has also risen to the middle class. The novel is riddled with middle-class markers, such as the ubiquitous white wine, Gruyère cheese, and careful choice of language. The novel shows how race, class, and generationality intersect in the making of identities—and of identity-related problems.

[10] The following passage has a similar effect: "'Did the police abuse you in any way?' Laurie looks up at his father. 'What?' 'I'm talking about racial abuse. Did the interviewing officer verbally abuse you in any way?' 'What are you on? The copper who interviewed me was black'" (Phillips 2009, 227).

predominantly white society, exemplified by the open racism that Keith encountered from his father-in-law and, it seems, significant parts of the English village where his wife Annabelle was born. Third, the dying Earl's rambling monologue, addressed to his son Keith, evokes memories of the Windrush generation of the early 1960s trying to gain a foothold in English cities, faced with bad housing and rampant racism.

7.4 Genealogies of Black Britain: Familial, Affiliative, Implicated, Cultural, Literary

Earl, Keith, and Laurie represent three generations of Black people in Britain, with their respective experiences and memories. At the same time, they form the tripartite genealogy of a British family of Caribbean descent. This diachronic perspective (which is co-present with the synchronic one, as genealogy intersects with generationality) raises a different set of questions: that of biological and social inheritance in the diaspora. Sonali Thakkar writes of the

> logic of diaspora, which pairs geographical displacement with cultural continuity and transmission. Continuity, frequently framed as familial transmission, is what supposedly allows for the transmission of identity *despite* dislocation. It is this emphasis on cultural reproduction as familial reproduction that makes diasporic discourse so dependent on family forms. (Thakkar 2011, 207–208)

In Keith's case, familial transmission turns out to be a key problem. *In the Falling Snow* places the focus on patrilineal genealogy and transmission. It is the men whose stories are told in detail and who are granted extended passages of focalization and intra-diegetic narration. However, transgenerational processes appear to be severely disrupted, as both fathers are—to a larger and lesser extent—absent. Earl spent years in a mental asylum and was only able to take his son Keith into his house when the boy was already thirteen; Keith split up with his wife when his son was fourteen.

Contrary to these masculine (dis)connections, the memory of Keith's loving stepmother Brenda comes into view as a generative force. Brenda died when Keith was at university. It is her photograph that he still keeps on the living room wall. When Keith exhorts his son to "put in more effort and try twice as hard as anybody else" (Phillips 2009, 167), he clearly echoes

Brenda's "Keep your chin up, love, your clothes nice and tidy, and your language decent... mind you come back with A's on that report card" (Phillips 2009, 16)—the only difference being that these exhortations are lost on his son. Given the fact that Brenda is female, white, and not even Keith's biological mother, the novel thus makes a strong point about the generative force of affiliative relationships and the power of transgenerational transmission beyond the biological and the racial.

The main genealogical theme of the novel, however, is Keith's "search for the father." Earl's stubborn silence about his migration to Britain and his family history prevent Keith from developing a sense of identity: "His father's silence has meant that his son has never been able to properly explain himself to anybody" (Phillips 2009, 285). It is only in the novel's powerful finale, on Earl's deathbed, that the old man finally discloses, in a long monologue addressed to Keith, what he had held secret all his life. Earl conveys his memories of being an immigrant in Britain in the 1960s, when he experienced extreme racial violence, which turns out to have been a trigger of his mental illness.[11] Earl also discloses his memories of Keith's mother Shirley, also an immigrant from the Caribbean. She got pregnant after one sexual encounter with Earl, and Earl did not accept her offer to marry. For Keith, and for the reader, Earl's monologue delivers the long-awaited solutions to many riddles in Keith's life. For Keith, it means the long-awaited possibility to reconnect with, imagine, and remember a diasporic genealogy.

Keith's search for familial genealogy broadens into an interest in *cultural* genealogies—a search for forefathers—when he embarks on a book project about the history of soul music. Keith is interested in "how black cultural heritage is passed on from one generation to the next." But the history of the black presence in Britain—all the way from the African soldiers "the Romans brought... to build Hadrian's wall"—offers little to inspire him. Instead, he "is trying to write about a deeper and more substantial tradition of cultural inheritance, and this means that he has to look across the Atlantic for models" (Phillips 2009, 95).[12] Keith's book project, which connects American

---

[11] English racists killed Earl's friend Ralph. Earl's mental illness is reminiscent of Frantz Fanon's (1967) work on the psychopathology of the experience of racism in *Black Skin, White Masks*. Brenda explains to Keith that "England had hurt his head" (Phillips 2009, 221). See also the discussion of Fanon's work in relation to postcolonial trauma in Craps (2013).

[12] This reflexivity does not mean that Keith is free from stereotypical thinking about generation elsewhere. In the subplot about Britain's more recent "first generation," that of immigrants from Eastern Europe in the wake of the 2004 enlargement of the European Union, Keith contemplates Danuta's Polish ancestry and thinks in all seriousness: "Home of Treblinka and Auschwitz. You don't change people's minds in a couple of generations" (Phillips 2009, 79). This is of course a highly

soul music with his British identity, suggests the kind of interactions that Paul Gilroy has described in *The Black Atlantic* (1996). In fact, Caryl Phillips has long been known as a Black Atlantic writer.[13] Unearthing the historical interconnections of the African diaspora in the Caribbean, the United States, and Britain has characterized much of Phillips's earlier work, most notably perhaps the novel *Crossing the River* (1993) and the travelogue *The Atlantic Sound* (2000), which both give evidence to the idea that the construction of a cultural genealogy of Black people in Britain requires remembering across and beyond the Black Atlantic.[14]

Despite Keith's focus on Black genealogies, what his family history displays is an instance of the entangled genealogies typical of modern postcolonial and multicultural societies. Ironically perhaps, but no longer uncommon as a genealogical constellation in British society, Annabelle's racist father, who had served the empire as a soldier, becomes grandfather to mixed-race Laurie. Laurie is thus caught up in a familial genealogy of what Michael Rothberg (2019) would call "complex implication," with not only victims, but also perpetrators, perpetuators, and beneficiaries of British colonialism and racism. Such entanglements—familial or affiliative, conflictual or unacknowledged, destructive or futural—have in fact been a major preoccupation of Phillips's literary oeuvre, and they structure novels such as *Cambridge* (1991) and *A Distant Shore* (2003). Small wonder that Phillips's writing has unfolded an unprecedented agency in the understanding of transcultural memory.[15]

The novel's structure performs yet another striking instance of genealogy—a *literary* one. Earl's extended monologue in his hospital bed, which amounts to a story-within-the-story (Phillips 2009, 269–282 and 287–319), is in its narrative form clearly a self-conscious reference, an homage to one of the founding figures of Black fiction in Britain: Sam Selvon, the author of *The Lonely Londoners* (1956). In this now-classic novel, Selvon gave literary shape to the Windrush generation in the 1950s. The novel revolves around the adventures of a group of young male immigrants from the Caribbean in postwar London, bound together by the

problematic statement that places the responsibility for the Holocaust perpetrated by Germans at the doorsteps of Polish families.

[13] Kırpıklı (2022); Rothberg (2009); Ward (2011),. For an overview of Phillips's oeuvre, see Ledent and Tunca (2012).

[14] See Ward (2007, 32).

[15] Another focus of Phillips's transcultural memory fictions is on Black-Jewish relatedness. Both Rothberg (2009) and Craps (2013) discuss the travel report *The European Tribe* (1987) and the novels *Higher Ground* (1989) and *The Nature of Blood* (1997) in this light.

generation-defining "communal voice" of character-narrator Moses Aloetta. Earl's monologue is reminiscent of Selvon's style. Just as Selvon's novel first and famously did, it features "modified forms of the oral vernacular" to create a distinctly Caribbean voice (Nasta 2002, 70), and it echoes the breathless extended stream-of-consciousness passage that can be found at the center of *The Lonely Londoners*.

Earl's monologue is a Windrush mini-narration. It is marked as such as it starts with a generation-defining voice: "I want to go home, Keith ... I'm not from here. I land in England on a cold Friday morning. It is April 15, 1960" (Phillips 2009, 269). This precision of historical reference echoes the oral testimonies of his generation, as they were given in the context of the Windrush anniversary (Phillips and Phillips 1998). The representation of Earl's memories draws on well-established *topoi* of Windrush remembrance, such as the Caribbean immigrants' realization upon arrival at the London docks that England was not full of the well-to-do white colonial administrators and landowners they knew back home: "The people don't look like the type of white men I used to see back home wearing club blazer and tie and walking about the place ramrod straight. Jesus Christ, I don't know England have such poor white men" (Phillips 2009, 269). All in all, Earl's monologue is much darker in tone and content than its genealogical pretext. The "sons of Empire" (Phillips 2009, 196), as Earl's friend Baron calls their group, with an ironic nod to genealogical empire metaphors, have not been able to make England their home. Earl's last words are a testament to his lifelong failure to cope with the realities of his life in England: "The idea of England is fine. I can deal with the idea. You understand me, son? I can deal with the idea" (Phillips 2009, 319).

In his 1999 essay "Following On: The Legacy of Lamming and Selvon," Caryl Phillips describes Selvon and George Lamming in a typical generational-genealogical figure as:

> our literary antecedents.... In the seventies and eighties I know that these writers had a profound effect on my generation, the second generation in this country who found themselves trying to deal with loneliness, ambivalence, and confusion about their relationship to British society. (Phillips 1999, 36)

The question of literary genealogy for Black writing—the existence and accessibility of a "legacy" and possibilities of "following on"—remains a pressing concern in Britain. In 2021, Bernardine Evaristo therefore introduced the book series *Black Britain: Writing Back* (Hamish Hamilton), which reissues forgotten works of Black writing, in order to actualize and shape a literary genealogy, and provide a sense of continuity, for Black British writers.

7.5 "In the Falling Snow": From Racial to Genealogical Metaphor

With "in the falling snow," the novel's title and main literary image, Phillips establishes yet another literary genealogy, one that reaches across the Black Atlantic. As Abigail Ward (2011) has pointed out, "in the falling snow" is an intertextual reference to a haiku written by the African American author Richard Wright, one of Phillips's main literary influences:

> In the falling snow
> A laughing boy holds out his palms
> Until they are white. (Wright 1961, 92)

Phillips retains Wright's thrust of the snow-metaphor as an image of Black people in a dominantly white environment, an image which reminds the reader of the continuity of racialized thinking in British society, while it implies—with the "laughing boy"—a certain levity.[16] In fact, Phillips's novel can be read as a diachronic phenomenology of "being in the falling snow," of being Black in Britain across three generations. At the same time, and in a double move, Phillips develops Wright's metaphor of race into a metaphor of generation. Being "in the falling snow" is turned into an image of familial genealogy, a condensed figure which captures the essential relatedness of father Earl and son Keith.

Memories of key incidents keep coming back to Keith's mind, in the form of textual blocks inserted into the flow of his thoughts—just as haunting memories come back to us, triggered either by internal or external cues. Keith's memories connected with the image of being "in the falling snow" are

---

[16] Ward (2011, 300) emphasizes that "the imagery is clearly loaded and evokes a contrast between black and white spheres . . . [in] other works by Wright, snow frequently symbolizes an unfeeling, white-dominated world." She suggests that the image of the laughing boy "perhaps chimes with Phillips's desire for a kind of racial 'transcendence,' or an understanding which goes beyond the confines of racial binaries."

introduced in the second part of the novel, when Keith, once again sitting alone in his apartment with white wine and cheese, contemplates Brenda's photograph on the wall. Memories of his childhood emerge. Keith remembers his thirteenth birthday, when his father suddenly turned up again after having spent a long time in a mental hospital. Earl gives his son Keith a birthday card. It is the time of the year when "the clouds were high and heavy with snow" (Phillips 2009, 88). One week later, Earl comes back to take his son to the movies (just as Keith later will take Laurie). The snow is now coming down: "huge white flakes were tumbling down from the sky and coating the pavement white" (Phillips 2009, 320).

This second encounter between Earl and Keith is narrated with a strong rhetoric of memory. Keith "*couldn't remember* if his father bought him any sweets or anything to drink, but he *clearly recalls* that..." (Phillips 2009, 320; my emphasis). Keith tried hard to remember. The past event obviously holds great significance for him. Eventually, a key moment of Keith's childhood emerges from memory:

> They began to walk back in the direction of the bus stop, past the parked cars that were already clad in snow, and as the flakes continued to fall on their bare heads he could feel his hand tight and safe in his father's hand. He looked behind him and saw two sets of footprints where they had walked, a large pair and his own smaller ones.... As they turned a corner, he tugged his father's hand. His father looked down at him and smiled. He pointed to the sky. "Look at all the snow!" His father continued to smile. (Phillips 2009, 320–321)

Suddenly, in the description of a rare moment of peace and happiness between father and son, all qualifiers that would point to the act of reconstructive remembering have disappeared. It seems as if the thirteen-year-old Keith was the internal focalizer—and not the middle-aged Keith who is actually doing the remembering. With the immediacy and vividness of the narrated events, the passage clearly represents what psychologists would call a "field memory," featuring emotional and sensory impressions as well as detailed "event-specific knowledge" (Schacter 1996, 21). Such intense recall of "personal event memories" (Pillemer 2001, 124) often comes with a sense of veridicality and "truthfulness." This is not necessarily the case. Even vivid field memories are (re)constructions. But they can refer to events that are perceived as "momentous," as "emotional or intellectual landmarks," in one's life (Pillemer 2001, 125). With the retrieval of the memory of walking in the falling snow alongside Earl, Keith appears to have worked his way to the very core of the meaning he attributes to their father-son relationship.

The two pairs of footsteps in the snow work as a genealogical image, indicating the movement of generations through time (older and larger footsteps next to younger and smaller ones). In fact, this metaphor is extended when Keith remembers standing at the door of Brenda's house and watching his father walk away: "As he walked, his father left behind a single set of footprints, and he remembered lingering by the doorstep and watching closely as the falling snow steadily erased all evidence of his father's presence" (Phillips 2009, 321). This is a powerful, condensed image of the transitory nature of all generations. The older generation inevitably disappears, is "erased" by nature. Afterward, "all evidence" of their "presence" is that which will remain in the autobiographical memories of a younger generation—just as the ones re-emerging in Keith's mind—and, importantly, in media, such as Earl's box of old photographs.

After Keith's retrieval of his momentous childhood memory, the narrative switches back again to the primary storyline. Keith learns that his father Earl has just died. Back at home, he realizes: "His father has gone and there is nobody ahead of him" (Phillips 2009, 326). A generational turnover has taken place. This means that Keith is now also confronted with the dynamics typical of the transition from communicative to cultural memory. After having listened to his father's oral memories at his hospital bed for several days and nights, what remains after his death as the sole source to an understanding of Earl's life are media of memory. The old photographs kept by Earl, which are mentioned repeatedly in the novel and which in the end "remain scattered on [Earl's] kitchen table," await, the reader is led to assume, Keith's perusal—as "*evidence* of his father's life" (Phillips 2009, 323–324; my emphasis).

Ironically, perhaps, it is not those photographs, but an altogether different one that is mentioned on the novel's last page: the picture of Annabelle's parents in the bedroom of the house Keith used to share with his wife. Her "father is looking confidently into the lens of the camera, while her mother's gaze is altogether more mournful" (Phillips 2009, 330). With this, the novel retains as a final image the certainties and the anxieties of empire, its continued presence in Britain, and its complex genealogies which are, for better or for worse, an integral part of Keith's own family. And although Keith muses that "[t]here is no reason for him to spend a night here in this small terraced house with all these people" (Phillips 2009, 330), the reader knows by then that these are indeed *his* people and that it is quite likely that Keith will stay and reunite with his wife.

With *In the Falling Snow*, Phillips, who was then mainly known as a writer of historical fictions, participates for the first time in the genre of the second-generation novel.[17] Being a "latecomer" to this genre means also that he inevitably transforms it. In this novel, we see a "second generation once removed"—to middle age, to a state in which the first generation is disappearing and can therefore no longer be held accountable (a theme also developed through the dementia Annabella's mother is suffering from), and to the new questions that arise in this situation, questions about the memories and identities of people of Caribbean descent in Britain, and about their abilities to place themselves in generational locations and in familial and cultural genealogies.

7.6 Conclusion: Fictions of Generational Memory Today

What we find in *In the Falling Snow* and increasingly in Black writing in Britain today is not only reflections on different immigrant generations, but also the problematization of generational identities and of transgenerational family dynamics within migratory settings, the unearthing of far-reaching cultural genealogies and postcolonial entanglements, and last but not least, critical perspectives on the biologist notions which pervade contemporary discussions of genealogy and transmission in multicultural societies. In short, a recent kind of Black writing produces fictions of generational memory in almost all aspects that the multifarious idea of generation implies. Novels such as *In the Falling Snow* can be read as seismographs of the shifting meanings of *generatio* in contemporary British society.

Fictions of generational memory are of course not only produced in Great Britain, but have also emerged in Germany (Eigler 2005; Eichenberg 2009), South Asia (Butt 2015), and elsewhere. They seem to be a truly global phenomenon, a specific literary mode to cope with generational, and hence

---

[17] Phillips's first two novels, *The Final Passage* (1985) and *A State of Independence* (1986), already featured immigration from the Caribbean to Britain (and back) as a theme, albeit not in the form of a second-generation novel. However, as Rini Vyncke (2010, 117) points out, "it might become even more interesting to compare *In the Falling Snow* (2009) further with two of Phillips's earlier plays. Both *Strange Fruit* (1981) and *Where There Is Darkness* (1982) deal with... intergenerational friction."

also mnemonic, transitions: from a generation of witnesses (of war, genocide, and migration) to their children and grandchildren, from "memory" to "postmemory" (Hirsch 2012), from "communicative" to "cultural memory" (J. Assmann 2011 [1992]). In our age of self-reflexive memory cultures, the ongoing shifts between generations become visible—and problematic—as mnemonic shifts. They affect how key events of the twentieth century (the Holocaust and the Second World War, decolonization and mass migration, the Partition of the Indian subcontinent, the Vietnam War, and so on) can be remembered today; and they evidently give rise to a type of literature that imaginatively addresses the set of problems connected with generation and memory.

PART III
MEMORY AND MEDIATION

Chapter 8
Literature, Film, and the Mediality of Cultural Memory

8.1 The Power of Fiction: Novels and Films as Media of Cultural Memory

Cultural memory is based on communication through media. Shared versions of the past are invariably generated by means of "medial externalization," the basic form of which is oral speech in face-to-face situations, and the basic setting arguably that of grandparents telling children about the "old days."

More sophisticated media technologies, such as writing, film, and the internet, broaden the temporal and spatial range of remembering. Cultural memory is constituted by a host of different media, operating within various symbolic systems: religious manuscripts, historical painting, autobiography, historiography, war movies, TV documentaries on streaming services, monuments, commemorative rituals, and contentious memory politics on Twitter/X. Each of these media has its specific affordances and limitations in the memory process. Each will leave its trace on the memory it co-creates with human and nonhuman actors within larger mnemonic assemblages. What kinds of cultural memory, then, are produced by literature and film?

Fictional media, such as novels and feature films, are characterized by their power to shape the collective imagination of the past in a way that is truly fascinating for the literary scholar—and somewhat alarming for the historian.[1] One of the best-known examples is Erich Maria Remarque's *Im Westen Nichts Neues* (1929; *All Quiet on the Western Front*).[2] When the novel appeared a decade after the end of the First World War, it immediately became a bestseller, was quickly translated into many languages, and was turned into an even more successful Hollywood movie, Lewis Milestone's

---

[1] See Rosenstone (1995); Kansteiner (2018).
[2] For the novels' generational dynamics, see Chapter 6, "Generation in Literary History."

Travels in Time. Astrid Erll, Oxford University Press. © Oxford University Press (2025).
DOI: 10.1093/oso/9780197767733.003.0009

All Quiet on the Western Front (1930). What was the First World War? For many people during the twentieth century, the answer would surely have been: "All Quiet on the Western Front."

In the twenty-first century, the First World War's centenary in 2014–2018 tremendously enlarged this memory stub, making accessible and bringing into circulation again many other elements of the archive. This is also because the centenary was the first major transnational commemorative event in the age of digital archives and social media.[3] But it is quite indicative that the major German contribution to the reawakening of First World War memories was a remediation of *All Quiet on the Western Front* (dir. Edward Berger, 2022) on Netflix (i.e., on a streaming service as the newest available media platform for the memory film). With its four Academy Awards and its continued availability on Netflix, this film has quite likely given a new lease of life to the "All Quiet" version of the First World War in transnational cultural memory.

Fictions, both novelistic and filmic, possess the potential to generate and mold images of the past which will often be retained by entire generations. Historical accuracy is not the major concern of such "memory-making" novels and films. Instead, they cater to the public with what is variously termed "authenticity" or "truthfulness." They create images of the past which resonate with cultural memory.[4] Usually, such fictions can neither be called "valuable literature," nor do they enter the canon of artistic masterpieces. They are memory-making and -shaping "collective texts."[5]

For the practice of literary and film studies, these insights from memory studies imply two methodological moves, or shifts in attention: first, from high culture ("the great tradition" of classical literature, the art-house film) to popular culture; and second, from the time-bound media of storage, which allow cultural memories to travel across centuries and even become

---

[3] On memories of the First World War on Twitter, see Clavert (2021); on nation-specific memory dynamics in a pan-European TV-miniseries, see Arnold-de Simine and Sindbæk Andersen (2017).

[4] Effects of "truthfulness" or "authenticity" that fictional mediations can have in memory culture do not emerge from their referentiality, but from their fit with collective memory (see Erll 2003). The pitfalls of referentializing reception are part and parcel of the dynamics of aesthetic media in memory culture. The critical debate ranges from Plato's suggestion to banish all poets from the ideal state (*The Republic*) all the way to how Netflix's *The Crown* (2016–2023) highlights the need for an "understanding of the conventions of the historical fiction genre, as well as the transmedial ramifications of streaming media productions" (Gambarato and Heuman 2022). For the potentialities of the "agency of the aesthetic" in memory culture, see Rigney (2021).

[5] See Erll (2011a, 64). The term "collective texts" refers to a way of reading in which literary works are actualized not so much as precious *objects* to be remembered themselves, but rather as *vehicles* for envisioning the past. Collective texts create, circulate, and shape contents of cultural memory.

themselves objects of remembrance (Shakespeare's historical plays would be an example), to the space-bound media of circulation, which can reach large audiences almost simultaneously, make cultural memories today, and may be forgotten tomorrow.[6]

The key question I am asking in this chapter is: What is it that turns *some* media (and not *others*) into powerful "media of cultural memory," meaning media which create and mold collective images of and narratives about the past? Using examples mainly from war literature and film, this chapter will provide three answers in three steps: I will look first at their *intra*medial "rhetoric of collective memory"; second, at their *inter*medial dynamics, that is, the interplay with earlier and later representations (remediation and premediation); and third, at the *pluri*medial constellations, in which memory-making novels and films appear and unfold their mnemonic agency. In short, I am concerned with phenomena *within*, *between*, and *around* those media which have the power to produce and shape cultural memory.

8.2 The Rhetoric of Collective Memory: Creating Modes of Remembering

Whenever the past is represented, the choice of media and forms has an effect on the kind of memory that is created. For example, a war which is orally represented, in an anecdote told by an old neighbor, seems to become part of lived, contemporary history; but as an object of a Wagnerian opera, the same war can be transformed into an apparently timeless, mythical event. In literature, as in film, there are different modes of representation which may elicit different modes of collective remembering in the audience.

Each memory-making medium has its specific "rhetoric of collective memory," constituted by one or more mnemonic modes. With regard to fictions of the First World War, I have distinguished five modes of a rhetoric of collective memory: the experiential, the mythicizing, the historicizing, the antagonistic, and the reflexive modes (Erll 2003). Such modes are a matter of "memory *in* literature."[7] They can be subjected to an *intra*medial analysis, using for example narratological categories (as I will do in the following). What is important to note is that a memory rhetoric can only create

---

[6] For the distinction between space-bound and time-bound media, see Innis (1951).
[7] Erll (2011a, 77–82).

a "mnemonic *potential*." This potential needs to be actualized by real readers in order to have an effect in memory culture.

Experiential modes are constituted by literary forms which represent the past as a recent, lived-through experience. Their rhetoric evokes a sense of remembering in the framework of "communicative memory."[8] Texts in which the experiential mode predominates tend to stage communicative memory's main source: the episodic-autobiographical memories of witnesses.

Typical forms of this mode of literary remembering are a "personal voice"[9] generated by first-person narration, thus imitating or indicating some kind of "life writing."[10] In the late 1920s, Siegfried Sassoon's and Robert Graves's war memoirs made use of this strategy.[11] But the experiential mode is not necessarily tied to first-person narration. Another typical form, used especially by modernist writers (such as Ford Madox Ford or Virginia Woolf[12]), is the stream-of-consciousness technique, which conveys the specific inner experientiality of the trenches, combat, and trauma.[13]

An experiential rhetoric can include addressing the reader in the intimate way typical of face-to-face communication; the use of the more immediate present tense; lengthy passages focalized by an "experiencing I" in order to convey embodied, seemingly immediate experience; circumstantial realism, that is, a very detailed presentation of everyday life in the past (Roland Barthes's *effet de réel* turns into an *effet de mémoire*); and, finally, the representation of everyday ways of speaking (sociolects, soldiers' slang, etc.) to convey the linguistic specificity and fluidity of a recent past.[14]

Mythicizing modes are constituted by literary forms that resemble representations of the past within the framework of Jan Assmann's "cultural memory," that is, the remembrance of foundational events which are situated in a faraway, mythical past, and have normative and formative significance

---

[8] On the Assmanns' distinction between communicative memory and cultural memory, see J. Assmann (2010). For a discussion, see Erll (2011a, 20–33); for communicative memory in the digital age, see Pentzold et al. (2023).
[9] On "personal," "authorial," and "communal voice," see Lanser (1992).
[10] On life writing and cultural memory, see Saunders (2010).
[11] Robert Graves, *Good-bye to All That* (1929) and Siegfried Sassoon, *Memoirs of an Infantry Officer* (1930). These memoirs present what Samuel Hynes (1997) has called "the soldiers' tale."
[12] Ford Madox Ford, *Parade's End* (1924–1928) and Virginia Woolf, *Mrs. Dalloway* (1925).
[13] Travel literature often operates with such features of the experiential mode. So do war novels. Much Holocaust fiction also resorts to strong experiential modes (but it often shows, reflexively, the limits of experience and its representation).
[14] This linguistic strategy can be studied in Frederic Manning's war novel *The Middle Parts of Fortune* (1929).

for a collectivity.[15] Typical of this tendency is Ernst Jünger's war novel *In Stahlgewittern* (1920; *The Storm of Steel*), in which German soldiers are transformed into figures of Germanic mythology. But also Francis Ford Coppola's highly acclaimed Vietnam War "anti-war" movie, *Apocalypse Now* (1979), mythicizes the historical events by means of intertextual references and the creation of a primordial atmosphere, using an array of visual and sound effects.

Historicizing modes convey literary events and persons as if they were objects of scholarly historiography: paying close attention to historical detail, including historical figures and events, working with footnotes, and so on. A historicizing rhetoric is dominant in the genre of the historical novel as it emerged in the nineteenth century. Walter Scott's *Waverley* (1814) is often seen as its founding text.[16] The novel's subtitle *'Tis Sixty Years Since* points to the typical historians' understanding of a "completed past" after three generations.[17] The genre of the historical novel has taken many twists and turns since Scott. Historical novels were the privileged "collective texts" during the nineteenth and twentieth centuries. In the 1980s and 1990s, they took a reflexive turn as postmodern "historiographic metafiction."[18] Around 2000, literary writing about the past veered away from historicizing modes and toward testimonial literature and experiential modes. This transition can be well observed in Pat Barker's *Regeneration* trilogy (1991–1995), historical novels on the First World War, conveyed in a strongly experiential mode.

Antagonistic modes come into being through literary forms that help to maintain one version of the past and reject another. Negative stereotyping (such as calling the Germans "the Hun" or "beasts" in early English poetry of the First World War) is the most obvious technique of establishing an antagonistic mode. More elaborate is the resort to biased perspective structures: Only the memories of a certain group are presented as true, while the versions articulated by members of conflicting memory cultures are

---

[15] Jan Assmann (1995 [1988], 132) defines "cultural memory" as follows: "The concept of cultural memory comprises that body of reusable texts, images, and rituals specific to each society in each epoch, whose 'cultivation' serves to stabilize and convey that society's selfimage. Upon such collective knowledge, for the most part (but not exclusively) of the past, each group bases its awareness of unity and particularity."

[16] See de Groot (2009); see Rigney (2012a) on the cultural memories of Walter Scott.

[17] For discussions about what constitutes "contemporary history," see Bevernage and Lorenz (2013).

[18] Hutcheon (1988); Wesseling (1991); Nünning (1997); Boccardi (2009); Jonston and Wiegandt (2017); Charbel (2020).

deconstructed as false. Authors of the "lost generation," Ernest Hemingway and Richard Aldington, for example, make ample use of these strategies.[19] Resorting to "we-narration" and establishing a "communal voice" (Lanser 1992) can underscore the antagonistic potential of a novel. This is actually one of the most striking narrative features in Remarque's requiem on the lost generation, *All Quiet on the Western Front* (1929). In this novel, "we-narration" creates a collective identity for a generation of young front-line soldiers, who are set apart from the old, war-mongering generation at home.[20] Antagonistic modes, which support identity-groups and their versions of the past, can also be found in feminist, imperial, and postcolonial writing, as well as in politically oriented *littérature engagée*.

Reflexive modes can be connected to each of the modes already mentioned. To put matters in the language of systems theory: Literature usually allows its readers both a first- and a second-order observation of the world.[21] It gives us the illusion of glimpsing the past (in an experiential, mythical, historicizing, or antagonistic way) and is—often at the same time—a major medium of critical reflection upon these very processes of representation. Literature is a medium that simultaneously builds and observes memory. It is a medium of memory-production and of memory-reflection.

Prominent reflexive modes are constituted by forms which draw attention to processes and problems of remembering. One of these forms is the explicit narratorial comment on the workings of memory, found, for example, in Marcel Proust's famous novel of memory, *A la recherche du temps perdu* (1913–1927). Other strategies include the montage of different fictional and nonfictional documents, which can be studied in Edlef Koeppen's *Heeresbericht* (1930; transl. *Higher Command*, 1931), the best German novel to have come out of the First World War. Even more experimental forms have appeared in the literature of the Second World War, such as Kurt Vonnegut's inversion of chronology in *Slaughterhouse-Five* (1969) as a way to represent the bombardment of Dresden. Historiographic metafiction (such as Michael Ondaatje's *The English Patient*, 1992), is a combination of historicizing and reflexive modes. Autofiction (such as W. G. Sebald's, Karl Ove Knausgaard's,

---

[19] Ernest Hemingway, *A Farewell to Arms* (1929), and Richard Aldington, *Death of a Hero: A Novel* (1929).
[20] For a highly antagonistic feminist rewriting of Remarque's novel, see Helen Zenna Smith [Evadne Price], *Not So Quiet... Stepdaughters of War* (1930); for a discussion of these two novels, see Chapter 6, "Generation in Literary History."
[21] See Luhmann (2000 [1997]).

and some of J. M. Coetzee's writing) is often a combination of experiential and reflexive modes.

These different modes of representing the past—here zooming in to everyday experience, there zooming out to timeless myth; here taking part in contestation, there staying aloof and adopting a reflexive stance—are not restricted to war writing, or even to historical writing. A rhetoric of collective memory can be found in all literary genres which represent the past, or more generally temporalities (from romance to gothic novels, crime thrillers, and science fiction). And it can of course also be found in other media such as feature films and TV series.

Neither is the number of mnemonic modes restricted to the five mentioned here. In fact, Anna Cento Bull and Hans Lauge Hansen have theorized an "agonistic mode."[22] I think that it should be possible to identify "relational modes," which can constitute multidirectional memory (*sensu* Rothberg 2009) in literary texts. Last but not least, modes of remembering need not necessarily be established by verbal, literary, and narrative forms. Nonfictional media such as historiography and journalism, as well as visual media such as painting and photography, have developed their own "rhetorics of collective memory."

8.3 Premediation and Remediation: The Intermedial Dynamics of Memory

Not only *intra*medial strategies, such as the rhetoric of collective memory, but also *inter*medial relations are involved in the process that turns fictions into media of cultural memory. Because remembered events are transmedial phenomena, their representation is not tied to one specific medium. They can be represented across the spectrum of available media.[23] And this is precisely what creates a powerful site of memory. The intermedial dynamics of cultural memory is usually characterized by a double movement, by the interaction of "premediation" and "remediation."

---

[22] See Bull and Hansen (2016). For current approaches to literature and memory, see Milevski and Wetenkamp (2022).
[23] See Ryan (2004, 2015) and Jenkins's (2006) work on "convergence culture" and "transmedia storytelling." Memory studies approaches are interested in the collective memory-making potential of transmedia dynamics. For a cognitive perspective on how individual rememberers actualize transmedia storytelling, see Alessio et al. (2024) on "spontaneous transmedia collocation."

"Remediation" was originally a term of new media studies, introduced by Jay David Bolter and Richard Grusin in 1999.[24] The concept was adapted and transformed for the uses of memory studies (Hoskins 2001; Erll and Rigney 2009).[25] Within memory research, remediation primarily describes the continuous transcription of memory content into different media. Memory content—stories and images about the past—is a transmedial phenomenon. It can be represented in oral speech and handwritten manuscripts or printed newspaper articles, in historiographies and novels, in paintings and photographs, in films and on websites. If we look at "Odysseus," "Napoleon," or "the Holocaust," we realize quickly that the images and stories retained in collective memory emerge and persist through their ongoing remediation. What is remembered about an ancient myth, a revolution, or a genocide thus usually refers not so much to what one might cautiously call "the original" or "the actual events," but instead to a palimpsestic structure of representations circulating in media culture. Repeated representation over decades and centuries in different media is what creates and stabilizes contents of collective memory.[26]

The term "premediation" draws attention to the fact that mediations which circulate in a given society provide schemata for future experience and its representation. In this way, the representations of colonial wars premediated the First World War; the First World War, in turn, was used as a model for the Second World War.[27] But not only depictions of earlier, yet somehow comparable events shape our understanding of later events. Media which belong to even more remote cultural spheres, such as art, mythology, religion, or law, can exert great power as premediators, too. John Bunyan's *The Pilgrim's Progress* (1678), with its "Valley of the Shadow and Death" episode, premediated many journals and letters written during the First

---

[24] In *Remediation: Understanding New Media* (1999, 55), Bolter and Grusin contend that "all mediation is remediation," that "each act of mediation depends on other acts of mediation. Media are continually commenting on, reproducing, and replacing each other, and this process is integral to media."

[25] For an in-depth discussion of remediation and premediation, see Erll (2017).

[26] Although not subscribing to strict media determinism, research on remediation in memory studies retains Bolter's and Grusin's (1999) original focus on the materiality and the technology of media. This is what distinguishes the term from other concepts of discursive and media filiations, such as intertextuality (Kristeva, 1969) or adaptation (Hutcheon, 2006). While not arguing in an overly determinist way that "the medium is the memory," media memory research does engage with the interesting question of how the "trace" of the medium may shape the memory it produces.

[27] This is my conceptualization of "premediation" (see Erll 2007, 2017). It diverges from the one developed by Richard Grusin (2004, 2010). For Grusin, premediation is a rather specific practice that emerged in the American media after 9/11. It describes the anticipation of further threats by means of incessant mediations of possible future wars and disasters.

World War, as Paul Fussell (1975) has shown. (At the same time, it was itself a remediation of biblical accounts.) In today's world, the cinema has emerged as a major premediating force. Movies, especially popular Hollywood films, provide globally circulating narrative schemata and scripts for life experience: for friendship, courtship, weddings, and also for war and terrorism.[28] The American understanding and representation of the events of September 11, 2001 (9/11) were clearly premediated by disaster movies, the crusader narrative, and biblical stories. Premediation therefore refers to cultural practices of looking, naming, and narrating. It is the effect of, *and* the starting point for, mediated memories.

Remediations tend to solidify cultural memory, creating and stabilizing certain narratives and icons of the past. Paradoxically, this will often also happen when antagonistic and reflexive forms of representation are used. Such invariably stabilizing effects of remediation can be observed in the emergence of "9/11" as an American, and indeed transnational, *lieu de mémoire*: The burning twin towers quickly crystallized into the one iconic image of the event, and this icon has been remediated ever since: in television news, photography, movies, comic strips, and so on. But such iconization is not restricted to visual media. Another example connected with 9/11 is the icon of the "falling man," which stands for those people who were trapped by the fire on the upper floors of the World Trade Center and decided to jump rather than die in the flames. The "falling man" was first represented by a photograph taken by Richard Drew. In September 2003, this photograph was remediated in a story written by Tom Junod and published in *Esquire* magazine. In March 2006, Henry Singer and Richard Numeroff turned the "falling man" into a documentary (*9/11: The Falling Man*). And in 2007, Don DeLillo's novel *Falling Man* appeared on the literary market.[29] These are only a few examples of the remediations of the "falling man," featuring text and image, as well as very different stories and meanings. All have contributed to the stabilization of the "falling man" as an icon of 9/11. In 2016, *Time* magazine stated that the falling man, whose identity is still unknown, had become "a makeshift Unknown

---

[28] Bourke (1999) shows how movies about the Second World War premediated the way that soldiers entered into battle in Vietnam (for similar results, see also Sturken, 1997; Welzer, 2002).
[29] Kristiaan Versluys, "9/11 in the Novel," in Matthew J. Morgan (ed.), *The Impact of 9/11 on the Media, Arts, and Entertainment: The Day That Changed Everything?* (New York: Palgrave Macmillan, 2009, 142–143).

Soldier"[30] in American culture—thus of course drawing on First World War commemorative practice as a premediator.

Remediation does not just consist in the repeated medial representation of images and narratives. It can also mean the incorporation of existent media products and technologies. It is especially in the cinema of cultural memory that we find such manifest forms of remediation. As Martia Sturken shows in *Tangled Memories* (1997) and Guy Westwell in *War Cinema* (2006), Hollywood war movies frequently incorporate existent documentary footage, and this integration of prior media serves to create an *effet de réel*: The fictional story seems indexically linked to the historical events it depicts.[31]

However, the boundaries between documentary material and fictional re-enactment are often blurred in the course of remediation. One example is the famous Iwo Jima photograph, which was taken by Joe Rosenthal on February 23, 1945. It shows a group of U.S. Marines raising the American flag on a Japanese island south of Tokyo. When it appeared in the *New York Times* shortly thereafter, it brought hope to the war-weary Americans. Still today, this photograph stands in U.S. memory for American heroism and the victory that is about to be won. Since its publication, the press photograph has been remediated countless times: by a memorial, several statues, books, songs, rituals, postage stamps, and other photographs. And it has been integrated (sometimes by filming the photograph itself, sometimes by re-enactment) into a great number of popular war movies, among them *Sands of Iwo Jima* (1949, with John Wayne). An impactful twenty-first-century remediation is Clint Eastwood's movie *Flags of Our Fathers* (2006), in which Hollywood stars re-enact the raising of the flag. A film still of this re-enactment, which precisely resembles the original photograph (except that it is in color), appears as the movie poster. It is probably only a question of time until the still of Eastwood's re-enactment will appear somewhere as authentic "source material" and will be itself remediated, in order to make yet another representation appear authentic.

Flags of Our Fathers is also an example of how specific media *technologies* can be remediated: The intentionally bleached-out colors remind the audience of the monochrome news coverage during the Second World War, and

---

[30] "The Story behind the Haunting 9/11 Photo of the Falling Man," *Time* (September 8, 2016), https://time.com/4453467/911-september-11-falling-man-photo/.

[31] On the logic of analog film and photography as "externalization" and "trace," see Ruchatz (2010); see also Sontag (2003). In our age of digital photography, the discussion of "deep fakes" is still oriented around the older, analog media-derived expectation that photography produces "traces" of the past.

of course also of Rosenthal's original black-and-white photograph. What is often integrated via remediation into filmic versions of the past is therefore not merely actual documentary material, but also its specific "look" (which usually derives from the media technology of the time, but also from historical aesthetics). Parts of the Vietnam War movie *Platoon* (1986), for example, imitate the shaky camera movement characteristic of war journalism at the front and thus the look of news coverage in the 1960s and 1970s. Another example is *Saving Private Ryan* (1998), a movie about the Second World War, for which key episodes were shot in the grainy style of 16mm color film, thus emulating the cinematography of 1940s documentaries (Westwell 2006, 78, 92).

It is the double dynamics of the premediation of remediation, of the medial preformation and reshaping of events, which links each representation of the past with the history of mediated memories. First and foremost, these processes make the past intelligible. At the same time, they endow medial representations with the aura of authenticity. Finally, they also play a decisive role in stabilizing the memory of historical events into *lieux de mémoire*.[32]

8.4 Film and Cultural Memory: Plurimedial Constellations

Judging from its prevalence and impact, "film" has become a leading medium of popular cultural memory. This is a development which started in the late 1970s (Kansteiner 2006) and has recently made a powerful transition into streaming media.[33] Even in today's digital media ecologies and despite competition from audiovisual content on YouTube and TikTok, the classic memory-making movie is still very much alive: Christopher Nolan's *Oppenheimer* (2024) won seven Oscars at the Academy Awards in 2024, and hundreds of millions of people watched the biopic worldwide.

Asking once again what it is that turns some movies (and novels) into powerful memory-making fictions, a preliminary answer can now be given: Certain intra- and intermedial strategies (as considered in sections 8.2 and

---

[32] On remediation of the filmic archive, see Brunow (2015); on remediation in literature and film, see Kilbourn and Ty (2013); on remediation in an age of streaming services, see Gambarato et al. (2022).

[33] See, for example, Shubhabrata Dutta's and Diksha Sundriyal's impressive list of "28 Best Historical Movies on Netflix (March 7, 2024)," (https://thecinemaholic.com/historical-movies-on-netflix/).

8.3 of this chapter) mark them out as media of cultural memory. However, such strategies endow fictions only with a *potential* for memory-making. This potential has to be *realized* (or actualized) in the process of reception: Novels must be read and films must be viewed by a community *as* media of cultural memory. Films that are not watched or books that are not read may provide the most intriguing images of the past, yet they will not have any effect in memory cultures—or at least not yet; as elements of the "archive" they can hold potentiality for future use. The specific form of reception which turns fictions about the past into memory-making fictions is not an individual, but a collective phenomenon. What is needed is a certain kind of *context*, in which novels and films are prepared and received as memory-shaping media.

Taking as an example filmmaking of the early twenty-first century, such contexts have been reconstructed in detail by an interdisciplinary group of researchers at the University of Giessen (Erll and Wodianka 2008). We took a close look at some popular German history movies, such as *Der Untergang* (2004, *The Downfall*), a film about the last days of Adolf Hitler, and *Das Leben der Anderen* (2006, *The Lives of Others*), a film about life in the German Democratic Republic. They were part of a boom of history films in the early twenty-first century, which could be observed especially in Germany. Movies, TV serials, fictional, documentary, and semi-documentary formats had virtually become obsessed with the representation of contemporary history. Films about the Nazis, the Holocaust, the Second World War, and its aftermath abounded.

Scrutinizing the cultural practices surrounding history movies, we determined that it is not primarily the intramedial and intermedial strategies that turn a "film about history" into a "memory-making film," but instead what has been established around them: A tight network of associated mediations prepares the ground for the movies, leads reception along certain paths, opens up and channels public discussion, and thus endows films with their mnemonic agency and meanings. With regard to the two examples mentioned above, we followed reviews in national and international newspapers and movie magazines, special features on TV, carefully targeted marketing strategies, merchandise, the DVD versions (including the "making of" segments, interviews with producers and actors, historical background information, etc.), awards (*The Lives of Others* received an Academy Award in 2007), political speeches, academic controversies (especially among historians with regard to *The Downfall*, on the question of the ethics of representing Hitler as the protagonist of a movie), the publication of a book about or a book based on the film (and its censorship, as in the case of *The Lives of Others*), and finally all those didactic formats which have turned each movie into teaching units in German classrooms.

All those advertisements, comments, discussions, and controversies constitute the collective contexts which channel a movie's reception and potentially turn it into a medium of cultural memory. Moreover, all these expressions are circulated by means of media. Therefore, we called these contexts "plurimedial constellations (or networks) of memory." To sum up: While the potential of fictions to be turned into media of cultural memory is developed by certain strategies on *intra*medial and *inter*medial levels, those potentialities can only be turned into actualities within *pluri*medial contexts. The "memory-making film" and the "memory-making novel" are made by the media constellations surrounding them.

8.5 Conclusion: Making Memory in a Digital Age

In our present age of digital media, literature and film have diversified into "twitterature," fan-fiction websites, YouTube shorts, and multiple other new media genres, that make and shape images and narratives of the past. How does the logic of memory-making media as described in this chapter play out in digital memory ecologies?[34]

In an important essay, Silvana Mandolessi contends that digital media do not mean the "end of collective memory" (*sensu* Hoskins 2017), but that strikingly:

> digital memory materializes and implements the theoretical claims made by Memory Studies since the field's inception: that collective memory may be conceived of as a process, mediated and remediated by multiple media with the participation of dynamic communities that perform rather than represent the past. (Mandolessi 2023, 1514)

In one sense, digital ecologies are a heightened state of what the memory process has always been. But there are also important differences from the

---

[34] On digital memory ecologies, see Hoskins (2017); on memory in a globital age, see Reading (2016).

broadcast age, as well as more broadly from the "Gutenberg parenthesis."[35] For Mandolessi (2023, 1514) these include "the new ontology of the digital archive" as an "archive in motion" (*sensu* Røssaak, 2010),[36] the "shift from narrative to database," "the reconfiguration of agency" as distributed between human and nonhuman actors, including algorithms and AI, as well as the "shift from mnemonic objects to mnemonic assemblages."

The digital memory ecology does not do away with the medial dynamics outlined above, but they may play out differently. A "rhetoric of collective memory," for example, can also be found on social media such as Twitter/X, Instagram, or TikTok, where it will be shaped by new affordances, such as the constraint of utter verbal condensation or the possibility of multimodality.[37] Commemorative initiatives such as @ichbinsophiescholl on Twitter or "Eva Stories" on Instagram tackle such new affordances as they try to mediate Holocaust memory.[38]

"Remediation" is the basic memory logic of the digital age (Grusin and Bolter 1999). Media of the historical past (from analog footage to material objects) are increasingly digitized. They become part of digital archives, which in turn enable further remediations by "prosumers" (e.g., of the two world wars on YouTube).[39] When it comes to externalizing autobiographical memories, remediation has turned into an everyday "retromedia practice," for example when users share old Polaroid photos on Instagram as part of their "digital memory work" (Annabell 2023).[40]

Rik Smit has proposed the term "platformization of memory" to express how profoundly digital platforms such as Google, Facebook, and Instagram shape all aspects of collective memory, from cognitive representations to archives. To "remember is increasingly to remember in and through

---

[35] For collective memory in a "post-broadcast age," see Edy (2014); for the "Gutenberg parenthesis" (i.e., the ca. 5,000 years when print was a leading medium), see Sauerberg (2009).

[36] Mandolessi (2023, 1516) explains that "the digital differs radically from traditional archival storage because what is stored is not an object but a code: a code is merely the potential to generate a representation, not the representation itself."

[37] On TikTok's "memefication" and "silly archive," see Lin and de Kloet (2023); on its "meta-memory," see Seet and Tandoc (2024); on memorial sites on YouTube, see Knudsen (2016).

[38] See Henig and Ebbrecht-Hartmann (2022); Thiele and Thomas (2023); for the logic of Holocaust memory on TikTok, see Divon and Ebbrecht-Hartmann (2022).

[39] See Brügger (2018); Makhortykh (2020). There are important differences between digital media as far as their "provenance" is concerned. Mandolessi refers to Brügger (2018, 5), when she distinguishes between "digitized media (nondigital media that have been digitized), born-digital media (media that have not existed in any form other than digital) and reborn digital media (born-digital media that have been collected and preserved, and that have been changed during this process)" (Mandolessi 2023, 1517).

[40] Annabell (2023, 2) studies how remediation is used by young women on Instagram to "refashion and reconfigure pre-digital mnemonic media practices and forms."

digital platforms. Memories have become data and data are turned into 'memories'" (Smit et al. 2024, 1).[41] Across such platforms, rather than emanating from one single memory-making medium, the production of memory needs to be located in ongoing interactive processes, such as sharing, liking, remediation, memefication, and algorithm-driven visibility.[42]

"Plurimedial constellations" have thus turned into "socio-technological assemblages."[43] The term, of assemblage, is very apt here. It highlights, as Mandolessi (2023, 1224) points out, the "entanglement of heterogeneous elements, including both human and non-human actors," and thus leaves room for the consideration of the agency of infrastructures and algorithms in the making of collective memory.[44]

Maurice Halbwachs began his work on the collective memory by highlighting the importance of the "social frameworks of memory" (*cadres sociaux de la mémoire*). Since the 1990s, research in the field of memory studies has been guided by the insight that these are in fact to a large degree "medial frameworks" (*cadres mediaux de la mémoire*), ranging from orality to email communication. Digital memory studies proponents such as Rik Smit (2024, 123) posit that social media platforms "act as new 'medial frameworks' of memory that support—infrastructurally speaking—and shape new forms, dependencies, and power dynamics when it comes to the keeping and representation of the past." We have thus entered the age of *cadres plateformisés de la mémoire*.

---

[41] Smit et al. (2024, 2) emphasize the "need to examine the ways in which the political economy and business models of contemporary platforms and digital technologies impact upon memory making." For foundational research on "mediated memories" and social media platforms as "socio-technical, performative infrastructures," see van Dijck (2007, 2010); van Dijck et al. (2018).

[42] See Birhane (2021); Jacobsen and Beer (2021).

[43] This is Makhortykh's term, who proposes that "platform-based memory infrastructures, which are distinguished by the integration of AI-driven systems in platforms' architectures for curating and creating memory-related content, can be viewed as socio-technical assemblages bringing together human and non-human memory actors" (Makhortykh 2023, 1508).

[44] And the "making" might better be seen as a "becoming": In socio-technical mnemonic assemblages, we grasp collective memory as a "provisional, contingent plurimedial configuration where the elements are interconnected in a process of becoming" (Mandolessi 2023, 1524). For an assemblage model approach to collective memory, which includes not only socio-technological, but also biological and mental aspects, see Chapter 13, "Ecologies of Trauma."

Chapter 9
Remediation across Time, Space, and Cultures
The Indian Rebellion of 1857–1858

9.1 Sites of Memory in Colonial Contexts: The "Mutiny" Myth and Its Medial Dynamics

How are sites of memory made and remade in antagonistic memory cultures, such as in settings of colonialism and postcolonialism?[1] How can we study collective memory in constellations, where one archive (the archive of the colonizer) is replete with written documents, highly accessible, and the source of a powerful and hegemonic canonical narrative of the past— while the other (the archive of the colonized) is to a large extent oral and thus less durable, dispersed across different languages, and endangered through repression by colonial authorities? What role do mediation, remediation, and premediation play in processes of imperial and subaltern, of postimperial and postcolonial memory-making?

The mnemohistory of the Indian Rebellion of 1857–1858 is a good testing ground for such fundamental questions of postcolonial media memory studies.[2] The rebellion has been framed by military historians as merely a colonial "small war" (Chakravarty 2014). But it affected India and Great Britain profoundly, and it shaped collective memories virtually across the globe over more than one and a half centuries.[3]

---

[1] As Ann Rigney (2010, 345) has pointed out, "the metaphor of 'memory site' can become misleading if it is interpreted to mean that collective remembrance becomes permanently tied down to particular figures, icons, or monuments."

[2] On the colonial archive, see Stoler (2008, 2016). On challenges of media memory studies in postcolonial settings, see Keightley (2022).

[3] As the multivolume project *Mutiny at the Margins* (2013–2017) shows, the events in India had an impact on people across the British Empire, from Jamaica to South Africa. See also Bhattacharya (2007); Pati (2007); Bender (2016). See Erll (2007) for a history of British and Indian mediated memories of the "Indian Mutiny" from 1857 to 2007. Overall, memory studies approaches to the Indian Rebellion are still rare, but the work by Wagner (2010, 2018) strongly speaks to the

Travels in Time. Astrid Erll, Oxford University Press. © Oxford University Press (2025).
DOI: 10.1093/oso/9780197767733.003.0010

The rebellion of 1857–1858 was an uprising against British colonial rule, which broke out in northern and central India in the spring of 1857. It started as a mutiny of discontented sepoy regiments (i.e., Indian soldiers in the service of the East India Company, which had, by that time, annexed the greater part of the subcontinent).[4] But the soldiers' uprising speedily turned into a "popular revolt,"[5] which also involved the tax-drained Indian peasants and disinherited Indian princes. One year later, in 1858, the British had re-established power, with hitherto unknown cruelty—for example, burning whole villages and executing every single man in them, in order to avenge British victims and to deter any other rebels.

In the history of British imperialism in India, the revolt turned out to be a watershed. It led to the transformation of an informal empire, which had been controlled for more than a hundred years by the East India Company, into the formal empire under the British crown: the British Raj in India, which would not end until almost a hundred years later, with Indian independence in 1947.

As a shared site of memory, the rebellion carries great significance in British as well as Indian memory cultures. In both countries, the uprising assumed the dimensions of a national myth. From an Indian nationalist perspective (permanently shaped by Savarkar's *The Indian War of Independence*, 1909), the rebellion of 1857–1858 is a foundational event in that it is understood as the first heroic revolt against foreign rule, which would lead to the freedom struggle and then to independence. From a British imperialist perspective, the events of 1857–1858 mark the beginning of and provide the legitimation for the British Raj. In the colonizers' view, with their uprising, the sepoys had shown the need for a strong British government on the Indian subcontinent.[6]

As these two different narratives already indicate, the events of the years 1857–1858 are not only a shared site of memory, but also very much a contested one. This contestation begins with the question of how to describe the Indian rebellion—a question that tends to be resolved rather differently

---

field's concerns. Pender (2022) is in fact the first to study commemorations of 1857–1858 across 160 years. For the first systematic survey of *Memory Studies in India*, see Parui and Raj (2025).

[4] The immediate cause of the rebellion of 1857 was that Hindu and Muslim sepoys refused to use the new Enfield rifle. The rifle had to be operated with greased cartridges, for which, as it soon turned out, the British had used cow's and pig's fat. This would have defiled Hindus and Muslims alike. Whether religious, conservative, or proto-nationalist impulses prevailed in the Indian rebellion is still discussed today.

[5] For this argument, see Mukherjee (1984).

[6] See Malik (2008); Metcalf (1995).

in Great Britain and in India. While in Britain the events still tend to be described with the derogatory term "Indian Mutiny" (thus implying insubordination and treachery on the Indian side), people in India usually prefer other terms, such as "Indian rebellion," "Indian uprising," or even "the first war of Indian independence."

Lieux de mémoire provide, as Pierre Nora maintains, "a maximum amount of meaning in a minimum number of signs."[7] In order to explain how such a condensation of meaning works, Ann Rigney has introduced the term "convergence" into the discourse of cultural memory studies.[8] Cultural memories tend to "converge and coalesce" into a *lieu de mémoire* (Rigney 2005, 18). Stories, iconic images, and *topoi* about the past flow together and are conflated into a site of memory. Thus, rather than as a static, fixed repository or a storehouse of memory, the *lieu de mémoire* should be conceptualized, in the words of Ann Rigney (2005, 18), as "a self-perpetuating vortex of symbolic investment."

But the convergence and condensation of meaning into a site of memory are only one direction of the process by which *lieux de mémoire* come into being. In fact, those individual rememberers who are confronted with a site of memory (standing in front of a memorial, participating in a commemoration, or just hearing the word "Indian Mutiny") will usually want to *unfold* meaning, to associate certain images and narratives with the specific site.

For example, the Victorians—and indeed up to the mid-twentieth century, mainstream British culture—associated the term "Indian Mutiny" with images of ferocious sepoys raping English women, British cantonments on fire, heroic Highland soldiers charging into battle, and with narrative plots such as "last-minute rescue," "the last stand," "faith and delivery," or "virtue rewarded." These are the key elements of the British imperialist "Mutiny" myth, which emerged during the nineteenth century and remained active well into the twentieth century.

However, the name of the event alone, or just one painting or memorial, obviously cannot suffice to evoke all these associations. They can only serve as "medial cues" which trigger possibly quite different memories in each observer—when connecting with images and narratives of the past that are

---

[7] Qtd. in Rigney (2005, 18). For a detailed account of the *lieux de mémoire* project, see Nora (1992).

[8] See Jenkins (2006) on "convergence culture."

already part of his or her memory.⁹ "Mutiny" memories can only emerge if the rememberer has read "Mutiny" novels, listened to atrocity stories, or was taught the imperialist version of the events as history in school, in short: if he or she is part of a media culture in which representations of the rebellion of 1857–1858 are constantly circulated in the form of "Mutiny" narratives and images.

This chapter will focus on the importance of media in creating and disseminating notions about the events of 1857–1858 and thus in constructing, maintaining, and transforming a site of memory which has been shared by British and Indian people over a time span of over one and a half centuries. Proceeding from the idea that it is the convergence of medial representations which turns an event into a *lieu de mémoire*, I will delineate some of the plurimedial networks which produced, questioned, and deconstructed the "Indian Mutiny" as a site of memory. I wish to draw particular attention to the diachronic dimension of these networks, or more precisely, to premediation and remediation.¹⁰ The rebellion of 1857–1858 is a perfect example of this memory-making interplay of premediation and remediation.

In what follows I will take a—necessarily highly selective—look at the premediation and remediation of some of the *topoi* and narratives which are staple ingredients of the British "Mutiny" myth. Probably the most tenacious notions about the "Mutiny" center on mini-narratives, such as "rape and revenge" and "treachery and massacre," as well as around some names and places fraught with meaning, such as "Nana Sahib," "Satichaura Ghat," and "Bibighar." Newspaper articles, eyewitness accounts, historiographical works, novels, and movies (among many other media) have contributed to infuse these elements of the "Mutiny" myth with meaning. The following is a reconstruction of some of the horizontal and vertical lines of representation, which connect British imperial mythmaking with colonial Indian countermemory, as well as popular Hollywood stories with new images of the revolt created in India's postcolonial Bollywood. It is the attempt to show how— via premediation and remediation—cultural memory operates across time, space, and cultures.

---

⁹ This model of the emergence of collective memories is indebted to the concept of "ecphory" (the synergistic combination of a memory trace with a retrieval cue), which goes back to biologist Richard Semon (1859–1918) and cognitive psychologist Endel Tulving. For the psychology of memory, see Tulving and Craik (2000).
¹⁰ For a discussion of these terms, see Chapter 8, "Literature, Film, and the Mediality of Cultural Memory."

9.2 Atrocity Stories and Premediation: The British Press of 1857

That the colonial British memory culture of the nineteenth century turned the events of 1857–1858 into a foundational myth, which contributed to grand-scale imperial self-fashioning and helped legitimize British rule in India, is well known (see Brantlinger 1988; Chakravarty 2005). With the help of exaggerated newspaper articles, biased historiography, and more than one hundred hugely popular "Mutiny" romances, a colonial narrative was created which had little to do with the actual events. The imperial myth prominently features the themes of Indian treachery, of terrible Indian atrocities, and—as far as the British side is concerned—of extreme heroism ("every man a hero, every woman a man," as one source phrases it).[11] From the colonizers' perspective, Indians had betrayed British benevolence by turning against their just, liberal, and progressive rulers. Back at home, in England, the rumors of massacres and the rape of British women struck at the heart of Victorian sensibilities. "Rape" became a symbol of what was understood as the Indians' transgressive assault against the British nation and an unforgivable inversion of colonial hierarchies.[12]

None of the elements of memory just mentioned can stand up to historical inquiry, even if one relies solely on British sources. The elements of the British myth are at best debatable, more often utterly wrong. For example, most of the rape stories belong to the "fictions connected with the Indian Mutiny," as Edward Leckey pointed out as early as 1859. Moreover, what was often forgotten was that some British atrocities preceded as well as surpassed those of the Indians, as Edward Thompson showed in detail in his *The Other Side of the Medal* (1925). British memory of the "Indian Mutiny"—up to 1947, and in a residual way also after Indian independence—is a case in point for the selectivity, unreliability, and political functions of cultural memory. And it is the product of a powerful imperial media culture.

The earliest and most important medium which turned the Indian uprising into a site of memory was the British press in the years 1857–1858. In many newspaper articles, one can sense an awareness that the current events already belonged to "world history." Back in London's Fleet Street, where

---

[11] *Calcutta Review* (LXI 1858, v). This is of course the dominant myth, created by a powerful imperial memory culture, which (and this is important for the approach delineated here) had an impact on British as well as Indian memory cultures. At the same time, there were certainly dissident voices in England which were highly critical of the British role in India (Sabin 2002, Herbert 2008).

[12] For a detailed and intriguing analysis of the figure of woman and the *topos* of rape in connection with the "Mutiny," see Sharpe (1993).

information about what happened in the faraway colony was scarce and unreliable, a rhetoric of prospective memory fashioned the events in India as a foundational, almost mythical event, and as an important lesson for "many generations to come."[13] The British press was also an important generator of those bloodcurdling atrocity stories which shape the image of the "Mutiny" in Britain to this day. Some examples may give a taste of the atrocity stories which were disseminated by British newspapers. The following text was originally published in the *Bombay Telegraph* and reissued in the *Times*:

> Children have been compelled to eat the quivering flesh of their murdered parents, after which they were literally *torn asunder* by the laughing fiends who surrounded them. Men in many instances have been mutilated, and, before being absolutely killed, have had to gaze upon the last dishonour of their wives and daughters previous to being put to death. But really we cannot describe the brutalities that have been committed; they pass the boundaries of human belief, and to dwell upon them shakes reason upon its throne. If ever a nation was made the instrument of an insulted Deity, that nation is England; and we trust that she will strike and spare not. (*Times*, September 17, 1857, 9)

Apart from the curious rhetorical device of introducing a *topos* of unspeakability (after *everything* seems to have been said), it is striking that this article ends with a fervent call for revenge. It is thus an early example of the rape-revenge plot connected with the events of 1857–1858, which can be found in most late nineteenth-century "Mutiny" romances, and which popular British memory would become obsessed with, until late in the twentieth century.

Along these soon conventionalized lines (treachery, massacre, mutilation, rape) went also the following atrocity story, again taken from the *Times*, which presents a veritable chamber of horrors:

> They took 48 females, most of them girls of [*sic*] from 10 to 14, many delicately nurtured ladies, – violated them and kept them for the base purposes of the heads of the insurrection for a whole week. At the end of that time they made them strip themselves, and gave them up to the lowest of the people to abuse in broad daylight in the streets of Delhi. They then commenced the work of torturing them to death, cutting off their breasts, fingers, and noses, and leaving them to die. One lady was three days dying. (*Times*, August 25, 1857, 6)

---

[13] This is a case of "mediated prospective memory," as discussed by Tenenboim-Weinblatt (2013).

Jenny Sharpe (1993, 66) has pointed out that the "eyewitness" who was responsible for this story was soon afterward exposed by Karl Marx in the *New York Daily Tribune* as "a cowardly parson residing at Bangalore, Mysore, more than a thousand miles, as the bird flies, distant from the scene of the action."

But where did these wild fantasies of rape and mutilation originate? The fact that a host of similar atrocity stories emerged simultaneously in many different places supports the idea that they are a result of premediation. Some of the atrocity stories seem to go back to the then current literary fashion of "Gothic horror." Most of them seem related to a Christian imagination, with its medieval and early Renaissance visions of hell, such as can be found in the works of Dante and Shakespeare, or—especially when it comes to children roasting over fire—in Hieronymus Bosch's paintings.[14] And mediated experiences of anti-colonial resistance, such as "The Black Hole of Calcutta" (1756) or the Haitian revolution (1791), were also reactivated.[15] All of these are texts, genres, and images to which an uninformed public resorts, in order to imagine and make sense of an exotic and dangerous reality that is barely understood. Such processes of premediation usually do not take place intentionally, though. Widely available media often provide their schemata inconspicuously. Premediation is a cultural practice of experiencing and remembering: the use of existent patterns and paradigms to transform contingent events into meaningful images and narratives.

Importantly, as the events of 1857–1858 were turned into an "Indian Mutiny," a powerful new premediator emerged. As Thompson (1925) already argued and as new historical research confirms, anxieties related to memories of the "Mutiny" became a major driver of political and military decisions in the British Empire, where fear, rumors, and perceived threats repeatedly led to preemptive violence. "Mutiny" memories thus unfolded their premediating agency over more than a century after the event.[16]

9.3 Mediating and Remediating "Satichaura Ghat": From Eyewitness Account to Historiography

Atrocities, massacre, and rape are staple elements of "Mutiny" memory to this day. A striking example of how a host of different medial

---

[14] Sharpe (1993, 65) points to "Dante, Ovid, and Shakespeare" as well as to the "Classical and biblical tradition" as premediators.
[15] See Erll (2007, 67); Bender (2016, 127).
[16] Kim Wagner calls this dynamic *The Great Fear of 1857* (2010); see also Bates (2011) and my discussion of the "Mutiny" as part of implicit collective memory in Chapter 12, "The Hidden Power of Implicit Collective Memory."

representations—from eyewitness accounts, newspaper articles, and historiography to novels, paintings, and movies—converged over a large time span into a powerful (yet in India and Britain rather differently interpreted) *lieu de mémoire* is the massacre of the "Satichaura Ghat," which took place in Cawnpore (Kanpur) on June 27, 1857.

Cawnpore was one of the British stations besieged by Indian rebels during the revolt (the other famous one is Lucknow Residency). Under the leadership of the rebel prince Nana Sahib, the Indian sepoys offered General Wheeler and the British residents of Cawnpore safe passage from their besieged entrenchment (the so-called Wheeler's entrenchment). They led them to the Ganges river, where boats were waiting for the defeated colonizers to take them to Allahabad, but fire was opened from an ambush as soon as the British boarded the boats. Several hundred British people were killed: the men instantly, the women several weeks later, after having been taken hostage in a nearby house called "Bibighar." The women's dead bodies were thrown into a well, which, under the name of the "Well of Cawnpore," was turned into one of the best-known memorials of the British in India.[17]

These seem to be the facts that can be established about "Cawnpore."[18] To this day, our knowledge of the Satichaura Ghat massacre rests on less than a handful primary sources. Of the four male British survivors, only two, Mowbray Thomson and W. J. Shepherd, wrote down their memories.[19]

The Indian rebels did not leave behind any written documents. This asymmetry in the archive remains a major problem for historians of "1857–1858" even today.[20] Indian historians (e.g., those of the Subaltern Studies group) usually refer back to the available but strongly biased imperial media representations as sources, but read them "against the grain."[21]

However, in the case of the Satichaura Ghat massacre, this dearth of sources from both sides offers a good opportunity for media memory studies, because the meager body of firsthand material makes "Satichaura Ghat" an excellent laboratory to observe *en détail* how the mediation and remediation of an event occurs.

Mowbray Thomson's "Mutiny" memoir, *Story of Cawnpore*, appeared in 1859. It has become, as Gautam Chakravarty (2005, 111) correctly observes, a "founding template," a text that almost all later remediations of

---

[17] For a fascinating discussion of this memorial and its afterlife, see Pender (2022).
[18] See Mukherjee (1998); Ward (1996).
[19] A further source are the memories of Amelia Horne (after her marriage, Amelia Bennett), published in 1858 under the pseudonym Amy Haines.
[20] See Wagner (2011, 762): "The dearth of contemporary Indian accounts to complement the exuberance of British ones remains a perennial problem facing historians desperately trying to imbue their analysis with a semblance of balance."
[21] For this method, see Guha (1983); Mukherjee (1984).

the massacre refer back to. Thomson was in one of the boats at the *ghat* (shore) when they were under fire and he survived by swimming down the Ganges river, by literally "beating the water for life" (Thomson 1859, 168).[22]

W. J. Shepherd's account of the Cawnpore massacre appeared in Lucknow as early as 1857, under the title *A Personal Narrative of the Outbreak and Massacre at Cawnpore during the Sepoy Revolt of 1857*. This is the first account to be published about the Satichaura Ghat massacre. However, Shepherd did not actually witness the massacre, but managed to escape the Wheeler's entrenchment as a spy dressed in Indian costume. (His masquerade was quickly discovered by the Indians and he was subsequently taken hostage by the Maratha chief Nana Sahib.) What he writes about "Satichaura Ghat" and "Bibighar" is therefore based on hearsay, and much seems to be wrong.[23] Nevertheless, Shepherd's account had a great impact on memory culture—because it appeared very early and because long passages from it were published in the *Times* (in November 1857). Shepherd's story was thus represented in *the* Victorian mass medium; as such, it was widely circulated and readily available to British audiences.

Because of its early appearance, Shepherd's account (but not Thomson's, which was not published until 1859) could enter the best-known historiography of the revolt, Charles Ball's popular, and often jingoistic, *History of the Indian Mutiny* (1858).[24] Ball's book is an example of what may be called "instant history-writing." It tells the story of the revolt even before the fighting was officially ended. Through their lack of hindsight and their determination to record every available representation of the revolt for future memory, such works of history fulfill, as Gautam Chakravarty (2005, 20) points out, "a mediatory function ... distilling a mass of heterogeneous primary material comprising letters, diaries, memoirs, newspaper reports, telegrams, civil and military despatches, parliamentary debates and, sometimes, rumour, and so preparing the ground for history writing in subsequent decades."[25]

---

[22] Later, Thomson exclaims: "how excellent an investment that guinea had proved which I spent a year or two before at the baths in Holborn, learning to swim!" (1859, 190) "Learning to swim" has, as P. J. O. Taylor (1996, 191–192) records, become one of the well-remembered anecdotes connected with the "Indian Mutiny."

[23] See Taylor (1996, 304–305). For Shepherd's reverberative error concerning the place to which the British women and children were brought after the massacre at the Satichaura Ghat, see further below.

[24] Ball does include, however, an earlier eyewitness account written by Thomson, misspelling his name as "Thompson" (Ball 1858, 384).

[25] This also shows clearly that historiography is inherently a "genre of remediation," a text type grounded on the integration of oral and written documents and other mediations of memory; or, as Ann Rigney puts it: "the historian's claim to speak with the authority of reality is paradoxically

Charles Ball's *History of the Indian Mutiny* (1858) is one of the most widely distributed, most richly illustrated, and certainly most popular histories of the revolt. Because of its extensive circulation, it has become an important source for all kinds of other narratives and images of the "Indian Mutiny." Ball's famous "Satichaura Ghat" illustration, for example (see Figure 9.1), is actually one of the most frequently reproduced images of the rebellion, even today (and often enough without any comment as to its source or its ideological implications). The "Ulrica Wheeler" myth, a story about the youngest daughter of General Wheeler, who is said to have killed several sepoys after being abducted by them and in order to "save her honor," also finds popular expression in one of Ball's illustrations (see Figure 9.2).

Ball drew largely on Shepherd's writing. Whole pages of his *History* consist of quotations taken from Shepherd's account in the *Times* (with Ball sometimes correcting obvious errors). Ball's history is therefore an extensive and literal remediation of Shepherd's eyewitness account. With its

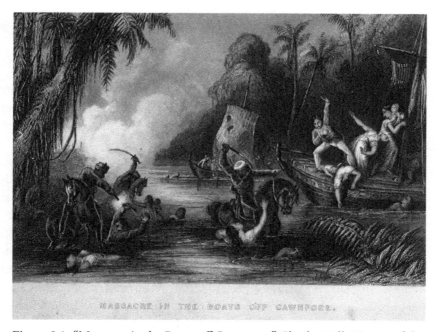

Figure 9.1 "Massacre in the Boats off Cawnpore." Charles Ball, *History of the Indian Mutiny* (1858, 336).

---

linked to his use of *other* discourses" (Rigney 1990, 13). Historiography is dependent on mediated mnemohistory.

Figure 9.2 "Miss Wheeler Defending Herself against the Sepoys at Cawnpore." Charles Ball, *History of the Indian Mutiny* (1858, 380).

wide distribution and huge popularity, the *History of the Indian Mutiny* transported Shepherd's personal memories of the events at Cawnpore as "History" into late nineteenth- and early twentieth-century memory cultures.

What is striking about Ball's *History* is its high degree of repetitiveness. For example, the episode of how British soldiers found the massacred bodies of English women and children in a well near the "Bibighar"—in what was to become the "Well of Cawnpore"—is told several times, each time by quoting a different eyewitness.[26] Such multiple convergent perspectives on the same event have (since the Gospels of the New Testament) an authenticating function. Moreover, the repetitions of certain episodes are in effect remediations. In Ball's *History*, we find the process of mnemonic coalescence in one single medium. No wonder that his book prepared the ground like no other for the emergence of the "Mutiny" as a site of British imperial memory.

In the following two sections, I examine how those early representations of the Cawnpore massacres, which were themselves interlinked in many

---

[26] See Erll (2007, 71–72).

complex ways, became an object for remediation in the late nineteenth century. How were the images and narratives created by Shepherd, Ball, and Thomson turned into the fundament of a both *shared* and *contested* site of memory (i.e., how did British *and* Indian writers refer to "Satichaura Ghat" and "Bibighar")? The subsequent section will move on to a different symbolic system of memory: to literature and to the most prominent literary genre of the nineteenth century, the novel.

9.4 High Imperialism, Remediation, and the Popular Novel: Henty's *In Times of Peril* (1881)

The most important and also, as far as cultural memory is concerned, most resonant period of British "Mutiny" writing is the latter part of the nineteenth century, an age of self-confident and aggressive imperialistic self-fashioning—not least in the medium of literature. In the 1880s, and even more so in the 1890s, the number of published "Mutiny" novels reached a peak. The literary market was flooded by popular romances and juvenile fiction addressing the events of 1857–1858. Examples include G. A. Henty's *Rujub the Juggler* (1893), H. C. Irwin's *A Man of Honour* (1896), J. E. Muddock's *The Great White Hand* (1896), and Flora Annie Steel's *On the Face of the Waters* (1897).

The turn from eyewitness account and history-writing to fiction and the greater freedom of representation associated with the latter result in a further amplification of the "Indian Mutiny" as a site of imperial memory. The "vicious" Nana Sahib's troops become more and more numerous. British soldiers appear more and more heroic. English women by the hundreds are abducted, raped, and/or killed by lecherous sepoys. This "larger than life" version of the "Indian Mutiny" (prepared and supported by other contemporary mediations, such as paintings, sermons, odes, monuments, and popular historiography) would thus enter popular memory and prove very persistent. Even a hundred years later, in contemporary British narrative history, traces of the high-Victorian myth-making can still be discerned.[27]

In 1881, G. A. Henty, one of the empire's most productive bards and successful "recruiting officer for a generation of schoolboys" (Turnbaugh 1975, 735) published *In Times of Peril*, a juvenile adventure novel with a highly

---

[27] For example, in Christopher Hibbert's historiography with the telling title *The Great Indian Mutiny* (1978) or in Saul David's military history *The Indian Mutiny* (2002).

184   TRAVELS IN TIME

propagandistic, didactic, and, not least, mnemonic dimension. The fictive teenage protagonists, the brothers Dick and Ned, take part in every major campaign of the "Indian Mutiny." They experience the siege and the storming of Delhi; they spend time in the Lucknow residency among the besieged and later take part in General Campbell's so-called second relief. They even witness the Satichaura Ghat massacre of Cawnpore:

> Dick and Ned Warrener were in one of the boats which were still ashore when the treacherous sepoys burst from their hiding-place. "The scoundrels!" burst from Ned indignantly; while Dick, seeing at a glance the hopelessness of their position, grasped his brother's arm.
> "We must swim for it, Ned, Take a long dive, and go under again the moment you have got breath."
> Without an instant's delay the brothers leaped into the water, as dozens of others were doing; and although each time their heads came up for an instant the bullets splashed around them, they kept on untouched until they reached the centre of the stream. (Henty 1881, 149–150)

The narrator's account of the boys' adventure echoes *The Story of Cawnpore* quite precisely, thus making the novel one of the numerous remediations of Thomson's textual "founding template." Even more interesting is what Dick and Ned can see with their own eyes, when after having "beaten water for life" (Dick tells his brother to "swim for it," thus recalling Thomson's anecdote) they reach the middle of the Ganges and look back at the Satichaura Ghat:

> They looked back, and saw the sepoys had many of them entered the river up to their shoulders, to shoot the swimmers; others on horseback had ridden far out, and were cutting down those who, unable to swim far, made again toward shallow water; while cannon and muskets still poured in their fire against the helpless crowds in the boats. (Henty 1881, 150)

This is a strikingly precise ekphrasis of Ball's Satichaura Ghat illustration (see Figure 9.1). What is rather strange, however, is that whereas the literary narrative thus evokes the well-known illustration in Charles Ball's *History*, the novel's own illustration of this scene (see Figure 9.3) seems to refer to a different point in the timeline of the massacre. This image, which can be found in the first edition of *In Times of Peril*, is in some ways clearly a

Figure 9.3 "Opening Fire on the Boats." G. A. Henty, *In Times of Peril* (1881, 148).

remediation of Ball's famous Satichaura Ghat image.[28] But more remarkable are the differences between Ball's and Henty's illustrations. The moment in time depicted in Henty's novel is the beginning of the massacre. The British are looking, surprised and shocked, in the direction from which the gunfire seems to come. The illustration in Ball's *History*, on the other hand, shows a later point in time, when the sepoys have followed the British into the water and are killing them with their swords.

This particular choice in the visual representation of the massacre fits well within the novel's overall structure. Even though the narrative does feature scenes in which British people are killed, the illustrations of *In Times of Peril* tell a different story: None of the novel's nineteen images represent the British being violated in any way.[29] On the contrary, the illustrations of *In Times of Peril* usually show colonizers successfully taking action. It is therefore the active and heroic part of the imperial "Mutiny" myth which is

---

[28] This assumption is supported by the fact that here, too, the form of the boats is historically *not* correct: The boats offered by Nana Sahib to the British had roofs which were to protect the white-skinned colonizers from the fierce Indian sun on their long ride to Allahabad (Ward 1996, 301). But the roofs appear neither in Ball's image nor in most of its remediations.

[29] In the "Satichaura Ghat" illustration (see Figure 9.3), there is a single figure in the boat who was apparently shot by the sepoys.

embellished by a specific blend of textual and visual remediation and variation. And this is of course a very appropriate kind of remembering in a novel which was clearly meant to instill imperialist values and norms in its young readers.

9.5 Affirmative Remediation and Subversive Premediation in Indian English Literature: Dutt's *Shunkur* (1877/1878)

The corpus of Indian representations and remediations of the "Mutiny" in the nineteenth century is less clearly defined and accessible than its British counterpart. Presenting an Indian perspective on the revolt was a dangerous thing to do for Indian novelists and historians under the Raj.

It was only in 1909, that is, more than fifty years after the revolt, that the nationalist classic by Vinayak Damodar Savarkar, *The Indian War of Independence* (1909), was published—and immediately banned by the British. Savarkar's pamphlet points to the enormous potential of "1857–1858" as a foundational event of an Indian nationalist memory culture, a potential to which Karl Marx had already drawn attention in 1858 when he called the rebellion the "first Indian war of independence" and emphasized the fact that, for the first time in history, Hindus and Muslims fought side by side against foreign rule.[30]

Not only because of British censorship, but probably also because of the low literacy rate in the nineteenth century, some of the most powerful media of Indian memories of "1857–1858" are to be found not in historical and literary writings, but mainly in oral media, such as ballads and folksongs. The collections of Scholberg (1993) and Joshi (1994) show that there were many ballads about Indian heroes of the revolt, such as the Rani of Jhansi, Tantia Tope, and Kunwar Singh (see also Nayar 2007).

With regard to literary representations of "1857–1858," Veena (1999, 1) maintains that the British had "complete control not only over Indian territory but also over the literary 'space' within which to write about it. It was

---

[30] Wagner (2011, 763) sums up the significance of Savarkar's book as "an important ideological tract of the early nationalist movement with very limited historical value as far as the events of 1857 are concerned." Pender (2022, 131) points out its relevance in a changing memory culture in the wake of the Indian independence movement: The "mutiny's jubilee year" of 1907 "witnessed the emergence of a rather more robust Indian counter-memory that not only challenged the hegemonic nature of British memory but more significantly British hegemonic control of India. Articulated as an inducement to further resistance and even as a guide for future insurrection, this counter-memory encouraged further acts of insubordination and resistance to British rule."

only after Independence that the literary space was opened up to accommodate the Indian perspective(s) on the events of 1857." Nevertheless, leafing through Scholberg's (1993) extensive bibliography, one realizes that there *are* Indian texts about the revolt which were published before 1947, in fact throughout the nineteenth and the early twentieth centuries. These have not been systematically analyzed. Considering the fact that the Indian texts recorded in Scholberg's bibliography are written in Indian regional languages such as Assamese, Bengali, Gujarati, Hindi, Kannada, Marathi, Oriya, Persian, Punjabi, Sindhi, Tamil, Telugu, and Urdu, it becomes clear that an understanding of Indian literary memory cultures and their representations of "1857–1858" must be an interdisciplinary project, one which would have to bring together scholars of various languages who engage with different regional literatures on 1857.

For a wide-ranging mnemohistory of "1857–1858," it is important to broaden the medial basis, integrating Indian newspaper articles, letters, ballads, images, and literary texts as representations of "1857–1858" in their own right.[31] This would mean drawing on the "archive" of recorded documents, as well as on the oral-performative, more ephemeral "repertoire" (to use a distinction made by Diana Taylor, 2003). Indian memories of the rebellion were mainly expressed in the form of a "repertoire." Pender (2022, 133) describes them as largely "unrecorded and leaving few traces of [their] existence."[32] But he also shows impressively that acts of vandalism against British "Mutiny" memorials (recorded, again, by British authorities) are an interesting source for understanding Indian counter-memories during the nineteenth century through "everyday acts of resistance" (Pender 2022, 135).[33]

---

[31] For important Indian sources made more recently available in English, see Kaushik (2008) and Farooqui (2010). Wagner (2011, 761) confirms: "New types of sources, such as oral accounts, folklore and songs, are increasingly used to explore popular histories and the memory of the Indian Uprising." Wagner (2018) breaks new ground for what might be called a "forensic memory-approach" (*sensu* Keenan and Weizman 2012) to "1857–1858" using a skull of an Indian rebel as a cue for a discussion of the events, also in light of the collection and exhibition of human remains in colonial and postcolonial contexts.

[32] About the "counter-commemorative landscape" Pender (2022, 132–133) states: "Whilst it would be naïve to imagine that Indian counter-memories did not exist, or failed to attach themselves to physical spaces, these memories were very often constructed from rather more furtive and entirely less enduring materials than their colonial equivalents and, as a result, often faded without ever leaving a trace within the imperial archive."

[33] This would culminate around the tenth anniversary of Indian independence in what a *Times* correspondent calls a "Holocaust of British Statues" in India (Pender 2022, 183). Today's memory activism and the decommissioning of monuments (Rigney 2023) draw on time-honored subaltern and postcolonial practices.

However, a few narratives that constitute an "Indian literary archive" do exist, and it is worthwhile taking a closer look at them: One of the best-known Indian works of fiction in English to have represented the events of 1857–1858 is Shoshee Chunder Dutt's short novel *Shunkur*, first published in 1877/1878. Shoshee Chunder Dutt (1824–1886) belongs to the famous Dutt family, a Bengali middle-class, Anglicized family of poets, journalists, and historians.[34] His writing can be placed at the beginning of the Bengal Renaissance. However, unlike more overtly nationalist Bengali writers, such as Bankim Chandra Chatterjee, Dutt did not turn to Bangla at some stage in his career, but chose to write exclusively in English throughout his life. In fact, "Shoshee's seemingly ambiguous poetic investment in the culture of the colonizer has meant that his prose, while representing some of the earliest fiction in English by a South Asian, has received scant attention in nationalist, Marxist and postcolonial literary histories" (Tickell 2005, 8). It is the aim of the following interpretation to uncover, with the help of concepts such as remediation and premediation, some of the anti-colonial criticism that even such an "elite Indian-English literary response" (Tickell 2005, 8) may express.[35]

Two main storylines can be distinguished in *Shunkur*. One is about Nana Sahib; the other is about the fictive character Shunkur. The Nana Sahib story features the Cawnpore massacres—as we have seen, a key element of the British memory of the "Indian Mutiny." Here, Dutt closely follows the *topoi* and narratives of the imperial media culture: Nana Sahib is depicted as an evil, decadent, and lecherous villain. The fictive story about Shunkur, however, is quite another matter. It begins in the Indian village Soorájpore. A young Indian woman shows compassion for two British soldiers on the run after the massacres at the Satichaura Ghat and offers them shelter in her house. The soldiers, Mackenzie and Bernard, however, reciprocate this good deed by raping the woman, who is so ashamed that she commits suicide. Her brother and her husband, Probhoo and Shunkur, find her dead body when they return from the market and vow revenge. They get involved in the revolt, fight on Nana Sahib's side, and find the rapists in the end. They kill the British villains and then, as their revenge is fulfilled, return to their village.

Shunkur is a good example of remediation on various levels. The way Nana Sahib is characterized as a villain and the introduction of the rape-revenge plot are remediations of the imperial British representation

---

[34] The historian Romesh Chunder Dutt is Shoshee Chunder Dutt's nephew.
[35] On Shoshee Chunder Dutt's writing, see also Mukherjee (2000).

of the "Indian Mutiny." Moreover, Dutt closely follows the British conventions of selection and highlighting. There are lengthy descriptions of the massacres at the Satichaura Ghat and in the Bibighar; and even the myth of "Ulrica Wheeler" is repeated in *Shunkur* (for Ball's illustration, see Figure 9.2). The sheer extent of Dutt's remediation becomes evident when his description of the Cawnpore massacres is compared with W. J. Shepherd's account in the *Times*:

W. J. Shepherd's "A Personal Narrative" in the *Times* (November 7, 1857, 7)	Shoshee Chunder Dutt's *Shunkur* (1885, 107)
The women and children, most of whom were wounded, some with three or four bullet shots in them, were spared and brought to the Nana's camp, and placed in a pukka building called "Subada Ke-Kothee."	Of the women and children several were wounded, and some of these were released from their sufferings by death, while the rest were confined in a puccá-house called "Subádá Kothee."
One young lady, however, was seized upon (reported to be General Wheeler's daughter) and taken away by a trooper of the 2nd Light Cavalry to his home, where she at night, finding a favourable opportunity, secured the trooper's sword, and with it, after killing him and three others, threw herself into a well and was killed.	One young lady only had been seized upon previously by a trooper of the 2nd Light Cavalry, and carried off to his own quarters, where she was violently treated; but, finding a favourable opportunity, she rose up at night, and securing her ravisher's sword, avenged herself by killing him and three others, after which she flung herself into a well, and was killed.

Quite obviously, Dutt copied Shepherd's account and integrated it into his literary text.[36] Such forms of plagiarism, though, are no anomaly in the history of remediating "1857–1858." As we have seen, Ball copied long passages from Shepherd's account into his *History of the Indian Mutiny*, and Henty drew on and amalgamated the representations of Thomson and Ball in only one page of his *In Times of Peril*. In *Shunkur*, however, the unmarked

---

[36] He also copied Shepherd's mistake. Shepherd (and after him Ball and Henty, but not Thomson) falsely assumes that the women were brought into the "Subádá Kothee" (instead of the nearby "Bibighar").

integration of British eyewitness accounts (along with all the imperialist stereotypes about Nana Sahib and "Cawnpore") is especially striking, because it seems that this nominally "Indian" version of the revolt is to a large extent nothing more than a remediation of British representations. The plagiarism can be understood as an example of "audience-tuning"[37] in the production of cultural memory: the adjustment of communication to (parts of) an intended audience. It serves as a *captatio benevolentiae*, indicating to a British readership, to which the novel was obviously also addressed,[38] that *Shunkur* is a "proper and authentic" account of the Mutiny, even though it was written by a colonial subject. What Homi Bhabha (1994) would call an instance of "colonial mimicry" is an effect of transcultural memory, and it operates by remediation. The novel thus may appear as yet another expression of a British-dominated memory culture, one that stabilizes the imperial *lieu de mémoire* through constant transcription, even across the boundaries of colonizer and colonized.

The storyline which features Shunkur's revenge, however, unfolds quite a different dynamics. It is a subversive version of Indian counter-memory. First of all, the adventures of Shunkur and Probhoo are an early representation of the "peasant armed," whom revisionist historiography of the revolt "discovered" only after 1947 and then turned into a central subject matter.[39] Dutt's fictional narrative imaginatively represents the lived experience of the host of peasants and small landowners who took part in the revolt, but whose testimony did not circulate within nineteenth-century British and Anglo-Indian memory cultures, because their memories were never written down in letters or autobiographies (as almost all of the British witnesses' were) and thus were never coded in one of the leading media of those cultures. Second, *Shunkur* inverts the British rape-revenge plot. Now it is the Indian woman, not the English woman, who is assaulted and must be revenged.

With regard to the simultaneous presence of British and Indian perspectives on the revolt in *Shunkur*, Meenakshi Mukherjee (2003, 95) concludes that "Dutt takes special care to distribute sympathy evenly between the

---

[37] This is a concept developed in psychology; see Echterhoff et al. (2005).

[38] Dutt is one of the first Indian writers to be published both in India and in Britain, thus reaching educated Indian elites and "Anglo-India" (the British then living in India), as well as an interested reading public back in the "colonial center," Great Britain.

[39] Notably in Eric T. Stokes's historiography *The Peasant Armed* (1986); see also Guha (1983) and Mukherjee (1984). *Shunkur* can also be placed in the tradition of Bengali literature on "peasant suffering," which was developed into a powerful trope of Bengali fiction from the mid-nineteenth century onward, especially by Dinabandhu Mitra's influential drama *Nil Darpan* [The Mirror of Indigo] (1858–1859). I am grateful to Indra Sengupta-Frey, who drew my attention to this fact.

British and the Indians. If officers like Bernard and Mackenzie are despicable enough to rape the woman who has given them shelter, Nanasaheb's treachery and promiscuity are foregrounded as if to provide a balance in villainy." Such an interpretation can certainly be backed by looking at the authorial narrator's comments, who is at pains to politely but firmly revise some British misconceptions about the revolt.

However, the Shunkur storyline goes beyond such a conciliatory endeavor, and it does so once again with a strategy of medial remembering. Except in this case, it is a canonical text of *Indian* memory cultures that the novel draws on. *Shunkur* can be read as a story of the rebellion which is premediated by the Indian epic *Mahabharata*'s mythical narrative about the beautiful Draupadi, who was married to the five brothers of the Pandava family: One of Draupadi's five husbands gambled away his land, his brothers, and his wife to the family of their cousins, the Kauravas. As a slave in the service of the Kauravas, Draupadi is almost raped by her husbands' cousins Duryodhana and Dushasana (but the Lord Krishna shows compassion and restores her garments as fast as they are torn). Draupadi's husband Bhima vows revenge and kills the cousins in the end. As Pamela Lothspeich (2007) has shown, the glorification of Draupadi as an allegory of "Mother India" can be traced back to late colonial Hindi literature, when many Draupadi parables were produced. Early twentieth-century drama, for example, drew on the myth of Draupadi's violation and used it as an allegory for the conquest of "Mother India" by the British. If we assume that *Shunkur* is an early version of such parables, then its rape-revenge plot is not only an inversion of a powerful British "Mutiny" *topos*. It has in addition a mythological dimension, which carries a proto-nationalist subtext—a subtext which the British reader would not necessarily expect or understand, if one goes by the medial mimicry on the text's surface.

Mukherjee (2003, 95) points out that "Shunkur's vendetta against those who raped his wife is made out to be a purely personal matter with no political overtones." This is what the ending of the novel in particular seems to point to. Shunkur's last words are: "there is no further motive for the life we were obliged to adopt; let us go back to our cheerless home" (Dutt 1885, 158). When read according to the conventions of Western-realist narratives of the nineteenth century, this is indeed a return to the apolitical sphere. On its surface, *Shunkur* neither comments on politics nor on the process of British-Indian history. But if we regard the novel as being premediated by the *Mahabharata*, then it is possible to decode from the literal story an allegorical dimension. After the "rape of Mother India" has been avenged and the perpetrators MacKenzie and Bernard (obviously standing for British imperialism) are taken to account, there is indeed nothing else to do than to "return home," that is, to try to resume the old ways of living. The novel's premediation by Indian myths thus defies British memory of the "Mutiny." It represents an alternative memory and performs an act of "remembering back" (Rothberg 2013). It provides a glimpse of a "future past" of the revolt of 1857–1858—the vision of an avenged "Mother India"— and inscribes this vision (however implicitly) into the Anglophone archive of "Mutiny" mediations.

9.6 "Mutiny" in Hollywood: *The Charge of the Light Brigade* (1936)

In the twentieth century, the "Indian Mutiny" continued to be constructed and reconstructed as a *lieu de mémoire*. New media (such as film, radio, television, and the internet), as well as an altered geopolitical landscape (decolonization, Indian independence in 1947), engendered new and altered forms of "symbolic investment."

Critical essays, such as Edward Thompson's *The Other Side of the Medal* (1925) and F. W. Buckler's *The Political Theory of the Indian Mutiny* (1922), and revisionist historiography, such as Eric Stokes's *The Peasant Armed* (1981) and Ranajit Guha's *Elementary Aspects of Peasant Insurgency* (1983), have challenged the imperial canon of events, heroes, and narrative structures, cherished myths, and *topoi*.[40] In the realm of literature, the late twentieth century saw a considerable increase of revisionist historical novels dealing with the Indian Mutiny (e.g., J. G. Farrell's *The Siege of Krishnapur*, 1973), of representations of the revolt in Indian English writing (Khushwant Singh's *Delhi*, 1989), in novels emerging from the Indian diaspora (Vikram Chandra's *Red Earth and Pouring Rain*, 1995), and from multicultural Britain (Zadie Smith's *White Teeth*, 2000). What they all have in common is that they move away from the imperial adventure and romance model of narrating the "Indian Mutiny" (of which Henty's novels are a good example) and open up new ways of remembering the revolt by using new narrative forms of representation (such as unreliability, multiperspectivity,

---

[40] For overviews of recent trends in the historiography of "1857–1858," see Wagner (2011) and Raugh (2017).

tales within tales, etc.).[41] In the remaining sections of this chapter, however, I will take a look at what has arguably become one of the most powerful media of symbolic investment into sites of memory: popular cinema.

Many of the most popular movies about imperial history emerged from the so-called Cinema of Empire (Richards 1973) during the 1930s and 1940s. But interestingly, it was not the British but rather the American film industry which set out to remember the "Indian Mutiny": Michael Curtiz's *The Charge of the Light Brigade* (1936) is a classic of the Empire Cinema made in Hollywood, and it is a striking cinematic version of the "Mutiny." Although the name "Cawnpore" never appears in this movie, with its plot of Indian treachery and rebellion *The Charge of the Light Brigade* certainly belongs in the long line of "Mutiny" remediations. More than five minutes of the film show a massacre of British civilians by Indian soldiers, a massacre which takes place after a long siege of an English station has ended and safe passage has been offered to the British by a rebellious Indian prince (see Figure 9.4).

Figure 9.4 *The Charge of the Light Brigade* (1936, dir. Michael Curtiz), massacre at the river.

---

[41] See Erll (2007). On literary memories of 1857–1858, see also Chakravarty (2005); Das and Arya (2009); Siddique (2012).

There is, once again, a British spy dressed in native garment who tries to leave the besieged station undetected, but is found out and killed by the rebels. Even the rape motif so dear to the British newspapers is integrated into the movie, when a Sikh tries to abduct the heroine (see Figure 9.5).

As the title of the movie, with its open reference to Alfred Lord Tennyson's famous poem about the Crimean War ("The Charge of the Light Brigade," 1854), already indicates, Curtiz's movie actually conflates two British sites of imperial memory, the "Indian Mutiny" and the "Crimean War." It is therefore a good example of further processes of convergence. To the Hollywood producers and American audiences, memories of British imperialism were foreign and not relevant to their identity. Thus, separate historical events could easily be amalgamated into one single *topos* of "violence and the British Empire." And apparently, their temporal sequence could also be altered: in Curtiz's movie, the Indian rebellion of 1857–1858 precedes the Crimean War of 1854–1856.

The fact that "Mutiny" narratives migrated to the Hollywood cinema of the 1930s points to yet another basic process of memory in media cultures:

Figure 9.5 *The Charge of the Light Brigade* (1936, dir. Michael Curtiz), abduction of white female by Indian rebel.

Mediations of the rebellion had by then turned into a powerful premediator. The "Mutiny" had become a narrative schema which could be used to create successful stories. In this sense, the rebellion is not only a *lieu de mémoire* shared by the British and the Indian people, but can be seen as a source of transnationally available patterns of representation.[42] As a transcultural schema, the "Indian Mutiny" had become decontextualized. In 1930s Hollywood, "Mutiny" does not refer to a specific historical event, perceived in a clearly demarcated spatiotemporal context and related to cultural identity. It had instead been turned into a narrative template used to tell stories of good and evil, valor and treachery—carrying with it, however, the ideology of a mnemonic form that was created in the context of British imperialism.[43]

But while in the United States the "Indian Mutiny" was used as an effective narrative schema for entertainment and box-office successes, the British government in India was rather sensitive about the revolt as a theme of popular cinema. As Prem Chowdhry (2000, 29) points out in his study on the historical reception of the Empire Cinema, *The Charge of the Light Brigade* was "considered by British officials in India a 'painful reminder of Indian history which has better left unrecalled.'" The reason for this hesitancy is, as Pender points out, a "significant shift in commemorative power" during the 1930s: "As Britain began to censor its own memory of the mutiny for fear that its expression would consolidate antiimperial sentiment and occasion new spaces of protest, an overtly nationalist memory of the War of Independence began to emerge from the shadows and dominate the imagination of many individuals engaged in the freedom movement" (Pender 2022, 132, 153).

It is for such political reasons that no "Mutiny" film emerged from the *British* Cinema of Empire during the 1930s and 1940s. Producers were very interested in the "Mutiny" as a theme, but British censorship intervened, for example in 1936 when plans for a movie called *The Relief of Lucknow* were made. The president of the British Board of Film Censors (BBFC), Lord Tyrrell, warned: "The B.B.F.C. has been advised by all the authorities

---

[42] In fact, the "Mutiny," and especially the figure of Nana Sahib, had soon become a favored subject of popular entertainment all over the world. In nineteenth-century Germany, for example, Theodor Fontane wrote about the Indian revolt, and in France, Jules Verne.

[43] In 1930s Hollywood, the Cinema of Empire is structurally and ideologically not very different from the major American genre of that time, the Western. According to the film historian Jeffrey Richards (1973, 3–4), "Americans do seem to have responded to Britain's folk myths in the same way that Britain responds to America's, the Westerns. There is in fact an area of cross-reference between the two genres."

responsible for the government of India, both civil and military, that in their considered opinion, such a film would revive memories of the days of conflict in India which it had been the earnest endeavor of both countries to obliterate with a view to promoting harmonious cooperation between the two peoples" (qtd. in Richards 1973, 42). And two years later, an official of the Government of India wrote about the same issue:

> May I say how extraordinarily dangerous I think any such film would be in India today. In the first place young nationalist India is extraordinarily sensitive about the whole Mutiny episode. To them it was the first wave of national movement for independence. . . . It would most certainly provoke a crop of films from Indian companies setting forth the Indian version of the Mutiny, and it would be extraordinarily difficult for the Government of India to censor or suppress them if it had allowed a British film of the Mutiny to appear. Further, Hollywood has long been itching to use the Mutiny as a theme. . . . There will be no means of stopping Hollywood from pouring out versions of its own which would probably infuriate both Britain and India. (qtd. in Chowdhry 2000, 30–31)

In these remarks, we can sense the power exerted by popular mediated memory. British officials feared both, a cinematic counter-memory made in India and an uncontrollable Hollywood machine, which might appropriate and commodify the memory of 1857–1858 without considering its political implications for the British Empire.

9.7 Bollywood "Films Back": Ketan Mehta's *The Rising* (2005)

My final example of a remediation of the Indian rebellion turns to the twenty-first century and to one of its biggest movie industries: Bollywood.[44] Just like the newspapers of the nineteenth century, Indian Bollywood movies reach large parts of the populace. Bollywood is not only the most powerful film industry in Asia. It also exports its products to Europe and the United States, where members of the Asian diaspora in particular account for its large audiences.

It is here (more than in the Anglophone novel) that memories of the 1857–1858 rebellion are still very much alive and continuously remediated,

---

[44] Kavoori and Punathambekar (2008); Anjaria (2021).

especially in the wake of its 150th and 160th anniversaries. *Umrao Jaan* (2006, dir. J. P. Dutta) and *Jaanisaar* (2015, dir. Muzaffar Ali) remediate a well-known Urdu novel about a courtesan in Lucknow (Mirza Muhammed Hadi Ruzwa's *Umrao Jaan Ada*, 1899). The fact that *Manikarnika: The Queen of Jhansi* (2019, dir. Radha Krishna Jagarlamudi and Kangana Ranaut) became one of the highest-grossing female-centric films in India is an indicator of the particularly strong resonance of the Rani of Jhansi figure in Indian collective memory today.

A highly controversial example of widely distributed Bollywood versions of 1857–1858 is Ketan Mehta's *The Rising* (2005). It is a film about Mangal Pandey, the first mutineer of 1857. *The Rising* is a clear instance of what may be called "filming back." It revises some of the most tenacious of the British myths: Instead of a drugged and ragged rioting sepoy (as borne out by colonial historical records), we see a proud and utterly sober Mangal Pandey (and when he consumes cannabis—"bhang"—he does so in the company of his British friend Gordon). While British accounts center on the rape of English women, *The Rising* depicts an organized setting up of brothels by the East India Company, where abducted Indian women have to be at the service of British soldiers. And whereas British historiography tends to describe the rebellion of 1857 as unorganized and chaotic, *The Rising* gives an account of a carefully planned, concerted action.[45]

This alternative version of the events of 1857–1858 presented by the movie drew some criticism, especially in Britain. In interviews given to several British newspapers in the summer of 2005, historian Saul David criticized the film, which was partly funded by the UK Film Council, for what he saw as its "historical inaccuracy."[46] But of course, *The Rising* is a *fictional* medium of memory. It is, moreover, part of the Mumbai film industry, which is famous for its highly melodramatic plots and black-and-white characterization, an aesthetic that starkly contrasts with classical Hollywood realism. Had it created a story in line with British military historiography, it would have failed dramatically *as a movie* (a movie, at that, directed primarily at Indian audiences). Cultural memory is produced not only by different media (oral speech, written documents, film) but also within different symbolic

---

[45] Historian Wagner (2010, 245) emphasizes that "there is little historical evidence to back up any of these revisionist interpretations of the events of 1857." More often than not, they are simple inversions of the British "Mutiny" myth.

[46] For example in an interview given to the *Sunday Telegraph* (August 14, 2005), which appeared under the sensational title "Lottery-Funded Film under Fire for Anti-British Bias" (see Hastings and Jones 2005).

systems (art, history, religion). Each of these has specific characteristics and limitations. A fictional film, even if it is a "history film," cannot be judged by using criteria that are derived from "history" as an academic discipline, because movies function according to a different symbolic system. This does not mean, however, that the production of cultural memory through literature, movies, and the arts cannot be criticized. What is needed is a different methodology, one which allows us to address the "ideology of memorial form" through, for example, an analysis of narrative voice, perspective structures, character constellations, the use of imagery, or (as in the following) medial structures and references.

The central message of *The Rising* is its linking of revolt and independence—in 1857 and 1947, respectively—as two national sites of memory. This linkage, which is still prevalent in postcolonial Indian memory cultures,[47] is made in *The Rising* verbally and visually. At the beginning of the movie, the following words appear on the screen:

> The man who changed history
> his courage inspired a nation
> his sacrifice gave birth to a dream
> his name will forever stand for FREEDOM

A key scene of the film is a British massacre of Indian peasants (see Figure 9.6). Historically, this episode is not recorded, or at least not as having taken place during the time immediately preceding the outbreak

Figure 9.6 *The Rising* (2005, dir. Ketan Mehta), massacre of Indian peasants.

---

[47] For a critical assessment of this version of Indian history, see Ray (2003).

of the mutinies in the spring of 1857. It does evoke, however, the time *after* the "Mutiny," the cruel British campaigns of counterinsurgency in 1858. Moreover, the episode recalls and inverts the British Satichaura Ghat myth, a technique similar to Dutt's inverted rape narrative. And finally, this scene is related to the palimpsest of new memories and medial representations which have emerged since Indian independence. It draws on the iconographic memory connected with the Indian freedom struggle, because it quite clearly is a visual echo of the Amritsar massacre in the Jallianwala Bagh (1919), which was similarly represented in countless movies about British India. The version most popular worldwide can be found in Richard Attenborough's *Gandhi* of 1982 (see Figure 9.7). The episode, in short, condenses the complex of "colonial violence" into one image.

It is in line with so many historical cross-references that we find in the final credits of *The Rising* the image of Mangal Pandey cross-faded with well-known images of Gandhi's freedom movement: Indians on a protest march, probably footage from the Quit India campaign of 1942 (see Figure 9.8). This is an apt visualization of the medial processes which are at the basis of all *lieux de mémoire*: images, *topoi*, and narratives about the past are brought together and "cross-faded," condensed into a single site of memory. Such a creation of a "maximum amount of meaning in a minimum number of signs" is made possible through the repeated representation of historical events, usually across the whole spectrum of culturally available media technologies and forms.

Figure 9.7 *Gandhi* (1982, dir. Richard Attenborough), the Jallianwala Bagh massacre of 1919.

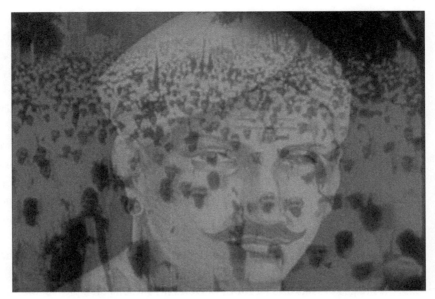

Figure 9.8 *The Rising* (2005, dir. Ketan Mehta), cross-fading of the image of Mangal Pandey with footage of Indian protest marches from the 1940s.

9.8 Conclusion: Memory in India Today

Sites of memory derive their meaning only within the context of (increasingly globalizing) media cultures. Medial representations surround, constitute, and modify memory. They function according to different technologies, affordances, symbolic systems, and within ever-changing sociopolitical constellations. Medial representations of the past, moreover, refer to one another, preform and reshape cultural memories, and they do so across the boundaries of time, space, and cultures. In this sense, all *lieux de mémoire* (and not only those "belonging" to two different nations) are "shared sites of memory." They are shared by different social classes, political camps, generations, religious groups, and regional cultures (above as well as below the level of the national), and not least by different media cultures—with their specific practices of representation and reception.

In twenty-first-century India, the events of 1857–1858 have become "the subject of enormous commemorative attention" (Pender 2022, 190). Indian memory entrepreneurs and activists since the 1970s have brought to the fore folk tales, ballads, and oral histories especially about Indian rebel leaders such as Tantia Tope, Mangal Pandey, and Rani Lakshmibai (the Rani of Jhansi). At the same time, the memory constellation in present-day India is highly diversified. The "respective acts of commemoration deployed by each group to celebrate 1857 is inextricably intertwined with specific conceptions of caste, class, gender, and religion" (Pender 2022, 218).

In the wake of the 150th and 160th anniversaries of the Indian Rebellion, memories of "Rani Lakshmibai" and "Uda Devi" are used to express Dalit memory, feminist memory, Hindu nationalist memory, or memories of intercommunal solidarity. It is this latter aspect in particular that also informs *The Rising*. Clearly, such memories in present-day India, which is deeply divided, unfold an enormous agency of a "past potentiality," pointing to the possibility of a collaborative effort of Hindus and Muslims, of men and women, of upper and lower castes and classes. Proponents of such hopeful versions of the past, such as journalist Amaresh Misra, understand their memory-making as a "new message of 'equality, tolerance, and unity based on the lessons of 1857'" (qtd. in Pender 2022, 218).[48]

Historians are more cautious. They point to evidence of divisiveness among rebels and warn against simplification: "Simply reversing the colonial hagiographies and exchanging Lawrence with Tantia Tope, or Nicholson with Mangal Pandey, does not advance our understanding of the past" (Wagner 2010, xxvi).

Ever since the beginning of the rebellion, the events of "1857–1858" have been turned into foundational myths. Such myths produce legitimacy— either for present politics or for alternative visions of the future—through the creation of genealogy and a sense of legacy. But questions remain, namely, a genealogy *of what*, a legacy *for what*? Is "1857–1858" a foundational event of extreme violence or of proto-national solidarity?

Any "foundational event" version of the rebellion will forever be at odds with the historiographic evidence of excessive violence on both sides. This is true for Indian memory cultures today, as it was for British imperial memory in the nineteenth century. A more productive way forward might be to recognize the Indian rebels as "implicated subjects" (Rothberg 2019), who were victims of British colonialism and *at the same time* may have become perpetrators, indiscriminately killing Anglo-Indian civilians; who may have acted together in solidarity in one place, but followed feudal or religious agendas in other places. There is simply not one sweeping moral narrative to be had,

---

[48] See Misra (2005, 2008).

if historical evidence is carefully taken into account. (And this is what the Indian Rebellion shares with most other violent conflicts.) But this does not disable the Indian rebellion as a site of memory. In fact, it can be a motor for the creation of a better future—provided that those who remember do so responsibly and acknowledge the particularity of the past potentialities that they mobilize.

Chapter 10
Plurimediality and Traveling Schemata

"District Six"

10.1 Aliens in Johannesburg: "District Six" in International Cinemas

In the year 1982 an alien spaceship appears over the South African city of Johannesburg (see Figure 10.1). The extra-terrestrials are in a state of utter destitution, many of them dead, sick, or malnourished. They are obviously unable to find their way home again. A camp is set up for these aliens just outside Johannesburg. It is called "District 9" (see Figure 10.2). In the decades that follow, the camp deteriorates into a slum area, ripe with violence, drug abuse and inter-species prostitution. Because of their crustacean-like appearance, the aliens are derogatorily called "prawns," and all humans in Johannesburg seem to agree that "the prawns must go." In 2010, the South African government decides on a relocation scheme and

Figure 10.1 *District 9* (2009, dir. Neill Blomkamp), the alien spaceship over Johannesburg.

Figure 10.2 *District 9* (2009, dir. Neill Blomkamp), District 9, shot on location in Chiawelo, Johannesburg.

contracts Multi-National United (MNU), a private company mainly interested in alien weaponry, to transfer the aliens to a new camp at a safe distance of 200 kilometers from the city: "District 10." Wikus van de Merwe (Sharlto Copley), a simple Afrikaner clerk at MNU, is to lead this operation, assisted by a brutal armed force—but he fails: While handing out eviction notices to the inhabitants of District 9, he accidentally touches a spray with alien DNA, mutates into an alien, is hunted by his own government, finds refuge in District 9, and learns to sympathize with the outcasts whom he finally helps to escape in their spaceship.

This is the story of *District 9*, a movie directed by the South African filmmaker Neill Blomkamp and produced by Peter Jackson. It came out in 2009 to great international acclaim. The movie starts as a mock-documentary, combining fictional interviews, television news footage, and videos from surveillance cameras (see Figure 10.3). This fictive footage, all edited at a rapid pace, reconstructs from the vantage point of a near future the fictional history of aliens in Johannesburg since 1982 and provides "evidence" of Wikus van de Merwe's actions and whereabouts up to the point at which he disappears from the radars of MNU and the South African government into District 9. Halfway through the movie, the mock-documentary mode changes into a conventional cinematic narrative. Wikus's unrecorded further fate, his transformation into an alien, is represented much in the style of alien movies from the 1980s.

Figure 10.3 *District 9* (2009, dir. Neill Blomkamp), forced removals viewed from surveillance cameras.

District 9, the alien movie set in Johannesburg, does something that seems worth drawing attention to in a book on traveling memory. This has to do with the obvious reference, in its title, to Cape Town's District Six. With its focus on a government scheme that aims at moving aliens dwelling in an inner-city slum area to an internment camp outside the city, the movie clearly refers to the history of apartheid and the ways in which it was acted out in South African cities. In enormous relocation schemes, the country's less-privileged people, mostly "black" and "coloured," were forcibly moved from inner-city compounds to townships at the fringes of the cities.

In a science-fiction setting and an allegorical framework, the movie re-enacts the violent history of apartheid, which, although it belongs to the past now, has permanently shaped the face of South African cities. It does so by substituting South Africa's history of racism with a present-day story about speciesism: humans of all races fight against aliens. In this fictional fight, those acquainted with South Africa's history of apartheid will find many ironic echoes—for example, an interviewee's wish to kill all aliens with a "selective virus" or Wikus's wholesale abortion in District 9 (once fantasies of radical white Afrikaners); the ubiquitous boards prescribing segregation (see Figure 10.4); the MNU's hypocritical argument to evict aliens for "humanitarian reasons"; the fact that the alien language features clicking sounds, which are also typical of Bantu languages, spoken for example by the Xhosa people who were victims of South African apartheid.

Figure 10.4 *District 9* (2009, dir. Neill Blomkamp), apartheid between humans and aliens.

In postcolonial studies, there has been work on how alien movies, from *Alien Nation* (1988) to *Independence Day* (1996), address, articulate, and reframe ideas and anxieties about race (for example, Sardar and Cubitt's *Aliens R Us*, 2002). It would certainly be interesting to study how this tried and tested allegorical pattern is transformed in *District 9*, which leaves the spectator feeling utterly alienated by the violence and mercilessness of the humans, but also reintroduces new racist patterns, for example in its depiction of Nigerians.

But the main aim of this chapter is to address a somewhat different question: If an alien movie is set in Johannesburg, if it half-mockingly, half-critically refers to segregation as it was practiced in South Africa, if it shows the dubiety and inhumanity of an apartheid legislation that enables forced removals, if, in fact, the movie is shot on location in a part of Soweto, the squatter camp of Chiawelo—then why is such a movie not called "Aliens in Soweto," or, for that matter, "Aliens in Sophiatown," thus referring to the inner-city districts and townships that actually belong to the city of Johannesburg and its apartheid history? Why "District 9"?

It seems that, rather than Sophiatown or Soweto, it is Cape Town's District Six that, since the end of apartheid, has been turned into a powerful transnationally available schema to draw on, when it comes to giving form to issues of racism, victimization, and segregation in urban space, and the forced removal of people from their original place.

According to cognitive psychology, schemata are patterns and structures of knowledge, on the basis of which we make assumptions regarding specific objects, people, situations, and the relation between them. Schemata reduce complexity and guide perception and remembering. As Frederic Bartlett showed as early as in 1932 (in *Remembering*), schemata are always culture-specific.[1] They emerge from socially shared knowledge systems. In our age of global media cultures and transnational migration, the circles or social frameworks (*sensu* Halbwachs 1925) of this sharing are ever-expanding. With migrants and mass media as their carriers, cultural schemata are set to "travel" and may thus acquire transcultural and transnational dimensions (Erll 2011b). They appear and are actualized in different local contexts across the world. In the form of traveling schemata, patterns of knowledge cut across boundaries of language, communities, and nations.

In order to describe the transnational dynamics of remembering connected with "District Six," I will, in the following, distinguish between two categories of schemata: visual schemata (*icons*), which are the result of iconization, and story schemata (*narratives*), which are the result of topization and narrativization. The focus will be on the medial—more precisely, plurimedial—production of key icons and narratives about District Six. The goal is to understand how the "District Six" schema has been set to travel: from Cape Town to Johannesburg, from South Africa to worldwide cinemas, from the serious, and violent, history of apartheid to the half-mocking imagination of an alternative alien present.

10.2 District Six and the History of South African Apartheid

When the apartheid regime came into power in South Africa in 1948, an array of new laws was brought about: The Prohibition of Mixed Marriages Act of 1949 put a ban on marriages between "white people" and people of other "races."[2] The Immorality Amendment Act of 1950 prohibited

---

[1] District Six can of course also be understood as *lieux de mémoire*, a site of memory in Pierre Nora's sense. With my discussion of "District Six" as a schema, I highlight the importance of medial *and* cognitive processes for memory and the insight that mnemonic contents can be set to travel only once they have been transformed into highly condensed patterns. Such patterns have variously been conceptualized in memory studies as schemata, symbols, memory figures, pathos formulas, or memory sites (see also Erll 2011a, 146; for a conceptualization of "schematic narrative templates," see Wertsch 2021).

[2] I quote the language of the apartheid regime here. On "non-racialism" and the persistence of "race" in South African politics and urban space, see Southall (2023).

extra-marital sexual relationships between "white" and "black" people. The Population Registration Act of 1950 meant that every person's race was classified and recorded in a national register. This register knew the categories of four racial groups: "native," "white," "coloured," and "Asian." The Group Areas Act of 1950 put all these forms of segregation into spatial practice. It created "apartheid" within the city itself, segregating people of different races into different urban spaces.

The aim of the Group Areas Act was to exclude non-whites from living in the most developed and attractive urban areas. They were forcibly removed from their neighborhoods and dumped in townships which were often far away from the city centers. Cape Town's District Six was declared a "white area" under the Group areas Act in 1966. In 1968 the forced removals started. The district's inhabitants were relocated in the Cape Flats-township complex, in a previously uninhabited flat and sandy area more than twenty kilometers southeast of Cape Town, often called "the dumping ground of apartheid." The forced removals stretched over a period of more than fifteen years. In the end, with the exception of some places of worship, all of the old houses were bulldozed.

Even today, District Six is an empty space within the city. Ironically, the district was never "redeveloped" into a white area. In the 1980s, the Hands Off District Six Campaign was formed and exerted strong pressure on the government. In 1994, with the end of apartheid, the National Congress recognized the claims of former residents and started to organize their return, which, however, is still in process.[3]

The specificity of District Six is that it was a multi-ethnic quarter with a long history. Already in the late nineteenth century it was a mixed community of former slaves, immigrants, merchants, and artisans. Many so-called Cape Malays, descendants of people who were brought from Malaysia to South Africa by the Dutch East India Company in the seventeenth century, had settled in the area. Next to them lived Xhosa people, Indians, and smaller groups of Afrikaners, people of British descent, and Jews. District Six, in short, featured almost all of the ethnic communities living in that part of South Africa at that time.[4]

---

[3] For an extensive social history of Cape Town, see van Heyningen et al. (1999); on memories of Apartheid and forced removals in Cape Town, see Field et al. (2007); on the Hands Off District Six Campaign, see Jeppie and Crain (1990). On the district's "deferred regeneration," see Field (2019).

[4] On the urbanism of District Six and its long history, see Pistorius et al. (2002).

In the 1960s, according to the South African government, District Six had deteriorated into a slum area, which had to be cleared. The government portrayed the district as a dangerous place, full of crime, gambling, drinking, and prostitution. This may have been true (the stories by Alex La Guma, for example, suggest that District Six was certainly not a convent), but for the government—with its obsession with racial purity and segregation—the "mixedness" of District Six seems to have been the greatest outrage. And of course, its location near the city center, Table Mountain, and the harbor meant that District Six could be turned into a valuable residential area for rich white people.

10.3 Mediations of "District Six"

How, then, did District Six turn from such a specific historical place into a traveling schema? The clue is mediation. This can already be sensed in the prime site of District Six remembrance, the District Six Museum, which was founded in 1994 and is located in the District's Central Methodist Church in Buitenkant Street, a former "sanctuary for political opponents and victims of apartheid" (Coombes 2003, 126).[5] Using the terms introduced by Jay David Bolter and Richard Grusin in their theory of remediation (1999), the District Six Museum tries to bring back the disappeared quarter by means of "hypermediation": Dating from its inaugural exhibition in 1994, *Streets: Retracing District Six*, its ground floor is covered with the painting of a large street map of District Six. There are columns of original street signs from the old district and large-scale photographic portraits of well-known former residents. The museum collection features more than 8,500 photographs of District Six and its families. It provides audiovisual material and oral history recordings. In 2000, the exhibition *Digging Deeper* created soundscapes out of the voices of ex-residents (Rassool 2006, 15). Some of these various media of collective memory are also available online on the museum's webpage, including a virtual walk through the district.

---

[5] In 1989, the District Six Museum Foundation was established, which had emerged from the Hands Off District Six Campaign. For a history of the museum, see Rassool and Prosalendis (2001). For a discussion of its uses of media and memory, see the chapter "District Six: The Archeology of Memory" in Coombes (2003); and the chapter "Working with Memory: The District Six Museum in the New South Africa" in McEachern (2002). On memory, space, and identity in Cape Town, see Murray et al. (2007). On the museum's participatory curation, see Soudien (2019).

Arguably, the museum has become such a powerful site of memory because it connects these manifold mediations with various forms of social performance. This social embeddedness can be traced back to the museum's origins in the Hands Off District Six Campaign, and this is evident even today by the museum's self-description as a "a living memorial" and its "archive as a living organism,"[6] by its strong reliance on visitors' and ex-residents' active participation, as well as by its emphasis on being a "community museum."[7] According to the historian Ciraj Rassool, one of the museum's trustees and most prolific scholars, the District Six Museum can thus be described as "a hybrid space," which combines "scholarship, research, collection and museum aesthetics with community forms of governance and accountability, and land claim politics of representation and restitution" (Rassool 2006, 15).

In the District Six Museum, a rich texture of medial representations, material traces of the past, and their various social uses (hyper-)mediates the district's history and seems to recreate the real to the extent that "soon after its creation, many visitors began to refer to the museum simply as 'District Six,' as the site of District Six's memorialization and commemoration had to perform the work of satisfying the desire for the real" (Rassool 2006, 13).

But also beyond this particular museum, there is a long history of District Six mediations. In painting, for example, artists such as John Dronsfield, Gregoire Boonzaier, Gerard Sekoto, and Kenneth Baker have captured versions of life in the district. Professional photographers, such as Cloete Breytenbach, Jillian Edelstein, Paul Grendon, Jan Greshoff, George Hallett, Jackie Heyns, Jimi Matthews, and Jansje Wissema, have substantially shaped the imagination of District Six. A key role in the memory of District Six is moreover played by different forms of entertainment: Hybrid Cape Jazz can be understood as a medial self-expression of the district's creole realities. A District Six musical was produced by David Kramer and Taliep Petersen in 1986. Short films about District Six, such as Lindy Wilson's documentary *Last Supper at Horstley Street* (1983) and Yunus Ahmed's *Dear Grandfather,*

---

[6] https://www.districtsix.co.za/permanent-exhibition-digging-deeper/ (March 27, 2024).

[7] "The museum's use of 'community' is not naive, but conscious and strategic. The museum insists on utilizing this concept as an organizational device, in asserting a particular politics of governance and institutional orientation, and in expressing a particular commitment to social mobilization, and to constructing and defending independent spaces of articulation and contestation in the public domain" (Rassool 2006, 17).

Your Right Foot Is Missing (1984), represent the time during and after the forced removals and their impact on resident families.[8]

Literature has had its share in the representation of District Six memories, too: Poetry on the topic was written by James Matthews, Adam Small, Dollar Brand (Abdullah Ibrahim), and Cosmo Pieterse. Peter Abraham's *Path of Thunder* (1948) is identified by Richard Rive (1990, 113) as the earliest published novel about District Six. The most famous works, however, emerged from the authors of the *Quartet* group,[9] most notably Alex la Guma's detective story *A Walk in the Night* (1962) and Richard Rive's fictional communal biography of the forced removals in *Buckingham Palace, District Six* (1986). In *Waiting for Leila* (1981), Achmat Dangor tells a love story against the backdrop of the district's destruction. More recently, different forms of life writing about District Six, often collective memoirs of families and communities, have come to the fore.[10]

10.4 Plurimedial Constellations

What all the above-mentioned representations of District Six constitute is a rich medial network, or, what I call a plurimedial constellation of memory.[11] The term emphasizes that it is never one single medium which "makes" a memory schema, but rather it is usually complex constellations of different media, which may refer to, imitate, or comment upon another. An integral part of such constellations is the social dimension: Media of memory can have an effect only through their social performance, the way they are produced, received, discussed, and handed on.

According to this model, the movie *District 9* is an integral part of the plurimedial constellation which creates, and constantly redefines, the memory of District Six—a constellation which is not only made up of different

---

[8] For more extensive accounts of representations of District Six, see Richard Rive's essay "District Six: Fact and Fiction" (1990), as well as McCormick (2002, 202–206).
[9] Alex La Guma, James Matthews, Richard Rive, and Alf Wannenburgh, whose short stories were collected and edited by Richard Rive in *Quartet: New Voices from South Africa* (New York: Crown Publishers 1963) and immediately banned by the apartheid government.
[10] For example, Hettie Adams's and Hermione Suttner's *Williams Street District Six* (1988), Andrina Dashwood-Forbes's *Birds on a Ledge* (1992), Linda Fortune's *The House in Tyne Street: Childhood Memories of District Six* (1996), Nomvuyo Ngcelwane's *Sala Kahle District Six: An African Woman's Perspective* (1998), and Noor Ebrahim's *Noor's Story: My Life in District Six* (1999). See also McCormick (2002, 203f.).
[11] For a definition of "plurimedial constellations," see Chapter 8, "Literature, Film, and the Mediality of Cultural Memory."

media produced and received at different times and the social practices connected to them, but which is moreover increasingly transnational in its scope. Worldwide political discussions about apartheid, the international news coverage of transition, truth, and reconciliation in South Africa, as well as the far-reaching media attention to new "Rainbow Nation" that gained added momentum during the 2010 FIFA World Cup, provided a medial framework within which representations of the memories of specific locales, such as that of District Six, can be received and understood in mnemonic communities across the globe.

Focusing on the important role that literary representations have played in the creation of "District Six" as a traveling schema, the following two examples serve to show how plurimedial networks extend into a transnational space. In the 1990s, South African poet and novelist Tatamkhulu Afrika, a former District Six resident, African National Congress (ANC) member, and political prisoner under the apartheid regime, wrote the poem "Nothing's Changed" about his return to District Six after the end of apartheid, only to find that segregation and the unequal distribution of wealth were still in place: "new, up-market, / haute cuisine, / guard at the gatepost, / whites only inn." The poem ends with the return of anger when the persona realizes that "nothing's changed": "I back from the glass, / boy again, / leaving small mean O / of small mean mouth. / Hands burn / for a stone, a bomb, / to shiver down the glass. / Nothing's changed" (Afrika 1994, 33–34).

In the United Kingdom, this poem became part of the GCSE (General Certificate of Secondary Education) English syllabus in 2009. It was included under the topic of "poems from different cultures." A generation of young Britains from all over the country studied this piece for their exams. This is a striking example of some of the processes typically involved in the production of traveling schemata: the creation of powerful mediations, their "travel" across the globe, and their social use in new local contexts. The case of "Nothing's Changed" gives rise to question of what it is that actually constitutes such a "transportable impact-medium." Although there are no general properties which make some media more memorable, movable, usable, and effectual than others, in the case of Tatamkhulu Afrika's poem, major factors seem to be a concise, in terms of linguistic register and evoked experience, rather easily "translatable" representation of "District Six"; the authenticity that will be ascribed to the poem by readers who are acquainted with the life of its author; and the fact that the reading and discussion of the poem have been firmly and strategically institutionalized in the educational sector.[12] Indeed, alongside the patterns of attention that are generated through global mass media and digital media, "old" mnemonic strategies, such as the formation of canons and syllabi, are still a major factor in the travel of memory across time and space.

A second example is the short story collection *Rosa's District 6* (2004) by Rozena Maart, a South African writer living in Canada. On the one hand, those short stories are part of a growing body of South African memory literature;[13] on the other hand, they testify to the importance of literary memories that emerge in contexts of migration. Diasporic writers can become carriers as well as mediators of transnational memory.[14] That this role is recognized and fostered in at least some parts of the world is shown by the fact that the collection's first story, "No Rosa, No District Six," originally published in 1991, won the Canadian *Journey Prize* in 1992. Such awards are another example of the strategic social uses of media of collective memory. They are a way of steering the economy of attention, by highlighting one topic of memory and not another.[15]

10.5 Iconization: Past Potentialities in Cloete Breyetenbach's *The Spirit of District Six*

The idea of plurimedial constellations implies that representations of memory are in many ways interconnected through forms of cross-reference and thus gain visibility and strength in international arenas of remembrance. Interestingly, Rozena Maart's collection participates in this mnemonic cross-referencing by the way in which the book's cover is fashioned. It features one of Cloete Breytenbach's famous photographs of District Six ("Seven Steps"; see Figure 10.5). Breytenbach (1933–2019) was a South African news

---

[12] Merry's (2006, 39) observation that "[a]s ideas from transnational sources travel to small communities, they are typically vernacularized, or adapted to local institutions and meaning" works also the other way round: As ideas or memories emerge from a local context and enter the transnational arena, they are remade for transnational audiences, transnationalized (i.e., translated from local specificities into languages and practices that render those memories widely intelligible and relevant, so that the work of vernacularization can commence in new local contexts). Laanes (2021) studies such processes with regard to interlingual translation.

[13] For accounts of literary memory in South Africa, see Nuttall and Coetzee (1998); Nuttall (2009).

[14] On diaspora and collective memory, see Baronian et al. (2007) and Hirsch and Miller (2011).

[15] Clearly, these types of promotion, as well as the above-mentioned forms of institutionalization and canonization, are key components of a power dynamics that makes certain memories travel and not others. As my examples show, much of the power of selecting and highlighting items of memory still resides at the national level, thus giving evidence to the significance of national boundaries and frameworks in the dynamics of transnational memory.

Figure 10.5 "Seven Steps" (Cloete Breytenbach, *The Spirit of District Six*, 1970); reproduced courtesy of CLOETE BREYTENBACH PHOTOGRAPHIC ARCHIVES.

photographer who worked for *Life Magazine*, *Daily Telegraph*, and *Bunte*, among others, and covered events in Africa, Europe, the United States, Vietnam, and Israel. His photographs of District Six were taken over a period of more than a decade, from 1959 to 1970.[16] His "District Six Collection" was

---

[16] Personal correspondence with Cloete Breytenbach (May 18, 2012).

published as a book in 1970, under the title *The Spirit of District Six* (Cape Town: Purnell), with an accompanying text written by Brian Barrow. This book has since seen six editions.

With the choice of one of Breytenbach's photographs as an illustration of her literary memories about District Six, Rozena Maart's collection clearly takes part in a larger, and indeed transnational, trend. In fact, it seems that today almost no representation of District Six can work without using this body of iconic images. Other examples include Alex La Guma's *A Walk in The Night* in the Trent Editions (2006), whose cover features Breytenbach's "Tram Ride" (see Figure 10.6). The cover of Richard Rive's *Buckingham Palace: District Six*, in the edition of the German Cornelsen Senior English Library of 2006, shows Breytenbach's image of "Richmond Street" (see Figure 10.7)—while the novel's original edition of 1986 (Cape Town: David Philip Publishers) had displayed a watercolored linocut by the South African painter Gregoire Boonzaier ("District 6," 1978), presumably a then-iconic representation of life in the district.

It seems as if, in the early twenty-first century, Breytenbach's photographic collection had become a nodal point in the plurimedial constellation constituting "District Six" as a memory schema. The images' tremendous, virtually worldwide significance as media of memory appears to have emerged in the late 1980s, perhaps with the reissuing of the 1970 collection in 1987 and 1997, which coincided with the international attention to the Hands Off District Six Campaign and the end of apartheid. Another important factor is international exhibition tours, in the course of which these photographs have traveled from Cape Town to Europe, Asia, and the United States.[17]

Breytenbach's photos have played a crucial role in the iconization and international circulation of the history of District Six and its meaning. These images appear whenever a condensed impression of past life in the district is required. They "travel" and materialize in intermedial combination with life writing, novels, and scholarly articles alike.[18]

To study iconization as a process of transnational memory, I draw on a definition proposed by the sociologist and memory scholar Claus Leggewie:

---

[17] To the question about international attention to his collection, Cloete Breytenbach stated in 2012: "There are increasing requests from TV producers, media publications etc. worldwide, for the use of images from the collection" (personal correspondence, May 18, 2012).

[18] For example, Breytenbach's "Tram Ride" and other photographs can be found in Ciraj Rassool's academic article "Making the District Six Museum in Cape Town" (2006). It seems that the historian Rassool uses them here not so much as historical sources in a strict sense, but as a "shorthand" for the richness of a past life in District Six which he wants to convey to the international readership that is targeted by the journal *Museum International*.

Figure 10.6 "Tram Ride" (Cloete Breytenbach, *The Spirit of District Six*, 1970); reproduced courtesy of CLOETE BREYTENBACH PHOTOGRAPHIC ARCHIVES.

Figure 10.7 "Richmond Street" (Cloete Breytenbach, *The Spirit of District Six*, 1970); reproduced courtesy of CLOETE BREYTENBACH PHOTOGRAPHIC ARCHIVES.

Iconization is an exaggerated form of visualization. An issue or process is represented in a particularly concise and sustained manner, and possibly surrounded with an aura. This is what the origin of the term "icon" suggests: an icon used to be a transportable cult image showing biblical scenes. . . . The *iconability* of images is furthered by their historical significance, certain visual properties, and by modalities of their reproduction. . . . Icons mobilize collective affects, they concentrate public attention, and they shape individual and collective memories. They have the power to do so, because they are displayed in a particularly intense, frequent, permanent, and widespread way, because they stand out of a mass of images due to their potential to be quickly recognized, and because they transgress social, political, and cultural boundaries. (Leggewie 2009, 9; my translation)

Cloete Breytenbach's photographs, which have come to stand for life in District Six before the forced removals, are clearly such icons, in Leggewie's sense. They visualize, in a concise, memorable, and recognizable way, certain ideas about the past of District Six, for example its multiculturality and joy of living (see esp. Figure 10.8, "Carnival in District Six" and Figure 10.9, "Sunday in District Six," as such iconic expressions). They highlight art, music, carnival, and street life as essential characteristics—or "the spirit"—of District Six. Arguably, the quality of these black-and-white photographs creates a certain aura around the past events. Having mainly been taken at the end of the "Golden" 1950s and in the 1960s (i.e., before the start and during the first phase of the forced removals,) these photographs function for today's viewers as symbolically charged medial "traces"[19] of (or "witnesses" to) the district's lost past.[20]

Breytenbach's photos are used as mnemonic traces of the "past potentialities" of peaceful and joyful multicultural life. For spectators, they raise the compelling question of "what might have been" had the removals not taken

---

[19] I use these terms in the sense of ontological theories of photography, e.g., by Roland Barthes (1980) and Susan Sontag (2003), whose work revolves around analog photography's indexical relationship to the past. In memory culture, photographs act as both "externalizations" and "traces" of the past (Ruchatz 2010), as consciously crafted monuments and as accidental documents. On how photography extends citizenship to the photographic subject, see Azoulay (2008).

[20] This after-the-fact significance is typical for photography as a medium of memory. Accordingly, Breytenbach states, "Only towards the end of my reportage of the area, by which time most of the structures in the district had been demolished, did I realise that the photographs could be of historical value" (personal correspondence, May 18, 2012).

PLURIMEDIALITY AND TRAVELING SCHEMATA 219

Figure 10.8 "Carnival in District Six" (Cloete Breytenbach, *The Spirit of District Six*, 1970); reproduced courtesy of CLOETE BREYTENBACH PHOTOGRAPHIC ARCHIVES.

Figure 10.9 "Sunday in District Six" (Cloete Breytenbach, *The Spirit of District Six*, 1970); reproduced courtesy of CLOETE BREYTENBACH PHOTOGRAPHIC ARCHIVES.

place. They thus become media of alternative future thinking, and arguably it is their aesthetic power to "break up time" which has set them on their transnational travels in the early twenty-first century.[21]

10.6 Topization and Narrativization: Stories of Urban Futures Past

In the production of traveling schemata, iconization is a key dynamic of visual media. In realm of language, powerful ideas about the past are often crystallized into *topoi*—concise commonplaces, often in the form of metaphors or clichéd phrases (see Erll 2011a, 70–72). One example of such topization is that of District Six's "lost multicultural community." Contained in this *topos* is a story-schema that can be unfolded by narrativization. To understand these processes, it is worth looking once more at Rozena Maart's collection *Rosa's District 6*. Maart's short stories unfold and put into narrative form those condensed *topoi* and icons that have become staple elements in the imagination of District Six. In the short story "The Green Chair," for example, the reader is presented with a description that elaborates the idea of a close-knit multicultural community:

> Pickled fish was a traditional District Six dish that was often eaten during the year but especially on Good Friday. . . . Christian families attended the three hour mass in the morning, and returned home to eat their pickled fish. Muslim families went to mosque in the morning and they too would go home to enjoy their pickled fish. . . . Food in District Six was not divided along religious lines. Many families kept halal homes because they had extended family that were Muslim, and eating was such an important part of District Six life, everyone wanted their friends and families to be able to eat at their homes. (Maart 2004, 16f.)

District Six appears here as a site of happy multicultural living-together. In fact, this claim is repeated incessantly, across the spectrum of available media. Again and again, District Six is called a "lively quarter," a "vibrant

---

[21] On "collective future thought," see Szpunar and Szpunar (2016); on "breaking up time" and alternative temporalities in historical thinking, see Bevernage and Lorenz (2013); on alternative histories and cultural memory, see Tabaszewska (2023).

quarter," a "cosmopolitan place," or, to quote from the text accompanying Cloete Breytenbach's photographs, "a happy, generous wonderful community" which "simply disappeared" (Breytenbach and Barrow 1997 [1970], 7).

Does this sound too good to be true? What could be the function of such a recurrent and highly schematized representation? Sandra Prosalendis, curator of the District Six Museum, explains that:

> District Six is remembered by many who had lived there as a place where they were able to cross religious, class and social boundaries. As a place where they were able to share their everyday experiences and to live not as "coloured," "whites," "Africans" or "Indians" but as South Africans. District Six occupies a special place in the history of South Africa. (Prosalendis 1999, 141; quoted in Coombes 2003, 212)

In her pertinent study *Visual Culture and Public Memory in a Democratic South Africa* (2003, 123), Annie E. Coombes describes "'District Six' as "a location that to all intents and purposes no longer exists in its former physical form, but that as a memory and a concept embodies all the attributes of a vibrant 'community' that refused the 'logic' of the apartheid state." But she also emphasizes that such a memory presumes "an (impossibly) harmonious and unified population prior to apartheid and possibly colonialism" (Coombes 2003, 126).

It is indeed remarkable that, as Richard Rive (1990, 10–12) muses, "so much attention has been focused on District Six and not on the many other similarly affected areas. What about Pageview in Johannesburg, South End in Port Elizabeth and Claremont and Simonstown in the Cape Peninsula?"[22] Rive also makes clear that District Six was not a romantic "fairyland," as a famous graffiti on one of its houses suggested, but "a ripe, raw and rotten slum. It was drab, dingy, squalid and overcrowded." However, it seems that, compared to other forced removals in South Africa, "this removal had more dramatic or melodramatic qualities than the others," not least because "District Six had a mind and a soul of its own. It had a homogeneity that created a sense of belonging.... It cultivated a sharp urban inclusivity, the

---

[22] This is indeed an important, if detrimental aspect of the powerful "District Six" schema. It may, as Anderson and Daya (2022) argue, "in fact enable the forgetting of removals and evictions in other, nearby spaces." Mnemonic schematization can lead to what psychologists call "retrieval induced forgetting" (Hirst and Coman 2018) on the level of culture. For a critical perspective on District Six as an icon of collective memory, see also Goldblatt (2021).

type which cockneys have in the East End of London and black Americans in Harlem." Therefore, in District Six, "there was no observable apartheid since the District was one, big apartheid."

What all this suggests is that "District Six" has become a narrative shorthand for a lost community flourishing in an urban space. Just like Breytenbach's ionic photographs, stories about District Six tend to refer to a past potentiality, to possibilities that existed in South Africa's past before the advent of apartheid, and that might have unfolded had history only turned out differently—in short, to a nostalgic urban future past.[23]

Traveling schemata can encapsulate complex and politically charged temporalities. As an over-determined memory schema which operates backward and forward in time, "District Six" is highly important for today's imagination of South Africa. It implies a narrative that is a warning *and* a promise. It explains at once what must never happen again *and* what might have been. And with its focus on what might have been (a future past) it creates a model for what might still come into being (a utopian future present). Much in this vein, ANC member Jeremy Cronin asserts: "We should certainly not romanticise the pre-apartheid past of Cape Town, but neither should we lose sight of the *proto-non-racialism* that was forged unevenly in localities all about our city, as Capetonians went about their daily lives" (Cronin 2006, 49, my emphasis).

10.7 Queering "District Six": The Kewpie Collection

Traveling schemata are expansive schemata. In 2018, with the District Six Museum exhibition *KEWPIE: Daughter of District Six*,[24] the iconization and narrativization of the district as an urban space of past potentialities took on new dimensions and resulted in a thorough queering of the mnemonic space (see Figure 10.10).

---

[23] On the concept of "futures past," see Koselleck (2004 [1979]). On "the future of nostalgia," see Boym (2001). What such a romanticizing vision of an urban future past tends to forget, however, is that the history of South African racism and segregation actually predates 1948. As early as in 1901, after an outbreak of the bubonic plague, black South Africans were forcibly removed from District Six to Ndabeni (Sambumbu 2010).

[24] The exhibition was curated by Tina Smith and Jenny Marsden (see Smith and Marsden 2020). For its webpage, see: https://www.districtsix.co.za/project/kewpie-daughter-of-district-six/; for the exhibition catalog *KEWPIE—Daughter of District Six* (2019), see: https://issuu.com/galagayandlesbianmemoryinaction/docs/kewpie_catalogue_-_digital_final_2020-07-21_pages.

Figure 10.10 Invitation to the opening of the exhibition *Kewpie: Daughter of District Six*, September 20, 2018, District Six Museum Homecoming Centre; reproduced courtesy of GALA Queer Archive and District Six Museum, South Africa.

Kewpie (1941–2012) was a celebrated drag queen who spent her life in District Six.[25] Her photos show everyday queer lives and nightlife events in District Six, involving a large cast of people from diverse ethnic backgrounds[26] (see Figures 10.11 and 10.12). But the photos also register the district's history of destruction, for example when a styled Kewpie steps on the rubble of torn down houses.

In 1997, Kewpie gave her collection of more than 700 photographs to the Gay and Lesbian Memory in Action (GALA) archive in Johannesburg. GALA describes these photos as "a collection from the apartheid era that depicts a queer, working class, coloured community," and it immediately introduces the *topos* of a lost urban past: The Kewpie collection is an "important resource that documents a community and place that has since been lost."[27]

Jack Lewis, who shot the documentary film *A Normal Daughter: The Life and Times of Kewpie of District Six* (2000), explains:

Before South Africa's apartheid government in the 1970's destroyed District Six, being gay, or "moffie," was an accepted part of this racially and religiously diverse community in Cape Town. Kewpie's hairdressing salon was the epicenter of this culture, a meeting place where the "girls" organized drag balls and cabaret performances, all of which are captured through her amazing collection of snapshots.[28]

After the exhibition at the District Six Museum's Homecoming Centre in 2018, memories of "Kewpie" gained enormous momentum across South

---

[25] "Kewpie was a hairdresser and iconic queer figure from District Six. A gender-fluid individual who identified by female pronouns, Kewpie was a seminal nightlife figure who organized balls and celebrations uniting the LGBTQI+ (Lesbian, Gay, Bisexual, Transexual, Queer, Intersex) community with the larger community of District Six." (South African History Online, https://www.sahistory.org.za/people/kewpie).

[26] "Most of the photographs in the collection were taken by Kewpie and friends, and show Kewpie's extensive social life and social circle, both within District Six and further afield. The photographs depict the carefully crafted public personas in her queer community, and also their private 'off-duty' lives" (GALA: "Kewpie Photographic Collection" https://gala.co.za/projects-and-programmes/a-daughter-of-district-six/).

[27] GALA: "Kewpie Photographic Collection," https://gala.co.za/projects-and-programmes/a-daughter-of-district-six/).

[28] https://africanfilmny.org/films/a-normal-daughter-the-life-and-times-of-kewpie-of-district-six/. In fact, it was Lewis who recognized the value of Kewpie's collection as an important archival source and facilitated its acquisition by GALA.

Figure 10.11 Kewpie in front of the salon "Kewpie's hairdressers," 1970s; reproduced courtesy of Kewpie Collection, GALA Queer Archive, Johannesburg, South Africa.

Figure 10.12 Kewpie and friends at a house party in Mount Street, 1971; reproduced courtesy of Kewpie Collection, GALA Queer Archive, Johannesburg, South Africa.

Africa—inspiring parades, art, and fashion[29]—and beyond. As in the case of Breytenbach's photos, iconic images from the Kewpie collection have been remediated on book covers (e.g., on the collection of queer writing by Africans, *They Called Me Queer*, eds. Kim Windvogel and Kelly-Eve Koopman, 2019).

With Kewpie's archive suddenly highly accessible in 2018, the schema of "the spirit of District Six," as iconized by Breytenbach's photographs, was expanded to include queer lives. The plurimedial constellation around "District Six" as a space of past multiculturality prepared the (visual and narrative) ground for remembering past sexual diversity. By the look of it, "the spirit of District Six" could seamlessly be broadened into the spirit of a "gay vicinity."[30]

This at least is suggested by the rhetoric of the District Six Museum, which states on its webpage that the Kewpie collection "reinforces historical understandings of District Six as a close-knit community where diversity was valued, while highlighting a lesser-known aspect of District Six history."[31] The exhibition catalog emphasizes the "extent of integration of queer people into the broader District Six community."[32]

Queer studies scholar Ramsden-Karelse (2023, 16) is more critical about this mnemonic extension of the "District Six" schema. She understands the Kewpie collection as a "precarious archive"[33] and argues that "Kewpie's account of the girls' experiences of precarity has been deemphasised in relation to its representation of freedom and flourishing. This occlusion, in the Collection's dissemination, seems informed both by desires of the disseminators and by the girls' uses of photography, for instance, to transform their conditions of precarity."

Photography's double logic in memory culture both as externalization and trace (Ruchatz 2010)—or of monument and document—becomes very clear in Ramsden-Karelse's careful argument. Kewpie and her friends used

---

[29] "The exhibition 'Kewpie: Daughter of District Six' unearthed an entire archive of local queer history. In 2018, the annual District Six Heritage Day Parade was dedicated to Kewpie and her contributions to the community and culture of District Six. The parade saw GALA and the District 6 Museum collaborate with The Death of Glitter (D.O.G) collective; a group of young queer artists from Cape Town. 'Kewpie: Daughter of District Six' toured Johannesburg in 2019" (South African History Online, https://www.sahistory.org.za/people/kewpie).

[30] This is Kewpie's dictum: "District Six was really my gay vicinity." See Corrigall and Marsden (2020).

[31] https://www.districtsix.co.za/project/kewpie-daughter-of-district-six/.

[32] *KEWPIE—Daughter of District Six* (2019, 42).

[33] Both in the sense of a "marginal archival source" and an archive that records the precarious lives of queer people (Ramsden-Karelse 2023).

photography as active, reality-constructing externalizations of a "livable" queer life. Through photography, the "girls" visually appropriated public space in apartheid-era South Africa, where their presence both as queer and colored people was prohibited. They thus created a "possibility of appearance" (Ramsden-Karelse 2023, 11).[34] In today's memory culture, however, Kewpie's photographs are largely read as documentary materials, as "traces" of a past reality. This also occurs in the face of the relative paucity of other traces of queer life in South Africa.[35]

The use of the Kewpie collection as a photographic memory trace has important political and transnational implications, which are explicitly stated by the District Six Museum, when it addresses the anti-queer propaganda (and legislation) across the African continent:

> Histories of queer lives like Kewpie's challenge the popular notion that homosexuality is un-African. They show a community and culture where gender non-conforming people, who often face prejudice and exclusion in contemporary South Africa, were largely accepted and loved as human beings with the right to express themselves as they wished.[36]

The African space where queerness is not un-African, is a lost space, with only mediated potentialities surviving. These survivals, or traces, in the local context of District Six are used for the project of building a better future. The affiliated "Salon Kewpie—The Legacy Project" (2023), for example, is an educational endeavor with the aim of creating a sense of queer history for present-day young (queer) people—a history that (though available in the GALA archives for more than twenty years) had apparently been utterly inaccessible until the exhibition of Kewpie's collection.[37]

---

[34] For a similar argument with regard to photography in Palestine, see Azoulay (2015).

[35] Ramsden-Karelse (2023, 15) emphasizes that Kewpie's photographic documents are "not corroborated by similar materials. This is perhaps a defining feature of archives of the precarious: the materials constituting these archives themselves exist and circulate precariously." Personal photography, but also life writing, and even literary texts can become an important archival source in such situations. Rozena Maart's cycle of short stories *Rosa's District Six*, for example, begins and ends with queer relationships. Its last story in particular ("The Bracelet") conveys a sense of the precariousness of queer life in Cape Town, when "moffie" Matthew explains: "People are only okay with 'moffies' because we form part of the entertainment, we play netball, provide fun and laughter, do women's hair" (Maart 2004, 209).

[36] https://www.districtsix.co.za/project/kewpie-daughter-of-district-six/.

[37] "The first iteration of *Salon Kewpie: The Legacy Project* consisted of a four-day educational programme culminating in the Kewpie Legacy Ball, held on Saturday 11 March 2023. Participating in the programme were 10 young LGBTIQ+ people of colour from communities historically subjected

The Kewpie exhibition effected a substantial queering of "District Six" as a mnemonic space, following the schema's logic of highlighting past potentialities—but with one important difference: The memory of queer communities also introduces new visions of genealogies of belonging to District Six that do not exclusively revolve around the (biological) children and grandchildren of those evicted from the district, but also extend to those who are ready to adopt an (affiliative) "queer postmemory."[38] As stated on the GALA webpage: "Now, a young generation of queer people based in Cape Town have adopted Kewpie as a local 'transestor' and look to her story as a basis for safe and creative spaces for the young queer community."[39] The Kewpie exhibition thus showcases and co-constructs queer afterlives in order to imagine queer futures.

10.8 Connective Schemata: Apartheid, Holocaust, Nakba

Traveling schemata are transnationally connective schemata. Their movement across time and space enables—and is enabled by—their capacity to connect with other memories. And indeed, the images and narratives associated with "District Six" resonate with discourses about racism, injustice, and forced removals all around the world. In recent years, for example, the memory of District Six has increasingly been invoked, in South Africa and elsewhere, in critical discourses about urban gentrification.[40] Most powerfully and repeatedly, however, "District Six" has been linked to that other "floating signifier" (Huyssen 2003, 99), the Holocaust.

The linkage between the experience of South African apartheid and the anti-Semitism of Nazi Germany can most prominently be found in Richard Rive's well-known novel *Buckingham Palace, District Six* (1986). It is embodied in the character of the Jewish landlord Solomon Katzen. The

---

to forced removals from areas such as District Six, Cape Town. On the Saturday, participants utilised the knowledge and experience they had gained during the week to make their Ballroom debut, walking in the opening category, 'Best Dressed Debutantes: Kiki House Debut'" (Youtube: https://www.youtube.com/watch?v=YOGhOxK9740).

[38] On the theory and practices of "queer postmemory," see Çalışkan (2019); see also Chapter 5, "Locating Family in Memory Studies"; on genealogy and memory, see Chapter 6, "Generation in Literary History."

[39] GALA: "Kewpie Photographic Collection," https://gala.co.za/projects-and-programmes/a-daughter-of-district-six/.

[40] See for example, the German documentary *Im Schatten des Tafelbergs* (2010, dir. Alexander Kleider and Daniela Michel; Engl. *When the Mountain Meets Its Shadow*).

novel tells the story of a mixed community living in "Buckingham Palace," the mock-name for a row of dilapidated houses in District Six. The narrative traces the history of the people living in those houses from the heyday of multicultural life in District Six in the 1950s all the way to the forced removals starting in 1968 and the final breaking up of the community fifteen years later. Halfway through the novel, it turns out that the owner of Buckingham Palace, Solomon Katzen, is a German Jew who fled the Nazi regime. Ironically, he finds himself now in a similar constellation, only with a reversal of roles:

> It is very funny for me. In Germany they treated me as an *untermenschen*. Here they force me to be part of the *herrenvolk*. But I cannot forget what they did to us in Germany. So my heart is with all the *untermenschen*, whoever and wherever they are.... They tell me that if I want to sell my houses in the District, I can only sell them to white people. If I want to sell my business, I can only sell it to white people. If anyone moves out of any of my houses, only white people can move in. So I have decided that while this evil law remains I will never sell my houses. (Rive 2006 [1986], 139)

In the field of cosmopolitan memory studies, the travels of the "Holocaust" as a mnemonic "template" to address genocide and the violation of human rights elsewhere is well-researched (Levy and Sznaider 2006 [2001]). It has been argued that such combinations and comparisons in memory discourse obscure the historical singularity and specificity of events such as the Holocaust or South African apartheid. However, the travel and linking of memory schemata may also create a greater visibility and understanding of injustices beyond local and national contexts (consider, for example, the significance of Rive's novel in the German schoolbook edition mentioned above) and potentially may engender solidarity among victim groups across the world (Rothberg 2009).

But the memory of "the Jewish connection to District Six is complicated," as Nudelman (2022, 40) points out. First, although Jews came in the late nineteenth century as poor immigrants to District Six, they were seen as "white" in the apartheid system and could therefore move to white areas after the district's demolition. Second, there is "the struggle between the predominantly Zionist ideals of the Jewish community and the anti-Zionist tendency within the Muslim community." And, due "in part to the

African National Congress's (ANC) close ties to the Palestinian Liberation Organisation, anti-Zionism has become widespread."

What does this mean for the logic of the traveling schema? "District Six" can be mobilized to remember the Holocaust as well as the Nakba and its aftermath. For example, Israel's controversial Prawer plan of 2011 to destroy Bedouin villages in the Negev and resettle their inhabitants was discussed in a South African opinion piece as follows: "Though comparing apartheid-South Africa with Israel-Palestine is heavily debated, the parallels between each country's policies of dispossession, especially when comparing District Six and the Naqab (Negev), are hard to miss" (Iraqi 2013).

Under the impression of the Israel-Hamas war (since October 2023) and South Africa's genocide case against Israel (since December 2023), the new director of the District Six Museum, Zeenat Patel-Kaskar, stated about Gaza that "the Palestinians and South Africa can draw parallels to loss and destruction" (Sambo 2024). In March 2024, people walked in Cape Town the length of the Gaza strip, chanting "from District Six to Palestine, forced removals are a crime" (Hirsch 2024). As a condensed schematic formula for segregation and forced removals, "District Six" has traveled to Gaza.

10.9 *District 9*: Transforming the Traveling Schema

Blomkamp's *District 9* taps the resources of traveling schemata much in the way described above. The movie's tacit allusion to District Six will be understood at least by parts of its international audiences and will add a semantic dimension to the film. Moreover, *District 9* uses the connective possibilities of the "District Six" schema, for example, when District 10, the place where the aliens are to be relocated, is described as a "concentration camp."[41]

However, although the movie's title and part of its storyline clearly refer to "District Six," *District 9* actually resists filling the schema according to the conventionalized ways: First of all, it does not describe "District 9" as the site of a diverse community harmoniously living together, but instead as home to a more or less homogeneous mass of aliens, which is "diversified" only by a group of fierce Nigerians who are both profiting from and fighting against

---

[41] This links the schema not only to the Holocaust, but also—geographically closer to South Africa—to the OvaHerero and Nama genocide perpetrated by the German Empire in 1904–1909 (in German South West Africa, today's Namibia). The Germans set up concentration camps, where the majority of African inmates died. On "documenting genocide" in *District 9*, see Conway (2017).

the extra-terrestrials. The movie does not romanticize slum dwellers. On the contrary, the aliens are shown, in their majority, to be rather witless, unruly, and violent. They seem utterly incapable of connecting with human society. District 9 is clearly *not* a past potentiality.

Second, *District 9* points to the difficulties of immigration in post-apartheid South Africa. Large numbers of immigrants and refugees, for example from Zimbabwe, have been greeted by South Africans with distrust and xenophobic violence and put into refugee camps much like the movie's aliens. Another dimension of the immigration theme is the movie's highly unfavorable representation of Nigerian immigrants. The Nigerians dwelling in District 9 are depicted as criminals and warlords, with strong leanings toward witchcraft and cannibalism. The chief of the Nigerian gangster gang in *District 9* is called Obasanjo, a name that is certainly reminiscent of the past Nigerian president, Olusegun Obasanjo. As a result, the Nigerian Minister of Information and Communications, Dora Akunyili, officially protested to the South African government about the movie and demanded an apology from its makers.[42]

Finally, the film seems to be a comment on the still drab realities in South African slums such as Johannesburg's Chiawelo, where the film was shot on location and from where many extras where recruited (see Figure 10.2). The South African newspaper *Global Post* commented: "In *District 9*, Chiawelo is depicted as a place so dire that it is only fit for alien refugees who landed in Johannesburg from another planet." For the inhabitants of Chiawelo, the movie thus produces the bitter "irony of living in what was shown in the movie as only habitable for aliens" (Conway-Smith 2009, see also Akpome 2017).

District 9 draws on the recognizability and power of the traveling schema "District Six," but it actualizes the schema in a rather complex and at times contradictory ways. It transforms the icons and narratives conventionally connected with the schema. It creates new images and tells new stories about new challenges.[43]

This, too, is a key process of memory in transnational media cultures. Instead of becoming inert by repetition, powerful traveling schemata are

---

[42] For a critical discussion of the movie's many problematic aspects, see Moses et al. (2010); on its "Afrophobia," see Mututa (2023).
[43] But of course, despite all its critical overtones (and racist undertones), Blomkamp's movie is first of all a medium of entertainment, an action-based alien film with many comical effects. This freedom and levity in the use of the "District Six" schema seems to suggests that at least part of the memory work and reconciliation process in South Africa may have been successful.

characterized by their ongoing transformation, by the way in which they are put to ever new uses and enable ever new images and stories to emerge—ranging, in the case of "District Six," from multicultural and queer potentialities to connections between apartheid, the Holocaust, and the Nakba, and eventually to an alien scenario that comments on immigration, poverty, and social tensions in present-day Johannesburg. Paired with this vital fluidity of the successful traveling schema, however, is an equally important degree of stability. From Richard Rive to Neill Blomkamp, the "District Six" schema remains essentially a tool to tell stories of diversity and racism, of victims and perpetrators, of displacement and return, of injustice and reconciliation, of futures past and futures present.

Chapter 11
The Ethics of Premediation in James Joyce's *Ulysses*

11.1 Premediation in Joyce's Book of Memory

For almost a century now, James Joyce's *Ulysses* (1922) has resonated across the world of literature as a narrative of memory and modernity. Along with Marcel Proust's *À la recherche du temps perdu* (1913–1927) and Virginia Woolf's *Mrs. Dalloway* (1925), it is one of the most significant inquiries of the novel into the workings of memory.

Ulysses is unparalleled in the range of the memory phenomena it explores. Through interior monologue and other formal innovations, it represents individual memory processes such as associative and involuntary remembering (Molly Bloom's monologue), traumatic and repressed memories (the death of Stephen's mother), and semantic memory (Bloom's retrievals of mostly wrong scientific information). At the same time, the novel is both shaped by and shapes cultural memory. It (re)creates sites of memory in Dublin. It evokes, recombines, consolidates, and ironizes mythical and religious, national and transnational (notably Greek, Irish, and Jewish) memories. With its vast variety of intertextual and intermedial references (from Shakespeare to Italian opera and women's magazines), it provides each new generation of readers a treasure trove of literary, musical, and popular memories (rendered accessible by an ever-increasing number of *Ulysses* commentaries). And with the *Odyssey* as its "continuous parallel" (Eliot 1923), it is arguably the most famous modern instance of long-term cultural remembering.

The memory concepts that can be found in *Ulysses* are, as John S. Rickard shows in *Joyce's Book of Memory* (1999), both traditional and contemporary. Through his Jesuit education, Joyce was conversant with the memory philosophies of Plato, Aristotle, and Augustine, and in his youth he was fascinated by Giordano Bruno's Hermeticism. The time of writing *Ulysses*

Travels in Time. Astrid Erll, Oxford University Press. © Oxford University Press (2025).
DOI: 10.1093/oso/9780197767733.003.0012

(eight years, 1914–1922, during which the Irishman James Joyce lived in self-imposed exile in Trieste, Zurich, and Paris) coincided with a peak period in the philosophy and psychology of memory. Joyce's contemporaries include Hermann Ebbinghaus, Sigmund Freud, William James, Henri Bergson, and also Theosophical writers such as Madame Blavatsky and Maurice Maeterlinck. Although *Ulysses* references such modern memory discourses in manifold ways (Lamarckian "race memory," Theosophical "universal memory," Freud's "mourning and melancholia," and Bergson's *durée* and *élan vital* are all palpable in the novel), and Joyce had many of the relevant books in his Trieste library, none of these authors can be perceived as a defining influence in *Ulysses*. Rather, as Rickard (1999) maintains, these ideas were in the air, part of the intellectual climate in early twentieth-century Europe, and as such ready to be taken up and processed by what Jacques Derrida has called James Joyce's "hypermnesiac machine" (1984, 147).

Joyce's *Ulysses* is not only time's witness of a particularly rich constellation of modernist thinking about memory, but also time's prophet—presciently exploring phenomena of collective memory and mediation, for which the early twentieth century had not yet developed a language. (Maurice Halbwachs's studies on collective memory would appear some years later, and concepts of mediated memory are by and large products of the late twentieth and early twenty-first centuries). In hindsight, it is quite ironic that Rickard (1999, 3) would write as recently as in 1999: "Joyce was profoundly interested in and affected by models of mind that we apparently can no longer take seriously. How many contemporary Westerners, for example, would be willing to concede the possibility of a human being's inheriting knowledge derived from his ancestors' or even his parents' experiences?"

Most of today's memory scholars (some of them "Westerners," others not), would quite likely react to Rickard's question with an emphatic "yes, we do"—though surely not by relying on concepts of innate ideas or racial memories that were the intellectual currency in the early twentieth century. Two decades after the publication of Rickard's study, and a century after Joyce's *Ulysses*, it has become clear that memory is more than a purely individual mental operation, as it was seen during the mainly behaviorist and cognitivist phases of memory psychology between the 1940s and the 1980s. With the resurgence of research on collective memory since the late 1980s, the question of how personal memories are shaped by social and cultural environments is back on the agenda.

THE ETHICS OF PREMEDIATION IN JAMES JOYCE'S ULYSSES

Working from the perspective of media memory studies, this chapter focuses on the question of how James Joyce's *Ulysses* represents *premediation*—a process that connects minds and media of collective memory. Premediation is one answer to the question of how our own experience is shaped by our ancestors' experience. It is the (usually non-conscious) process by which images and narratives recalled from representations circulating in media culture turn into powerful schemata and preform imagination, experience, memory, storytelling, and action. It is a forward-facing, generative dynamic of memory.

This chapter discusses two problematic forms of premediation presented in *Ulysses*. In the episodes "Calypso" and "Ithaca," hypermediated orientalist and anti-Semitic schemata shape the characters' thinking and acting. How does *Ulysses* represent individual memory in a culture saturated with mediations? And what are the ethical stakes of the novel's "mimesis of premediation"? To what extent are the characters in Ulysses navigated by premediation? How can they take over the wheel and navigate themselves—challenging, even breaking what I call the hidden power of implicit cultural memory?[1]

The last part of this chapter moves on from "literature as mimesis of memory" to "the memory of literature."[2] It asks what happens once we apply the concept of premediation to the literary text itself and consider the references to the *Odyssey* in *Ulysses* as a case of premediation—thus opening up once more the discussion about the nature and functions of the Homeric parallel in Joyce's novel and showing how new concepts of memory and mediation can elucidate this famous case of intertextuality or "classical reception."[3] I will address the ethical dimensions of what I take to be a specifically modernist form of classical reception: the turn from remediation to premediation, which establishes a new temporal regime. Discussing the ethical stakes of premediation both on the level of narrative representation and in the novel's intertextual relations, this chapter aims to contribute to the study of "narrative ethics" in the sense of Lothe and Hawthorn (2013).

---

[1] See Chapter 8, "Literature, Film, and the Mediality of Cultural Memory," for a discussion of premediation; and Chapter 12, "The Hidden Power of Implicit Collective Memory," for forms of implicit memory.

[2] For this distinction between the literary representation of memory ("mimesis of memory"), on the one hand, and intertextuality as a form of literature's memory, on the other hand, see Erll (2011a, 66–82).

[3] On the intersections of classical reception studies and memory studies, see Chapter 3, "Homer—A Relational Mnemohistory."

It asks how premediation operates in narrative-fictional texts, how it is shown to create (sometimes non-conscious, even unwanted) effects, and how it is consciously used and self-critically reflected upon.

11.2 Somewhere in the East: Navigating Premediation

In the "Calypso" episode, the novel's fourth chapter, Bloom makes his first appearance. A modern Odysseus figure, the Irish-Jewish Leopold Bloom is cast as a traveler. Yet physically Bloom merely moves through his native Dublin on June 16, 1904, the one day that comprises the novel's temporal setting, the day that has been turned into "Bloomsday."[4] Bloom's travels take place in the mind, but also among Dublin society and across the material geography of the Irish capital, then still under British rule and in an age of rapid modernization.

Bloom is setting off from his home in Eccles Street on a warm June morning, heading toward Dlugacz's, the butcher's, in order to buy a pork kidney for his breakfast. While walking, he indulges in a mental journey that brings him to the Near East.[5]

> Somewhere in the east: early morning: set off at dawn. Travel round in front of the sun, steal a day's march on him. Keep it up for ever never grow a day older technically. Walk along a strand, strange land, come to a city gate, sentry there, old ranker too, old Tweedy's big moustaches, leaning on a long kind of a spear. Wander through awned streets. Turbaned faces going by. Dark caves of carpet shops, big man, Turko the terrible, seated crosslegged, smoking a coiled pipe.
>
> ...
>
> Night sky, moon, violet, colour of Molly's new garters. Strings. Listen. A girl playing one of those instruments what do you call them: dulcimers. I pass.

---

[4] See King (2014) for a thoughtful discussion of the commemoration of Bloomsday in the present age of Irish multiculturalism.

[5] Bloom's "reverie" is a "mental transportation," an "exploratory" and "productive simulation," as Patrick C. Hogan (2014, 54–57) puts it, in the terminology of cognitive theory. Such a cognitive approach, however, cannot account for the fact that Bloom's "productive simulation" is at least partly co-produced by an environment of mediated memories. Yet I agree with Hogan (2014, 6) that Joyce's *Ulysses* is a case of "critical psychological realism," which enables the "mimetic reading" which I (and Hogan, too) conduct—while at the same time acknowledging that memory in *Ulysses* also exceeds the mimetic, for example in the novel's own intra-textual memories.

Probably not a bit like it really. Kind of stuff you read: in the track of the sun. (*Ulysses* 4.84–100[6])

The episode shows how mental travels such as Bloom's are *navigated by* schemata, which usually remain non-conscious. These schemata, as becomes apparent in the quoted scene, are often derived from media culture, from the "kind of stuff you read."

There are two main reasons why Bloom's mind would wander in the Near East while he is walking through his Dublin neighborhood on a sunny morning in early summer. First, as a Jewish-Irish character, he vaguely envisions Palestine as his diasporic homeland (at Dlugacz's he will pick up and contemplate a Zionist advertisement). Second, Bloom likes to indulge in erotic fantasies about his wife Molly, and these are often steeped in oriental imagery, a predilection that turns Bloom into both an orientalized and orientalizing character throughout the novel. It is about Molly that Bloom invariably thinks as he leaves his home.

The text provides signals that Bloom's imagination is prompted by several external and internal cues. When he leaves the house to buy breakfast, he can hear his wife turning and the marital bed jingling. This reminds Bloom of Gibraltar, where Molly grew up and her father Major Tweedy bought the bed.[7] Molly returns in Bloom's mental travel as a sexualized, oriental fantasy, when his imagination of a violet Eastern sky triggers the memory of Molly's new violet garters. With the Jewish homeland (Bloom will discard such *nostos* a few minutes later) and Molly's exotic eroticism never far from his mind, the sight of the morning sun and the sensation of a "happy warmth" (*Ulysses* 4.81) seem to have worked as external cues initiating Bloom's mental travel "somewhere in the east."[8]

But as much as these are Bloom's very individual, favorite mental pathways, there is also a strong aspect of collective memory in this scene. The images of the East that Bloom conjures up do not come to him by chance but are significantly *premediated* by literature and popular media culture.

---

[6] All quotations from *Ulysses* refer to Joyce (1986).
[7] Gilbert (1955 [1931], 5) describes Molly as "of mixed Spanish, Jewish and Irish extraction." Bloom often imagines her as "Moorish," turbaned, or in red slippers.
[8] In Joyce's time, Freudian and Jungian concepts of the unconscious would have been at hand for a description of this scene, as well as Ebbinghaus's and Proust's ideas of association and involuntary memory. Today, it could also be described as a combination of *involuntary autobiographical* (Berntsen 2012) and *involuntary semantic memories* (Kvavilashvili and Mandler 2004). But what is important here is that these involuntary memories *premediate* a *new* experience or fantasy.

The dulcimers, for example, seem to be an echo of Samuel Taylor Coleridge's romantic orientalist poem—Hugh Kenner (1987, 69) sees "Bloom, no doubt fumbling for a classroom memory of 'Kubla Khan.'" But the major source of premediation in this scene are Victorian travel accounts. Bloom knows this very well: "kind of stuff you read: in the track of the sun." This is a reference to Frederick Diodati Thompson's popular late Victorian travel account *In the Track of the Sun: Diary of a Globetrotter* (1893), which is listed in the "Ithaca" episode as one of the books in Bloom's house. Premediation becomes palpable here. It is represented by interior monologue, and it is explicitly reflected upon by the central character.

"Calypso" thus emerges as an episode about media and collective memory. It provides a literary representation of the process of *premediation*, of the formative power of schemata derived from media culture, and of the way such schemata may preform experience, shape imagination, reshape memory, influence visions of the future, and possibly also trigger action.

As William C. Mottolese has shown, Bloom's mind will return to Thompson's book again in "Nausicaa" and "Circe"—both episodes featuring erotic fantasies.[9] What is striking, however, is that in "Calypso" Bloom's mental travel is navigated not so much by verbal echoes from Thompson's book but by visual ones. Mottolese (2008, 102) emphasizes that *In the Track of the Sun* is an "extremely visual book." It features seventy-nine full-page photographs and illustrations of sights from virtually across the world as it was "seen" in the late nineteenth century, often through a colonial and voyeuristic gaze. "In the pages of *In the Track of the Sun*, Bloom would have encountered numerous images in word, photo, or illustration that appear in some form in *Ulysses*. Not surprisingly, ... Bloom remember[s] the visual images more than the words" (Mottolese 2008, 12).

A comparison of Thompson's chapters on Egypt, Palestine, and Turkey with Bloom's interior monologue as he is taking his early morning walk reinforces the sense that Bloom's orientalist imagination is highly visual (see Figures 11.1, 11.2., 11.3, and 11.4). Much of the passage quoted above turns out to be ekphrasis, a textual rendering of Thompson's pictorial representations of Eastern settings. Bloom's imagination is premediated by Thompson's orientalizing images—which themselves are premediated in

---

[9] Mottolese (2008, 109) points to Thompson's voyeuristic, erotic gaze, often focusing on strange, naked women.

THE ETHICS OF PREMEDIATION IN JAMES JOYCE'S *ULYSSES* 241

Bedouin sheik from the neighbourhood of Ghaza.

Figure 11.1 "Bedouin sheik from the neighbourhood of Ghaza," reproduced from Frederick Diodati Thompson, *In the Track of the Sun*, 1893, 165; public domain, The Internet Archive: https:archive.org/details/intrackofsun0000f red/page/216/mode/2up.

242 TRAVELS IN TIME

A Turkish and an Egyptian woman.

Figure 11.2 "A Turkish and an Egyptian Woman," reproduced from Frederick Diodati Thompson, *In the Track of the Sun*, 1893, 174; public domain, The Internet Archive: https://archive.org/details/intrackofsun0000fred/page/216/mode/2up.

THE ETHICS OF PREMEDIATION IN JAMES JOYCE'S *ULYSSES* 243

Interior of a Jewish house at Damascus.

Figure 11.3 "Interior of a Jewish House at Damascus," reproduced from Frederick Diodati Thompson, *In the Track of the Sun*, 1893, 206; public domain, The Internet Archive: https://archive.org/details/intrackofsun0000 fred/page/216/mode/2up.

The Via Dolorosa, Jerusalem.

Figure 11.4 "The Via Dolorosa, Jerusalem," reproduced from Frederick Diodati Thompson, *In the Track of the Sun*, 1893, 186; public domain, The Internet Archive: https://archive.org/details/intrackofsun0000fred/page/216/mode/2up.

that they are firmly grounded in Victorian conventions of visualizing the East.[10]

Even more than ekphrasis, the "somewhere in the east" passage has the feel of a *mise-en-scène*, with its spatial and temporal markers ("somewhere," "at dawn"), information about costume ("turbaned faces"), the key characters' appearance (Turko is a "big man") and posture ("seated crosslegged"). This hints at a further dimension of premediation, one that Bloom also seems to be aware of: Victorian exotic pantomimes like *Turko the Terrible*.[11]

"Turko the Terrible" is one of the leitmotifs of *Ulysses*, and it is one of the first links that the novel establishes between its two protagonists, Stephen and Bloom. In the first episode, "Telemachus," Stephen Dedalus thinks of the pantomime when he imagines his mother's secrets and youth memories (*Ulysses* 1.258).[12] This happens just a little time after Bloom conjures up

---

[10] *In the Track of the Sun* features many canonized sights, and its mode of representation is the orientalist picturesque (Metcalf 1989). Thompson's verbal discourse, by contrast, especially in the chapters on Egypt and Palestine, is utterly racist and full of invectives against the people then living in the Near East—material, that is, which appears hard to stomach for Bloom, who is a pragmatic humanist and partly identifies himself as Jewish.

[11] Victorian pantomines were musical comedies, a popular pastime for families.

[12] "She heard old Royce sing in the pantomime of *Turko the Terrible* and laughed with others" (*Ulysses* 1.257–258).

"Turko" in order to further navigate his mental travel (and the figure will return in one of Bloom's fantasies in "Circe"). *Turko the Terrible* was a very successful pantomime in late nineteenth-century Dublin, one that Bloom and Mrs. Dedalus are likely to have attended as adolescents.[13] For the fictional(ized) Dubliners of 1904, *Turko the Terrible* is thus a shared media event of the recent past. It has generated shared media schemata (which pious Mrs. Dedalus is possibly putting to different uses than Bloom).

Ulysses displays many such examples of premediation: music and opera ("Sirens"), canonical literature (Stephen's *Hamlet*), Victorian women's magazines ("Nausicaa"), religious texts such as the Bible and the Haggadah, and last but not least, the media products that Bloom encounters on June 16, 1904 (the Zionist advertisement and the *Titbit* magazine's prize story that Bloom famously wipes himself with)—all these shape the ways in which characters experience, think, remember, imagine, project, and eventually act. As in the example of Bloom in "Calypso," the effect of premediation varies according to the parameters of the character's individual mind style. At the same time, individual minds are shown to be steeped in the collective dimension of past and present media culture, which provides resources for remembering and imagination.

Ulysses is not secretive about the power of premediation. Bloom self-reflexively ponders on the impact that travel books like *In the Track of the Sun* have on his imagination ("kind of stuff you read"), and—in an Edward Saidian twist *avant la lettre*—he is also critically aware of the fact that reality is "probably not a bit like" the hypermediated orientalist, actually often crudely racist discourse and images derived from Thompson's book.

This is one of the ethical dimensions of premediation in *Ulysses*. The novel shows how premediation shapes its characters' mental operations, mostly in a non-conscious fashion. But it also shows that characters can become aware of premediation and realize how it forms and sometimes distorts their vision of reality. Bloom's capacity to indulge in a premediated orientalist fantasy and simultaneously take a step back and critically assess its origins and adequacy—to be navigated by but also to navigate premediation—is part of Bloom's much-hailed humanism.

---

[13] See Gifford and Seidman (1988, 18): "A pantomime by the Irish author-editor Edwin Hamilton (1849–1919), adapted from William Brough's (1826–70) London pantomime *Turko, the Terrible, or, the Fairy Roses* (1868). Hamilton's version was an instant success at the Gaiety Theatre in Dublin during Christmas week 1873. It was repeatedly updated and revived in the closing decades of the century. Its frame was essentially a world of fairy-tale metamorphoses and transformations—as King Turko (Royce) and his court enjoyed the magic potential of the Fairy Rose."

It does not seem a coincidence that Bloom's navigation of premediation appears on the very first pages of "Calypso," the episode that introduces and interrelates two core themes of *Ulysses*: orientalism (*sensu* Said 1978) and Bloom's Jewishness.[14] The episode suggests that Bloom's experience of marginalization in Dublin society due to what Davison (1998, 7) calls his "non-Jewish Jewishness" may have engendered in him a greater sensibility for the mediatedness of ideas about the (oriental and otherwise) Other. Arguably, the ethical capacity of navigating media schemata is part of Bloom's "cunning"—his central character trait, which connects this modern Ulysses with Joyce's understanding of both Odysseus and modern European Jewry (see Davison 1998, 114).

Reading *Ulysses* through the lens of premediation sheds new light on Joyce's famous saying that "imagination is memory" (Budgen 1970, 187). This refers not only to Joyce himself and his encyclopedic memory, from which he could consciously draw and form his materials. It also refers to the common rememberer, who will often, just like Bloom, be hampered by "defective mnemotechnic" (*Ulysses* 17.766), but whose mind will nevertheless be steeped in collective memory produced in media culture, and whose remembering and imagination are more often than not navigated by non-conscious premediation—not an unproblematic process and one, as the "Calypso" episode shows, that raises diverse ethical questions.

11.3 The "Ballad of Little Harry Hughes": The Hidden Power of Implicit Cultural Memory

Joyce famously called his *Ulysses* an "epic of two races,"[15] and the novel's exploration of the Jewish-Irish analogy comes to a climax in the penultimate

---

[14] Both dimensions have been addressed in Joyce studies since the late 1990s (see Davison 1998; Kershner 1998; Reizbaum 1999). Davison (1998, 7) explains that "[t]o Joyce, Bloom represented the urban Westernized Jew, lost to Judaism but still somehow inwardly Jewish." With wonderful Joycean irony, this in-betweenness is expressed in Bloom's hybrid breakfast dish: of non-kosher pork, Bloom (whose father came from Hungary) prefers the inner organs, a staple in "Eastern European Yiddish diet" (Davison 1998, 201). Bloom thus inhabits an ambivalent position, which will make him—as the day proceeds—a target of the anti-Semitic sentiment prevalent in Dublin's Catholic and nationalist society. In the cultural logic of the early twentieth century, both Bloom's Jewishness and his Irishness move him close to images of the Oriental: "He is a citizen of the British Empire yet outside it, an Irishman but a Jew, a European but an Oriental both because he is a Jew and because he is Irish" (Kershner 1998, 291). However, the sources of his orientalist imagination are, as Kershner (1998, 293) points out, "entirely and explicitly intertextual" (i.e., a matter of premediation and not of firsthand experience). "[A]fter all, a century of Romantic narratives has helped to persuade him that Molly, like anything shamefully desirable, is Moorish" (Kershner 1998, 292).

[15] In a letter to Carlo Linati, dated September 21, 1920: "l'epopea di due razze (Israele-Irlanda)." See Ellmann (1992, 270f.)

episode, "Ithaca," when Bloom and young Stephen Dedalus sit at night in Bloom's kitchen, quoting to each other ancient Hebrew and Irish verse, comparing Irish and Hebrew script, and finding as "points of contact" (17.745) between the Jewish and the Irish people "their dispersal, persecution, survival and revival" (17.755f.). What Bloom and Stephen engage in could be described as an attempt at "multidirectional" remembering—at understanding different histories of suffering through the lens of each other (Rothberg 2009). This "memory work" culminates in an exchange of songs. Margot Norris (2009, 65) writes about the dynamics of this episode: "Rhetorically, the narrator here shapes a crescendo of communicative possibility that leads to a climax of meaningful understanding and exchange that will take form as a celebration in song."

Such communicative and commemorative possibilities, however, come to an abrupt end when Stephen sings the popular anti-Semitic "Ballad of Little Harry Hughes." Bloom had started the exchange with a song in Hebrew, the opening lines of the Zionist anthem "Hatikvah" (7.763f.). After singing, Bloom appears to "encourage his guest to chant in a modulated voice a strange legend on an allied theme" (17.795f.). Stephen answers with the ballad about the little boy Harry who falls victim to murder after he destroys the windows of a Jewish house while playing ball. The daughter of the house lures him inside and cuts off his head with a penknife. This is an exemplar, as Norris (2009, 69) reminds us, of "the very genre of blood libel that started pogroms" all over Europe ever since the Middle Ages.[16]

The narrative mediation of this episode takes place in the form of a catechism, questions asked and answers provided by an anonymous narrative instance—"catechism (impersonal)" as Joyce calls it in the Gilbert schema[17]:

> Recite the first (major) part of this chanted legend.
> *Little Harry Hughes and his schoolfellows all*
> *Went out for to play ball*

---

[16] Blood libel "served as a pretence for plundering Jewish neighbourhoods or expelling Jews from the country (such stories figured in the expulsion of Jews from Spain under Ferdinand and Isabella)" (Mahaffey 1999, 261). Blood libel was often connected to the Jewish feast of Passover. The Christian children's blood was allegedly worked into Passover-matzah. Abby Bender (2014, 67) argues that the Ithaca episode "both formally and ritually enacts various moments of the Passover ceremony." She explains the memory-logic of Stephen's choice of a song about blood libel as follows: "[B]y recounting the story of a Jew's daughter who murders little Harry and thus reproducing the claim of Jewish monstrousness, Stephen provides the historically traditional version of Passover, not in Jewish memory, but in Western history—a history that . . . makes diasporic Jews into tragic victims, not models of national self-determination" (Bender 2014, 75). See also Weitzman et al. (2023) on the history of "blood libel" and its appearance in different regions.

[17] Gilbert (1955 [1931], 32). I discuss the role of these schemata in the next section.

248 TRAVELS IN TIME

> *And the very first ball little Harry Hughes played*
> *He drove it o'er the jew's garden wall.*
> *And the very second ball little Harry Hughes played*
> *He broke the jew's windows all.*

[A musical score of this first stanza is inserted here.]

How did the son of Rudolph receive this first part?
With unmixed feeling. Smiling, a jew, he heard with pleasure and saw the unbroken kitchen window.

Recite the second part (minor) of the legend.

> *Then out there came the jew's daughter*
> *And she all dressed in green.*
> *"Come back, come back, you pretty little boy,*
> *And play your ball again."*
> *"I can't come back and I won't come back*
> *Without my schoolfellows all,*
> *For if my master he did hear*
> *He'd make it a sorry ball."*
> *She took him by the lilywhite hand*
> *And led him along the hall*
> *Until she led him to a room*
> *Where none could hear him call.*
> *She took a penknife out of her pocket*
> *And cut off his little head.*
> *And now he'll play his ball no more*
> *For he lies among the dead.*

[A musical score is inserted here.]

How did the father of Millicent receive this second part?
With mixed feelings. Unsmiling, he heard and saw with wonder a jew's daughter, all dressed in green. (17.801–831)

There is no doubt about Bloom's utter surprise at the anti-Semitic twist of the song, which he apparently had not heard before, or about his deep hurt. Whatever Bloom may have thought to be an "allied theme" (his Zionist song could have elicited a song about the Irish freedom struggle), he certainly was not prepared for that.[18] While he receives the first rather innocent stanza "with unmixed feeling," still "smiling," and confidently positioning himself as "a jew" (the catechist question frames him as Rudolph's, that is his Jewish father's, son) inside a Jew's house, mapping the ballad's story-world onto his own surroundings (he looks at his own "unbroken" window), he hears the second part "with mixed feelings" and "unsmiling." Bloom is still immersed in the ballad's story-world, reliving the events with his inner senses, now hearing and seeing "a jew's daughter," whom (as the catechism's question implies) he must associate with his own daughter Milly, who turns, as the song proceeds, into a murderess.

It is notoriously difficult to gauge *why* Stephen chooses this outrageous song, which he knows must hurt his host deeply (especially after their conversation in the cabman's shelter, when Bloom had confided in him the anti-Semitic attacks he had suffered earlier that day). Further, *what* actually happens (what is said and done, what is merely imagined, what the thoughts and motivations of both characters are) is similarly difficult to decide due to the narrative form of the "Ithaca" episode, with its questions and answers that often appear convoluted, ambiguous, or seem to lead far away from what is actually happening on the story level—a complex type of unreliable narration.[19]

But what is clear is *how* the ballad is presented: in a hyper-remediated way: Among the myriad songs remediated in *Ulysses*, the "Ballad of Little Harry Hughes" is the only one whose representation includes not only the full lyrics (all five stanzas appear printed in italics) and the handwritten musical notation,[20] but also yet another rendering of the lyrics (of the first and second stanza) in Joyce's own handwriting underneath the musical notation. This is an excess of remediation, the repetition of older mediations in a range of different semiotic systems. Clearly, this form of representation underlines the "vivacity of the song" (Brannigan 2010, 54), and it also

---

[18] In one sense, Stephen's song is indeed about an "allied theme." It represents the very anti-Semitism that led to the Zionism referenced in Bloom's song. (I am grateful to Leona Toker for this insight.)

[19] Karen Lawrence (1981, 182) calls this "a mechanism of avoidance." Norris (2009, 57) highlights the performative and ethical functions of this narrative strategy: "narratorial practices of avoidance, particularly when they concern Bloom's Jewishness, function performatively by acting out serious questions whose answers will be far more problematic and ambiguous than any devised by a religious catechism."

[20] The musical annotation was provided by Joyce's friend Jacques Benoît-Méchin (see Gifford and Seidman 1988, 579).

"aggressively makes it impossible for the reader to miss, misunderstand, or misconstrue the literal wording of the ballad" (Norris 2009, 67).

Yet such excess of remediation also points to the ballad's sheer cultural presence. It does not appear to be a tune that Stephen has to unearth from the past with difficulty; quite the opposite, it seems easily accessible. Repeated remediation of a memory content signals that it holds a key place in collective memory. Moreover, it is exactly such hyper-remediation that produces premediation. Much-mediated memories tend to stick in people's minds. Their patterns (a plot, a character constellation, stereotypes, a melody, a rhyme-scheme) can become unstuck and travel to new situations as premediating schemata. Premediation (here a phenomenon of "memory in mind") thus follows from remediation (as a phenomenon of "memory in or across media").

To disentangle some of this scene's media logic: first, what Stephen does on the story level is a typical form of remediation. He is singing an old song again, that is, practicing the very kind of remediation that memory studies hold to be constitutive of the life of memory contents in culture. Songs that are not sung again and again will be forgotten, or relegated to the archive, and with them the messages that they carry. Second, what the novel does on its textual and visual surface is a triple remediation: representing a historically extant song as printed text, handwritten text, and musical score. The novel *Ulysses* thus contributes to the perpetuation of this anti-Semitic song in cultural memory, but it does so in a highly critical and reflexive way, exhibiting the (detrimental) power of continuously remediated memory matter to *premediate* present experience, meaning-making, and action.

What history, what histories of mediation, lie behind the remediation of the "Ballad of Little Harry Hughes" in *Ulysses*? Francis James Child's *English and Scottish Popular Ballads* (Vol. III, Part I, 1904), which Joyce, as Mahaffey (1999, 261) argues, doubtlessly knew, meticulously collects the different versions of this ballad. Its story seems to go back to the famous murder case of eight-year-old Hugh of Lincoln, who went missing in the summer of 1255. His dead body was found in the courtyard of a certain Copin (or Jopin), a Lincoln Jew, most likely placed there by the unknown murderer who calculated (correctly, as it turned out) on the anti-Semitic atmosphere in England under Henry III. Under torture, Copin confessed to a ritual murder in which Jews from all over England had allegedly participated.[21] This

---

[21] Child quotes from the medieval chronicle *Chronica Majora* that Copin confessed that "almost all the Jews in England had been accessory to the child's death, and almost every city of England where Jews lived had sent delegates to the ceremony of his immolation, as to a Paschal sacrifice,"

is, as Göller (1987, 19) argues, an early version of "the idea of a Jewish world conspiracy"—as it would gain currency again during the Great Depression of 1929, and only a few years later be used to legitimize the genocidal anti-Semitism of Nazi Germany. The story of Little Harry exemplifies the sheer historical depths from which premediating plots and stereotypes can emerge, and (in hindsight even more so) the dangerous potential they may carry.[22] In the aftermath of Copin's confession and execution, more than eighty Jews were arrested and eighteen hanged. Henry III confiscated the Jews' possessions and turned them into royal property, thus profiting significantly from the blood libel. Harry became a Christian child martyr, and although he was never canonized, pilgrimages took place to sites associated with him.

The story of Little Harry Hughes of Lincoln is a densely remediated one—over more than seven centuries and across a spectrum of impactful media.[23] The case was narrated in over thirty medieval chronicles, most notably in Matthew Paris's contemporary *Chronica Majora*, in the *Annals of Waverly*, and the *Annals of Burton*.[24] An early Anglo-French ballad retains the chronicles' key elements, yet later English-language ballads "must, in the course of five hundred years of tradition, have departed considerably from the early form; in all of them the boy comes to his death for breaking a Jew's window, and at the hands of the Jew's daughter" (Child 1904, 239). In Joyce's time, not only popular English ballads, but also nursery rhymes and visual representations, had produced many variants of the story of Little Harry, while retaining central motifs such as the ball game or the killing with a pen-knife. In some strands of the ballad corpus, the story became connected with an initiation or seduction story (see Göller 1987, 25f.), which is clearly present in the variant that Stephen sings—not surprisingly, given the young poet's difficult relationships with women (see Mahaffey 1999, 262f.).

Francis Child (1904, 240) explicitly criticizes the anti-Semitic thrust of the song: "These pretended child murders, with their horrible consequences, are only a part of a persecution which, with all moderation, may be rubricated as the most disgraceful chapter in the history of the human race." He is aware

---

as "the Jews crucified a boy every year, if they could get hold of one, and had crucified this Hugh" (Child 1904, 236).
[22] On medieval stereotypes and modern anti-Semitism, see Chazan (2023).
[23] The story itself is premediated by an array of earlier medieval atrocity stories about children crucified by Jews.
[24] For summaries of their different versions, see Child (1904, 234–238). In the late fourteenth century, Chaucer's Middle English "The Prioress's Tale" (part of *The Canterbury Tales*, 1387–1400) combines the legend with a miracle tale. Parts of the story thus entered the canon of English literature.

of the ongoing impact of the story-pattern and confirms that at his time, in the late nineteenth century, "[t]he charge against the Jews of murdering children for their blood is by no means as yet a thing of the past" (Child 1904, 242). His long list of blood libel in recent history all over Europe includes cases in Neuhoven [sic] near Düsseldorf (Germany, 1834), in Rhodes (1840), in Tisza-Eszlar (Hungary, 1882), and in Smyrna (1883)—all followed by massacres of Jews, often in hundreds.[25] A few decades later, in Joyce's time, anti-Semitism was still virulent, in fact exacerbated by a recycling of the blood libel discourse. In the wake of the Dreyfus affair, Catholic journals "reintroduced the medieval myth of Jewish sacrifice of Christian children and the drinking of their blood during Passover feast" and the resuscitation of such accusations had "devastating effects in rural communities throughout Europe" (Davison 1998, 18f.). As late as 1911, there was a case of blood libel in Kiev that was discussed all over Europe, and in 1919 Joyce went to a protest meeting about a "false accusation of ritual murder" (Davison 1998, 19; see also Reizbaum 1999, 13).

It is through histories of remediation that stories such as those of Jewish blood libel solidify into cultural memory. Different media display different capacities in the process: Over centuries, medieval chronicles were seen as reliable historiography. Ballads and nursery rhymes are easily memorable and address children at an early age, shaping their minds (Rubin 1995). Modern journals (Catholic or other) can be powerful opinion makers. In the early twentieth century, multiply remediated anti-Semitic memories thus were present, easily cued and accessed, discharging an energy that appears faster than light in preforming thoughts about and actions toward Jews.

Stephen draws on this repertoire immediately, almost mechanically. There is nothing that indicates that his selection was premeditated or that he had thought of "Little Harry" earlier that day. His choice of the "Ballad of Little Harry Hughes" appears in answer to questions raised by his present situation: What comes to your mind when you sit in "a Jew's house"? When attention is drawn to "the Jew's young daughter"? (Bloom repeatedly mentions his Milly.) Blood libel. The story of Little Harry. The ultimate trigger eliciting the anti-Semitic ballad from Stephen's memory appears to be Leopold Bloom's reassuringly meant words after his suggestion to sing

---

[25] Bloom's sharp analysis of the staying power of atrocity tales like that of blood libel is astute but omits the mediation part: "the incitations of the hierarchy, the superstition of the populace, the propagation of rumour in continued fraction of veridicity, the envy of opulence, the influence of retaliation" (*Ulysses* 17.844–847).

a song on an "allied theme": "Reassuringly, their place, where none could hear them talk, being secluded" (17.797). The idea of a secluded place, where Stephen could not be heard by any other Dubliner, reappears in Stephen's commentary on the song, when he speaks of "a secret infidel apartment" to which Harry is led.[26]

With the "Ballad of Little Harry Hughes," James Joyce's *Ulysses* points to the enormous longevity and power of popular anti-Semitism in cultural memory. As Bender (2014, 75) points out, it "illustrates a hyper-memory that persists through the centuries." This "hyper-memory" is fueled by and takes effect through the twin dynamics of remediation and premediation. It is exactly to this dual dynamics that the "Ithaca" episode draws attention: by its striking hyper-remediation of the ballad; by its repetition (in the episode's setting, in the ballad's story-world, in Stephen's commentary) of the schema "secluded Jewish apartment," which seems to trigger the age-old story in Stephen's mind; and by the reluctance of the narrative instance to provide a clear motivation for Stephen to sing the ballad (typically, phenomena such as long-term priming and mind popping are non-declarative; see Kvavilashvili and Mandler 2004).

Premediating schemata like these are sticky, hard to transform or to get rid of. These forms of collective memory are very different from the explicit, voluntary, conscious, often ceremonialized forms of commemoration that are usually the focus of memory studies. They seem to belong to the strata of implicit, involuntary, non-conscious memory that are created in the *longue durée* of memory culture and can take unexpected and uncontrollable effects in social interaction. This is what I call the hidden power of implicit cultural memory.

What is the ethical dimension of this complex scene? "Ithaca" shows the hidden power of anti-Semitic premediation even in someone as critical and free-thinking as Stephen, who earlier that day had answered so nonchalantly "who has not?" to headmaster Deasy's anti-Semitic invective, "they sinned against the light" (2.373, 2.361). Margot Norris (2009, 56, 75) ascribes an "ethical effect" to this "sabotaged climax": "By shocking the reader ... Joyce forces us to explore why such outbursts are produced, to reexamine their

---

[26] Stephen's cryptic commentary, which has generated its own history of interpretation (see Norris 2009, 68f.) runs as follows: "One of all, the least of all, is the victim predestined. Once by inadvertence, twice by design he challenges his destiny. It comes when he is abandoned and challenges him reluctant and, as an apparition of hope and youth holds him unresisting. It leads him to a strange habitation, to a secret infidel apartment, and there, implacable, immolates him, consenting" (*Ulysses* 17.832–837). Across the novel, the "victim predestined" turns into a sliding signifier, referring to Harry, Stephen, and also to Bloom. See also Davison (1998, 233f.).

historical origins, and to worry about their pernicious future effects not only on Leopold Bloom, but more widely on an entire European population."

In fact, detrimental or pernicious premediation is a force that can sabotage what is appreciated as cosmopolitan or "multidirectional" memory today (Levy and Sznaider 2006 [2001]; Rothberg 2009). "Ithaca" points to the (often hidden, non-conscious) limits of multidirectional remembering. Cosmopolitan potentials are clearly palpable in the Irish-Jewish memory exchange between Bloom and Stephen. But, as Bender (2014, 76) points out, "[w]hether self-consciously or not, Stephen ultimately forces us to confront our uncritical celebration of the solidarity of the oppressed; he reveals that analogies between peoples may be meaningful, but still they must happen within history, not outside it. The ballad brings a tolerated antisemitism in to the present."

However grave and justified the concerns about the hidden power of implicit cultural memory, this is not a one-way road to inevitable mnemonic perdition. Interestingly and importantly, Göller (1987, 31) points to the "opposing forces" in the mnemohistory of the "Ballad of Little Harry Hughes." The first chronicler of the story, medieval monk Matthew Paris, uses the Latin word *deliramenta* (hallucinations) to describe the mental state in which Copin confessed to the Jewish blood ritual, "thus casting doubt on the veracity of the crown witness." In a long-term cultural memory perspective, Göller also looks at what came *before* the medieval story of Little Harry (possibly a fairytale-like proto-version of a story about initiation, without any anti-Semitic motif) as well as *after* its transformation into popular English ballads: in some strands of the Anglophone ballad corpus, notably in American variants, the anti-Semitic motif was elided.

Ironically, it is exactly this American part of the corpus that comes closest to Stephen's version. Stephen's variant of the "Ballad of Little Harry Hughes" is very similar to what Child (1904, 251) lists as version "N," a ballad that was recorded in New York and appears in Newell's 1884 *Games and Songs of American Children*. Newell encountered this ballad as "a song of negro children in New York," and he traces its source back to an Irish immigrant grandmother, surmising that "a thirteenth-century tradition, extinct perhaps in its native soil, had taken a new lease of existence" (Newell 1884, 75). This case is in itself a striking example of traveling memory and transcultural remediation.[27] The only glaring difference between the "Irish-Black American" variant "N" and the one that Stephen sings is that the ballad

---

[27] Newell's tale about how he found the ballad in New York is also included in a footnote of Child's *Popular Ballads* (Child 1904, 254). If Joyce was indeed acquainted with Child's collection, then he

found in New York had elided the anti-Semitic dimension and turned into "Little Harry Hughes and the Duke's Daughter" (Newell 1884, 75). In comparison, the fact that Stephen retains and repeats the ballad's anti-Semitic slant stands out even more prominently.

Stephen, a character who, like Bloom, both navigates and is navigated by premediation, would have had a *choice*: a choice of singing the song again, but differently. The American variant shows that it is indeed singable without the anti-Semitic motif. But Stephen does not draw on (or come up with) the possibility of what Gifford and Seidman call a "genteel avoidance of the ballad's 'antisemitism'" (1998, 579).

The "Ballad of Little Harry Hughes" in the "Ithaca" episode shows that premediation is not a blind fate to be accepted in increasingly hypermediated memory cultures. It is the effect of a process of remediation in which everyone is implicated, in which different variants can almost always be imagined or retrieved, and in which we all have the choice of what to transport, what to elide, what to ignore—only, however, on the condition that non-conscious schemata are made conscious, and then (self-)critically scrutinized, thus breaking the hidden power of implicit cultural memory.

11.4 Premediated by the *Odyssey*: *Ulysses* and a New Temporal Regime

Premediation is not only imaginatively explored in *Ulysses*, it is also one of the novel's structuring principles. *Ulysses* is premediated by the *Odyssey*. Joyce's novel does not repeat or rewrite the Homeric epic. Instead, it draws on the resources of the *old* story's mnemohistory in order to tell a *new* story for a new time. Arguably, with its specific way of referencing the *Odyssey*, Joyce's *Ulysses* established premediation as the major mode of mnemonic relationality between modernists and the ancients. In this way, *Ulysses* significantly contributed to the creation of modernism's new temporal regime[28]—the regime of premediation.

Controversial discussions about *Ulysses*'s relation to the Homeric pretext started with the publication of the novel—and this controversy is still ongoing. While Valery Larbaud (1922) saw the ancient epic as an indispensable

---

would have been aware of this backstory of transcultural memory and of the different narrative possibilities of the "Ballad of Little Harry Hughes."

[28] I use the concept "temporal regime" to describe how cultures conceive of the relationality of past, present, and future; see also Hartog (2017) and Assmann (2020).

"key" to *Ulysses*, Ezra Pound (1922) declared it a mere "scaffold."[29] T. S. Eliot (1923, 483) identified a "mythical method" in Joyce's "manipulating [of] a continuous parallel between contemporaneity and antiquity" and described the Homeric references as "simply a way of controlling, of ordering, of giving a shape and a significance to the immense panorama of futility and anarchy which is contemporary history."

Joyce himself furthered the idea that the *Odyssey* could be seen as a pre-mediating schema for *Ulysses*, sending Carlo Linati (in 1920) his famous "summary—key—skeleton—scheme,"[30] which assigns each chapter a title referring to episodes from the *Odyssey*. This scheme suggests correspondences between characters and events of *Ulysses* with elements from the *Odyssey*. The word "schema" entered the terminology of Joyce-research by way of the "Linati-schema" and later the "Gilbert-schema," both of which are often used schematically indeed to discuss parallels between the *Odyssey* and *Ulysses*. However, the effects of the *Odyssey*'s presence in *Ulysses* are not at all schematic in the sense of a simple, mechanical key-lock relation. They are often highly complex, ambiguous, and allusive. As a result, interpretations that try to follow the Odyssey-as-schema concept too closely may appear counterproductive and even ridiculous.[31]

In Joyce's time, Immanuel Kant's philosophy and early Gestalt psychology were available as sources for notions of schema and schema-like phenomena. Much like the thinking about memory, the idea of schema was in the air. While Joyce was writing *Ulysses*, the British psychologist Frederic Bartlett had begun to develop his influential theory of narrative schemata, which he would set out in his 1932 monograph, *Remembering*.[32] However, Bartlett's concept of schema, as Brady Wagoner has shown, is anything but schematic. Instead, it implies an "embodied, dynamic, temporal, holistic, and social, ... living, moving process" (Wagoner 2017, 155, 122).[33] If we consider that the

---

[29] "[A] scaffold, a means of construction, justified by the result and justifiable only by it" (Pound 1954 [1922], 70).

[30] Joyce's original Italian terminology is "sunto-chiave-scheletro-schema," and later in the letter he refers to "mio schema" (Ellmann 1992, 270).

[31] Kenner (1987, 3f.) writes about Stuart Gilbert, whose guide to *Ulysses* was the first book-length study of the novel to appear (in 1931) as a "quasi-authorised guide" based on Joyce's typewritten schema: Gilbert "seems to have been solemn and naive, which was unlucky because *Ulysses* is neither." Kenner adds that "[r]esponding to early accusations of formlessness, Gilbert adduced a schematic formality from which understanding took several decades to recover" (Kenner 1987, 170).

[32] Similar ideas were advanced in the 1930s by Jean Piaget and Lev Vygotsky (see Wertsch 2002).

[33] Bartlett himself was unhappy with term "schema," realizing that it could be understood as static structure (as it in fact has later come to be understood), yet noting that it is "very difficult to think of any other descriptive word" (Bartlett 1932, 201).

process of schema building is more often than not a mediated one, then the schema as "an embodied, dynamic, temporal, holistic" *and mediated* process quite aptly describes the presence of the *Odyssey* in *Ulysses*. The *Odyssey* is a malleable resource, shaped and reshaped by time and media, embodied as personal memory of author and readers, and used as a narrative schema in an "effort after meaning" (Bartlett 1932, 20)—much in the way evoked by T. S. Eliot as a pursuit of shape and significance, though not in static predetermined ways.

It is my contention that the idea of the *Odyssey*-as-schema for *Ulysses* can only be recovered if we understand "schema" in an extended Bartlettian sense as a dynamic temporal and mediated phenomenon—as a force of mnemohistory that derives from remediation and drives premediation. In fact, many problems with the *Odyssey* in Joyce research originate in the interpreters' problematically static concept of "schema." In *Ulysses*, the *Odyssey* does *not* appear as a fixed Homeric pre-text, a static structure, a rigid template or script, with clearly defined slots to be filled in.[34] Instead, the reader encounters great complexity, for example, when Molly appears as both a Penelope (albeit an unfaithful one) and a Calypso. Similarly, the Linati-schema lists "the departing wayfarer" as the "meaning" of the "Calypso" episode, but Bloom (the novel's Ulysses) does not fare very far (but makes it only around the corner to the pork butcher). And the reunion of father Ulysses and son Telemachus that readers would expect in an "Ithaca" episode does not really seem to be a slot well filled-in by the anti-Semitic song that Stephen sings to Bloom.

One explanation for these complexities is what Joyce refers to as "two plane"[35]—the novel's ironic double structure, which shows how the modern world looks incongruent when matched to ancient terms, and vice versa. But "ancient" and "modern" are not just two pillars with a gap of two and a half millennia between them. What is at stake in the discussion of the presence of the *Odyssey* in *Ulysses* is an understanding of the process of literature in memory culture, particularly in its *longue durée* encompassing antiquity and modernity. Seen through the lens of memory studies, Homer's *Odyssey* is for *Ulysses* not a timeless myth *outside of history* but a remediated and

---

[34] The vocabulary here comes from schema-theories developed in the fields of cognitive psychology and computer science in the 1970s, for example Schank and Abelson (1977).
[35] In fact, Joyce preferred the description "two plane" (a term coined in conversation by T. S. Eliot) to what Eliot eventually advanced as the "mythical method" (see Ellmann 1992, 297). "Two plane" seems to imply that the stories of the ancient hero Odysseus and modern Bloom must be seen on par: Bloom sheds new light (often comic, tragic, or ironic) on Odysseus and vice versa. See Erll (2024b) on Joyce's allegorical method and its relation to "Odyssean mnemohistory."

premediating story, whose transmission is firmly located *within history*. It is mnemohistory.[36]

A significant part of the *Odyssey*'s mnemohistory consists in remediations—in the history of mediating the story of Odysseus again and again, from orality to literacy, from manuscript to print, in translations, adaptations, rewriting, across time, space, and cultures. *Ulysses* shows on almost every page that it refers not to a single stable pre-text but to a rich history of what has come to be called in classics departments "classical receptions." Joyce's choice of the title for his novel—*Ulysses* rather than "Odysseus"—already indicates that it deals with a mnemohistory, evoking not only Joyce's first encounter with the *Odyssey* as a schoolboy in the form of Charles Lamb's *Adventures of Ulysses* (1808), whose episodic structuring is remediated in *Ulysses* (Erll 2019b), but also Virgil's remediation of Homer's epics, the *Aeneid* (29–19 BCE), which firmly established Odysseus's Latin name Ulixes/Ulysses in mnemohistory.

James Ramey (2007, 98) emphasizes that Joyce's method consists in "allusions to earlier allusions to the same myth." And he points out that "[r]ather than simply knowing and using the *Odyssey* as a template, Joyce became a Homerist." In his influential book *The Ulysses Theme*, W. B. Stanford (1954, 274) records: "Professor Stanislaus Joyce has kindly informed me that his brother had studied the following writers on Ulysses: Virgil, Ovid, Dante, Shakespeare, Racine, Fenelon, Tennyson, Phillips, d'Annunzio, and Hauptmann, as well as Samuel Butler's *The Authoress of the Odyssey* and Bérard's *Les Pheniciens et l'Odyssee*, and the translations by Butler and Cowper." Thus Joyce's is not just the learnedness of a "Homerist," but also the mnemohistorian's keen awareness of an old story's versions and variants, its mediated and transcultural[37] lives in mnemohistory—"literary metempsychosis," to use Ramey's (2007) term.[38] *Ulysses* exemplifies on the level of media culture what Bartlett writes about schemata in the individual mind: they are

---

[36] Leah Culligan Flack (2015, 4–6) points to "the misconception [which] exists to this day that the *Iliad* and *Odyssey* serve primarily as ahistorical, mythological touchstones for modernist writing." Her argument focuses on the strategic, political use of Homeric references (and their cultural authority) as "a tactical defense of modernist writing."

[37] Joyce focuses on the transcultural dimension of this mnemohistory, by, for instance, using the idea of Phoenician influence on Homer's *Odyssey* that he found in Victor Bérard's (1902) work, or in the novel's frequent references to Sindbad as another Odyssean story.

[38] "Metempsychosis," a keyword in *Ulysses*, is indeed an apt description of the afterlives of literary memory, as studied for example by Ann Rigney (2012). Ramey (2007, 99) argues that Joyce "frees himself from a mechanical reliance on the *Odyssey* as an authoritative source" and instead positions himself within a "transhistorical textual community."

"active developing patterns," "an active organization of past reactions, or of past experiences" (Bartlett 1932, 201).

Bartlett's idea of schemata also includes the possibility of reflexivity, which the psychologist somewhat ominously calls the capacity of "turning around upon one's schemata"—something which today, as Wagoner (2017, 124) points out, would be described as "meta-memory" or "meta-cognition." The schema becomes "not merely something that works the organism, but something with which the organism can work" (Bartlett 1932, 208), much in the way that Bloom both is navigated by but also navigates his schemata in his mental travels "somewhere in the east." With its host of incongruous effects, *Ulysses* can also be said to "turn around upon" the *Odyssey* as its premediating schema, showing the intricacies and ironies of the premediating power of what has come to be called the Western canon.

Steeped in a mnemohistory of over two and a half millennia, *Ulysses* reconfirms and establishes anew the Homeric story as a cultural schema, but in a way that flexibly adapts the schema to modernity. It draws on the *Odyssey*'s potentialities for premediating new stories in a new time, on the wealth of possibilities emerging from a mnemohistory of receptions and remediations as dense, versatile, and transcultural as that of few other stories. But *Ulysses* also self-consciously "turns around upon" this schema, in its ironic (sometimes comic, sometimes tragic) "two plane-effects" as well as by mixing the schema of the *Odyssey* with other schemata, derived from mnemohistories of the Bible, Shakespeare, Dante, and by assembling premediating schemata as diverse and incongruous as that of "Homer," "Turko," and "Little Harry."[39]

Joyce's *Ulysses* was a major catalyst of Odyssean memory in the twentieth century.[40] From here, the *Odyssey* would make its way into an "Age of Extremes" (Eric Hobsbawm), as one of the most powerful premediating forces shaping the experience of modernity's uncertainties, of travel and exile, of war and genocide (see Hall 2008). The fundamental move from remediation to premediation that Joyce's *Ulysses* effected by turning the *Odyssey* into a flexible cultural schema (by *not* repeating, translating, rewriting, or adapting the old text, but instead by making its memory *preform* a modern story) marks a significant change in the temporal regime

---

[39] Wagoner (2017, 125) explains that Bartlett emphasizes the "interplay of different schemata": "when we recall an event or more complex material, multiple schemata come into play, supporting or checking each other at different points."

[40] Alongside other modernists, of course (see also Flack 2015; Graziosi and Greenwood 2010).

from Victorianism to modernism. Flack (2015, 3) aptly describes this as one "of the central paradoxes of modernist writing: the vital presence of classical literature in a movement nominally dedicated to the modern and the new." Casting aside epochs of the more recent past (such as Victorianism), many modernists embraced antiquity, yet according to a new temporal logic. While remediation and premediation are two aspects that always interplay in the mnemohistorical process, modernism placed its accent more firmly and self-reliantly on forward-facing premediation than any earlier epoch. This new relation to the past was expressed by Osip Mandelstam (1997, 71) in 1923: "We are free from the burden of memories. On the other hand, we have so many rare presentiments: Pushkin, Ovid, Homer." It is in this sense—in the turn from remediation to premediation—that Ezra Pound's (1935) "make it new" can be reconciled with the strong presence of the classical past in modernist literature, not least in Joyce's *Ulysses*.

Ulysses firmly established the *Odyssey* as a premediating memory in the age of modernism, even after much of the aura of classics was lost with the civilizational break of the First World War. The novel opened up a horizon of narrative possibilities,[41] a horizon which already seemed to imply later modern writers such as Jorge Luis Borges and Derek Walcott and their radically new ways of telling stories about the modern world. *Ulysses* launched modernism's new temporal regime by showcasing on virtually every page how "turning around upon" received schemata would not repeat the Old, but produce the New. This is the epistemological and ethical significance of the novel's premediation.

---

[41] Piero Boitani (1994) would argue that Homer's *Odyssey* itself already held diverse narrative potentialities, which would be unfolded over reception history. Seen in this way, Joyce's *Ulysses* is (like Dante) one of the major junctures in reception history, a catalyst that actualized such potentialities and turned them into possibilities for later writers.

PART IV
DIALOGUES WITH PSYCHOLOGY

Chapter 12
The Hidden Power of Implicit Collective Memory

12.1 "Unusual Suspects": Moving beyond Commemorative Memory

"Round up the Unusual Suspects!" Vered Vinitzky-Seroussi's (2011) exhortation is the starting point of this article. Certain forms of collective memory are by now very well-researched. Among the "usual suspects" of interdisciplinary memory studies are forms of explicit, identity-creating, and often official commemoration—acts of memory in any case, which actors are aware of. Such conscious acts of memory are an important, visible, and much-discussed part of memory culture. But they do not represent the entire range of possible relations between minds, media communication, and (social) environments.

In fact, as Michael Schudson (1997, 3) remarked, conducting memory studies exclusively as commemoration studies is a bit like the drunk man who only looks for his car keys under the street lamp. In other words: "Not all of what societies remember is recalled through or in relation to self-conscious or dedicated memory projects. Instead, the past is often incorporated into the present in ways that do not aim at commemoration" (Schudson 2014, 85). Schudson thus draws an important distinction between "commemorative memory," on the one hand, and a whole variety of other forms of collective memory, which he subsumes under the term "non-commemorative memory."

This chapter builds on such calls to move beyond the predominance of memory studies as commemoration studies. For reasons of terminological precision and interdisciplinary interconnectability (outlined below), it suggests a distinction between explicit and implicit forms of collective memory. It proposes "implicit collective memory" as a cover term for the myriad possibilities of the past affecting the present in ways that most people remain unaware of.

Travels in Time. Astrid Erll, Oxford University Press. © Oxford University Press (2025).
DOI: 10.1093/oso/9780197767733.003.0013

Memory studies has not even begun to systematically address the usually hidden but powerful dynamics of implicit collective memory. In what follows, I will discuss the role of media communication for processes of remembering that remain non-conscious on a collective level. And to show that implicit phenomena are (and have always been) an equally quite hidden key concern of memory studies, I will engage with perspectives from a wide range of memory research in various disciplines.

12.2 What Does "Implicit Memory" Mean? Psychological Perspectives

In cognitive psychology, where the term was coined (Graf and Schacter 1985), "implicit memory" refers to processes of individual memory that subjects are not conscious of. Cognitive psychology posits different systems of memory. Endel Tulving (1983) famously differentiated between semantic memory ("knowing that") and episodic memory ("remembering"). Both are forms of explicit memory, which enables conscious (declarative, intentional) recall. Implicit memory, on the other hand, is behind all non-conscious acts of memory, which can range from procedural memories (i.e., for tying shoelaces or riding a bike, "knowing how") all the way to effects of perceptual and conceptual priming (see Schacter 1987; on procedural vs. declarative memory, see Squire 1987).[1]

Priming is a standard psychological method to make implicit memory empirically observable in the laboratory. One typical example of (perceptual) priming research in cognitive psychology is the word-stem completion task, where participants are first shown a list of words and later asked to quickly generate words from the first three letters (so that ele__ could be completed into elephant, elevator, etc.). The result is that participants tend to resort to the words seen earlier, but without being aware of the connection. Importantly, amnesiacs, who cannot have conscious memory for the

---

[1] See also Schacter (1996). For a use of memory systems to describe mental representations of collective memory, see Manier and Hirst (2010). I have applied these categories to further distinguish between different social functions of collective memory. According to this model (Erll 2011a, 108), there are two explicit forms of collective memory: first, "collective-episodic (or: autobiographical) memory," which means that remembered items are related to time and collective identity (often, but not exclusively, in the mode of commemorative memory), and, second, "collective-semantic memory," which refers to the production of cultural knowledge and accentuates its temporal dimension. (For sociology of knowledge approaches to memory, see the entries in Olick et al. 2010; Savelsberg 2021).

previously shown lists of words, perform on this task just as well as healthy people.[2] Put in a nutshell, when seen through the lens of priming, implicit memory appears, in the words of cognitive psychologist Henry L. Roediger (1990), as a form of "retention without remembering." Similarly, social psychologist Don Carlston (2010, 4) explains in the *Handbook of Implicit Social Cognition*: "Although measured in a variety of ways, implicit memory has been defined fairly consistently as influences of past experience on later performance, in the absence of conscious memory for the earlier experience."

In a broader memory studies perspective, there are some particularly relevant effects of priming, among them the "mere exposure effect" (Bornstein and Craver-Lemley 2017), and the "validity effect" (Renner 2017), that is, the fact that what is seen and heard again and again, often without awareness, seems familiar, is liked, and is even considered true. Behavioral economist Daniel Kahneman (2011, 85) explains: "A reliable method to bring people to believe in false statements is frequent repetition, because familiarity cannot easily be distinguished from truth." Priming can also lead to "mental contamination" (Schacter 2002, 301), for example by sexist and racist stereotypes, as well as to non-conscious forms of plagiarism: cryptomnesia.[3]

One reason for all these effects is that implicit memory involves source amnesia. The source of a piece of information and its status (Is it someone's lived experience or hearsay? Is the source reliable or unreliable, fictional, or factual?) do not seem to play a great role whenever items are encoded and activated unintentionally. What is retained in the framework of implicit memory feels familiar (pleasant, natural, true) and can even assume the subjective, "episodic" quality of personal experience.[4]

In a psychological perspective, implicit memory is an apparatus of automatic, "fast thinking," as Kahneman calls it in *Thinking, Fast and Slow* (2011). He posits a psychological "double process model" and distinguishes between

---

[2] For an overview, see Roediger (1990).

[3] A caveat may be in place here: The more spectacular research on "social" or "behavioral" priming, as it was conducted in the 1980s and 1990s (e.g., Bargh et al.'s [1996] "Florida experiment" where students walked slower after being primed on words connected to old age), has now come under severe criticism as many of its findings could not be replicated (see Chivers 2019). On the one hand, there is now a call in psychology for greater methodological rigor when studying what is seen as universal mental patterns. On the other hand, there is an emerging insight that certain priming effects occur only in subsets of people (Chivers 2019, 202). This latter point resonates well with memory studies' emphasis on the social situatedness and particular ecologies of each act of memory.

[4] "The experience of familiarity has a simple but powerful quality of 'pastness' that seems to indicate that it is a direct reflection of prior experience" (Whittlesea et al. 1990, 716).

controlled (conscious, intentional) and automatic (non-conscious) forms of human information processing. For social psychologist John Bargh, automatic cognitive processes have four characteristics: "lack of awareness, lack of intentionality, lack of controllability, and high efficiency (nonreliance on cognitive resources)" (Carlston 2010, 40; Bargh 1994).

"High efficiency" is a central attribute of implicit memory. At the same time, such powerful "fast" forms of memory often remain entirely hidden. They are non-conscious, unintentional, and uncontrollable. This is why, in his now-classic introduction to the psychology and neuroscience of memory, *Searching for Memory* (1996, 161), Daniel Schacter writes about "the hidden world of implicit memory." Moving on to the broader field of memory studies, and with a nod to Schacter, I point to "the hidden power of implicit collective memory," thus accentuating not only the invisibility, but also the agential, forward-pushing, future-making capacities of implicit collective memory.

12.3 A Hidden Power: Implicit Memory as a Collective Phenomenon

But how can we start thinking about implicit memory as a *collective* phenomenon? To begin with, it is worth recalling what is meant by "remembering" and "forgetting," when these processes are not just understood as phenomena of individual psychology but seen in their (actual) distribution across assemblages of biological, mental, sociocultural, and material elements. For memory studies, "memory" exists only in this extended form as an "ecology of memory" (Hoskins 2016; see also Sutton et al. 2010). "*Collective* memory" is therefore a tautology. I use the term only to be clear and also with a nod to a terminological tradition going back to Maurice Halbwachs (1925), who claimed that all memory is always already collective memory.[5]

Collective *remembering* does not mean that all individuals would have identical mental representations in their minds. Instead, it means that certain versions of the past are actualized again and again within social groups (via discourses, media, practices), and that they are well-networked with other topics. Similarly, collective *forgetting*, as Guy Beiner (2018) has shown,

---

[5] Reformulated in the terms of current posthumanism: "Memory" emerges as dynamic co-construction (or "sympoiesis"; Haraway 2016) and as an effect of distributed agency (Bennett 2010).

does not mean that all traces, all knowledge of a past event would be lost. It means that within *certain* social frameworks, there are no acts of remembering that are traceable. For example, memories of particular past events can be avoided, kept secret, tabooed, or may seem difficult to articulate in public. But often, memories of such events will "live on" within familial or local frameworks—or within the semantic collective memory of science (as has been the case with the Spanish flu; see Beiner 2021). The logic of collective memory thus implies, in Barry Schwartz's (2009, 23) words, that "remembering and forgetting are distributed unevenly among different communities, groups, and individuals."

Implicit collective memory has to be conceptualized according to this logic, too. What the majority of people remain unaware of can be quite obvious to some observers: Cultural stereotypes, tabooed pasts, emotional regimes, non-conscious master narratives—for some people, such as newcomers to a society or critical observers, the daily activations and effects of implicit collective memory immediately catch the eye. Certain actors will moreover work quite intentionally with implicit collective memory: journalists using framing techniques; politicians who play with historical allusions; film industries and advertising agencies who exploit cultural schemata and narrative habits. Last but not least, it belongs to the tasks of critical media, art, and literature to make the dynamics of implicit collective memory visible—and thus potentially transformable.[6]

How can we then draw a distinction between forms of memory that are collectively non-conscious and those that belong to explicit knowledge? Here, as elsewhere in memory studies, functional definitions are key: Within social groups, the explicit and the implicit are particular usages and effects of collective memory, and not separate systems. (Whether forms of explicit and implicit memory are located within different regions of the brain and thus dissociable is still a question under discussion; see Carlston 2010.) This means that certain remembered items can be the object of knowledge or official commemoration at one point in time, while at another point in time they unfold their world-making power in an unnoticed way.

A striking example is the presence of colonial monuments or racist forms of speaking in postcolonial societies (for their role in Brexit, see Rasch and Ward 2019). Such "colonial remains" can stay implicit—unnoticed by

---

[6] See Chapter 11, "The Ethics of Premediation in James Joyce's *Ulysses*" on how Joyce's novel performs this particular memory work. On the agency of the aesthetic in general, see Rigney (2021).

most—for a long time, until their power of stabilizing and transmitting forms of (direct and structural) violence across generations is exposed. In this way, memory activists (such as Black Lives Matter) have made explicit in recent years what had long been a powerful, but largely implicit presence (see Otele et al. 2021; Rigney 2023). In our self-reflexive memory cultures of what Ulrich Beck (2006) has termed "second" or "reflexive modernity," the transformation of implicit collective memory into explicit knowledge and commemoration has been a key concern. This operation was already at the heart of Victor Klemperer's (2013 [1947]) analysis of the language of the "Third Reich" (LTI, *lingua tertii imperii*) and its detrimental non-conscious afterlives. Another example of a transforming agent between implicit and explicit collective memory is all feminist work that exposes and seeks to rectify the (let's hopefully say: often) non-conscious gender biases of historiography and science (Reading 2016).

But how is implicit collective memory transmitted from generation to generation when it is never explicitly addressed? Schematization seems to be a powerful process in the travels of implicit collective memory. Examples of schematized memorata are visual icons, narrative patterns, stereotypes, metaphors, world-models, values and norms, and certain ways of acting or "doing" things (on *habit memory*, see Connerton 1989).[7] They are often loaded with affect. Think of the discursive formula "dying for the fatherland," the millennia-old iconic image of the Pietà, the binary of light versus darkness, the narrative pattern of "rise and fall," the stereotype of the "yellow peril" (actualized again during the COVID-19 pandemic). Such potentially perilous packages of schema-cum-affect are passed on—often (though not exclusively) non-consciously—from human to human, from generation to generation. Media in all their forms and appearances play a decisive role in the process: Implicit collective memory is *mediated and remediated* via gesture and mimics, via orality and literacy, via analog and digital media.

With implicit collective memory, I describe the recurrent use of mostly schematized memorata, which remains—for a majority of the group or society—unintentional, non-conscious, and not visible. As the examples above show, with the collective dynamics of non-awareness come questions of ethics. What responsibilities arise from not-remembering and not-knowing?[8] Such ethical questions can be addressed with Michael Rothberg's

[7] On the role of narrative schemata for memory, see Bartlett (1932); Bruner (2003); and Wagoner 2017); on "metaphors we live by," see Lakoff and Johnson (1980).
[8] On "agnotology," see Proctor and Schiebinger (2008).

(2019) concept of the "implicated subject," which helps describe actors' differentiated ability and willingness to be aware of the past and its continuous presence. The accent of the present intervention, however, is on the *generative power* of implicit memory: while remaining unexposed, it is likely to produce more of the same in the future.

How has research in different disciplines addressed the phenomena that I suggest bringing and thinking together under the banner of "implicit collective memory"? In what follows, I will discuss narrative templates, media framing and priming, and premediation as concepts for the study of implicit memory—thus staging a dialogue between psychology, anthropology, sociology, communication studies, media culture studies, and mnemohistorical research.

12.4 A Perspective from Anthropology and Cognitive Psychology: National Narratives

National narratives are a striking example of the hidden power of implicit collective memory.[9] In *How Nations Remember* (2021), anthropologist James Wertsch studied the differences in national narrative templates between Russia and the United States. Collaborating with cognitive psychologists on an interdisciplinary survey study (Abel et al. 2019), Wertsch and his colleagues could show how Russian narrative templates about the Second World War are fundamentally different from those of not only the United States, but also most other nations. Abel et al. (2019) asked more than 100 people from each of eleven countries to state what they thought were the ten most important events of the Second World War. The results are striking: Even in China and Japan, subjects produced items that are largely in consensus with the American perspective on the Second World War. Among the most important events range Pearl Harbor, D-Day, the Holocaust, and Hiroshima and Nagasaki. In Russia, however, the results are very different: With an extraordinary level of consensus (and in combination with the greatest general knowledge about the war, which was also tested), Russian subjects usually did not mention Pearl Harbor or the dropping of atomic bombs, but came up with the following core set of events: the Battle of

---

[9] For foundational studies on the role of narrative for history and memory, see Ricœur (1984) and White (1973). On the role of national basic narratives for European memories of the Second World War, see Welzer (2007).

Stalingrad, the Battle of Kursk, the Siege of Leningrad, the Battle of Moscow, the German invasion of the Soviet Union, and the Battle of Berlin.

How can such differences be explained? And what holds this stable set of remembered events together? Analyzing Putin's uses of historical memory, Wertsch (2021, 25) argues that these are basic elements of a story that "positions Russia as a victim of attacks by alien enemies." Importantly, this is a narrative pattern that most people in Russia do not (always) seem to be aware of. But it guides not only the way they select remembered events, but also how they imagine the future. According to Wertsch, for Putin the narrative template of Russian victimhood is a "fast cognitive tool": "It is a narrative tool that could almost be said to be doing some of his thinking and speaking for him" (Wertsch 2021, 24). Wertsch's book came out just a couple of months before Russia's invasion of Ukraine. It shows not only the extent to which the war in Ukraine is a war of differing collective memories, but also how memory studies contribute to a better understanding of how implicit memory operates through narrative and can be used and abused as part of aggressive politics.[10]

But how do such largely invisible narrative templates circulate in society? How are they passed on, across decades and centuries? In the case of Russia, Wertsch (2021, 14) discerns a dynamics where the template of national victimhood permeates major societal spheres and communication media (from family conversations to textbooks to popular culture and the national press). But what about the striking transnational consensus on the "American narrative"? With regard to subjects in Germany, Italy, or China, it remains a conundrum why they should remember "Pearl Harbor" and not, say, the "Battle of Kursk." At least part of the answer must lie in globalizing media culture, where American historical narratives have been widely disseminated via Hollywood films such as *Pearl Harbor* (2001, dir. Michael Bay). The crucial point here is that their enormous influence on viewers' images of history remains, in the sense of a "collective source amnesia," largely unknown to audiences and under-researched in media studies.[11]

What remains equally unknown to most people is the selectivity, narrativity, and perspectivity of their own images of history. Wertsch

---

[10] For further cognitive psychological research on national narratives, see Roediger and Wertsch (2022); Roediger and Zerr (2022); Yamashiro et al. (2022). For a folkloric studies perspective on implicit memories of earthquakes in Turkey, see Gülüm (2024).

[11] On the logic of the "memory film," see Chapter 8, "Literature, Film, and the Mediality of Cultural Memory."

(2021, 13) emphasizes that "narrative tools often operate under the radar of conscious reflection, leaving us with the impression that we have a direct, unmediated picture of reality." He reminds us of the words of narrative psychologist Jerome Bruner: "Common sense stoutly holds that the story form is a transparent window on reality, not a cookie cutter imposing a shape on it" (Bruner 2003, 6–7). Most of the time, we don't even see which cutter we hold in our hands. But the fact that we successfully used it yesterday and the day before makes it more likely that we will use it tomorrow, too. This is the forward-facing power of implicit collective memory.

12.5 Perspectives from Sociology and Communication Studies: Framing and Priming

As outlined above, anthropology and cognitive psychology can contribute their insights about narrative schemata and templates to the project of tracing the hidden power of implicit collective memory. Promising perspectives from sociology[12] and communication studies include research on framing and priming. While communication studies research on priming is based on psychological models, the concept of framing has its own tradition in sociology, going back all the way to Erving Goffman, Emile Durkheim, and Georg Simmel.

Metaphors of the frame and framing are used in many different ways today: in communication studies (as "media frames"), in political philosophy (Judith Butler's "frames of war," 2009), and last but not least in memory studies, where Halbwachs's *cadres sociaux* (social frameworks) remain a key concept.

For Erving Goffman, the founding figure of sociological frame analysis, "framing" means "the organization of experience." "Observers actively project their frames of reference into the world immediately around them" (Goffman 1974, 11, 39). Such mental frames are acquired in the socialization process. The production of realities by means of framing is an active process, but not necessarily a conscious one. On the contrary, our functioning in the everyday world is contingent on our automatic usage of frames.

---

[12] For discussions among cultural sociologists about how to conceptualize "implicit culture," see Olick and Simko (2021) and Lizardo (2022). Important building blocks for the sociological study of implicit memory are Zerubavel's (2008, 2015) works.

This understanding resonates strongly with Maurice Halbwachs's theory of collective memory. The concept of the frame was so important to Halbwachs that he devoted an entire monograph to it: *Les cadres sociaux de la mémoire* (1925, The social frameworks of memory). Halbwachs's metaphor of the *cadres sociaux* merges into one term the social and mental properties of the "frame": It is via the people who surround us (French: *cadres sociaux*) that we acquire our socially shaped mental frameworks of remembering (again, French: *cadres sociaux*). But these social and mental frameworks not only enable and shape acts of remembering. They also—and this is what Goffman will accentuate fifty years later—lead the understanding of new experience along certain paths. For Halbwachs, frames remain largely a hidden power. In *La mémoire collective*, he states that a "social current of thought" is "ordinarily as invisible as the air that we breathe. In normal life we recognize its existence only when we resist it" (Halbwachs 1997 [1950], 70; my translation).

Being a sociologist, Halbwachs directs his attention to the social dimension of memory. But in a hypothetical anecdote about a "walk through London," he imagines how media such as the words of his architect friend or Charles Dickens's novels shape his current experience as he is walking through the city (Halbwachs 1997 [1950], 52–53). Halbwachs thus exemplifies something that media memory studies (e.g., Edy 2006; Erll 2011a, 129) have emphasized again and again: Social frameworks are mediated phenomena. They are medial frames, *cadres médiaux*. Social relations and meanings are constituted and transmitted through oral speech, letters, or books; and in the age of digital media they have acquired an intrinsically mediated form (van Dijck 2007; Hoskins 2017). Medial frameworks both shape collective remembering of the past and have a forward-facing power, as we see in Halbwachs's anecdote, where media preform his perception of London. It can be supposed that in everyday life (i.e., without the sociologist's introspection) they will do so in a mainly non-conscious way.

In the late twentieth century, communication studies adopted the concept of framing in order to understand the logic of the news.[13] For Robert M. Entman (1993, 52), "[f]raming essentially involves selection and salience. To frame is to select some aspects of a perceived reality and make them more salient in a communicating text in such a way as to promote a particular

---

[13] For a comprehensive overview of communication studies approaches to collective memory, see Pentzold and Lohmeier (2023).

problem definition, causal interpretation, moral evaluation, and/or treatment recommendation for the item described." In this usage, framing becomes a conscious strategy on the production side. But its power nonetheless resides in the non-conscious effects of news framings on the reception side.

Framing and priming have become key concepts of communication studies and media effects research.[14] The two terms describe different phenomena involved in the dynamics of implicit collective memory. Both are metaphors. John Sonnett (2019, 227) explains that "framing" is based on a spatial and visual metaphor (the framing or arranging of paintings), while "priming" is based on a temporal and sequential metaphor (only *after* the presentation of a piece of information can certain effects come to pass). Therefore, research on framing is typically interested in the "how" of communication (and collective memory), while research on priming asks about the "what."[15]

12.6 The Challenge: Implicit Collective Memory across the *longue durée*

Psychology, sociology, and communication studies have shown that framing and priming are social and medial phenomena, and that their effects remain implicit for most of the actors involved. The possibility of linking these approaches with memory studies depends on questions of time: It is only when their power to frame and to prime persist beyond the moment that mediations can shape collective memory. But the problem is that in most psychological experiments, priming effects are counted merely in minutes and hours.[16]

Communication studies has tried to model the temporal stability of frames as "chronic accessibility," which can be heightened by "frequent

---

[14] See Lecheler and De Vreese (2019); Roskos-Ewoldsen et al. (2009); Tewksbury and Scheufele (2009).

[15] Vincent Price and David Tewksbury (1997) further differentiate between "applicability" and "accessibility" of frames. "Applicability" is concerned with the semantic uses and usability of a frame (how?), while "accessibility" points to the temporally restricted activation potentials of a prime (what? when?) (see also Scheufele 1999). In communication studies, framing is thus about the ways in which mediations can shape and change perceiving and understanding, while priming is about the automatic activation of non-consciously existent memorata, which may include frames. Media can prime people on certain frames.

[16] An interesting exception is perceptual priming (see Mitchell 2006).

priming" or "repetitive framing" (Roskos-Ewoldsen et al. 2009, 83). Christian Baden and Sophie Lecheler (2012, 359) have made an important foray into the theoretical modeling of the duration of framing effects. They emphasize, much in the sense of memory studies, that "the social relevance of framing effects hinges upon their ability to persist." But empirical research on media framing so far has only provided evidence for effects that last ten days to a maximum of three weeks (Schemer 2013, 161).

From a memory studies perspective, this sounds sobering. Vastly different temporal horizons are at stake in the study of collective memory. Memory studies is concerned with the question of how medial (pre)formations can exert effects over years, decades, centuries, even millennia—and that means, not only across the life spans of individual subjects, but also across multiple generational thresholds: the *longue durée* of collective memory.[17]

The narrative patterns of the *Odyssey* or of Exodus, the iconic formula of Pietà, and anti-Semitic stereotypes have quite obviously been "chronically accessible" over long periods of time. But what connections must be made to turn the psychological, sociological, and communications studies concepts discussed here into useful tools for the study of the long-term dynamics of collective memory?

Two aspects need to be taken into account. First, examples ranging from Homeric myths and their narrative templates to Christian iconography, all the way to tenacious stereotypes and conspiracy theories, show that long-term memorata are always built up plurimedially. They are transmedial phenomena, remediated again and again across the spectrum of available media.[18] This is, second, a social process through and through: Interaction, collaboration, dialogue, negotiation, agonism—the entire spectrum of the dynamics of social memory-making needs to be taken into account here. Psychological research on implicit memory, on the contrary, tends to focus solely on individual memory performance and not on the question of how memorata can be shared and thus become part of collective memory. More generally, in mainstream psychology, social interaction tends to be seen as

---

[17] The term *longué durée* was introduced by *Annales*-historian Fernand Braudel in the 1950s. He studied long-term changes, across centuries and millennia, of social structures that people do not become aware of. Today, the term is taken up again by critical historians (Guldi and Armitage 2014) in order to address the long and slow processes underlying climate change or social inequalities.

[18] For "remediation," "premediation," and "plurimediality," see Chapter 8, "Literature, Film, and the Mediality of Cultural Memory."

"memory contamination," rather than (as in the field of memory studies) as a means of "memory production."[19]

Implicit collective memory is produced and passed on in complex social and plurimedial constellations—often across the *longue durée*. This insight opens up an entirely new range of questions: How do such constellations come into existence? How is it that certain framings become strong primes, preforming action again and again in social groups? What media technologies and genres tend to have enough authority and power to disseminate frames and make them appear "applicable"? What forms of institutionalization, canonization, dissemination, educational politics, or marketing make the "chronic accessibility" of certain primes possible? Such questions necessitate the combination of psychological memory studies with the conceptual toolbox, archives, and methods of media culture studies and mnemohistory. An example of such a combination will be presented in the following section.

12.7 Perspectives from Mnemohistory: Remediating and Premediating Colonial Violence

European postcolonial memory cultures remain a strong residue of implicit collective memory. European societies are replete with mostly nonconscious and unacknowledged afterlives of its empires—all across Portugal, Spain, Italy, France, Belgium, the Netherlands, the United Kingdom, Denmark, and Germany. This is why research fields such as postcolonial studies and new imperial history have a lot to offer the study of implicit collective memory.[20] Research on "postcolonial melancholia" (Gilroy 2004), "colonial durabilities" (Stoler 2016), and "embers of empire" (Ward and Rasch 2019) address the ways in which implicit legacies of colonialism (affective, archival, discursive) continue to shape mentalities and guide political action long after decolonization.

Part of these largely invisible and unspoken legacies are ways of framing violent events of colonial history. In Germany, for example, for over a century the Herero and Nama Genocide of 1904–1908 (in what is now Namibia)

---

[19] But for an overview of existent cognitive psychology research on collective memory, see Hirst et al. (2018). For the social contagion of memory paradigm, see Meade and Roediger (2002).
[20] See, for example, Schwarz (2011); Craps (2013); Rothermund (2015); Bijl (2016); Teichler (2021); Adebayo (2023); Mwambari (2023).

had been framed as merely a "small war" in a "short German colonial history" (de Wolff 2021). The case I discuss in this section concerns British imperial and postimperial memory, where an "insurgent frame" has lingered for at least two centuries. This frame has many mnemohistorical sources, but one particular important genealogy points back to the Indian rebellion of 1857–1858.

The press coverage of the 1857–1858 rebellion in northern India is a case in point for the potential tenacity of initial press framings, and for the quite seamless migration of frames from colonial to postcolonial times. The rebellion brought together Indian soldiers, farmers, and princes of different ethnicities and religions against the British, and it was so successful that it almost cost them their Raj. The British called the rebellion a "Mutiny" and thus inserted a powerful framing into British imperial mnemohistory that still reverberates today. The term "mutiny" implies an unlawful uprising, as well as an event that is restricted to the military. Both interpretations of the events of 1857–1858 are debatable.

Anglo-Indian and British press texts that immediately covered the "mutiny" for the imperial metropolis worked with selections, highlighting, word choices, and narrative structures that could still be felt decades, even a century later, in the ways in which the years 1857–1858 were presented in British historiography and across broader media culture. The first reports printed in the *London Times* about the rebellion in northern India were real or feigned eyewitnesses accounts. Their framing is unequivocally one-sided: The rebellion was cast as a perfidious mutiny of ungrateful, religiously fanatical, and cruel subjects against the just colonial rule of the unsuspecting and benevolent British. Atrocity stories became the most powerful genre in the "Mutiny" coverage. The rape and killing of British women and children were specifically highlighted and embroidered with gory details. In 1857, Karl Marx, who offered an alternative framing of the events as the "first Indian war of independence," had already exposed one of the "eye-witnesses" featured in the *Times* as a liar (Sharpe 1993, 66). However, the early British press framings and their narrative plots migrated untarnished, sometimes word-for-word, first into imperial historiography, then into English novels and theater of the nineteenth century, early cinema, as well as—after Indian independence in 1947—into postimperial historiography, fiction, and television.

Those "Mutiny" frames erupted again with a vengeance in 2005 in a debate around a Bollywood movie of the rebellion (*Mangal Pandey:*

The Rising, 2005, dir. Ketan Mehta). In unison with a diverse range of newspapers, and backed by the comments of eminent British historians, the *Daily Mail* (August 19, 2005) criticized the movie as "fanatically anti-British." "Fanatical"—for over 150 years, this had been a standard attribute to frame resistance against British colonial rule. Under the workings of implicit collective memory, a filmic twentieth-century rendition of the "Mutiny" seems to have turned into yet another mutiny.[21]

What I only sketch here (a more comprehensive account can be found in Chapter 9, "Remediation across Time, Space, and Cultures: The Indian Rebellion of 1857–1858") is the dynamics of remediation in memory culture: the transcription of memorata into ever-changing new media, a process in which traces (here: framings) of older mediations travel along, often unheeded, across potentially very long stretches of time. Remediations are a vital agent in the dynamic plurimedial constellations which emerge around remembered events and keep them on the agenda of memory culture. With time, remediations lead to mnemonic premediation. Much-repeated frames, narrative schemata, or visual patterns become "household items" of a media culture. They can become detached (unlocked, unbound) from the stories they were originally used to convey, and reattached to new experience, which they then medially preform (that is, shape even before the events take place). Think of Bruner's cookie cutters.

In the case of the "Mutiny," such mnemonically preformed events can include debates about the relative merits of a Bollywood drama. But more deadly, among the events that were quite possibly premediated by "Mutiny"-memory, is the Amritsar massacre of 1919, a decisive turning point in the Indian independence movement of the early twentieth century. Facing a crowd of largely peaceful protesters, Colonel Dyer of the British Indian Army had his soldiers open fire and kill hundreds of Indians, who couldn't escape from the enclosed compound of the Jallianwala Bagh, where they had gathered. In a perceptive book about the "shadows of the Mutiny" in the British Empire, *The Other Side of the Medal* (1925, 53–54), historian Edward

---

[21] Sociological approaches (e.g., Alexander 2012) might see here a typical case of the production of "cultural trauma." But apart from the fact that the term "trauma" sounds cynical in contexts where imperialists fashion themselves as innocent victims, the theory of cultural trauma is concerned with "publicly available narratives of collective suffering" (Alexander 2012, 29). It thus uses a different lens for potentially identical archives: It is concerned with the visible social construction of an explicit and painful memory, while the approach advocated here focuses on the implicit afterlives and potentially perilous agency of such constructions. (On new approaches to cultural trauma, see the articles in Hirst 2020).

John Thompson surmised that the massacre was a knee-jerk reaction, the result of "inherited thought concerning the Mutiny," and evidence of "the workings of imperfectly informed minds obsessed with" the stories about Indian atrocities of seventy years earlier.[22] Seen from hindsight, the framings of mid-nineteenth-century media culture were thus still palpable in the early twentieth century, and they are still active today, over one hundred and fifty years later. Surely, they were themselves the result of centuries-old dynamics of premediation. Already in the eighteenth century, Indian peasant uprisings had been framed by British colonizers as outpourings of religious fanaticism (see Guha 1983).

"Implicitness" on a collective level does not mean ignorance of all. Perhaps some imperial historians used the gory and one-sided early press framings of the "Mutiny" quite deliberately. Perhaps some journalists today critically revisit the old press archives. And perhaps some are astutely aware of the plurimedial mnemohistory of the rebellion and understand the logic of the "Mutiny cookie cutter." But what is crucial is that the majority of people in British postimperial memory culture are not aware of the chains (or better, cascades) of imperial remediations. They suffer from what might be termed collective source amnesia.

Thinking and talking about colonialism, actors in postcolonial memory cultures (not just in Britain, but also, say, in Germany or Russia) are often "thought and spoken" by implicit mnemohistories. A word choice like "fanatic" for the description of colonial subjects taking collective action may thus feel natural to some people—and in the logic of implicit memory, therefore also "true." These are "mere exposure effects" and "validity effects" on a collective level—effects which are prepared in the *longue durée*, by the self-reinforcing dynamics of much (re)mediated frames.

For mnemohistorical research, framing and priming are thus very relevant concepts. But they have to be "translated" according to different dynamics on different scales of the complex ecologies of collective memory: for example, into "remediation" (as a form of plurimedial repetitive framing in the *longue durée*) and into "premediation" (as a form of media priming, which is based on *longue durée* frames). Mnemonic premediation

---

[22] Such mechanisms are also suggested in E. M. Forster's famous Raj-novel, *A Passage to India* (1924; for a discussion see Brantlinger 1988). Interestingly, these books addressing phenomena of implicit collective memory of colonialism appeared around 1925, the *annus mirabilis* of collective memory research, when Maurice Halbwachs's *Les cadres sociaux de la mémoire* was published.

has effects on individual minds (fast accessibility and seeming "fitness" of a frame for many people in memory culture). At the same time, mnemonic premediation becomes visible in mediations, when certain discernible framings, schemata, or narrative patterns migrate to new topics. It thus has a side that can be researched by cognitive psychologists, and a side that can be studied by the mnemohistorian.

12.8 Perspectives for Memory Research: Beyond the Street Lamp

What are the consequences of the hidden power of implicit collective memory for interdisciplinary memory research? Implicit collective memory remains largely an invisible agent. In everyday life, most people will neither notice its power to shape perception and action nor realize that there are sometimes enormous differences between implicit repertoires of different social groups. Think of Russian and "Western" narratives of the Second World War (Abel et al. 2019). Research into implicit collective memory means making visible what remains invisible to most people—and thus moving out of the (academically quite safe) light cone of a street lamp that illuminates only explicit (and mostly commemorative) memory.

Implicit collective memory is, contrary to commemoration, not primarily backward-looking, but fundamentally a preforming, a forward-facing dynamics. In cognitive psychology, priming is defined as the influence of past experience on subsequent action. A mnemohistorical perspective shows that new experience and action are often mnemonically premediated, that is, implicitly preformed by the mediations of (sometimes *longue durée*) collective memories, in which subjects participate. What is ultimately at stake with the term of "implicit collective memory" is the social, medial, and for most people non-conscious aspects of a cultural remembering-imagining system (Conway et al. 2016). Implicit collective memory is a form of "collective future thinking without thinking."[23]

What significance does existent research on memory cultures (*sensu* A. Assmann 2011 [1999] and J. Assmann 2011 [1992]) have for the study of implicit collective memory? It is indispensable, because the non-conscious

---

[23] On collective future thought, see Szpunar and Szpunar (2016).

is mostly a long-term effect of active memory culture and its key processes: remediation, canonization, institutionalization, commemoration, and the wide dissemination of certain memorata. It is not surprising that some of the most influential long-term frames spring from canonized texts such as the Bible, from frequently remediated national myths, much-used textbooks, and from globally disseminated Hollywood movies. The resources of implicit collective memory emerge from explicit memory culture.

The term "implicit collective memory" is proposed here as an umbrella term for a wide array of phenomena, which all share a certain source (they derive from mediated collective memory), mode (most people remain unaware of them), and function (they preform thought and action). The term aims to bring together research from different quarters and traditions in order to study a transdisciplinary phenomenon. Among these traditions are not only those discussed in this chapter: cognitive psychological, sociological, and communication studies approaches to priming and framing; anthropological approaches to national narratives; mnemohistorical research on remediation and premediation. Implicit collective memory is moreover discernible as one of the key concerns of social movement studies (Lorenzo Zamponi's "repertoires," 2018), research on conspiracy myths (van Prooijen and Douglas 2017), recent discussions in the philosophy of history about the "presence" of the past (Bevernage and Lorenz 2013), as well as postcolonial and decolonial debates about the continuities of imperial practices and forms of thinking (Stoler 2016). Last but not least, the implicit poses a key challenge to theories of new media. It has been addressed as "the digital unconscious" (Monk 1998), is part of what Andrew Hoskins calls the "new grey in digital memory" (Hoskins and Halstead 2021), and of what Rik Smit (2024) addresses as the "platformization of memory."

The preoccupation with implicit forms of collective memory can boast a long tradition—perhaps an even longer one than the study of commemorative memory. A key figure is surely Aby Warburg (2000 [1924]), whose understanding of the afterlives of antiquity gestures far beyond a deliberate recourse to a "classical tradition." Warburg describes the workings of visual "pathos formula" as a non-conscious activation of older forms and affects in new artworks. As we have seen, Halbwachs was also interested in invisible "social currents." And Frederic Bartlettt's (1932) foundational research in experimental psychology is fundamental, too, for an understanding of non-conscious narrative schemata that seem specific to particular (memory) cultures.[24]

For many humanities scholars, the "collective non-conscious" may be suggestive of the psychoanalytic "unconscious" and the ways it has been used for the description of social processes. Well-known examples include C. G. Jung's (2014) quite problematic "collective unconscious," a concept developed in the early 1900s, as well as Sigmund Freud's mass psychology (2004 [1921]; 2010 [1939]). In memory studies, psychoanalytical thought has long played a key role in attempts to describe the dynamics of difficult non-conscious collective memory—all the way from Theodor W. Adorno's deliberations on the afterlife of fascism (Adorno 1977 [1959]) to Marianne Hirsch's (2012) "postmemory" as a form of unintentional transgenerational transmission of traumatic memory.[25]

Why then "implicit collective memory" and not "the collective unconscious"? My use of a technical term coming from cognitive psychology is meant to act as a reminder that there is no easy equation between the Freudian unconscious, on the one hand, and the social effects of past experience and media reception that most people remain unaware of, on the other. It moreover directs attention to a possible dialogue between memory studies and recent cognitive science approaches to the "new unconscious."[26]

But the essential rationale for the term "implicit collective memory" is pragmatic. As Daniel Schacter reminds us, the "nonconscious world of implicit memory revealed by cognitive neuroscience differs markedly from the Freudian unconscious," because it is "far more mundane" than the Freudian drama about the forces of repression. Implicit memories "arise as a natural consequence of such everyday activities as perceiving, understanding, and acting" (Schacter 1996, 190–191). What is at stake

---

[24] For individual implicit memory, Schacter (1987, 502) shows that philosophers, psychologists, neurologists, and psychiatrists from the seventeenth century onward became interested in how "memory for recent experiences was expressed in the absence of conscious recollection." He discusses, among others, René Descartes, Gottfried Wilhelm Leibnitz, Erasmus Darwin, Maine de Biran, Johann Friedrich Herbart, William Carpenter, Ewald Hering, Sergei Korsakoff, Pierre Janet, Sigmund Freud, Henri Bergson, Hermann Ebbinghaus, and William McDougall.

[25] For psychoanalytic approaches to historical consciousness, see Rüsen and Straub (2011 [1998]).

[26] See Hassin et al. (2005). Moreover, applied in a conversation with posthuman studies, the term opens up the possibility of studying the bio-technological co-production of forms of non-conscious memory. Katherine Hayles (2017) theorizes a "cognitive non-conscious" in humans, but also in technological systems, and in the realm of plants and animals, that is, in a "planetary cognitive ecology."

is an understanding of the quantitatively most frequent memory processes. Implicit memory—in its cognitive as well as in its social or medial instantiations—is not a pathology, but a basic and ubiquitous dynamic that first of all enables memory ecologies to function. What is therefore needed is a better understanding of the hidden power of everyday, automatic forms of collective remembering across its various dimensions. What is not needed is a playoff between, say, psychoanalysis and the cognitive sciences. Instead, only a joining of forces from different quarters will enable us to make sense of the invisible phenomena of collective remembering—of those "unusual suspects," which are not found under the Freudian, or any other, single street lamp.

Upon closer inspection, implicit collective memory has in fact already emerged as a key concern of present-day interdisciplinary memory studies—but in a characteristically unexamined way. Jeffrey Olick's (2016, 60) studies on the path-dependency of social memory points in the direction of implicit collective memory, as does Robyn Fivush's and Azriel Grysman's (2022) distinction between explicit and implicit gendered narratives, and Barbie Zelizer's (2022) discussion of framing as part of "journalism's backstage." Implicit collective memory is, in the words of Eviatar Zerubavel (2008, 2015), the "elephant in the room" of memory studies, so far remaining "hidden in plain sight."

The greatest challenge of research on implicit collective memory is of a methodological kind: How can we make hidden phenomena graspable, and thus researchable? Perhaps, to begin with, by creating connections between the rich methodological repertoires that already exist in memory studies across its diverse disciplines and that range from experimental and quantitative methods all the way to archival, discourse-analytic, and narratological approaches, and finally to the possibilities that digital humanities now open up. The conundrums of implicit memory phenomena provide one more reason to turn the multidisciplinary field of memory studies into a site of intensified interdisciplinary collaboration.

Chapter 13
Ecologies of Trauma

13.1 Where Trauma and Culture Meet

Where do trauma and culture meet? Over the past three decades, the study of cultural trauma has been moving along two major paths: there is, first, the broad and diversified field of what Lucy Bond and Stef Craps (2019) call "cultural trauma studies"; and second, the more clearly defined sociological theory of "cultural trauma" (Eyerman 2019). The former has its roots in an early 1990s dialogue on psychoanalysis and poststructuralist theory that was conducted by scholars affiliated with Yale University, including Cathy Caruth, Shoshana Felman, and Geoffrey Hartman (see Caruth 1996; Felman and Laub 1992). Cultural trauma studies has since brought forth many different branches, such as Marianne Hirsch's (2012) "postmemory," as well as critiques of "trauma culture" (Luckhurst 2008) and important forays into forms of transcultural trauma by Stef Craps (2013) and Michael Rothberg (2009, 2019). The sociological theory of cultural trauma, on the other hand, goes back to a research group at Stanford University in 1999–2000, involving, among others, Neil Smelser, Ron Eyerman, and Jeffrey Alexander, who all work with the concept of cultural trauma from a social constructivist viewpoint.

While cultural trauma studies have never lost sight of trauma as a psychic injury—yet tend to focus on its cultural, mediated, and socially shared dimensions—the sociological theory of cultural trauma is based on a strict distinction between individual and collective levels. It puts an emphasis on trauma as social construction. For Jeffrey Alexander (2012, 101), "collective traumas are reflections neither of individual suffering nor actual events, but symbolic renderings that reconstruct and imagine them." Cultural trauma is, according to Neil Smelser's (2004, 44) definition, "a memory accepted and publicly given credence by a relevant membership group."[1]

---

[1] Smelser's (2004, 44) full definition is: "a memory accepted and publicly given credence by a relevant membership group and evoking an event or situation which is (a) laden with negative affect,

As Smelser's wording suggests, and as trauma scholars like Craps, Rothberg, and others have shown, research on cultural trauma—no matter in what particular variation—can be located within the larger field of memory studies and tends to be seen as a specific form of cultural memory. But this does not make matters any simpler, as the definition of both concepts is a subject of ongoing and heated discussion.[2] It is from this broader memory studies perspective that this chapter aims to tackle what appear to be unresolved questions about cultural trauma: Where do trauma and culture meet? How do we address trauma as physical, psychic, and cultural phenomena in one framework? How do we navigate between individual and collective levels without making category mistakes? How can we usefully integrate recent research on the extended mind and on memory ecologies and assemblages into the study of cultural trauma? What is the significance of narrative templates in the traveling and translation of trauma across time, media, and social scales? Last but not least, what is—and what should be—the role of "collective identity" in research on memory and trauma?

Admittedly, this is a veritable odyssey of conceptual questions, and it will be fittingly attended by tracing the *Odyssey* as a narrative template: I will follow Homer's perennial story as a powerful cultural tool for expressions of trauma across time and space, drawing on examples ranging from antiquity to the present day.[3]

13.2 Toward an Assemblage Model of the Extended Mind

Proliferating research on cultural trauma across diverse disciplines has contributed to a more general understanding of what this chapter describes as "ecologies of trauma": the insight that traumata—from the individual trauma addressed by psychotherapists to the so-called collective trauma studied by sociologists—are experienced, felt, perceived, understood,

---

(b) represented as indelible, and (c) regarded as threatening a society's existence or violating one or more of its fundamental cultural presuppositions."

[2] For overviews of cultural trauma studies, see Leys (2000), Bond and Craps (2019).

[3] As the Homeric question remains unresolved to this day, I use the term "Homer" to refer to what was most probably an oral tradition turned into the written epics *Iliad* and *Odyssey* during the seventh century BCE. Throughout, I will discuss the narrative agency of the *Odyssey* as told in the Homeric poem, not taking into account other narrative traditions (such as the counternarratives by Dares and Dictys, or Dante's particular version of Odysseus; see Stanford 1963 [1954]); see also Erll (2024a); and Chapter 3, "Homer—A Relational Mnemohistory."

negotiated, and healed within sociocultural, spatiotemporal, and human-nonhuman contexts.[4]

But is such an integrated vision, as suggested by the term "ecologies of trauma," advisable at all? Or will considering both individual *and* collective dimensions of trauma invariably mean reintroducing what Jeffrey Alexander so successfully dispensed with: the problematic conflation of a person's psychic injury with political memory and questions of representation? This "category mistake" was astutely observed by Wulf Kansteiner (2004) in poststructuralist trauma theories arising in the wake of Cathy Caruth's influential *Unclaimed Experience* (1996). Alexander follows the path of radical social constructivism when he emphasizes the strict separation of individual and collective levels and their different logics:

> *Individual* victims react to traumatic injury with repression and denial, gaining relief when these psychological defenses are overcome, bringing pain into consciousness so they are able to mourn. For *collectivities*, it is different. Rather than denial, repression, and "working through," it is a matter of symbolic construction and framing, of creating stories and characters, and moving along from there. (Alexander 2012, 3)[5]

Or, reformulated in the words of systems theorist Elena Esposito, "from the functioning of the brain and consciousness *nothing* can be deduced regarding the functioning of society" (Esposito 2002, 18; my translation and emphasis). Indeed, thinking in simple analogies can be highly misleading when it comes to an understanding of trauma in individual and collective dimensions. The same goes for memory more generally. Memory studies is not an exercise in finding correspondences between processes on different scales, as in a "great chain of (mnemonic) being"; it is not a neat Renaissance-style relating of microcosm and macrocosm, even if terminology such as "*cultural* trauma" and "*collective* memory" may suggest just that.

But if no analogies can be drawn between individual and social levels, why use the term "cultural *trauma*" at all to capture what appears to be quintessentially a politics concerning negative emotional memories?

---

[4] On "memory ecologies," see Hoskins (2016). More broadly, on the environmental or ecological turn in collective memory studies, see Gülüm et al. (2024)

[5] Kansteiner (2004, 186) maintains that "nations can repress with psychological impunity: their collective memories can be changed without a 'return of the repressed.'"

Why describe social processes using a concept that was developed with a view to psychic phenomena? (In fact, why further metaphorize what is already a metaphor, as the term "trauma" was originally used just for physical wounds?) The wording chosen by the sociological strand of cultural trauma theory seems to assign affective and emotional states, as well as cognitive agency, to representations and collectivities (for example, when Alexander maintains that cultural trauma leaves "indelible marks" on "group consciousness"[6]). Philosopher Robert A. Wilson (2005) warns that "by attributing cognitive agency to things that merely have functional agency, we magnify or heighten our sense of what those agents can do." This leads to a fundamental question of cultural trauma research: What does the "cultural" actually do?

Of course, these are general questions that memory studies at large has continually been confronted with. Perhaps a broader memory studies perspective may therefore be helpful in addressing them. Many scholars maintain that collective or cultural memory is *not* a mere metaphor. But how exactly the relation between "memory in the head" and "memory in the wild," to use a phrasing suggested by Amanda Barnier and Andrew Hoskins (2018), should be conceptualized is the subject of ongoing debate.

Arguably, the problem could in the first place be the very distinction. Referring to Jeffrey Olick's influential discussion of "collected memory" versus "collective memory" (1999), which has done a lot to chart the multidisciplinary field of memory studies, William Hirst and Charles B. Stone (2015, 105f.) argue that such a separation of spheres unnecessarily implies an "ontological distinctiveness."[7] They claim that "when the mind is appropriately conceptualised, ... the distinction between collective and collected memories collapses"—with the effect that everybody (the sociologist, the psychologist, the neuroscientist, the art historian) is dealing with "simply one memory." But what does "appropriate conceptualization" mean? Hirst and Stone refer to the "extended mind" and, pointing to Gregory Bateson's example of the blind man with a cane, they ask "why not go beyond the

---

[6] This is part of Alexander's (2012, 6) definition of cultural trauma: "Cultural trauma occurs when members of a collectivity feel they have been subjected to a horrendous event that leaves indelible marks upon their group consciousness, marking their memories forever and changing their future identity in fundamental and irrevocable ways."

[7] Indeed, Olick (1999, 336) claims that these are "radically distinct ontological orders." But I see Olick's distinction rather as perspectives on, or roads into, the field of memory studies: either via the phenomenon of the mind-that-collects or via public symbols—or: via bottom-up or top-down approaches, as Hirst et al. (2018) argue. But both spheres are deeply interconnected, and indeed each is unable to produce memory without the other (see Erll 2011a, 97–98).

surface of the skin and include the cane" when explaining how the blind man navigates his way through the world? Theories of the extended mind consider how the social and material world always plays into cognition, how memory is produced in complex ecologies made up of inner and outer resources.

In their work on the extended mind, the philosophers and psychologists Sutton et al. (2010, 524) address the vexed question of how to relate individual and collective, inner and outer, cognitive and social dimensions of memory. In doing so, they make a useful distinction between two options of understanding this relation, delineating "two primary routes to extended cognition." The first assumes "*complementarity* of disparate inner and outer resources," and the second "*parity* or functional equivalence of neural and external components."

Thinking of memory in terms of parity of levels implies thinking in analogies, and this will generate all kinds of epistemological problems. There just is no functional equivalence or "isomorphism" (Sutton et al. 2010, 525) between such different levels as the biological and the social, or the medial and the mental. They may be connected in the production of memory, yet each will operate according to its own logic.

But how can we account for the remarkable, often seemingly miraculous, similarities between levels? Images of the past are constructs (no matter how true to the past events they may seem to be), and this has been shown both for the neuronal level and for media culture. Both for individuals and for societies, narrative memory serves to construct a sense of identity. And as far as traumatic memories are concerned, although social constructivism warns us against making such linkages, it seems that not only individuals but also groups have a tendency to "act out" a past that has not been "worked through." This was argued by Sigmund Freud in *Moses and Monotheism* (1939), where the psychoanalyst imagined the murder of an Egyptian Moses by the Israelites as the original but repressed sin of the Jewish people, passed down through the generations as an inheritance of guilt and trauma, and it is a common way of thinking about transitional societies—in Latin America, South Africa, Eastern Europe, and elsewhere.[8]

---

[8] Studying the Moses myth from Egyptian antiquity to Freud, Jan Assmann (1997) has shown how the "return of the repressed" across the *longue durée* follows a complex cultural logic with mental, material, narrative, and social aspects: An event such as Akhenaten's new monotheistic religion possibly causes multiple individual traumatizations among people living in Egypt in the fourteenth century BCE. It is subsequently officially censored, but stories of trauma are unofficially passed on

But these surprisingly analogical patterns may have more to do with the inherent connectedness of individual minds with their larger environments than with a miraculous synchronicity of otherwise disparate systems. While the idea of *parity* will inevitably lead to category mistakes, thinking of such phenomena in terms of *complementarity* might be a route toward understanding memory (including traumatic memory) as extended across diverse dimensions of a complex ecology.

In other words, the complementarity approach paves the way for an understanding of memory as emerging from relations between biological, mental, material, medial, and sociocultural phenomena. Rather than entities placed on hierarchical levels, these diverse phenomena might better be conceived of as elements in constellations of an extended mind. Drawing on an emerging discussion in memory studies and tapping the conceptual repertoire of actor-network theory (ANT), they are "mnemonic actors" within a "flat ontology of memory"—parts of what Red Chidgey calls a "memory assemblage" (Chidgey 2019).[9]

But what is a memory actor? First of all, it is an actor that never acts alone. Memory is a relational process, or in the words of Donna Haraway (2016, 61), a case of "sympoiesis"[10]; from the paper and ink we use to memorize lists of words to the way parents help children in scaffolding their autobiographical memory, and to the interplay of objects, infrastructures, and people in the creation of an archive. In ANT, as Annemarie Mol (2010, 257) explains, the "semiotic understanding of relatedness" inherited from Saussure, structuralism, and poststructuralism "has been shifted on from language to the rest of reality." Elements in a memory assemblage are related to, connected

---

through the generations. These remain "dislocated" as they are not part of, and cannot be integrated with, canonical memory. They emerge again and again, and attach themselves to events and persons (like Moses and the Jews) that had not been part of the historical events in the first place.

[9] "To take a note from Latour, scales of memory do not move from the personal-local-national-global, getting increasingly larger and more complex. Instead, multiple scales and sites occupy and inhabit every assemblage as forces that work in concert, proximity and conflict with each other" (Chidgey 2019, 11). Hirst and Stone (2015, 106) suggest a need to "take a systems approach, in which memorising and remembering occurs within a system that includes individuals, and the environmental and social context." Actor-network theory is such a "systems approach," but one that does not fall back into cloudy concepts of "the cultural" or "the social"; is immune against thinking in analogies *and* the strict separation of elements assigned to different ontological levels; and at the same time helps conceptualize objects, archives, and landscapes not as mere *ancillae* to individual remembering but as mnemonic actors in their own right.

[10] "Nothing makes itself; nothing is really autopoietic or self-organizing" (Haraway 2016, 58). According to Haraway, "M. Beth Dempster suggested the term sympoiesis for 'collectively producing systems that do not have self-defined spatial or temporal boundaries. Information and control are distributed among components'" (Haraway 2016, 61). As the "partners do not precede the relatings" in such systems, "relationalities *are* the objects of study" (Haraway 2016, 64).

with, other elements, and only as part of such associations can they become mnemonic actors. In this view, the prefrontal cortex, an affect-laden flashback, the dyad of husband and wife, the knot in the handkerchief, the book, and the screen of a digital device can all be seen and studied as actors. An actor is, according to Latour, "any thing that does modify a state of affairs by making a difference" (Latour 2005, 71). Agency, for Latour, does not derive from one actor alone, but from the "actor-network." An actor is therefore only "what is *made* to act by many others" (Latour 2005, 46). Actors in the perspective of ANT do not necessarily have cognitive agency, intentionality, affect, emotion, and responsibility, but they are functional parts of a network. The emphasis placed by ANT and new materialism on what Jane Bennett (2010, ix) in *Vibrant Matter* calls and theorizes as "*distributive* agency" helps reconceive what has been seen as ontologically distinct vertical planes (biological, individual, and social dimensions of memory) as actants on *one* horizontal plane, within *one* ontology, and *one* ecology of memory—acting together, albeit according to different logics.

This perspective not only enables us to see Bateson's blind man and his cane as an actor-network, but also makes us consider the particular logic and agency of the cane within this network. This strengthening of the material is an important way of tackling the risk of extended mind-approaches "looping back to the self again" (Barnier and Hoskins 2018, 387). In the perspective proposed here, statues and libraries surely don't "have" memory, but they can have mnemonic agency as parts of a memory assemblage. Memory emerges from associations of biological, mental, social, and material actors in particular assemblages. Such assemblages are transient and need to be continuously performed, or they will dissolve.

ANT and new materialism make it possible to frame the emergence of memory as an effect of relationalities, entanglements, or intra-action.[11] These approaches thus enable a better understanding of the "extended mind" within complex memory ecologies.[12]

---

[11] See Karen Barad (2007, ix): "To be entangled is not simply to be intertwined with another, as in the joining of separate entities, but to lack an independent, self-contained existence.... Individuals do not pre-exist their interactions; rather, individuals emerge through and as part of their entangled intra-relating."

[12] This perspective also resonates with Stef Craps's call for "memory studies to start to think ecologically (rather than merely socially)" (Craps et al. 2018, 500). While Craps is interested here in the Anthropocene, a move from the mental to the social (via the transcultural) to the ecological is also implied in uses of the term "ecological" in psychological and media memory research (Graumann 1986; Hoskins 2017). Memory emerges from and needs to be located within complex ecologies that include immediate social and material environments, digital and other media, as well as human-nonhuman and nature-culture complexes.

Let's come back to cultural trauma. In the perspective suggested here—memory emerging from mnemonic assemblages in a flat ontology—the "cultural" of cultural trauma no longer need be discussed either as "some force behind" trauma or as a traumatized supra-individual consciousness. Instead, the focus can turn to how particular cultural phenomena work with other entities as an "actor-network," and how traumatic memories and memories of trauma emerge from these relations in "ecologies of trauma."

13.3 Narratives as Actors: Following the *Odyssey*

Representation—and narrative representation in particular—holds great significance in all theories of trauma. It is through forms of narrative that trauma is mediated, discussed, healed, and possibly also transferred, shared, or vicariously experienced. Narrative resources play a key role in trauma studies—all the way from Freud's emphasis on narrative healing to the poststructuralist suspicion of all-too-simple, harmonizing narratives (and the concomitant emergence of fragmented trauma fictions), and eventually to the sociological focus on how groups imagine cultural trauma into being by creating "narratives about social suffering" (Alexander 2012, 2).

According to anthropologist James Wertsch (2002, 2021), narrative templates are tools of collective memory. They are also tools of expressing and understanding trauma, or "actors," in the sense of ANT. Drawing on Latour's (2005, 11) imperative to "follow the actors" and "trace actors' new associations," this chapter asks: What happens when we follow narrative patterns as "mnemonic actors" that are used to frame a past-that-continues-to-hurt? What happens when we study how they travel and are translated across different dimensions in ecologies of trauma—from individual to group, from fictional character to nation, from medium to mind, from the local to different regions, across languages, and across time?

The following discussion will draw on one of the oldest narrative templates for framing individual and collective traumas of displacement—an odyssey. Tracing the odyssey template across different times, places, media, and collectivities will, first, show how Homer's *Odyssey* is used as an ancient narrative resource for modern trauma therapy. Second, asking how claims about traumatization are rhetorically moved from individual to collective scales leads to discussing the *Odyssey*'s significance for the articulation of diaspora as "cultural trauma." Third, problematizing identity positions in trauma discourse shows how Homer's *Odyssey* already imagines transcultural trauma and leads to asking why, in today's art and media culture, the odyssey template is frequently used to frame the traumata of refugees. The chapter ends with a critical discussion of the notion of "collective identity," that seemingly indispensable—but arguably rather detrimental—companion to all thinking about cultural trauma and collective memory.

13.4 Combat Trauma, Ancient and Modern: Jumping with Homer

Clinical psychoanalyst and bestselling author Jonathan Shay is not afraid of time-jumps. In his books *Achilles in Vietnam* (1995) and *Odysseus in America* (2002), he conducts close readings of the Homeric epics *Iliad* and *Odyssey* (both from the seventh century BCE), and draws analogies to American soldiers returning from Vietnam and other theaters of war. Like Achilles, they suffer most from betrayals by their commanders and the loss of their closest comrades. Like Odysseus, they have to face long "trials of homecoming."

Traumatization of soldiers in war (variously called shell shock, war neurosis, combat fatigue, or PTSD) has constituted a significant empirical foundation of trauma theory in the twentieth and twenty-first centuries. It is also a case in point for an understanding of ecologies of trauma. Each war seems to have generated its own version of soldiers' trauma. Veterans of the First World War showed different symptoms (such as paralysis of limbs) than those of the Vietnam War (nightmares, flashbacks), and their problems were named and treated differently. Apparently, different times and different sociocultural and military contexts produce different types of trauma. What this suggests is that there might be a "changing same"—a tendency of soldiers to become traumatized in battle, with culturally distinct manifestations of such traumatization: ecologies of trauma.

However, using a 2,700-year-old narrative to understand contemporary veterans' traumata seems like a rather bold stroke. Does Shay commit major category mistakes between different ontological, temporal, and cultural levels by using literature as evidence for real-world psychological processes, by drawing analogies between the archaic and the modern period, between ancient Greeks and present-day Americans? Of course, Shay's is unmistakably a mode of reading myths that has a long tradition in the field of psychoanalysis, going back all the way to Freud (for example, to his readings of the Oedipus myth). But cross-cultural research on trauma has challenged such universalizing notions of trauma and human nature. Drawing on the work of anthropologist Allan Young, Bond and Craps (2019, 106) remind us that while "trauma tends to be thought of as a timeless, acultural, psychobiological phenomenon, . . . it is actually a discursive invention that arose in a particular historical context." Trauma is tied to modernity and the West, cultural trauma studies suggest. But, if we follow Shay, it can be found in places as remote as ancient Greece.

These different standpoints on the relativity or universality of trauma as psychic process are probably unresolvable. But as a particular memory assemblage, the use of the *Odyssey* in current post-traumatic stress disorder (PTSD) therapy is an interesting example of the transtemporal dynamics, or "cross-temporal networks" (Felski 2011, 577), of narrative in the conception and healing of trauma. It shows how age-old templates can travel across time and space, and then be put to use as "actors" in present situations to do their therapeutic work—quite regardless of whether they were intended as trauma narratives in the first place, or even referred to actual traumatic experience. Conversely, traveling on to classics departments, the Homeric template enriched with psychoanalytic meaning has prompted philologists to look anew at their historical texts.[13]

Such a pragmatic approach is also put forward by classicist Joel Christensen, who understands the stories that Odysseus tells to his benevolent hosts, the Phaeacians (the "Apologue," books IX–XII), as a "therapeutic narrative." Curiously enough, almost all of Odysseus's adventures at sea are told not by the epic narrator but in a long inset by the protagonist-as-eyewitness to his empathically listening hosts. This embedded narrative is a highly personal, and hence subjective, potentially unreliable, and indeed possibly therapeutic story of individual experience—the first one of such a considerable length known in the ancient literatures of Europe and the Near East. For Christensen (2018, 24), "Odysseus's therapeutic narrative illustrates the enduring and mutually beneficial power of epic and modern psychology to reinforce and elucidate one another. . . . Audiences leave these tales with the

---

[13] See the deepened discussion in Meineck and Konstan (2014). Such double temporal moves are a key concern of the field of classical reception studies.

stories' models in their minds, and can use them to tell their own stories and explore their own worlds." (See also Christensen 2022.)

From this perspective, understanding trauma emerges as an ongoing, relational process within a transtemporal assemblage. Shay's approach to modern trauma using Odysseus thus need not be reduced to the problematic attempt to find sameness or analogies between psychic processes on different temporal and cultural levels. Instead, it can be seen as an active intervention in the circulation of story models, a work of translation, of interpreting and putting ancient narrative resources to new uses. This is not because the old is "just like" the new, but rather because the old can serve as a narrative model to frame the new. The *Odyssey* works here not as a mirror, but as a narrative tool—and a sense of its potential political agency within the actor-network is conveyed in the foreword to *Odysseus in America*, where U.S. Senators Max Cleland and John McCain (both Vietnam War veterans) confess to its "compelling insights into our own experience" (Shay 2002, XI).

But a narrative like the *Odyssey* does not just leap from out of nowhere into a present memory assemblage. The condition for this is a long process of cultural memory:[14] more than two and a half millennia of receptions, transcriptions, translations, and remediations, during which the epic emerged, shaped and altered by each new memory assemblage. Only therefore, and only in this way, are both of Homer's epics available today as narrative resources to address trauma. This is the deep historical dimension of the odyssey template as an "actor" in ecologies of cultural trauma.

13.5 Displacement as Cultural Trauma: Framing Diaspora with the *Odyssey*

Contrary to what modern travel and entertainment industries feature under names like "Odyssey cruises" may imply, Homer's Odysseus is not a man who travels for fun. His is a form of what today might be called "forced displacement." After his sack of Troy, with the famous ruse of the Trojan horse, Odysseus's fleet is tossed and torn across a mythical Mediterranean Sea for ten years. All the while, Odysseus longs for his home, kingdom, and wife. The reason for his involuntary exile is not connected to trade, labor,

---

[14] I use the term "cultural memory" here in the specific sense of J. Assmann (2011 [1992]).

religious persecution, or genocide (some of the driving forces of modern diasporas). It is revenge: the wrath of the sea god Poseidon, whose one-eyed son, Polyphemus, Odysseus has blinded.

As my modernizing summary of Homer's *Odyssey* already indicates, the poem lends itself to a reading through the lens of modern knowledge about migration and diaspora. The reason for this is not only that it is a story about involuntary and unforeseeable travels and dangerous encounters, but that it also features hospitality as a key theme—that first question of all ancient and modern travelers: How will they be received by hosts and host societies?

The *Odyssey* is thus an almost three-millennia-old narrative template for the articulation of the trauma of forced displacement and the hope of return ("Ithaca"). But interestingly, for most of this time it was not used as such. Instead, the biblical narrative of Exodus proved much stronger. From the nineteenth century onward, "Exodus" was taken up by members of the African diaspora in the Americas to address their histories of forced displacement and slavery as cultural traumata. Exodus remains a powerful narrative template for African Americans to the present day, and it has informed, for example, many of President Obama's speeches (Hartnell 2011). Of course, one reason for this preference of Exodus over *Odyssey* is the sheer diffusion of biblical stories. But arguably, the greater traction of the story about the Israelites' exodus from Egypt (as told in the Five Books of Moses) is also due to the fact that it focuses on a clearly defined collectivity (the Israelites) and conveys a strong sense of shared cultural identity, whereas the *Odyssey* focuses on Odysseus as an individual and his cross-cultural encounters.

It is therefore not surprising that two of the best-known literary articulations of exile-as-trauma that draw on the *Odyssey* refer to individual experience. The Roman poet Ovid resorted increasingly to Homer's Ulysses (as Odysseus is called in the Latin tradition) when in his letters he lamented his banishment from Rome to Tomis on the Black Sea (today's Constanța in Romania). Du Bellay's famous sonnet "Heureux qui comme Ulysse, a fait un beau voyage" (*Les Regrets*, 1558) was written when the Renaissance poet was sent from his rural French home to the unloved metropolis of Rome to act as secretary to Cardinal du Bellay (Stanford 1963 [1954], 142, 176). These are literary articulations of painful but entirely individual displacements. The narrative schema is not (yet) used as a template for displacement as cultural trauma in the sense of Jeffrey Alexander—but it is clearly a cultural tool for the articulation of experiences with a traumatic quality.

It was only in the early twentieth century that Odysseus was turned into the forefather of modern exiles by such writers as James Joyce and Ezra Pound. Since the mid-twentieth century, members of the African diaspora in the Americas have increasingly reimagined themselves in Odyssean terms, and have successfully framed, and made legible for others, the trauma of transatlantic slavery and the continued experience of oppression. Of paramount importance in this respect are the writers and artists Ralph Ellison, Derek Walcott, Wilson Harris, and Romare Bearden. In his New World epic, *Omeros* (1990), Walcott gave shape to the cultural trauma of the diaspora in the Caribbean, using Homer's *Odyssey* as narrative template.[15] More than anything else, perhaps, Odysseus stands today for multiply displaced people, tossed across the Atlantic, faced with monstrous, Cylopean white colonizers, yet still nurturing the hope of eventually coming "home"—not so much to an ancestral Africa, but, following Walcott, in the Caribbean's rich creolized traditions.

In many ways, this "Caribbean odyssey" might seem an articulation of cultural trauma in the social constructivist sense. It exhibits some salient features of the literary field as one of cultural trauma's "institutional arenas" where "new master narratives of social suffering" (Alexander 2012, 19) are produced and disseminated. Walcott was awarded the Nobel Prize for *Omeros* in 1991, and his writings have become canonical literature, central items of university syllabi across the English-speaking world. The ascription of literary value, canonization, and the transnational spread of stories (also in translation) belong to the powerful "aesthetic" and "mass media" aspects of cultural trauma in the social constructivist sense (Alexander 2012, 20, 22).

But perhaps the writers of earlier centuries were quite right; if anything, then Odysseus's displacement constituted a personal trauma. Only by expanding the individual case to the collective dimension could Odysseus become the man who stands for a social group, turned into a modern creolized Caribbean Everyman. This upscaling, the broadening of the odyssey narrative from a story of individual to collective displacement, was effected—as it is so often in creative literature—by means of allegory.

Reading Homer allegorically has a long tradition that reaches back into antiquity, and was one of the methods of the Stoics and early Christian interpreters to endow the pagan epic with new meanings and thus keep it alive in

---

[15] On the history and uses of Greek antiquity in the Caribbean, see Greenwood (2010).

the literary tradition—a key method in the cultural memory process. In the twentieth century, it is through allegory that Odysseus's individual trauma of displacement has come to express the traumata of African slaves in the Americas. The key is "national allegory," a literary form that Fredric Jameson has (controversially) identified as postcolonial literature's major strategy (for his new reflections on allegory, see Jameson 2019).

Walcott's *Omeros* is quite explicit about allegory. The narrator himself draws attention to the allegorical dimension of his New World epic, pointing to the "Homeric association" (Walcott 2008 [1990], 31) of his St. Lucia, a Caribbean island so much fought over by European colonial powers that it was once called "Helen of the West Indies." Fisherman Philoctete, who suffers from a wound in his leg, "believed that the wound came of the chained ankles of his ancestors" (Walcott 2008 [1990], 19). Here, the fictional character himself finds a metaphor for slavery's trauma (the physical wound created by slave shackles) and suggests an extension from individual pain (as physical trauma) to psychological, collective, and transgenerational trauma. While starting, as all national allegory does, from simple analogical thinking (the individual and his/her experience stand for the nation and its history), *Omeros* does not stay there. In the frameworks of its extended narrative allegory, the epic describes ongoing structural violence, the legacy of slavery, which renders Philoctete a poor man troubled by a sense of rootlessness and turns the tourists, who want to take a picturesque photo of the scarred black man, into wealthy Americans. The island's wholesale "touristification" (Carrigan 2012) reveals continuities of inequality across time, the stuff that "slow violence" (Nixon 2011) is made of.

In *Omeros*, cultural trauma therefore emerges not as simple correspondence between individual and collective experience, and also not as a phenomenon of "collective consciousness" (which does not get any more convincing by calling it *asabiyya*; see Jameson 2019, 196). Instead, in its extended narrative, the epic shows how its characters' personal and particular traumata emerge from political and sociocultural constellations of injustice, discrimination, and economic deprivation evolving across time. These dynamics were pointed out as early as the 1950s by Martinique-born psychoanalyst Frantz Fanon, for example in *Black Skins, White Masks* (1952), who, as Bond and Craps (2019, 109) maintain, "can be credited with recognizing the social nature of . . . traumas and the need for structural and material change in order for genuine healing to take place." While *Omeros* clearly suggests allegory as a reading mode, and has contributed to the transnational communication of slavery and uprooting as "cultural trauma," a much more nuanced picture of the multiple actors constituting an ecology of trauma emerges from its narrative representation.

13.6 Transcultural Trauma: Trojan Women and Syrian Refugees

The most intriguing points about Homer's *Odyssey* and its relevance for an understanding of ecologies of trauma are its transcultural dimensions and uses. Two of these will be discussed in the following: first, the articulation of transcultural trauma in the *Odyssey* (Trojan women); and second, the uses of the poem in today's European discourses about the trials of refugees from Africa and the Middle East (Syrian refugees). After having examined ecologies of trauma with a view to jumps across time and across social scales, this last example considers jumps across identity categories.

There is one passage in the *Odyssey* that still today comes as a surprise. When Odysseus is at a banquet at the court of the Phaeacians and hears the blind bard Demodocus sing about his own feats in the Trojan War, he breaks down and cries. He is "melting into tears," sobbing uncontrollably. Astonishingly enough, the epic narrator describes Odysseus as weeping like a Trojan woman.

> Odysseus was melting into tears:
> His cheeks were wet with weeping, as a woman
> weeps, as she falls to wrap her arms around
> her husband, fallen from fighting for his home
> and children. She is watching as he gasps
> and dies. She shrieks, a clear high wail, collapsing
> upon his corpse. The men are right behind.
> They hit her shoulder with her spears and lead her
> to slavery, hard labor, and a life
> of pain. Her face is marked with her despair.
> In that same desperate way, Odysseus
> was crying.[16] (*Odyssey* 8.521–533)

---

[16] I use Emily Wilson's (2017) vigorous translation of the *Odyssey*, a key actor in the reassembling of Homer for the present age (see also Erll 2024a).

This astounding passage has troubled interpreters for millennia. Classical philologist William H. Race (2014, 55) remarks that this passage is "a virtual lexicon of words for grief." The discursive representation of emotions—also across translations—remains a key to the mediation of trauma. But whose trauma is represented here? Odysseus's extreme grief is one thing, and he may indeed be overcome by what Race (2014, 56) identifies as "veterans' sudden rush of sorrow and grief at revisiting intense combat situations." Another thing is that this passage is rendered by the epic narrator in a curious literary form, what Margret Foley (1978) called a "reverse simile." In Homeric reverse similes, women are compared with men, humans are compared with animals. But this is the only simile in the epic, where the suffering of a Greek is compared with the suffering of Trojans. The heroic city-destroyer is compared with his hapless female victims. This suggests that after his ten-year odyssey, the king of Ithaca is now in a position similar to the Trojan women who lost everything (family, property, freedom) but their lives.

Given that throughout the *Odyssey* (contrary to what we find in the *Iliad*), the epic narrator focuses purely on the perspective of Odysseus and other Greeks, this is an amazing act of acknowledging other peoples' history (and ancient audiences understood the Trojan War as history), of empathy and imaginative investment that modern readers may not expect in an "archaic tale." It produces a version of "transcultural trauma" in the emphatic sense of acknowledging and empathizing with the suffering of others. Seen with Judith Butler, Homer provided his audiences with the "frames of war" that made Trojan lives "grievable."[17] It is true that in this simile, the traumatic experience of Trojan women is used to express the grief of Odysseus. But it seems inevitable that audiences also consider the simile the other way around and wonder about the Trojans and their trials. It also seems inevitable that they are reminded of the connection between Odysseus as perpetrator and the Trojan women as his victims. Different types of mnemonic relationality produce different types of trauma in this passage—including an excitingly early form of transcultural trauma.

---

[17] Butler (2009, 1) criticizes the "selective and differential framing of violence...through which we apprehend or, indeed, fail to apprehend the lives of others as lost or injured (lose-able or injurable)." Her particular use of the framing-concept (which memory studies has inherited from Halbwachs) thus raises questions about transcultural trauma: our relation to the suffering of individuals seen as distant others and how their experiences can be rendered memorable, their traumata acknowledged.

These "tears of Trojan women" are a seed of the literary imagination that was richly developed later in Greek antiquity, when, under the impression of the Persian and Peloponnese wars, Sophocles and Euripides repeatedly imagined in their tragedies, with great empathy, what defeat in war meant for non-Greek peoples, centering their dramas around Persian and Trojan women. But when Homer's *Odyssey* entered Latin literature, writers like Virgil and Seneca took over the compassion for Trojan victims—but in a framework where Romans identified with the Trojans as their alleged ancestors. This actually meant *arresting* the Homeric potential of transcultural trauma; for what is lamented in Virgil's *Aeneid* (29–10 BCE) or in Seneca's *The Trojan Women* (ca. 54 CE) is an imagined "we," not a victimized "other." This brings what had originally been a remarkable feat of the transcultural imagination back to the more banal, antagonistic, and exclusionary logic of "cultural trauma" as described by Alexander and others.

What the travels of the "tears of Trojan women" through literary history hint at is the perennial question of who can and should remember whose traumata, and from what position: the various forms of mnemonic relationality, and the possibilities and limitations of jumps across identity categories of self and other. It also shows how traveling representations of cultural trauma can change quickly from empathetic investment to self-serving self-fashioning, to weapon and war cry.

But the potential of the *Odyssey* to frame transcultural trauma appears to have survived. It has emerged again during the so-called refugee crisis in Europe. The odyssey template increasingly pops up across a wide spectrum of mediations (news media, literature, art, performance, films, and such) to frame the traumatic experiences of today's refugees in the Mediterranean; from Patrick Kingsley's popular piece of new journalism, *The New Odyssey: The Story of Europe's Refugee Crisis* (2016), to Ai Wei Wei's artwork "Odyssey" (2018). But what does it mean to frame Syrian and African refugees with narrative patterns that possibly would not come to their own minds when articulating their traumata? (And this is not because Homer's epics were "Western tales" or "Western heritage," but because there is no strong tradition of remediations of the *Odyssey* in Arab literatures; it is a common heritage that so far has not been claimed; see Appiah 2018). It is a move that is clearly addressed to European audiences, using the Homeric template as a tool of familiarization, of communicating traumatic experiences that may not be easily intelligible to these audiences, and endowing them with the status of a foundational significance. It is an attempt at constructing "transcultural trauma" much in the cultural trauma-logic of Jeffrey Alexander.

13.7 Coda: Against Collective Identity, for Relational Memory

Two things about framing ecologies of trauma with the *Odyssey* as narrative tool are striking. First, it is a traveling resource, from Greece to Rome to the Caribbean, and to Europe and the Middle East, and back again. The uses of a narrative template that has migrated through time and space point to the more general process of "traveling memory" (Erll 2011b). Cultural trauma, too, that seemingly fenced and group-specific form of memory, is more often than not a product of such traveling memory.

Second, the *Odyssey* as narrative template produces cultural trauma *without* a strong sense of collective identity. The poem itself does not feature strong "we-identities." After the fall of Troy, the Hellenic tribes separate in conflict with each other before they embark on their respective returns home (*nostoi*). Odysseus's crewmen appear anxious, self-serving, and critical of their leader, while the Ithacans at home are depicted as a divided, quarrelsome lot. And after having lost all his men, Odysseus in fact spends most of his ten-year errancy alone. Despite all the allegorization of Odysseus's individual experience into a cultural experience, what the odyssey narrative could never really do is frame a strongly bounded cultural, national, or nationalist trauma. It is just too volatile as a template, too focused on movement and encounter to serve as a schema expressing clear-cut and stable identities.[18]

Arguably, this is a good thing. The *Odyssey* enables a thinking of traumatic histories without the "lies that bind," as Anthony Kwame Appiah (2018) calls the diverse fictions of identity—whether they concern gender, class, religion, ethnicity, nation, or culture. Categorical constructions of pure collectivities and their eternal antagonism, or of blameless victims, are difficult to make with the *Odyssey*. Odysseus himself is as often perpetrator as he is victim (the Cyclops episode is the best-known in this regard; see Adorno and Horkheimer 2009 [1948]). When seen through the trauma lens, the *Odyssey*

---

[18] Jan Assmann's (2011 [1992]) discussion of the Homeric epics as foundational and identity-building texts in ancient Greece refers in the case of the *Odyssey* more to the epic as a canonized medium of memory than to the contents of its story.

displays multiple traumatizations of various "implicated subjects" (Rothberg 2019). In this it seems closer to the truth of most histories at the basis of cultural trauma, complex and messy as they are. As Walcott's Caribbean example shows, this insight need not lead to a depoliticization of cultural trauma narratives, but to greater nuance, and thus the sustainability of their claims.

All this does not really facilitate a vision of the odyssey template in strictly binary terms, with ingroup bias and outgroup exclusion, clear-cut definitions of self and otherness. Homer's epics are less concerned with "collective identity" (Greek, European, Western) than commentators from 1800 onward would have us believe—possibly because they lived in an age of national identity formation, and this was therefore their lens for perceiving Homer (just as my lens may be the relational and the transcultural).

In other words, at the beginning of cultural narrations of (memories of) war, travel, displacement, and encounter lie two epics that offer the possibility of conceptualizing identity not—or at least not strongly and exclusively—as binary, antagonistic, and heterological, but as *relational*. And as the "tears of Trojan" women show, the *Odyssey* also enables an understanding of trauma as relational. Craps and Bond (2019, 110) alert us to the fact that Cathy Caruth had already pointed to the "inherent relationality of trauma." In *Unclaimed Experience* she states that "history, like trauma, is never simply one's own, that history is precisely the way we are implicated in each other's traumas" (Caruth 1996, 24). Though history is of course also how we are implicated in each other's joy, growth, or well-being, it is clear that there is no simplistic concept of collective identity at the beginning of trauma theory in the 1990s.

This emphasis on relationality is an extremely important point for the field of memory studies at large, where it seems that no definition of "collective memory" can do without "collective identity" as its companion term, a field that seems to rely on the idea that collective memory *must* be intimately connected with, stabilize, or affirm collective identity—all the way from social psychology to sociology and to cultural history. Transcultural approaches to the study of memory have already worked against the idea of memory staying put within bounded, naturalized collectives and has emphasized solidarity across national, ethnic, or religious groups (Rothberg 2009; Erll 2011b; Craps 2013).

But there is reason to question even more fundamentally the collective memory–collective identity bind. Of course, there is a memory-identity nexus in discussions of individual memory, from Locke onward. But just as no one would want to associate all forms of individual memory with identity (it seems to be a product of autobiographical memory and not, say, of priming), there may be modes of collective memory that do not bear on collective identity at all. Mathematical formulas mediated in society and transmitted across time are a case of collective memory without collective identity. Of course, knowledge and habits acquired in a certain sociocultural context shape people. But calling such sociocultural shaping "collective identity" means widening out the term to such an extent that its meaning becomes diluted. Jan Assmann (2011 [1992], 114) usefully distinguishes between collective identity as a "basic structure" and as a "form of enhancement" through reflection. As a *basic structure*, "culture and society convey or generate an identity that is always personal though not necessarily collective. The individual's self-awareness is influenced by them, but this does not mean that (s)he will automatically have a sense of belonging to a particular society and its culture." *Enhancement* only takes place with the emergence of a "we-consciousness," that is, a sense of belonging and solidarity with a collectivity.

Identity itself is a rather recent concept, and "collective identity" even more so (Niethammer 2000). Could it be that the very idea of collective identity is yet another one of the "lies that bind?" But even Appiah, who masterly and sweepingly deconstructs categories of gender, religion, ethnicity, nation, class, and culture, does not touch the underlying concept of collective identity. It seems difficult to question these days. Appiah can't help stating that, however fictitious particular collective identities may turn out to be, there is the basic phenomenon of "clannishness," and that "the assertion of identity always proceeds through contrast or opposition" (Appiah 2018, 202).

But while "opposition" in the structuralist sense is a truism (we always discriminate—we make differences—in order to be able to grasp the shape of a concept, and of ourselves), this basic meaning of the term tends to slide away in today's discourse about memory and identity toward "opposition" in the social or political sense. This bears the danger of naturalizing certain habits of nineteenth- and early twentieth-century Europe, where the strongest affirmations of national identity went hand in hand with the strongest denigration of other nations. But should a practice of 200 years ago (and yes, re-emerging in our current age of populism) really inform the academic concepts we create to address the challenges of the twenty-first century? Doesn't the construction of self-images equally "always proceed" through a recognition of similarities with others, indebtedness, interaction, and cooperation? And have not these relational operations often enough shown their power to transversally cut through seemingly different constituencies, and been the very condition for the emergence of the new?

What does all this mean for the study of cultural trauma? There are potentially traumatizing events (such as floods, earthquakes, volcanic eruptions, tsunamis, and other natural catastrophes) that are not primarily perceived and represented according to an identity/alterity binary, along antagonistic lines, or in an accusatory logic. Understanding the expression of and coping with such traumata will point researchers in the directions of cooperation, sharing, and resilience (Lindsey et al. 2016). Research in narrative psychology on emotional memories has shown that one can better cope with difficult experience as more perspectives are integrated into one's narrative about the past (Habermas 2019). Accentuating such multiperspectival memory implies turning away from the logic of exclusionary collective identities and toward the logic of relationality.

This is also a question of what anthropologists would describe as emic and etic perspectives. While historical actors such as populist politicians will insist on strong collective identities (emic perspective), a researcher-observer may quickly identify cracks in the identificatory armor (etic perspective). The question is whether academia wants to submit its research to what Amartya Sen (2006) has called "civilizational incarceration." We may be incarcerated, day after day, by politicians, activists, and marketing experts (with both laudable and not so laudable intentions). But scholars should be able to demonstrate how to break out of the cage of collective identity.

Don't get me wrong. Now more than ever, it remains of paramount importance to critically study constructions of memory that go hand in hand with strong, bounded, and antagonistic collective identities, and that use cultural trauma as political weapons. These practices are currently (re-)emerging across the globe. But as general academic concepts, memory and trauma should remain open—returning to the vocabulary of ANT—to other possibilities of conceiving associations between social actors.

This is also a question of mental models. Conceiving of memories as assemblages within a flat ontology, with dynamically changing associations, helps us leave behind models that turn memories into monad-like entities (some "individual," others "collective") and put them into hierarchically stacked containers with identity labels. Memory—also traumatic memory—in fact is Odyssean, replete with unforeseeable travels, strange encounters, and new connections in unknown lands.

Across time, the Homeric *Odyssey* as narrative template has shown its agency in assemblages of traumatic memory, but it has tended to resist association with strong concepts of collective identity. It has played an important role in the articulation of individual traumatic experience and its communalization (from Odysseus at the Phaeacians to Ovid, Du Bellay, and Shay's Vietnam veterans). But it has never worked particularly well for antagonistic narrations of "cultural trauma" in the sense of Alexander et al. (2012)

It seems that the trauma of displacement and the hope of return—that core Odyssean story—just cannot be narrated with Homer's poem, whenever clear-cut collective identities need to be foregrounded. This task is fulfilled much more effectively by the Exodus narrative, with its slots for two antagonistic groups (Israelites versus Egyptians), its unbridgeable ethnic and religious boundaries, its "linear and uncomplicated movement from bondage to freedom, from Egypt to the promised land" and its seductive "suggestion of the conjunction of innocence and power" (Hartnell 2011, 4–5). Exodus has lent itself particularly well to articulations of collective identities based on traumatic histories, by very different groups with very different political agendas, and it has seen the most intriguing narrative inversions—all the way from Puritan settlers' stories of American exceptionalism to the Back-to-Africa movement and Afrocentrist claims to an Egyptian heritage. Transculturalizing the antagonistic story of Exodus, on the other hand, has been the agenda of a debate across time that was reconstructed by Jan Assmann in *Moses the Egyptian* (1997). In retelling the story of Moses as that of a man deeply influenced by Egyptian society and religion—that biblical "Other"—thinkers from Maimonides to Schiller to Freud dreamed the dream of revoking the Mosaic distinction (Assmann 1997, 166), the distinction between truth and untruth, and between the associated collectivities.

The Homeric *Odyssey* engenders exactly such narrative possibility to produce stories of relationality. Odysseus's versatile character, multidirectional movements, and cross-cultural encounters lend themselves to framing entangled histories and transcultural memories. A sense of transcultural trauma—acknowledging both the pain of others and the fundamental relationality of one's own painful history with that of perceived others—is a precious legacy of Homer's *Odyssey* (most powerfully expressed in the "tears of Trojan women"), which was richly taken up in different ecologies of memory across time and is just now re-emerging in the European refugee crisis.

Chapter 14
Flashbulb Memories

An Interdisciplinary Research Program
(with William Hirst)

14.1 Introduction

It is a common experience: Telling others about where you were when you learned about the attack of September 11, the death of Michael Jackson, or the verdict of Derek Chauvin, George Floyd's murderer. Despite their negatively charged nature, people seem to enjoy telling these stories and listening to others tell their story. Since Brown and Kulik's (1977) landmark article, psychologists have referred to the memories on which these recollective narratives are based as "flashbulb memories" (FBMs). FBMs are memories for the circumstances in which you learned about a public, emotionally charged event. The public event serving as the basis of these memories is often traumatic, but there is a pressure—even, possibly, a pleasure—in sharing with others one's FBMs. FBMs have become so much a part of our understanding of what makes a public event important that commentators will often underscore the importance of an event, as they did in the spring of 2021 with the Chauvin verdict, by noting that people will always remember where they were when hearing the breaking news.

This chapter explores the potentials of interdisciplinary research on FBMs, using the concepts of narrative, identity, and (aesthetic) media as its searchlights. It is written by a cognitive psychologist and a literary and cultural theorist. Both work in the multidisciplinary field of memory studies. Over the past three decades, this field has seen vibrant research on collective memory across the humanities and the social sciences (see Olick et al. 2010; and the SAGE journal *Memory Studies*, since 2009). Interdisciplinary perspectives are a defining feature of memory studies, where memory is seen as a biological, mental, sociocultural, *and* material phenomenon. Unfortunately, as yet, there has been no sustained dialogue on collective memory between cognitive psychology (Hirst et al. 2018), on the one hand, and cultural memory studies (J. Assmann 2011 [1992]; Erll 2011a), on the other.

The present chapter is an effort to put into practice the interdisciplinary vision that characterizes the field of memory studies. We hope to show that the point of view adopted by memory studies affords new questions about FBMs that more siloed disciplinary lines of research neglect. For us, a memory studies–oriented investigation puts at the center of any discussion of FBMs the relation between autobiographical recollections and what has become known as "collective memory."

A possible minimal definition of collective memory is that it largely consists in knowledge (usually, but not exclusively) about the past, which is shared within collectivities and which bears on social identities. Collective memories often take the form of narratives and images. They find representation in *minds* (as "socially framed" memories; see Halbwachs 1925), in *mediations* (orality, writing, the digital, etc.), and in *social interactions and institutions*. These are not fundamentally separate ontological planes. On the contrary, it is the ongoing interplay between minds, mediations, and social interactions that produces and maintains collective memory. Different disciplinary approaches to collective memory (psychological, cultural, or social) are therefore just that: different entry points into the highly complex process of collective memory.

In what follows, we first explore how psychology has studied FBMs as a distinctive form of autobiographical memory and then discuss possible new approaches suggested by interdisciplinary memory studies. We will show that FBMs are not just individual phenomena in the "mental black box," but in fact are part of the collective memory process. FBMs are fundamentally narratives, and the stories we tell about them bear on social identities, on the transnational travels of FBMs, and on their transgenerational afterlives. Historical media cultures and aesthetic forms, in turn, enable and shape the narrativization of FBMs.

A caveat may be in place here: Whereas readers from the social sciences could find some of the arguments derived from cultural theory "speculative," readers from the humanities might be taken aback by what they likely perceive as an overly "empiricist" approach of psychological research. The important point is to acknowledge that memory studies involves disciplines with very different research traditions and methodologies—and to see this diversity not so much as a confusion of research protocols than as a chance of cross-pollination.

14.2 Flashbulb Memories Explained

The two psychologists who introduced in 1977 the term "flashbulb memories" (FBM), Roger Brown and James Kulik, coined it in order to capture their impression that people had taken a photograph of the moment when they received the news of the death of Martin Luther King, Jr., or of John F. Kennedy. Flashbulb memories are memories of a reception event. They differ from firsthand autobiographical memories—that is, memories one might form if one actually experienced the event itself, rather than learned about it from someone else or some external source. As autobiographical memories, they also differ from event memories, that is, memories of the facts concerning the FBM-eliciting event (e.g., with respect to the attacks of 9/11, that four planes were involved). The events eliciting FBMs are, by definition, public, inasmuch as in order for people to form a memory of the circumstances of learning of an event, an external source must have communicated the news to them.

FBM-eliciting events studied to date include assassinations and other politically charged proceedings; major public occasions, such as the World Cup; and national disasters, such as earthquakes.[1] Although most studies have investigated negative events, positive events can also elicit FBMs (e.g., the fall of the Berlin Wall).[2] The public does not need to be as large as a nation. People can have FBMs of an event experienced within a family setting, such as learning of the death of a parent (Rubin and Kozin, 1984).

Brown and Kulik (1977) posited that a separate memory mechanism might be involved in the formation and retention of FBMs. They labeled the mechanism "Print Now!," thereby underscoring the putatively indelible, vivid, and elaborated nature of FBMs. Brown and Kulik wrote that FBMs had a "primary, 'live' quality that is almost perceptual" and that they were as "unchanging as the slumbering Rhinegold" (Brown and Kulik 1977, 74, 86).

Much of the subsequent psychological work focused on testing this claim.[3] This research has shown substantial declines in the consistency of FBMs over time, thereby bringing into question Brown and Kulik's original claim. What makes FBMs distinctive, however, is the confidence with which people hold these memories (Talarico and Rubin 2003). If the psychological study

---

[1] See Luminet and Curci (2009, 2018); see Hirst and Phelps (2016) for a review.
[2] See Bohn and Berntsen (2007); see Stone and Jay (2018) for a review.
[3] See, for example, Neisser and Harsh (1992); Finkenauer et al. (1998); Curci and Luminet (2006); Hirst et al. (2009, 2015); Conway (2013).

of FBM tells us anything to date, it is that simply repeating a confidently held memory again and again over years, if not decades, does not ensure its accuracy.

14.3 Collective Memories and Narratives Aligned

Surprisingly, although FBMs involve public events, and as such might be thought to intersect in some way with collective memories, psychologists rarely mentioned this possibility. One exception is Ulric Neisser, a central figure in the early development of cognitive psychology. In 1982, he reflected on the distinctive role of FBMs as a meeting point of different memory narratives. He wrote:

> [One] recalls an occasion where two narratives that we ordinarily keep separate—the course of history and the course of our lives—were momentarily put into alignment. Details are linked between our own history and History.... [Flashbulb memories] are the places we line up our own lives with the sources of history itself and say "I was there." (Neisser 1982, 47–48)

Seen through the lens of memory studies, Neisser seems to juxtapose two forms of collective memory. "History" (with a capital "H") usually emerges when public events are turned into official, commemorative, and hegemonic collective memory. Historiography participates in the process, but does not remain the only, or the most powerful medium (see also Burke 1989). "History" is the result of "communication across time," often taking narrative form (J. Assmann 2011 [1992]). It is not a once-and-for-all fixed product, but a process (Olick 2007). It is dynamic and subject to ongoing change (Rigney 2005). And it will be actualized in mediations and social interactions *as well as* in individual recollections. As a mental phenomenon, Neisser's "History" is part of what Manier and Hirst (2010) call "lived collective memories" (i.e., memories of public events that people lived through). People do not need to experience them directly, but they nevertheless need to be aware of them and engage with them to at least a limited extent.

Neisser's "our own history" translates into socially shaped autobiographical memories, which are, as psychologists have shown, also highly constructed and often narrative in shape.[4] Although personal in nature,

---

[4] For psychological work on memory and narrative, see, for example, Bruner (1990); Fivush and Haden (2003); McLean et al. (2007); McAdams (2008); Brockmeier (2015); Schiff (2017); Habermas (2019); Wertsch (2021).

autobiographical memories are "socially framed," as Halbwachs (1925) cogently argued. They are, moreover, inextricably shaped by media and are themselves mediated in settings of conversational remembering (Hirst and Echterhoff 2012).

Neisser is treating flashbulb memories, then, as points of convergence between narratives on two different *scales* of collective memory. In doing so, he anticipated recent work in transnational memory studies, which has evoked the concept of "scale" in order to address the interplay of collective memories in diverse dimensions, such as the intimate, the familial, the local, the urban, the regional, the national, and the transnational.[5] With different spatial and group-related scales come different modes of remembering (e.g., the institutional, the mass mediated, and the interactional). Neisser draws attention to the fact that FBMs connect socially framed memory on the "History" scale of usually national or transnational memory with socially framed memory on the smallest scale of the socially situated individual. His idea of "narrative alignment" resonates with current research in cultural memory studies on memorability: Events become particularly memorable when they are represented (often narratively) across diverse scales and according to different modes of memory (Rigney 2016).

Neisser also anticipates the role that FBMs may play in acts of witnessing (Hirst et al. 2020). Concerns about "witnessing" have dominated memory studies from the 1990s onward. Neisser's idea "that we line up our own lives with the sources of history itself and say 'I was there'" describes the act of witnessing to an important event. It also underscores the important but epistemologically problematic status of the witness as a historical source, as it was discussed in particular in the aftermath of the Holocaust (Lustiger Thaler and Knoch 2017), but also with regard to child abuse (Loftus and Ketcham 1994). FBMs constitute a type of "witnessing at a remove"—a phenomenon which is discussed in media studies as "secondary witnessing" or "media witnessing" (Frosh and Pinchevski 2009), and in psychology as "vicarious memory" (Pillemer 2009).

The "elephant in the room" for memory studies, which has been much preoccupied with trauma (Bond and Craps 2019), will be the question of whether and how FBMs are similar to or even connected with "traumatic witnessing" (Felman and Laub 1992). In a dialogue with the social constructivist theory of "cultural trauma" (Alexander 2012), psychologists Hirst, Cyr, and Merck (2020) have argued that FBMs are often the earliest stage in the construction of cultural trauma.

---

[5] See De Cesari and Rigney (2014); Kennedy and Nugent (2016).

A different, and more difficult, question is whether FBMs are a type of traumatic memory for the individuals who hold them. There is extensive debate as to what events might be considered traumatic, and hence the source of "traumatic memories" (e.g., Haslam 2016). It might therefore be more fruitful to ask whether FBMs can elicit post-traumatic stress disorder (PTSD). As it is captured in the *Diagnostic and Statistical Manual of Mental Disorders* (2013), the standard in the United States for classifying mental disorders, PTSD is usually associated with directly experienced events. When directly experienced, the events eliciting FBMs no doubt can result in PTSD (Conway and Loveday 2015). The question here is whether these emotionally charged events can also elicit PTSD even when they are only indirectly experienced, as is the case for most people reporting FBMs. The issue is worth considering. Epidemiological studies have established that secondary witnesses can exhibit symptoms of PTSD, although these usually resolve themselves after a few months (Galea et al. 2002). Moreover, brain-imaging studies of those close to Ground Zero showed long-term enhanced activity levels of the amygdala, a brain structure involved in emotional processing and memory. This finding suggests that the emotionality associated with the event can linger (Sharot et al. 2007). These studies do not definitely speak to the issue of FBMs and PTSD, however. For the present, what we want to maintain here is that there are many ways in which emotionally charged events can manifest as memories: through the memories underlying PTSD, through FBMs, and no doubt through many other means.

14.4 Between Photographic Image and Tellable Story

Brown and Kulik (1977, 74) claimed that an FBM "is very like a photograph that indiscriminately preserves the scene in which each of us found himself when the flashbulb was fired." But evocative as this visual metaphor may be (and as much as it may capture the phenomenological qualities of FBMs in the individual rememberer), it is also misleading, from both cognitive psychology and literary theory perspectives. In a psychological perspective, episodic memories—memories of lived experience, whose recall involves, according to Tulving (1983), a "mental time travel"—are not photographic, but rather reconstructive, (re)created with each recall from diverse memory traces and present cues.

From a literary theory perspective, a photographic image alone might not be sufficient to account for the mnemonic power ascribed to FBMs. Research on photography and memory has shown that images must be connected with narratives in order to turn into meaningful and socially relevant memories. In the case of family photography, for example, old pictures come to life only through the surrounding stories of family members (see Hirsch 1997). Without context or prior knowledge on behalf of viewers, a single photographic image may hold the *potential* for a narrative, but will not tell an *actual* story. Narratologist Werner Wolf (2003) holds that a single monophase image may "induce narration," but because of its atemporality, it can never "represent" a narrative. (This is a discussion leading back to Lessing's comparison of the relative merits of the visual and literary arts in *Laokoon*, 1766.)

For the rememberer, an FBM may involve a vivid image of a reception context and thus invite a comparison with photography, but in fact, FBMs derive their meaning and longevity only through *narrative*. What makes FBMs distinctive is that, as Neisser underscored, unlike many stories of a personal nature, stories about FBMs achieve their narrative interest because of the alignment between personal "history" and "History" writ large. A story in which you recount that your mother called you and woke you up is of little interest. It might happen with disturbing frequency. But a story in which she went on to tell you that the United States was under attack suddenly makes this story compelling.

In the perspective of literary theory, these properties of FBMs can be described with the concepts of "narrativity" and "tellability." Out of context (i.e., not connected to the public event and its collective memory), FBMs have a very low degree of *narrativity*. In cognitive narratology, "narrativity" means the possibility to evoke a story in readers' minds.[6] A simple "my mother woke me up" or "I stood there and saw this" usually does not evoke a story. It can only do so when listeners know the larger story of the public event. It is only when put in a larger "collective" context, and only when listeners activate their preexisting knowledge about the event, that flashbulb memories unfold their narrative potential.

"Good" stories or "tellable" stories are stories that "have a point." In conversational storytelling analysis, "tellability" is connected to relevance

[6] See Ryan (2006); Herman (2008, 2013).

theory and refers to "features that make a story worth telling, its 'noteworthiness.'" Tellability "is dependent on the nature of specific incidents judged by storytellers to be significant or surprising and worthy of being reported in specific contexts, thus conferring a 'point' on the story" (Baroni 2014, 836; for a memory studies perspective, see Savolainen 2017). Put simply, for a person who knows nothing about recent world history, the statement "On November 9, 1989, I saw footage of Berlin on television. I saw Trabbis crossing the border" does not flesh out into a narrative, nor does it become clear what the point of the tale could be.

But the narrativity and tellability of FBMs depend not only on grounding the autobiographical in the collective; they also depend on rooting the collective in the autobiographical. Memory for most news events covered by the media is quite poor (Abel and Berntsen 2021). But material becomes much more memorable if one can relate it to oneself (Kuiper and Rogers, 1979). FBMs are not simply stories about a public event, they are stories about the rememberer witnessing the public event. People are generally interested in personal accounts of historical events. Documentarians routinely elicit personal recollections from "witnesses" (on personalization of history in television documentaries, see Kansteiner 2006). Although those telling their FBM story did not personally witness the event, they nevertheless can say that "they were there."

14.5 We-Narratives: Flashbulb Memories and Social Identity

Flashbulb memories may be personal memories, but they speak to the rememberer's social identity and sense of belonging.[7] In psychological research, social identity involves a sense of belonging to a group and the extent to which one's sense of self is shaped by this group membership (Tajfel and Turner 2004). In the perspective of cultural narratology (Erll 2011a, 157–160), FBMs could be described as "we-narratives," or more precisely, as first-person narratives embedded in larger "we-narratives."

Several psychological studies have shown that FBMs are community-specific.[8] Such a cultural and comparative perspective on FBMs was already present in Brown and Kulik (1977), when they showed that in the mid-1970s

---

[7] See Neisser (1982); Hirst and Meskin (2018).
[8] See, for example, Conway et al. (1994); Curci et al. (2001); Kvavilashvili et al. (2003); Tinti et al. (2009).

their African American participants had FBMs of the assassination of Malcolm X (1965), whereas their European American participants did not. In today's perspective, after decades of memorialization of Martin Luther King, Jr., and his assassination as a major national event (Polletta and Maresca 2021), it is sobering to see that in Brown and Kulik's (1977, 89) study only 13 of 40 whites could report an FBM of King's assassination (1968), as compared to 30 out of 40 Blacks.

But FBMs are not just community-specific. They can also serve as markers of community membership; that is, they can be community-defining. On many occasions, it is not just a few individuals from the affected community but the community as a whole that possesses an FBM. Almost everyone in the United States formed a flashbulb memory of 9/11 (Hirst et al. 2015). People believe that when an individual loses their memory of 9/11—perhaps because of aging—they lose their identity as a member of the affected community (Merck and Hirst 2022).

Of course, it is sometimes difficult to determine which communities might be expected to have an FBM as an identity-defining feature. Some events are consequential to many different communities, not just one; 9/11 is a case in point. But even in this instance, emotional intensity associated with the attack declined over time less markedly for citizens of the country under attack, the United States, than for non-U.S. citizens (Curci and Luminet 2006). Moreover, after a year and a half had passed, the level of social sharing of FBMs reported by U.S. citizens was greater than the level reported by non-U.S. citizens. Americans still wanted to tell their stories about learning of 9/11, whereas non-U.S. citizens did not to the same degree.

In other words, even for something of international importance, such as 9/11, for many public, emotionally charged events, especially those that might be candidates for a cultural trauma (in the sense of Alexander 2012), the presence of FBMs, especially detailed ones, appears to be an indicator, if not a defining feature, of community membership. To be considered a "proper American," you are expected to have an FBM of 9/11 (see Hirst et al. 2020). FBMs have the function of asserting and maintaining group membership and of bolstering social identities.

But a caveat is in order, for the relation between FBMs and social identity can become complex for those who live on the margins of an affected community or combine multiple cultural identities and "mnemonic memberships." To use a fictional example: Mohsin Hamid's 2007 novel *The Reluctant Fundamentalist* suggests a scenario where cultural hybridity leads to the insertion of the FBM into a very different narrative with a very different meaning. The protagonist (a Pakistani-born but U.S.-educated Wall Street banker) watches the live images of the burning Twin Towers in a hotel room on a job in the Philippines. This scene is clearly staged as a "Print Now!"-moment in the novel's retrospective dramatic monologue. But the protagonist does not react in the way readers would expect. He expresses a different affect and feels a sense of satisfaction. In the course of the story, the protagonist will distance himself from the American narrative of 9/11, self-identifying more and more as a Muslim, eventually returning to Pakistan, and possibly (the novel's open ending does not disclose it) becoming a terrorist himself.

What this fictional example suggests is that the possession of an FBM alone is not a sufficient indicator for a particular social identity and membership in a mnemonic community. The determining factor appears to be the shape—and the normative message—of the "Historical" narrative into which the FBM is embedded.

14.6 Can Flashbulb Memories Travel?

Although, on the one hand, FBMs seems to garner their strength and pervasiveness in national or group-specific frameworks that afford a sense of social identity, today's global media culture, which makes it possible to witness almost any event in real time, raises the question about the transnational and transcultural dimensions of FBMs.[9] Such a question emerges almost immediately when taking the perspective of transcultural memory studies, a field which has been invested for more than a decade in the study of dynamics of remembering that transcends—"travels" across or beyond— taken-for-granted frameworks such as the nation, ethnic groups, or religious communities (see Erll 2011b). Memories of the Holocaust in particular have been shown to travel globally (Levy and Sznaider's "cosmopolitan memories," 2006), to engender empathy in groups that appear to have no connection to the relevant events (Landsberg's "prosthetic memory," 2004), and to be brought into relation with memories of colonialism, sometimes creating forms of "differentiated solidarity" (Rothberg's "multidirectional memory," 2009).

---

[9] On transnational memory, see De Cesari and Rigney (2014); on transcultural memory, see Crownshaw (2011a).

So, (how) can FBMs travel? To be sure, the FBM as a mental phenomenon, with its particular phenomenology (elaborateness, vividness, ease of retrieval) remains with the original rememberer. But what can be shared are representations, which may convey a sense of the specificity of the witnessing moment and the "flashbulb-ness" of its memory.

We distinguish two major forms of the movement of FBMs: First, people can travel or migrate, carry their FBMs with them, and articulate them as oral narratives in new places. In such cases, in particular, the transmission of FBMs depends on their tellability: Listeners can get excited about personal stories of hearing about, say, a volcano explosion or a *coup d'état* in a faraway part of the world, if the interlocutor also provides a bit of the relevant "History," which gives listeners a sense of the significance and consequentiality of an event they had not known about. Interestingly, immigrant children are more likely to know about their parents' experience in the "old country" if it was beset with war or other political conflict (Svob and Brown 2012).

Second, media representations travel in global media cultures, and media reception shapes individual memory.[10] Landsberg's "prosthetic memories" are a good tool to think with here. Using movies and exhibitions about the Holocaust and of slavery as examples, Landsberg suggests that these highly experiential mediations can engender "prosthetic memories," which, "like an artificial limb, are actually worn by the body" of distant audiences. Prosthetic memories have the power to "produce empathy and social responsibility as well as political alliances that transcend race, class, and gender" (Landsberg 2004, 20, 21). Seen from a cognitive psychology perspective, prosthetic memories could be described as a type of "vicarious memory" (Pillemer 2009) that comes to be represented in the mind as "distant collective memories" (Manier and Hirst 2010)—with "distance" referring here not to time, but to (social) space. They are affectively charged semantic memories about "other people's histories." While hinting at similar mechanisms, Landsberg's cultural theory-concept of "prosthetic memory" is characteristically more normative (highlighting ethical and political stakes) than its counterparts from cognitive psychology.

But how are traveling FBMs connected to social identities? Perhaps, "social identity" is not a precise enough tool to address the kinds of mnemonic relationalities woven by traveling memories. Rothberg's (2019) notion of "long distance solidarity" better captures the possible effects of

---

[10] On transcultural memory and reception, see Törnquist-Plewa and Sindbæk Andersen (2017).

traveling FBMs. As such terms suggest, humanities' research on the transnational and transcultural dynamics of memory often takes an explicitly ethical, even normative stance (which largely is absent from cognitive psychology research), looking for the political potentials of productive forms of collective memory. A typical question arising in a humanities' perspective on traveling FBMs would be: Can listening to a flashbulb narrative by an American media witness of 9/11 produce empathy and a sense of solidarity in distant listeners, especially when they connect it—"multidirectionally" (*sensu* Rothberg, 2009)—with their own experiences of terrorism?

14.7 Transgenerational Dynamics

FBMs travel not only across space and social groups, but also across time. Articulated as narratives in oral conversations, written down or mediated in film, FBMs can cross the generational threshold and reach people who were not yet born or were too young during the FBM-inducing event.

To understand the different paths along which FBMs can be passed on, it is useful to draw on Jan and Aleida Assmann's distinction between "communicative memory" and "cultural memory" (J. Assmann, 2011 [1992]). Communicative memory encompasses a temporal horizon of several generations. The contents of communicative memories are often passed on orally, as well as by other personal and more "fluid" media, such as letters, diaries, or—today—via WhatsApp messages and Facebook entries. Cultural memory can cross much wider temporal horizons of hundreds and thousands of years, provided that its messages are encoded into "stable" media.

Although the details of the Assmanns' distinction between two registers of collective memory are much discussed,[11] their general point remains useful for any exploration of memory: There are shorter-term collective memories passed on between living generations and longer-term collective memories that can only be represented and passed on via stable mediations.

A classic example of an FBM that has been passed on across more than one hundred and fifty years, in the mode of canonized cultural memory, is Walt Whitman's poetry. Whitman begins one of his four commemorative poems of Abraham Lincoln with "When lilacs last in dooryard bloom'd," referring to the circumstances in which he learned of Lincoln's assassination.

---

[11] For psychology, see Stone et al. (2018); for cultural studies, see Erll (2011a, 28–33).

The assassination occurred on April 14, 1865, a time when, indeed, lilacs were in bloom. As Whitman subsequently wrote: "I remember where I stopped at the time, the season being advanced, there were many lilacs in bloom. By one of the caprices that enter and give tinge to events without being at all a part of them, I find myself always reminded of the great tragedy of that day by the sight and odor of these blossoms. It never fails" (Whitman 1882, 320). His personal recollection of learning of the assassination is lastingly connected to the public tragedy itself.[12] With his narrative poem, he passes on his FBM of Lincoln's death, potentially across hundreds and thousands of years.

Arguably, there is an entire archive to be discovered of historical witnesses and their flashbulb narratives. How did news of the French revolution reach Goethe, Schiller, and other Romantics across Europe? Do their autobiographical writings convey FBMs? Are representations of FBMs found more often since the eighteenth century, the great age of self-consciousness? Are there differences between Western and non-Western cultures? (see Wang and Aydin 2018). Can we trace their phenomenology in ancient and medieval texts and objects?[13]

The intergenerational transmission of FBMs (the pathways of communicative memory) are to date not well explored. But there is some evidence with regard to 9/11 FBMs. Meyler et al. (2022) solicited from children who were nine years old or younger at the time of the 9/11 attack what they knew about 9/11, as well as what they knew about their parents' experience of 9/11. Although they were not always accurate, nor very detailed in their reports, 89 percent of the children could report on their parents' FBMs. (By accuracy, we mean the extent to which the child's report about the parental FBM corresponded to the parent's report.) The distribution of accuracy was bimodal, with 39 percent of the children reporting the parental FBM accurately and in detail, and 51 percent reporting an accurate FBM, but with only minimal detail. Whereas 11 percent of the children claimed not to have any knowledge of the parental FBM, only 2 percent of the parents thought that their children would not know their FBMs. As a testimony to the transmission of affect between parent and child, a strong correlation

---

[12] See also the psychologist F. W. Colegrove's (1899) study on how U.S. citizens remembered how they learned about Lincoln's assassination. Thirty-three years after the event, 71% could give many details of their reception circumstances. According to Luminet and Spijkerman (2017, 348), Colegrove was "a precursor for the field of flashbulb memories."

[13] Luminet and Spijkerman (2017) is one of the few studies of historical FBMs. It traces FBMs of the First World War Armistice (November 11, 1918) in Belgium in memoirs and diaries.

existed between the parents' self-report of their emotional state at the time of the attack and the children's report about how their parents felt at the time. Interestingly, neither the age of the child, nor the amount of 9/11 talk between child and parent, nor the amount of media attended to by the child affected the accuracy or knowledge of parental FBMs.

Results such as these suggest that flashbulb narratives can travel between generations. What seems to make at least FBMs of portentous events such as 9/11 highly transmissible is their affect and their high relevance for social identities. Moreover, Meyler et al.'s (2022) research suggests that they are more or less unconnected to other modes of memory transmission (media reception, familial conversations about the past). A systematic revisiting of multigenerational interviews that were made over the past decades, for example in the field of oral history, might provide further insights in the (non)specifity of the transmission of FBMs between generations.

14.8 Media History

FBMs and media culture are inextricably connected. Already in 2009, the editor of the journal *Memory Studies*, sociologist and media theorist Andrew Hoskins, identified research on FBMs as a "fertile ground for interdisciplinarity" (Hoskins 2009).[14]

It is not surprising that the concept of FBM came up at the height of the global mass media regime. In the 1970s (the time of Brown and Kulik's coinage of the FBM concept), TV sets were widespread household items. The witnessing of events in the news had become a daily family ritual. The "live broadcasting of history" produced FBM-inducing "media events" (Dayan and Katz 1992). And the restricted number of public broadcasters before the rise of cable television channels ensured that widespread FBMs were likely based on the same footage.

In our post-broadcast era, the emergence of FBMs follows a different logic. Satellite and cable TV, streaming services, the internet and social media have changed the parameters for FBMs. According to Hoskins (2009, 148), "FBMs are no longer forged under a 'scarcity-led' broadcast environment that was

---

[14] On memory studies with a focus on media theory, see Erll (2011a, 113–143; Garde-Hansen (2011; Neiger et al. (2011); on digital memories, see Hoskins (2017) and Mandolessi (2023); on their interrelatedness with personal memories, see van Dijck (2007).

so central to the initial development of the concept. Rather, digital abundance is the new driver of our new media ecology in which FBMs emerge and re-emerge today." We now live in a "high choice media environment" (Prior 2010), which leads to what Jill A. Edy (2014, 73) calls "memory silos."[15] Research is needed to find out whether this also leads to "flashbulb memory silos."

Since Marshall McLuhan (1964), media theory holds that "the medium is the message," and consequently one could surmise that the medium also influences the formation and phenomenology of FBMs. In the present age, FBMs will typically be formed with a smartphone in hand (see the study by Talarico et al. 2019). The new media ecology has turned FBMs into a matter of secondary "witnessing in times of social media" (Schankweiler et al. 2018). But the contents of this mediated witnessing may be very diverse, depending on which media and memory silos one inhabits. FBMs are more and more related to what Hoskins calls the "memory of the multitude" rather than to a mainstreamed collective memory.[16]

14.9 Flashbulb Memories and the Agency of the Aesthetic

As our occasional examples have already indicated, literature and the arts play an important role in exploring the phenomenology of FBMs. This is particularly true for poetry and narrative fiction, with their unique forms of representing consciousness that provide them with a niche in the cultural imagination of the memory process. As Walt Whitman's poem "When Lilacs Last in the Dooryard Bloom'd" suggests, there may even be a literary subgenre of flashbulb-poetry, most likely to be found in commemorative poetry carrying titles such as "upon hearing...," "upon reading...."

In the twentieth century, the beginnings and endings of wars and conflicts have yielded literary flashbulb moments in poetry.[17] Auden's "September 1, 1939" (1940), for example, starts with a clear sense of the time and place of hearing the news about the German invasion of Poland: "I sit in one of the dives / On Fifty-second Street /.../ The unmentionable odour of death /

---

[15] "A memory silo may emerge if distinct groups of people within a social system come to share a collective memory unique to them and are unaware that this memory is not typical beyond the boundaries of their group" (Edy 2014, 74).
[16] "Collective memory has its limits. Memory of the multitude does not" (Hoskins 2017, 106).
[17] For the following examples, we are indebted to Daniel Dornhofer's encyclopedic memory of English poetry.

Offends the September night." First World War poet Siegfried Sassoon refers in "Everyone Sang" (1919) to what must have been for many a memorable sensory detail of armistice in 1918: "Everyone suddenly burst out singing."[18]

Aesthetic media can also take a more reflexive, even critical stance on FBMs—a mode found in particular in 9/11 fiction and film. In his comic board book *In The Shadow of No Towers* (2004, 1), Art Spiegelman depicts in a short (just three panels long) comic strip the phenomenology and political effects of 9/11 FBMs among Americans. In the first panel, a nuclear American family sits drowsily on a sofa in front of a television set. In the second panel, news of 9/11 come as a shocking, literally hair-raising event. This is clearly an FBM-inducing situation with the relevant affect. In the third panel, the family sits in exactly the same sleepy position and posture. But their hair remains raised, which indicates the pervasive sense of anxiety and insecurity in post–9/11 American culture that Grusin (2010) has described. One thing has changed in the living room: There is now an American flag on the wall. A strong sense of national identity has been produced or reaffirmed with the FBM. The FBM of 9/11 seems to have led to a mixture of anxiety and nationalism.[19] But "the new normal" (that's the panel's title) does not entail a greater degree of (mental or political) activity.

Literature and film are, moreover, important media to imagine and critically reflect upon the traveling and transnational dimensions of 9/11 FBMs. We have already pointed to Mohsin Hamid's novel *The Reluctant Fundamentalist* (2007). Another relevant work is the film *11'09"01 September 11* (2002), a collection of eleven short films on 9/11 which attempts to capture international perspectives on the event (in eleven minutes and just one frame each). Several clips are about the (im)possibilities of creating FBMs across the world (e.g., among children in an Afghan refugee camp in Iran; this is Samira Makhmalbaf's contribution). The UK-related clip by Ken Loach makes a multidirectional argument (in the sense of Rothberg 2009) by substituting the usual FBM-inducing images of the falling Twin Towers with the memory images that Chilean refugee Pablo, who is stranded in Great Britain, retains of Chile's *coup d'état* of 1973. This coup against Salvador Allende also happened on a September 11 and was backed by the

---

[18] See Luminet and Spijkerman (2017) for FBMs in memoirs related to the First Word War and the striking accuracy of memories for weather.

[19] The psychological theory of "affiliation under stress" might account for these dynamics (Taylor 2006).

U.S. government. The clip connects two different histories and two different victim groups, asking about the implication of the U.S. in violent histories across the world. This political message is underscored by showing an alternative set of FBM-inducing images.

But aesthetic media do not just engage in the *representation* of the phenomenology of FBMs and in the *critical reflection* of their political dimensions. As part of media culture, they are also powerful *agents* in their own right, when it comes to the creation, consolidation, and reconsolidation of FBMs. Hence, Rigney's (2021) concept of the "agency of the aesthetic" is particularly applicable here. Literature and film can keep up the high degree of tellability of FBMs by remediating again and again the historical events and their witnessing. For 9/11, blockbuster movies like *United 93* (2006) or documentaries like *Fahrenheit 911* (2004) seem to have unfolded such agency (Hirst et al. 2009, 2015).

Moreover, aesthetic media may exert their power not just after the fact, when FBMs are already in place, but sometimes even *before* an event is witnessed via media. This dynamic has been discussed as "premediation" (see Erll 2017; Grusin 2010). While FBMs are phenomenologically characterized by the rememberer's great confidence in the accuracy and consistency of the memory, they are also quite likely—as any other perception, experience, and memory—socially framed and preformed, in particular by culturally available narratives and images. Thus, when first seeing the images of 9/11, many people had associations of an alien attack, or of a "Third World War," as they had seen them in science fiction movies like *Independence Day* (1996). Schemata derived from such aesthetic images and narratives may have shaped individual receptions. The question is whether and to what extent such aesthetically preformed (mis)conceptions remain an important part of the FBM ("at first I thought this was . . ."; "It felt like . . .").

14.10 Conclusion

In setting out to write this chapter, the two authors explored the benefits of interdisciplinary perspectives as envisioned by scholars in the field of memory studies. We specifically wanted to investigate how such a perspective might reshape the lens through which one studies and understands the phenomenon of FBMs. When Roger Brown and James Kulik brought the phenomenon to the attention of their fellow psychologists, their chief interest—as well as that of the psychologists who followed in their lead—was in whether a distinctive cognitive mechanism drove the phenomenon. They rested their claim on the seeming accuracy of FBMs. Since then, at least in the hands of psychologists, research has mainly focused on empirically testing Brown and Kulik's claim: Are FBMs accurately recalled, even after decades? Do they remain vivid and confidently held over the long term? How do they differ from "ordinary autobiographical memories"? Does one really need to posit a new cognitive mechanism, or can one account for the characteristics of FBMs by employing what is known about "ordinary memory processes"?

To a large extent, these questions have been resolved. Study after study has established that FBMs decay over time—at least their accuracy does. The consensus is that ordinary memory mechanisms may be sufficient to account for FBMs' characteristics. Brown and Kulik raised the question; the field of psychology subsequently answered it.[20]

But to those outside the field of psychology, the issue of underlying cognitive mechanisms, while important, does not seem to address why FBMs are of enduring interest. Though people are always amazed to discover how unreliable their confidently held and vivid FBMs might be, this observation cannot account for why they want to tell their FBM story nonetheless.

The interdisciplinary lens of memory studies provides a means of opening up questions about FBMs beyond the ones that have occupied psychologists since Brown and Kulik's seminal article. It brings in a discussion of narrative and an understanding of FBMs as "good" and "tellable" stories that can convey a sense of "living in history" (Brown et al. 2009) and fulfill the important anthropological function of what theoretician of history Jörn Rüsen (2017) has described as giving meaning to temporal experience. A memory studies lens, moreover, shows that FBMs are part of—and propped up by—collective memory, and it highlights the important functions that FBMs seem to have for social identities. It helps us think about how FBMs might "travel"—across national boundaries and across generations. It underscores the role of (new) media, as well as the need to consider the "agency of the aesthetic." Connecting psychology with narrative, cultural, and media research, an integrated memory studies approach finds a place for a range of disciplines to cooperate in building the broader and more panoptic study of FBMs—FBMs 2.0, if you like.

---

[20] See critically on the "flashbulb memory game," Curci and Conway (2013).

Afterword

Traveling On

How will the field of memory studies travel on? Memory studies is an expansive, multi-paradigmatic field that brings together in dialogue a great number of disciplines and subfields, all the way from the theory of history to queer studies, from cognitive psychology to media studies, and from archaeology to political sciences. Dialogue is its major mode, strength, and potential. To be successful, conversations on such a broad and international platform need to be free of jargon and disciplinary narcissism, and ready to engage in cross-disciplinary perspective-taking and academic translanguaging.

But what holds the field together, apart from its interdisciplinary and international ethos? I think it is a special "take" on phenomena. Basically any phenomenon can be seen through the lens of memory research: the photograph you spot in a newspaper, the new law your government has just passed, the name of the street you are living in, the dish you are eating, the stereotypical phrase that is just popping up in your mind. In that sense, Konstantina Tsoleridou is certainly right, when she posts (about my courses at university) a meme called "Memory Is Everywhere" (see Figure 15.1).

Memory research temporalizes. It assumes a temporal perspective on phenomena. This concerns both the ontological question of the phenomenon's existence in time, as well as the epistemological question about the ways in which it has been framed and reframed as a phenomenon with pasts, presents, and futures. Temporalizing is the signature operation of the field of memory studies.

But with the idea of collective memory—whether we like it or not—comes a seduction: the allure of analogical thinking. We operate with a term that refers traditionally (think Plato and Aristotle), in some academic quarters still today (think mainstream neurosciences), and in public understanding almost exclusively, if erroneously, to a purely individual phenomenon. However, serious collective memory research cannot be based on an "individual memory first" logic that entails the transfer of insights about neuronal

Figure 15.1 Konstantina Tsoleridou, "Memory Is Everywhere," meme, reproduced courtesy of Konstanina Tsoleridou.

and mental processes to other domains. This would mean committing an analogical fallacy.

Is the solution, then, a radical disengagement between different dimensions of memory, severing the individual from the social, the mental from the medial? Such a move can help to focus on the logic of particular aspects of collective memory (this book zooms in on literary and medial dynamics). But the various dimensions of collective memory are in fact interrelated. They are co-constructive to an extent that (as Maurice Halbwachs already argued) *no* individual memory is thinkable without social groups, and similarly, *no* higher mental process remains untouched by media culture. Disengagement is an important heuristic tool (no scholar can "do it all"). But as the credo of an entire field, it would lead to many silos of memory research standing next to each other—and to a truncated vision of the memory process. As it travels on, the field of memory studies must nagivate between the Scylla of analogical fallacies and the Charybdis of silofication.

If we boldly conceive of collective memory as a distributed phenomenon that cuts across biological, mental, social, cultural, material, and medial dimensions, then the nature of the intersections between these dimensions must be on the agenda of our inquiry. This means that social and cultural scholarship cannot afford—or only at their peril—to ignore what psychology and the neurosciences have to say about memory, and vice versa.

Last but certainly not least, memory studies is not only an expansive but also a hybrid field. Collective memory is part of public and political discourse as well as an object of academic inquiry. Over the past decade, in particular, many hybrid forms of "doing memory" have emerged—all the way from academically inspired curatorial practice to memory scholar-activists. Memory research stretches between a more analytical and a more normative pole; it holds cold and hot options. This book clearly leans more toward the "cold" endeavor of conceptualization and comparative mnemohistory, but without overlooking the ethical and political implications of all academic work.

I want to end with a "hot" demand for the possibility of "cold" research. Today more than ever, in an age of rampant memory abuse and aggressive memory antagonisms, there is the need for a rigorously academic field of memory studies with the time, resources, freedom, and new generations of researchers to develop a deeper understanding of how humans make time and are made by time. Collective memory has made our societies—all societies—possible in the first place. It has fueled the project of the European Union, the human rights regime, and advocacy for the recognition and repair of violent pasts. But it also fuels the rise of populism, the Russian War in Ukraine, and the Israeli/Palestinian conflict. Environmental and anthropocenic memories and anxieties, the new challenges of AI-generated memories, the persistence of long-term narrative, aesthetic, and affective patterns that (for better or worse) shape our thought and action—these are just some of the pressing issues that show how urgently we need a better understanding of the logics, the uses and abuses, the possibilities and limitations of collective memory worldwide.

Acknowledgments

Memory studies is a collaborative science. All essays printed in this book are the result of stimulating international and interdisciplinary dialogues. I am immensely indebted to a number of research networks, where I could develop and discuss my ideas—and to many people engaged in and for these networks.

Between 2003 and 2007, I worked at the Interdisciplinary Research Center "Memory Cultures" (*Sonderforschungsbereich Erinnerungskulturen*) at Justus Liebig University Giessen, and this in many ways planted the seeds of my thinking about memory, which would grow in the decades to come. I had the wonderful luck to work in a project led by Ansgar Nünning, where we gauged the potential of cultural memory studies as a field, explored imperial memories of the Indian Rebellion of 1857–1858, and theorized the intersections between literature and memory. Together with Stephanie Wodianka and a working group called "Time, Media, Identity," I conceptualized the "memory film." Jürgen Reulecke's work on "generationality" inspired me to explore literary generations.

In 2007, a workshop with Ann Rigney's Utrecht-based project on "The Dynamics of Remembrance" made it possible for us to think through the mediation and remediation of cultural memory. The workshop also marked our first meeting with Andrew Hoskins and Jeffrey Olick—the beginning of an ongoing exchange about the digital and sociohistorical dimensions of memory. Two decades of joint research and publications with Ann Rigney have left their intellectual and stylistic marks on my work, for which I am deeply grateful.

A one-year fellowship at the "Netherlands Institute of Advanced Study" (NIAS, 2009–2010) and the discussions in its "Memory Group" and the theme group "The Reception of Netherlandish Art in Asia" gave me the time and mental space to develop the idea of "traveling memory." The conversations with Michael North, Pamela Pattynama, and Ann Rigney were particularly important. I first presented the concept of traveling memory at the 2010 London conference on "Transcultural Memory," which was organized by Lucy Bond, Rick Crownshaw, and Jessica Rapson—a foundational event in the emergence of (transcultural) memory studies as an international field.

A constant source of inspiration and exciting insights into cutting-edge memory research remains the international "Mnemonics-Network for Memory Studies," which has been hosting annual summer schools for doctoral candidates since 2012. I am indebted to its initiator Stef Craps for bringing together a bunch of world-leading memory scholars. The chapters on generationality and genealogy had their first iteration in a Mnemonics-keynote I gave at Ghent University in 2013.

The "Network in Transnational Memory Studies" (NITMES, 2012–2015), led by Ann Rigney, provided many opportunities for discussions with Aleida Assmann, Rosanne Kennedy, Michael Rothberg, and Barbara Törnquist-Plewa—as well as some memorable swimming sprees. The chapter on "District Six" as a traveling schema goes back to our dialogues on transnational memory.

The large European COST-network "In Search of Transcultural Memory in Europe" (2012–2016), led by Barbara Törnquist-Plewa and Tea Sindbæk Andersen, not only provided the possibility to see and feel European memory in places like Budapest, Copenhagen, Dublin, Krakow, Skopje, and Sofia. It also involved the gift of meeting a large number of fabulous scholars and friends. "Traveling Memory in European Film" emerged from this network, from discussions about the migration film with Dagmar Brunow, Sébastien Fevry, and Erin Högerle, as well as from a memorable conference in Jerusalem, hosted in 2013 by Vered Vinitzky-Seroussi.

The founding of the "Memory Studies Association" (MSA) in 2016, by Jeffrey Olick, Aline Sierp, and Jenny Wüstenberg, brought many of the existing networks together into a common space that has since been open to even broader conversations, increasingly including colleagues from beyond Europe. The essay "Memory Worlds in Times of Corona" was originally an afterword to a special issue dedicated to the 2019 MSA-conference in Madrid, and it is clearly shaped by the theoretical nudges of its organizers, Francisco Ferrándiz, Marije Hristova, and Johanna Vollmeyer.

Since 2019, and starting from a panel at the MSA Madrid, I have been conducting with William Hirst the project of "Breaking down the Silos," which brings social and cultural scholars together with psychologists in a sustained exchange about collective memory. The chapters on "Ecologies of Trauma" and on "Flashbulb Memories" emerged from the many "Silos"-roundtables and the preparation of the 2022 conference at Goethe University Frankfurt. At roughly the same time, the McDonnell Foundation's "Collective Memory Research Group," led by James V. Wertsch and Henry L. Roediger III, became a home for truly interdisciplinary research on collective memory. Ideas for the chapter "The Hidden Power of Implicit Collective Memory" sprang from this context. The McDonnell project has also provided funding for a survey study on transnational flashbulb memories that I am honored to conduct together with Magdalena Abel, William Hirst, and Piotr Szpunar—an opportunity to put conceptual thought about interdisciplinarity into practice.

Since 2022, the Hessen-wide project "Transformations of Political Violence" (funded by BMBF, the German Federal Ministry of Education and Research) has opened up the possibility for media scholar Kaya de Wolff and me to engage in a dialogue with colleagues from peace and conflict studies. Together, we think through the memory-violence nexus and develop the idea of "memory *before* violence."

Over all these years, the "Frankfurt Memory Studies Platform" (FMSP), operative since 2011 and hosted by the Frankfurt Humanities Research Center, has been a vibrant hub of interdisciplinary and international memory research. I don't have the space here to name all the students and researchers based at Goethe University and the many international fellows who have inspired discussions at FMSP, and who embody for me the future of memory studies—but a big and deep-felt thanks goes to my co-leader of FMSP, Hanna Teichler, with whom it is just a pleasure to make memory studies happen. Our long-standing collaboration with the Historical Museum Frankfurt, and in particular with Angela Jannelli, has kept us acutely aware of the local and urban aspects of traveling and transnational memory. More recently, the "Actualizations Group," grounded in the philologies at Goethe University, has provided a new home for exploring the literary past in the present. Last but not least, I am grateful to Nadia Butt for turning Frankfurt with me into a site of explorations on transculturality, travel, and memory.

Chapters 3, 11, and 13 could not have been researched and written without the generous funding by Volkswagen Foundation, which awarded me an Opus Magnum in 2016-2017.

Konstantina Tsoleridou greatly helped me in the editing process—and contributed a memorable meme.

Johanna Bühler painted the cover image. I am overjoyed that my daughter's version of Odyssean memory has become part of this book.

*

I would like to thank Jeffrey K. Olick for giving me the idea for both the book and its title, and James Cook for his readiness to set up with us the Oxford UP series "Studies in Collective Memory." I am immensely grateful to Emily Benitez for her unfailing support in the editorial process.

All individual chapters in this collection of essays are revised and updated versions of earlier publications. I am grateful to the relevant presses and publishing houses as well as to my co-author William Hirst to grant me the rights to reproduce (parts of) the following texts:

"Travelling Memory." *Parallax*. Special Issue, *Transcultural Memory*, edited by Rick Crownshaw, 17(4) (2011): 4-18 [Chapter 1].

"Travelling Memory in European Film: A Morphology of Mnemonic Relationality." Special Issue, *Audiovisual Memory and the (Re-)Making of Europe*, edited by Astrid Erll and Ann Rigney. *Image & Narrative* 18(1) (2017): 5-19 [Chapter 2].

"Homer—A Relational Mnemohistory." Special Issue, *Cultural Memory after the Transnational Turn*, edited by Astrid Erll and Ann Rigney. *Memory Studies* 11(3) (2018): 274-286 [Chapter 3].

"Memory Worlds in Times of Corona." Special Issue, *Reframing Time and the Past*, edited by Johanna Vollmeyer, Francisco Ferrándiz, and Marije Hristova. *Memory Studies* 13(5) (2020): 861-874 [Chapter 4].

"Locating Family in Cultural Memory Studies." Special Issue, *Families and Memories: Continuities and Social Change*, edited by Irene Levin, Nicole Hennum, Claudia Lenz, and Tone Schou Wetlesen. *Journal of Comparative Family Studies* 42(3) (2011): 303-318 [Chapter 5].

"Generation in Literary History: Three Constellations of Generationality, Genealogy, and Memory." *New Literary History* 45(3) (2014): 385-409 [Chapter 6].

"Fictions of Generational Memory: Caryl Phillips's *In the Falling Snow* and Black British Writing in Times of Mnemonic Transition." In *Memory Unbound: Tracing the Dynamics of Memory Studies*, edited by Lucy Bond, Stef Craps, and Pieter Vermeulen. New York: Berghahn, 2017, 109-130 [Chapter 7].

"Literature, Film, and the Mediality of Cultural Memory." In *A Companion to Cultural Memory Studies*, edited by Astrid Erll and Ansgar Nünning. Berlin: De Gruyter, 2010 [2008], 389-398 [Chapter 8].

"Remembering across Time, Space and Cultures: Premediation, Remediation and the 'Indian Mutiny.'" In *Mediation, Remediation, and the Dynamics of Cultural Memory*, edited by Astrid Erll and Ann Rigney. Berlin: De Gruyter, 2009, 109-138 [Chapter 9].

"From 'District Six' to *District 9* and Back: The Plurimedial Production of Travelling Schemata." In *Transnational Memory: Circulation, Articulation, Scales*, edited by Chiara de Cesari and Ann Rigney. Berlin: De Gruyter, 2014, 29–50 [Chapter 10].

"Homer, Turko, Little Harry: Cultural Memory and the Ethics of Premediation in James Joyce's *Ulysses*." *Partial Answers* 17(2) (2019): 227–253 [Chapter 11].

"The Hidden Power of Implicit Collective Memory." *Memory, Mind & Media* 1, e14 (2022): 1–17 [Chapter 12].

"Travelling Narratives in Ecologies of Trauma: An Odyssey for Memory Scholars." Special Issue on *Cultural Trauma*, edited by William Hirst. *Social Research* 87(3) (2020): 533–563 [Chapter 13].

"Flashbulb Memories: An Interdisciplinary Research Programme." *Narrative Inquiry* 33(2) (2023): 398–420 (with William Hirst) [Chapter 14].

Bibliography

Abel, Magdalena, and Dorthe Berntsen. 2021. "How Do We Remember Public Events? Pioneering a New Area of Everyday Memory Research." *Cognition* 214: 104745. https://doi.org/10.1016/j.cognition.2021.104745.

Abel, Magdalena, Sharda Umanath, Beth Fairfield, Masanobou Takahashi, Henry L. Roediger, and James V. Wertsch. 2019. "Collective Memories across 11 Nations for World War II: Similarities and Differences Regarding the Most Important Events." *Journal of Applied Research in Memory and Cognition* 8 (2): 178–188. https://doi.org/10.1016/j.jarmac.2019.02.001.

Adams, Bert N., and Jan Trost, eds. 2004. *Handbook of World Families*. Thousand Oaks, CA: Sage Publications.

Addis, Donna Rose. 2020. "Mental Time Travel? A Neurocognitive Model of Event Simulation." *Review of Philosophy and Psychology* 11: 233–259. https://doi.org/10.1007/s13164-020-00470-0.

Adebayo, Sakiru. 2023. *Continuous Pasts: Frictions of Memory in Postcolonial Africa, African Perspectives*. Ann Arbor: University of Michigan Press.

Adorno, Theodor W. 1977 [1959]. "Was bedeutet: Aufarbeitung der Vergangenheit?" In Adorno: *Gesammelte Schriften, Vol 10.2*. Frankfurt am Main: Suhrkamp. 555–572.

Adorno, Theodor W., and Max Horkheimer. 2009 [1948]. *Dialectic of Enlightenment: Philosophical Fragments*. Stanford, CA: Stanford University Press.

Afrika, Tatamkhulu. 1994. "Nothing's Changed." In *Tatamkhulu Afrika: Maqabane*. Belville: Mayibuye Books. 33–34.

Akpome, Aghogho. 2017. "'Zones of Indistinction' and Visions of Post-Reconciliation South Africa in District 9." *Safundi: The Journal of South African and American Studies* 18 (1): 85–97. 10.1080/17533171.2016.1249167.

Alexander, Jeffrey C. 2012. *Trauma: A Social Theory*. Cambridge: Polity.

Alfandary, Rony, and Judith Tydor Baumel-Schwartz, eds. 2023. *Psychoanalytic and Cultural Aspects of Trauma and the Holocaust*. London: Routledge.

Alibhai-Brown, Yasmin. 2001. *Mixed Feelings: The Complex Lives of Mixed Race Britons*. London: Women's Press.

American Psychiatric Association. 2013. *Diagnostic and Statistical Manual of Mental Disorders: Fifth Edition (DSM-5)*. Washington, DC: American Psychiatric Publishing.

Anastasio, Thomas J., Kristen Ann Ehrenberger, Patrick Watson, and Wenyi Zhang. 2012. *Individual and Collective Memory Consolidation: Analogous Processes on Different Levels*. Cambridge, MA: MIT Press.

Anderson, Benedict. 1991. *Imagined Communities: Reflections on the Origin and Spread of Nationalism*. London: Verso.

Anderson, Molly, and Shari Daya. 2022. "Memory Justice in Ordinary Urban Spaces: The Politics of Remembering and Forgetting in a Post-Apartheid Neighbourhood." *Antipode* 54 (6): 1673–1693.

Anjaria, Ulka. 2021. *Understanding Bollywood: The Grammar of Hindi Cinema*, 1st ed. London: Routledge. https://doi.org/10.4324/9780429293726.

Annabell, Taylor. 2023. "Scrolling Back: Remediation within and through Digital Memory Work." *Memory, Mind & Media* 2: e10. https://doi.org/10.1017/mem.2023.6.

Antonini, Alessio, Sam Brooker, and Lovro Škopljanac. 2024. "Spontaneous Transmedia Co-Location: Integration in Memory." *Memory, Mind & Media* 3 (e7): 1–14.

Appadurai, Arjun. 1996. *Modernity at Large: Cultural Dimensions of Globalization*. Minneapolis: University of Minnesota Press.

Appiah, Kwame Anthony. 2018. *The Lies That Bind: Rethinking Identity*. New York: Liveright.

Arana, Victoria R., and Lauri Ramey, eds. 2009. *Black British Writing*. New York: Palgrave Macmillan.

Araujo, Ana Lucia. 2012. *Politics of Memory: Making Slavery Visible in the Public Space*. New York: Routledge.

Araujo, Ana Lucia. 2021. *Slavery in the Age of Memory: Engaging the Past*. London: Bloomsbury Academic.

Armitage, David. 2012. "What's the Big Idea? Intellectual History and the *longue durée*." *History of European Ideas* 38 (4): 493–507.

Arnold-de Simine, Silke, and Tea Sindbæk Andersen. 2017. "Between Transnationalism and Localization: The Pan-European TV Miniseries 14—Diaries of the Great War." *Image & Narrative* 18 (1): 63–79. https://www.imageandnarrative.be/index.php/imagenarrative/article/view/1480.

Assmann, Aleida. 2011 [1999]. *Cultural Memory and Western Civilization: Functions, Media, Archives*. Cambridge: Cambridge University Press.

Assmann, Aleida. 2014. "Dialogic Memory." In *Dialogue as a Trans-Disciplinary Concept: Martin Buber's Philosophy of Dialogue and Its Contemporary Reception*, edited by Paul Mendes-Flohr. Berlin: De Gruyter. 199–214.

Assmann, Aleida. 2020 [2013]. *Is Time Out of Joint?: On the Rise and Fall of the Modern Time Regime*. Ithaca, NY: Cornell University Press.

Assmann, Corinna. 2018. *Doing Family in Second-Generation British Migration Literature*. Berlin: De Gruyter.

Assmann, Jan. 1995. "Collective Memory and Cultural Identity." Translated by John Czaplicka. *New German Critique* 65 (65): 125–133. https://doi.org/10.2307/488538.

Assmann, Jan. 1997. *Moses the Egyptian: The Memory of Egypt in Western Monotheism*. Cambridge, MA: Harvard University Press.

Assmann, Jan. 2006. *Religion and Cultural Memory: Ten Studies*. Translated by Rodney Livingstone. Stanford, CA: Stanford University Press.

Assmann, Jan. 2010. "Communicative and Cultural Memory." In *A Companion to Cultural Memory Studies*, edited by Astrid Erll and Ansgar Nünning. Berlin: De Gruyter. 109–118.

Assmann, Jan. 2011 [1992]. *Cultural Memory and Early Civilization. Writing, Remembrance, and Political Imagination*. Cambridge: Cambridge University Press.

Aubert, Nathalie. 2015. "'We Have Nothing Better than Testimony': History and Memory in French War Narratives." *Journal of European Studies* 45 (4): 287–300. https://doi.org/10.1177/0047244115599144.

Aydemir, Murat, and Alex Rotas, eds. 2008. *Migratory Settings*. Amsterdam: Rodopi.

Azoulay, Ariella. 2008. *The Civil Contract of Photography*. New York: Zone Books.

Azoulay, Ariella. 2015. *Civil Imagination: A Political Ontology of Photography*. London: Verso.
Bachmann-Medick, Doris, ed. 2016. *Cultural Turns: New Orientations in the Study of Culture*. Berlin: De Gruyter.
Baden, Christian, and Sophie Lecheler. 2012. "Fleeting, Fading, or Far-Reaching? A Knowledge-Based Model of the Persistence of Framing Effects." *Communication Theory* 22 (4): 359–382. https://doi.org/10.1111/j.1468-2885.2012.01413.x.
Baer, Alejandro, and Natan Sznaider. 2018. *Memory and Forgetting in the Post-Holocaust Era: The Ethics of Never Again*. London: Routledge.
Ball, Charles. 1858. *The History of the Indian Mutiny: Giving a Detailed Account of the Sepoy Insurrection in India; and a Concise History of the Great Military Events Which Have Tended to Consolidate British Empire in Hindostan*. Vol. 2. London: London Printing and Publishing Company.
Barad, Karen. 2007. *Meeting the University Halfway: Quantum Physics and the Entanglement of Matter and Meaning*. Durham, NC: Duke University Press.
Barad, Karen. 2017. "Troubling Time/s and Ecologies of Nothingness: Re-Turning, Re-Membering, and Facing the Incalculable." *New Formations* 92: 56–86.
Barclay, Katie, and Nina Javette Koefoed. 2021. "Family, Memory, and Identity: An Introduction." *Journal of Family History* 46 (1): 3–12. https://doi.org/10.1177/0363199020967297.
Bargh, John A. 1994. "The Four Horsemen of Automaticity: Awareness, Intention, Efficiency, and Control in Social Cognition." In *Handbook of Social Cognition*, edited by Robert S. Wyer and Thomas K. Srull. New York: Erlbaum. 1–40.
Bargh, John A., Mark Chen, and Lara Burrows. 1996. "Automaticity of Social Behavior: Direct Effects of Trait Construct and Stereotype Priming on Action." *Journal of Personality and Social Psychology* 71: 230–244.
Barnier, Amanda J., and Andrew Hoskins. 2018. "Is There Memory in the Head, in the Wild?" *Memory Studies* 11 (4): 386–390.
Barocas, Harvey A., and Carol A. Barocas. 1979. "Wounds of the Fathers: The Next Generation of Holocaust Victims." *International Review of Psycho-Analysis* 6 (3): 331–340.
Baroni, Raphaël. 2014. "Tellability." In *Handbook of Narratology*, edited by Peter Hühn, Jan Christoph Meister, John Pier, and Wolf Schmid. Berlin: De Gruyter. 836–845. https://doi.org/10.1515/9783110316469.836.
Baronian, Marie-Aude, Stephan Besser, and Yolande Jansen, eds. 2007. *Diaspora and Memory: Figures of Displacement in Contemporary Literature, Arts and Politics*. Amsterdam: Rodopi.
Barriales-Bouche, Alejandra, and Marjorie Salvodon, eds. 2007. *Zoom In Zoom Out: Crossing Borders in Contemporary European Cinema*. Newcastle: Cambridge Scholars.
Barthes, Roland. 1980. *La chambre claire: Note sur la photographie*. Paris: Gallimard.
Bartlett, Frederic C. 1954 [1932]. *Remembering: A Study in Experimental and Social Psychology*. Cambridge: Cambridge University Press.
Bates, Crispin, ed. 2011. *New Perspectives on 1857: Anticipation and Experiences in the Locality*. Delhi: Sage.
Bates, Crispin, gen. ed. 2013–2017. *Mutiny at the Margins: New Perspectives on the Indian Uprising of 1857*. 7 vols. New Delhi: Sage.
Bayer, Gerd. 2010. "After Postmemory: Holocaust Cinema and the Third Generation." *Shofar* 28 (4): 116–132.

Beck, Ulrich. 2006. *The Cosmopolitan Vision*. Cambridge: Polity Press.
Beck, Ulrich. 2007. "The Cosmopolitan Condition: Why Methodological Nationalism Fails." *Theory, Culture & Society* 24 (7–8): 286–290. https://doi.org/10.1177/02632764070240072505.
Beck, Ulrich. 2009. *World Risk Society*. Cambridge: Polity Press.
Becker, Annette. 2003. *Maurice Halbwachs: Un intellectuel en guerres mondiales 1914–1945*. Paris: Agnès Viénot.
Beiner, Guy. 2018. *Forgetful Remembrance: Social Forgetting and Vernacular Historiography of a Rebellion in Ulster*. Oxford: Oxford University Press.
Beiner, Guy, ed. 2021. *Pandemic Re-Awakenings: The Forgotten and Unforgotten Flu of 1918–1919*. Oxford: Oxford University Press.
Bender, Abby. 2014. "A Bloomsday Seder: Joyce and Jewish Memory." In *Memory Ireland*. Vol. 4, *James Joyce and Cultural Memory*, edited by Katherine O'Callaghan and Oona Frawley. Syracuse, NY: Syracuse University Press. 62–78.
Bender, Jill C. 2016. *The 1857 Indian Uprising and the British Empire*. Cambridge: Cambridge University Press.
Bennett, Jane. 2010. *Vibrant Matter: A Political Ecology of Things*. Durham, NC: Duke University Press.
Bérard, Victor. 1902. *Les Phéniciens et l'Odyssée*. Paris: Armand Colin.
Berghahn, Daniela. 2013. *Far-Flung Families in Film: The Diasporic Family in Contemporary European Cinema*. Edinburgh: Edinburgh University Press.
Bergmann, Martin S., and Milton E. Jucovy, eds. 1982. *Generations of the Holocaust*. New York: Columbia University Press.
Berlinerblau, Jacques. 1999. *Heresy in the University: The Black Athena Controversy and the Responsibilities of American Intellectuals*. New Brunswick, NJ: Rutgers University Press.
Bernal, Martin. 1987. *Black Athena: The Afroasiatic Roots of Classical Civilization*. New Brunswick, NJ: Rutgers University Press.
Berntsen, Dorthe. 2012. *Involuntary Autobiographical Memories: An Introduction to the Unbidden Past*. Cambridge: Cambridge University Press.
Berntsen, Dorthe. 2017. "Flashbulb Memories and Social Identity." In *Flashbulb Memories: New Challenges and Future Perspectives*, edited by Olivier Luminet and Antonietta Curci. Hove: Psychology Press. 182–200.
Bevernage, Berber, and Chris Lorenz, eds. 2013. *Breaking Up Time: Negotiating the Borders between Present, Past, and Future*. Göttingen: Vandenhoeck & Ruprecht.
Bhabha, Homi K. 1994. *The Location of Culture*. London: Routledge.
Bijl, Paul. 2016. *Emerging Memory: Photographs of Colonial Atrocity in Dutch Cultural Remembrance*. Amsterdam: Amsterdam University Press.
Birhane, Abeba. 2021. "Algorithmic Injustice: A Relational Ethics Approach." *Patterns* 2 (2): 1–9.
Bloch, Marc. 1925. "Mémoire Collective, Tradition et Coutume." *Revue de Synthèse Historique* 40: 73–83.
Bloom, Harold. 1975. *A Map of Misreading*. New York: Oxford University Press.
Boccardi, Mariadele. 2009. *The Contemporary British Historical Novel: Representation, Nation, Empire*. Basingstoke: Palgrave.
Bohn, Annette, and Dorthe Berntsen. 2007. "Pleasantness Bias in Flashbulb Memories: Positive and Negative Flashbulb Memories of the Fall of the Berlin Wall among East

and West Germans." *Memory & Cognition* 35 (3): 565–577. https://doi.org/10.3758/BF03193295.
Boitani, Piero. 1994. *The Shadow of Ulysses: Figures of a Myth*. Oxford: Oxford University Press.
Bolter, J. David, and Richard A. Grusin, eds. 1999. *Remediation: Understanding New Media*. Cambridge, MA: MIT Press.
Bond, Brian. 2014. *Britain's Two World Wars against Germany: Myth, Memory and the Distortions of Hindsight*. Cambridge: Cambridge University Press.
Bond, Lucy, and Jessica Rapson, eds. 2014. *The Transcultural Turn: Interrogating Memory Between and Beyond Borders*. Berlin: De Gruyter.
Bond, Lucy, Stef Craps, and Pieter Vermeulen, eds. 2016 *Memory Unbound: Tracing the Dynamics of Memory Studies*. New York: Berghahn.
Bond, Lucy, and Stef Craps. 2019. *Trauma*. Abingdon: Routledge.
Bornstein, Marc H., and Linda R. Cote. 2013. *Acculturation and Parent-Child Relationships: Measurement and Development*. London: Routledge.
Bornstein, Robert F., and Catherine Craver-Lemley. 2017. "Mere Exposure Effect." In *Cognitive Illusions: Intriguing Phenomena in Thinking, Judgment, and Memory*, edited by Pohl RF. London: Routledge. 256–275.
Bourke, Joanna. 1999. *An Intimate History of Killing: Face-to-Face Killing in Twentieth-Century Warfare*. New York: Basic Books.
Boym, Svetlana. 2001. *The Future of Nostalgia*. New York: Basic Books.
Bradd, Shore, and Sara Kauko. 2017. "The Landscape of Family Memory." In *Handbook of Culture and Memory*, edited by Brady Wagoner. Oxford: Oxford University Press. 85–116.
Brannigan, John. 2010. *Race in Modern Irish Literature and Culture*. Edinburgh: Edinburgh University Press.
Brantlinger, Patrick. 1988. *Rule of Darkness: British Literature and Imperialism, 1830–1914*. Ithaca, NY: Cornell University Press.
Brems, Elke. 2019. "Our Shared History: Some Thoughts on Translation and Cultural Memory." In *Translation in and for Society: Sociological and Cultural Approaches in Translation*, edited by Beatriz Martínez Ojeda, María Luisa, and Rodríguez Muñoz. Córdoba: Ediciones Universidad de Córdoba. 207–222.
Breytenbach, Cloete, and Brian Barrow. 1997. *The Spirit of District Six*. 1970. Cape Town: Human & Rousseau.
Brockmeier, Jens. 2015. *Beyond the Archive: Memory, Narrative, and the Autobiographical Process*. New York: Oxford University Press.
Brown, J. Dillon, and Leah Reade Rosenberg, eds. 2015. *Beyond Windrush: Rethinking Postwar Anglophone Caribbean Literature*. Jackson: University of Mississippi Press.
Brown, Norman R., Peter J. Lee, Mirna Krslak, Frederick G. Conrad, Tia G. B. Hansen, Jelena Havelka, and John R. Reddon. 2009. "Living in History: How War, Terrorism, and Natural Disaster Affect the Organization of Autobiographical Memory." *Psychological Science* 20 (4): 399–405. https://doi.org/10.1111/j.1467-9280.2009.02307.x.
Brown, Roger, and James Kulik. 1977. "Flashbulb Memories." *Cognition* 5 (1): 73–99. https://doi.org/10.1016/0010-0277(77)90018-X.
Browning, Robert. 1975. "Homer in Byzantium." *Viator* 6: 15–34.
Brügger, Niels. 2018. *The Archived Web: Doing History in the Digital Age*. Cambridge MA: MIT Press.

Bruner, Jerome S. 1990. *Acts of Meaning: Four Lectures on Mind and Culture.* Cambridge, MA: Harvard University Press.
Bruner, Jerome S. 2003. *Making Stories: Law, Literature, Life.* Boston: Harvard University Press.
Brunow, Dagmar. 2015. *Remediating Transcultural Memory: Documentary Filmmaking as Archival Intervention.* Berlin: De Gruyter.
Bryceson, Deborah Fahy, and Ulla Vuorela, eds. 2002. *The Transnational Family: New European Frontiers and Global Networks.* Oxford: Berg.
Bryld, Claus, and Anette Warring. 1998. *Besættelsestiden Som Kollektiv Erindring: Historie- Og Traditionsforvaltning Af Krig Og Besættelse 1945–1997.* Frederiksberg: Roskilde Universitetsforlag.
Buckley-Zistel, Susanne, Kaya de Wolff, Astrid Erll, Sybille Frank, Nicolai Hannig, Sabine Mannitz, Mariel Reiss, Jona Schwerer, Sara-Luise Spittler, Monika Wingender. 2024. "Memory before Violence." Frankfurt a.M.: TraCe Working Paper X.
Budgen, Frank. 1970. *Myselves When Young.* New York: Oxford University Press.
Budgen, Frank. 1973 [1934]. *James Joyce and the Making of Ulysses.* Bloomington: Indiana University Press.
Bull, Anna Cento, and Hans Lauge Hansen. 2016. "On Agonistic Memory." *Memory Studies* 9 (4): 390–404. https://doi.org/10.1177/1750698015615935.
Burke, Peter. 1989. "History as Social Memory." In *Memory: History, Culture and the Mind,* edited by Thomas Butler. New York: Blackwell. 97–113.
Burkert, Walter. 1992. *The Orientalizing Revolution: Near Eastern Influence on Greek Culture in the Early Archaic Age.* Cambridge, MA: Harvard University Press.
Büscher, Monika. 2020. "A Great Mobility Transformation." In *12 Perspectives on the Pandemic: International Social Science Thought Leaders Reflect on Covid-19,* edited by Gerhard Boomgaarden. Berlin: De Gruyter. 58–63.
Butler, Judith. 2009. *Frames of War: When Is Life Grievable?* London: Verso.
Butt, Nadia. 2015. *Transcultural Memory and Globalised Modernity in Contemporary Indo-English Novels.* Berlin: De Gruyter.
Çalışkan, Dilara. 2019. "Queer Postmemory." *European Journal of Women's Studies* 26 (3): 261–273. https://doi.org/10.1177/1350506819860164.
Campbell, Sue. 2003. *Relational Remembering: Rethinking the Memory Wars.* Lanham, MD: Rowman & Littlefield.
Carlston, Daryl C. 2010. "Models of Implicit and Explicit Mental Representation." In *Handbook of Implicit Social Cognition: Measurement, Theory, and Applications,* edited by Bertram Gawronski and B. Keith Payne. New York: Guilford Press. 38–61.
Carrier, Peter. 2000. "Places, Politics and the Archiving of Contemporary Memory in Pierre Nora's *Les lieux de mémoire*." In *Memory and Methodology,* edited by Susannah Radstone. Oxford: Berg. 37–58.
Carrigan, Anthony. 2012. *Postcolonial Tourism: Literature, Culture, and Environment.* New York: Routledge.
Carsten, Janet. 2007. *Ghosts of Memory: Essays on Remembrance and Relatedness.* Malden, MA: Blackwell.
Caruth, Cathy. 1996. *Unclaimed Experience: Trauma, Narrative, and History.* Baltimore, MD: Johns Hopkins University Press.
Cassirer, Ernst. 1944. *An Essay on Man: An Introduction to a Philosophy of Human Culture.* New Haven, CT: Yale University Press.

Catlin, Jonathon. 2021. "When Does an Epidemic Become a 'Crisis'? Analogies between Covid-19 and HIV/AIDS in American Public Memory." *Memory Studies* 14 (6): 1445–1474. https://doi.org/10.1177/17506980211054355.
Cazzolla Gatti, Roberto. 2020. "Coronavirus Outbreak Is a Symptom of Gaia's Sickness." *Ecological Modelling* 426: 109075. doi:10.1016/j.ecolmodel.2020.109075.
Chakrabarty, Dipesh. 2000. *Provincializing Europe: Postcolonial Thought and Historical Difference*. Princeton, NJ: Princeton University Press.
Chakravarty, Gautam. 2005. *The Indian Mutiny and the British Imagination*. Cambridge: Cambridge University Press.
Chakravarty, Gautam. 2014. "Mutiny, War, or Small War? Revisiting an Old Debate." In *Mutiny at the Margins*. Vol. IV, *Military Aspects of the Indian Uprising*, edited by Gavin Rand and Crispin Bates. London: SAGE. 135–146.
Chamberlain, Mary, and Selma Leydesdorff. 2004. "Transnational Families: Memories and Narratives." *Global Networks* 4 (3): 227–241. https://doi.org/10.1111/j.1471-0374.2004.00090.x.
Charbel, Felipe. 2020. "The New Faces of the Historical Novel." *História da Historiografia: International Journal of Theory and History of Historiography* 13 (32): 19–46. https://www.redalyc.org/articulo.oa?id=597763218002.
Chazan, Robert. 2023. *Medieval Stereotypes and Modern Antisemitism*. Berkeley: University of California Press.
Chidgey, Red. 2019. *Feminist Afterlives: Assemblage Memory in Activist Times*. Basingstoke, UK: Palgrave Macmillan.
Child, Francis J. 1904. *The English and Scottish Popular Ballads: Edited from the Collection of F. J. Child by Helen Child Sargent and George Lyman Kittredge*. Vol. 3. Boston: Houghton Mifflin.
Chivers, Tom. 2019. "A Theory in Crisis: What's Next for Psychology's Embattled Field of Social Priming." *Nature* 576 (7786): 200–202.
Chowdhry, Prem. 2000. *Colonial India and the Making of Empire Cinema: Image, Ideology and Identity*. Manchester: Manchester University Press.
Christensen, Joel. 2018. "The Clinical Odyssey: Odysseus's Apologoi and Narrative Therapy." *Arethusa* 51 (1): 1–31.
Christensen, Joel. 2022. *The Many-Minded Man: The "Odyssey," Psychology, and the Therapy of Epic*, Ithaca, NY: Cornell University Press.
Clavert, Frédéric. 2021. "History in the Era of Massive Data." *Geschichte und Gesellschaft* 47 (1): 175–194.
Clifford, James. 1986. "Partial Truths." In *Writing Culture: The Poetics and Politics of Ethnography*, edited by James Clifford and George E. Marcus. Berkeley: University of California Press. 1–26.
Clifford, James. 1992. "Traveling Cultures." In *Cultural Studies*, edited by Lawrence Grossberg, Cary Nelson, and Paul A. Treichler. New York: Routledge. 96–116.
Colegrove, Frederick W. 1899. "Individual Memories." *The American Journal of Psychology* 10 (2): 228–255. https://doi.org/10.2307/1412480.
Connerton, Paul. 1989. *How Societies Remember*. Cambridge: Cambridge University Press.
Conway, Daniel. 2017. "Framing a New Reality: Documenting Genocide in *District 9*." *International Journal of Philosophy and Theology* 78 (4-5): 444–455. 10.1080/21692327.2017.1338158
Conway, Martin A. 2013. *Flashbulb Memories*. London: Psychology Press.

Conway, Martin A., Stephen J. Anderson, Steen F. Larsen, C. M. Donnelly, M. A. McDaniel, A. G. R. McClelland, R. E. Rawles, and R. H. Logie. 1994. "The Formation of Flashbulb Memories." *Memory & Cognition* 22 (3): 326–343. https://doi.org/10.3758/BF03200860.

Conway, Martin A., and Catherine Loveday. 2015. "Remembering, Imagining, False Memories & Personal Meanings." *Consciousness and Cognition* 33: 574–581. https://doi.org/10.1016/j.concog.2014.12.002.

Conway, Martin A., Catherine Loveday, and Scott N. Cole. 2016. "The Remembering-Imagining System." *Memory Studies* 9 (3): 256–265. doi:10.1177/1750698016645231.

Conway-Smith, Erin. 2009. "District 9 Puts Spotlight on South Africa's Housing Crisis." *Global Post*, September 17. http://www.globalpost.com/dispatch/south-africa/090916/district-9-hits-south-africa.

Cook, Pam. 2005. *Screening the Past: Memory and Nostalgia in Cinema*. London: Routledge.

Coombes, Annie E. 2003. *History After Apartheid: Visual Culture and Public Memory in a Democratic South Africa*. Durham, NC: Duke University Press.

Corrigall, Malcolm, and Jenny Marsden. 2020. "District Six Is Really My Gay Vicinity: The Kewpie Photographic Collection." *African Arts* 53 (2): 10–27. doi:10.1162/afar_a_00525.

Cosenza, Maria Emilio. 1910. *Petrarch's Letters to Classical Authors: Translation and Commentary*. Chicago: University of Chicago Press.

Coser, Lewis A. 1992. *Maurice Halbwachs: On Collective Memory*. Chicago: University of Chicago Press.

Craps, Stef. 2013. *Postcolonial Witnessing: Trauma Out of Bounds*. Basingstoke, UK: Palgrave Macmillan.

Craps, Stef. 2023. "Ecological Mourning: Living with Loss in the Anthropocene." In *Critical Memory Studies: New Approaches*, edited by Brett A. Kaplan. London: Bloomsbury Academic. 69–77.

Craps, Stef, Rick Crownshaw, Jennifer Wenzel, Rosanne Kennedy, Claire Colebrook, and Vin Nardizzi. 2018. "Memory Studies and the Anthropocene: A Roundtable." *Memory Studies* 11 (4): 498–515. https://doi.org/10.1177/1750698017731068.

Creet, Julia, and Andreas Kitzmann, eds. 2014. *Memory and Migration: Multidisciplinary Approaches to Memory Studies*. Toronto: University of Toronto Press.

Cronin, Jeremy. 2006. "Creole Cape Town." In *A City Imagined*, edited by Stephen Watson. Johannesburg: Penguin Books. 45–54.

Crossley, Nick. 2012. *Towards Relational Sociology*. London: Routledge.

Crownshaw, Rick, ed. 2011a. *Transcultural Memory*. Special Issue of *Parallax* 17 (4). https://doi.org/10.4324/9781315540573.

Crownshaw, Rick. 2011b. "Perpetrator Fictions and Transcultural Memory." *Parallax* 17 (4): 75–89. https://doi.org/10.1080/13534645.2011.605582.

Curci, Antonietta, and Martin A. Conway. 2013. "Playing the Flashbulb Memory Game: A Comment on Cubelli and Della Sala." *Cortex: A Journal Devoted to the Study of the Nervous System and Behavior* 49 (1): 352–355. https://doi.org/10.1016/j.cortex.2012.05.004.

Curci, Antonietta, and Oliver Luminet. 2006. "Follow-Up of a Cross-National Comparison on Flashbulb and Event Memory for the September 11th Attacks." *Memory* 14 (3): 329–344. https://doi.org/10.1080/09658210500340816.

Curci, Antonietta, Olivier Luminet, Catrin Finkenauer, and Lydia Gisle. 2001. "Flashbulb Memories in Social Groups: A Comparative Test-Retest Study of the Memory of French President Mitterand's Death in a French and a Belgian Group." *Memory* 9 (2): 81–101. https://doi.org/10.1080/09658210042000120.

Daković, Nevena. 2007. "Borders in/of the Balkan Road Movie." In *Zoom In, Zoom Out: Crossing Borders in Contemporary European Cinema*, edited by Alejandra Barriales-Bouche and Marjorie Salvodon. Newcastle: Cambridge Scholars. 70–88.

Daniel, Ute. 2001. *Kompendium Kulturgeschichte. Theorien, Praxis, Schlüsselwörter*. Frankfurt am Main: Suhrkamp.

Danieli, Yael, ed. 1998. *International Handbook of Multigenerational Legacies of Trauma*. New York: Plenum Press.

Das, G. K., and Sushma Arya, eds. 2009. *Literature of Resistance: India, 1857*. Delhi: Primus Books.

Das, Santanu. 2018. *India, Empire, and First World War Culture: Literature, Images, and Songs*. Cambridge: Cambridge University Press.

Das, Santanu, Anna Maguire, and Daniel Steinbach, eds. 2022. *Colonial Encounters in a Time of Global Conflict, 1914–1918*. Abingdon, Oxon: Routledge.

Dasgupta, Sundeep. 2008. "The Visuality of the Other: The Place of the Migrant between Derrida's Ethics and Rancière's Aesthetics in Calais: The Last Border." In *Migratory Settings*, edited by Murat Aydemir and Alex Rotas. Amsterdam: Rodopi. 181–194.

Davison, Neil R. 1998. *James Joyce, Ulysses, and the Construction of Jewish Identity: Culture, Biography, and 'the Jew' in Modernist Europe*. Cambridge: Cambridge University Press.

Dayan, Daniel, and Elihu Katz. 1992. *Media Events: The Live Broadcasting of History*. Cambridge, MA: Harvard University Press.

Deane-Cox, Sharon and Anneleen Spiessens, eds. 2022. *The Routledge Handbook of Translation and Memory*. London: Routledge.

De Cesari, Chiara, and Ann Rigney, eds. 2014. *Transnational Memory: Circulation, Articulation, Scales*. Berlin: De Gruyter.

De Groot, Jerome. 2009. *The Historical Novel*. London: Routledge.

de Wolff, Kaya. 2021. *Post-/koloniale Erinnerungsdiskurse in der Medienkultur: Der Genozid an den Ovaherero und Nama in der deutschsprachigen Presse von 2001 bis 2016*. Bielefeld: Transcript.

DeLillo, Don. 2007. *Falling Man*. New York: Scribner.

Denis, Philippe. 2021. "Family Memories and the Development of the Genocide Ideology in Rwanda." In *Family Memory: Practices, Transmissions and Uses in a Global Perspective*, edited by Radmila Švaříčková Slabáková. New York: Routledge. 147–161.

Derrida, Jacques. 1984. "Two Words for Joyce." In *Poststructuralist Joyce: Essays from the French*, edited by Derek Attridge and Daniel Ferrer. Cambridge: Cambridge University Press. 145–159.

Dilthey, Wilhelm. 1957 [1875]. *Die Geistige Welt. Einleitung in die Philosophie des Lebens. Erste Hälfte: Abhandlungen zur Grundlegung der Geisteswissenschaften, Gesammelte Schriften*. Stuttgart: Teubner.

Diner, Dan. 2007. *Gegenläufige Gedächtnisse. Über Geltung und Wirkung des Holocaust*. Göttingen: Vandenhoeck & Ruprecht.

Divon, Tom, and Tobias Ebbrecht-Hartmann. 2022. "Performing Death and Trauma? Participatory Mem(e)ory and the Holocaust in TikTok #POVchallenges." *AoIR Selected Papers of Internet Research* 11(1): 1–5. doi:10.5210/spir.v2022i0.12995.

Donati, Pierpaolo. 2011. *Relational Sociology. A New Paradigm for the Social Sciences*. London: Routledge.
Donnell, Alison. 2019. "Looking Back, Looking Forward. Revisiting the Windrush Myth." In *The Cambridge History of Black and Asian British Writing*, edited by Susheila Nasta and Mark Stein. Cambridge: Cambridge University Press. 195–201.
Dorr, Maria Elisabeth, Astrid Erll, Erin Högerle, Paul Vickers, and Jarula M. I. Wegner, eds. 2019. *Remembering between Travel and Locatedness: New Horizons in Cultural and Media Memory Studies*. Special Issue of *Journal of Aesthetics & Culture* 11.
Draaisma, Douwe. 2012. *Why Life Speeds Up as You Grow Older: How Memory Shapes Our Past*. Cambridge: Cambridge University Press.
Dutt, Shoshee Chunder. 1885 [1877]. "Shunkur: A Tale of the Indian Mutiny." In *Shoshee Chunder Dutt: Bengaliana: A Dish of Rice and Curry and Other Indigestible Ingredients*. Calcutta: Thacker & Spink. 87–158.
Eakin, Paul John. 1999. *How Our Lives Become Stories: Making Selves*. Ithaca, NY: Cornell University Press.
Ebbrecht-Hartmann, Tobias. 2011. "Begegnungen und Unterbrechungen: Europäische Gedächtnisräume in Romuald Karmakars *Land der Vernichtung* und Robert Thalheims *Am Ende kommen Touristen*." In *Kino in Bewegung: Perspektiven des Deutschen Gegenwartsfilms*, edited by Thomas Schick and Tobias Ebbrecht-Hartmann. Wiesbaden: VS Verlag für Sozialwissenschaften. 157–184.
Ebbrecht-Hartmann, Tobias. 2021. "Commemorating from a Distance: The Digital Transformation of Holocaust Memory in Times of COVID-19." *Media, Culture & Society* 43 (6): 1095–1112. https://doi.org/10.1177/0163443720983276.
Echterhoff, Gerald, and Martin Saar, eds. 2002. *Kontexte und Kulturen des Erinnerns: Maurice Halbwachs und das Paradigma des kollektiven Gedächtnisses*. Konstanz: UVK.
Echterhoff, Gerald, E. Tory Higgins, and Stephan Groll. 2005. "Audience-Tuning Effects on Memory: The Role of Shared Reality." *Journal of Personality and Social Psychology* 89 (3): 257–276. https://doi.org/10.1037/0022-3514.89.3.257.
Eckstein, Lars. 2006. *Re-Membering the Black Atlantic: On the Poetics and Politics of Literary Memory*. Amsterdam: Rodopi.
Eddo-Lodge, Reni. 2017. *Why I'm No Longer Talking to White People about Race*. London: Bloomsbury Circus.
Edmunds, June, and Bryan S. Turner. 2005. "Global Generations: Social Change in the Twentieth Century." *The British Journal of Sociology* 56 (4): 559–577. https://doi.org/10.1111/j.1468-4446.2005.00083.x.
Edy, Jill A. 2006. *Troubled Pasts: News and the Collective Memory of Social Unrest*. Philadelphia: Temple University Press.
Edy, Jill A. 2014. "Collective Memory in a Post-Broadcast World." In *Journalism and Memory*, edited by Barbie Zelizer and Keren Tenenboim-Weinblatt. Basingstoke: Palgrave Macmillan. 66–79.
Eichenberg, Ariane. 2009. *Familie-Ich-Nation. Narrative Analysen zeitgenössischer Generationenromane*. Göttingen: V&R Unipress.
Eigler, Friederike Ursula. 2005. *Gedächtnis und Geschichte in Generationenromanen seit der Wende*. Berlin: Erich Schmidt.
Eliot, T. S. 1923. "'Ulysses,' Order, and Myth." *The Dial* 75 (5): 480–483.
Ellmann, Richard, ed. 1992. *Selected Letters of James Joyce*. London: Faber and Faber.

Emonds, Friederike B. 2011. "Revisiting the Memory Industry: Robert Thalheim's *Am Ende Kommen Touristen*." *Colloquia Germanica* 44 (1): 55–78.
Entman, Robert M. 1993. "Framing: Toward Clarification of a Fractured Paradigm." *Journal of Communication* 43 (4): 51–58.
Eriksen, Anne. 1995. *Det Var Noe Annet under Krigen: 2. Werdenskrig I Norsk Kollektivtradisjon*. Oslo: Pax Forlag.
Erll, Astrid. 2003. *Gedächtnisromane: Literatur über den Ersten Weltkrieg als Medium englischer und deutscher Erinnerungskulturen in den 1920er Jahren*. Trier: WVT.
Erll, Astrid. 2006. "Re-Writing as Re-Visioning: Modes of Representing the 'Indian Mutiny' in British Literature, 1857 to 2000." *European Journal of English Studies* 10 (2): 163–185. https://doi.org/10.1080/13825570600753485.
Erll, Astrid. 2007. *Prämediation—Remediation: Repräsentationen des Indischen Aufstands in Imperialen und Post-Kolonialen Medienkulturen (von 1857 bis zur Gegenwart)*. Trier: WVT.
Erll, Astrid. 2009. "Narratology and Cultural Memory Studies." In *Narratology in the Age of Cross-Disciplinary Narrative Research*, edited by Sandra Heinen and Roy Sommer. Berlin: De Gruyter. 212–227.
Erll, Astrid. 2011a. *Memory in Culture*. Basingstoke: Palgrave Macmillan.
Erll, Astrid. 2011b. "Travelling Memory." *Transcultural Memory*, edited by Rick Crownshaw. Special Issue *Parallax* 17 (4): 4–18.
Erll, Astrid. 2012. "War, Film and Collective Memory: Plurimedial Constellations." *Journal of Scandinavian Cinema* 2 (3): 231–235.
Erll, Astrid. 2015. "Transcultural Memory." In *Critical Encyclopedia of Testimony and Memory*. http://memories-testimony.com/en/notice/transcultural-memory/.
Erll, Astrid. 2017. "Media and the Dynamics of Memory: From Cultural Paradigms to Transcultural Premediation." In *The Oxford Handbook of Culture and Memory*, edited by Brady Wagoner. Oxford: Oxford University Press. 305–324.
Erll, Astrid. 2019. "Odyssean Travels: The Migration of Narrative Form (Homer – Lamb – Joyce)." In *Narrative in Culture*, edited by Astrid Erll and Roy Sommer. Berlin: De Gruyter. 241–267.
Erll, Astrid. 2023. "Literary Memory Activism." In *The Routledge Handbook of Memory Activism*, edited by Yifat Gutman and Jenny Wüstenberg. London: Routledge. 411–416.
Erll, Astrid. 2024a. "Game-Changing Homeric Memory: Odysseys Before and After Joyce." *Textual Practice* 38 (1): 34–52.
Erll, Astrid. 2024b. "Transculturality and the Eco-Logic of Memory." *Memory Studies Review* 1. 1–19.
Erll, Astrid, and Ansgar Nünning, eds. 2010 [2008]. *A Companion to Cultural Memory Studies*. Berlin: De Gruyter.
Erll, Astrid, and Ann Rigney, eds. 2009. *Mediation, Remediation, and the Dynamics of Cultural Memory*. Berlin: De Gruyter.
Erll, Astrid, and Ann Rigney, eds. 2017. *Audiovisual Memory and the (Re-)Making of Europe*. Special Issue *Image & Narrative* 18 (1).
Erll, Astrid, and Ann Rigney, eds. 2018. *Cultural Memory Studies after the Transnational Turn*. Special Issue of *Memory Studies* 11 (3).
Erll, Astrid, and Stephanie Wodianka, eds. 2008. *Film und kulturelle Erinnerung: Plurimediale Konstellationen*. Berlin: De Gruyter.

Erll, Astrid, and William Hirst, eds. 2025. *Cognition, Culture, and Political Momentum: A Companion to Interdisciplinary Memory Research*. New York: Oxford University Press (in preparation).

Esposito, Elena. 2002. *Soziales Vergessen: Formen und Medien des Gedächtnisses der Gesellschaft*. Frankfurt am Main: Suhrkamp.

Evaristo, Bernardine. 2019. *Girl, Woman, Other*. London: Hamish Hamilton.

Eyerman, Ron. 2019. *Memory, Trauma, and Identity*. London: Springer.

Eyerman, Ron, and Bryan S. Turner. 1998. "Outline of a Theory of Generations." *European Journal of Social Theory* 1 (1): 91–106. https://doi.org/10.1177/136843198001001007.

Fanon, Frantz. 1967. *Black Skin, White Masks*. New York: Grove Press.

Farooqui, Mahmoo. 2010. *Besieged: Voices from Delhi 1857*. Delhi: Penguin Books India.

Felman, Shoshana, and Dori Laub. 1992. *Testimony: Crises of Witnessing in Literature, Psychoanalysis, and History*. New York: Routledge.

Felski, Rita. 2011. "Context Stinks!" *New Literary History* 42 (4): 573–591.

Fevry, Sébastien. 2014. "Immigration and Memory in Popular Contemporary French Cinema: The Film as 'Lieu d'Entre-Mémoire.'" *Revista de Estudios Globales & Arte Contemporáneo*. Special Issue *Memoria y el Otro. Memorias Translocales y Transdisciplinares* 2 (1): 239–263. https://doi.org/10.1344/regac2014.1.13.

Fevry, Sébastien. 2015. "Calais comme lieu d'entre-mémoire." *EspacesTemps.net*. http://www.espacestemps.net/en/articles/calais-comme-lieu-entre-memoire-2.

Fevry, Sébastien. 2017. "Immigration and 'Mythological' Memory in French Cinema: How References to Homer and Ovid Refigure the European Perception of Exile." *Image & Narrative* 18 (1): 20–32.

Field, Kendra T. 2022. "The Privilege of Family History." *The American Historical Review*, 127 (2): 600–633. https://doi.org/10.1093/ahr/rhac151.

Field, Sean. 2019. "Uncanny District Six: Removals, Remains, and Deferred Regeneration." In *The Routledge Handbook of Memory and Place*, edited by Sarah De Nardi, Hilary Orange, Steven High, and Eerika Koskinen-Koivisto. London: Routledge. 31–41.

Field, Sean, Renate Meyer, and Felicity Swanson, eds. 2007. *Imagining the City Memories and Cultures in Cape Town*. Cape Town: Human Sciences Research Council (HSRC) Press.

Figes, Orlando. 2007. *The Whisperers: Private Life in Stalin's Russia*. London: Allen Line.

Finkenauer, Catrin, Olivier Luminet, Lydia Gisle, Abdessadek El-Ahmadi, Martial Van Der Linden, and Pierre Philippot. 1998. "Flashbulb Memories and the Underlying Mechanisms of Their Formation: Toward an Emotional-Integrative Model." *Memory & Cognition* 26 (3): 516–531. https://doi.org/10.3758/BF03201160.

Fivush, Robyn. 2019. *Family Narratives and the Development of an Autobiographical Self: Social and Cultural Perspectives on Autobiographical Memory*. New York: Routledge.

Fivush, Robyn, and Azriel Grysman. 2022. "Narrative and Gender as Mutually Constituted Meaning-Making Systems." *Memory, Mind & Media* 1 (E2): 1–14. doi:10.1017/mem.2021.4.

Fivush, Robyn, and Catherine A. Haden, eds. 2003. *Autobiographical Memory and the Construction of a Narrative Self: Developmental and Cultural Perspectives*. New York: Psychology Press.

Flack, Leah Culligan. 2015. *Modernism and Homer: The Odysseys of H.D., James Joyce, Osip Mandelstam, and Ezra Pound*. Cambridge: Cambridge University Press.

Fludernik, Monika. 1996. *Towards a "Natural" Narratology*. London: Routledge.
Foley, Helene P. 1978. "'Reverse Similes' and Sex Roles in the *Odyssey*." *Arethusa* 11 (1–2): 7–26.
François, Étienne, and Hagen Schulze. 2001. *Deutsche Erinnerungsorte*. Vol. 3. München: C. H. Beck.
Frayn, Andrew, and Fiona Houston. 2022. "The War Books Boom in Britain, 1928–1930." *First World War Studies*, 13(1), 25–45. https://doi.org/10.1080/19475020.2022.2129718.
Freud, Sigmund. 2004 [1921]. *Mass Psychology and Other Writings*. London: Penguin.
Freud, Sigmund. 2010 [1939]. *Moses and Monotheism*. Trans. Katherine Jones. Mansfield Centre, CT: Martino Publishing.
Fridman, Orli, and Sarah Gensburger, eds. 2023. *The Covid-19 Pandemic and Memory: Remembrance Commemoration and Archiving in Crisis*. Basingstoke: Palgrave Macmillan.
Frosh, Paul, and Amit Pinchevski, eds. 2009. *Media Witnessing: Testimony in the Age of Mass Communication*. Basingstoke: Palgrave Macmillan.
Fuchs, Anne. 2010. *After the Dresden Bombing Pathways of Memory 1945 to the Present*. Basingstoke: Palgrave Macmillan.
Fussell, Paul. 1975. *The Great War and Modern Memory*. Oxford: Oxford University Press.
Gadamer, Hans-Georg. 1960. *Wahrheit und Methode*. Tübingen: Mohr.
Galea, Sandro, Jennifer Ahern, Heidi Resnick, Dean Kilpatrick, Michael Bucuvalas, Joel Gold, and David Vlahov. 2002. "Psychological Sequelae of the September 11 Terrorist Attacks in New York City." *New England Journal of Medicine* 346 (13): 982–987. https://doi.org/10.1056/NEJMsa013404.
Gambarato, Renira Rampazzo, and Johannes Heuman. 2023. "Beyond Fact and Fiction: Cultural Memory and Transmedia Ethics in Netflix's *The Crown*." *European Journal of Cultural Studies* 26 (6): 803–821. https://doi.org/10.1177/13675494221128332.
Gambarato, Renira Rampazzo, Johannes Heuman, and Ylva Lindberg. 2022. "Streaming Media and the Dynamics of Remembering and Forgetting: The Chernobyl Case." *Memory Studies* 15 (2): 271–286. https://doi.org/10.1177/17506980211037287.
Gansera, Rainer. 2007. "Zur Disco am Lagerzaun vorbei." Interview with Robert Thalheim, Hans-Christian Schmid and Britta Knöller. *Süddeutsche Zeitung*, August 16, 2007. Available at: http://www.sueddeutsche.de/kultur/die-macher-von-am-ende-kommen-touristen-zur-discoam-lagerzaun-vorbei-1.256149.
Garde-Hansen, Joanne, Andrew Hoskins, and Anna Reading, eds. 2009. *Save As—Digital Memories*. Basingstoke: Palgrave Macmillan.
Garde-Hansen, Joanne. 2011. *Media and Memory*. Edinburgh: Edinburgh University Press.
Gedi, Noa, and Yigal Elam. 1996. "Collective Memory—What Is It?" *History & Memory: Studies in Representation of the Past* 8 (1): 30–50.
Geertz, Clifford. 1973. *The Interpretation of Cultures: Selected Essays*. New York: Basic Books.
Gensburger, Sarah. 2016. "Halbwachs' Studies in Collective Memory: A Founding Text for Contemporary 'Memory Studies'?" *Journal of Classical Sociology* 16 (4): 396–413. https://doi.org/10.1177/1468795x16656268.
Gensburger, Sarah, and Jenny Wüstenberg, eds. 2023. *De-Commemoration. Removing Statues and Renaming Places*. New York: Berghahn.

Ghosh, Vanessa E., and Asaf Gilboa. 2014. "What Is a Memory Schema? A Historical Perspective on Current Neuroscience Literature." *Neuropsychologia* 53 (1): 104–114.
Gifford, Don, and Robert J. Seidman, eds. 1988. *Ulysses Annotated: Notes for James Joyce's Ulysses*, 2nd ed. Berkeley: University of California Press.
Gilbert, Stuart. 1955 [1931]. *James Joyce's Ulysses*. New York: Vintage.
Gilroy, Paul. 1993. *The Black Atlantic: Modernity and Double Consciousness*. Cambridge: Harvard University Press.
Gilroy, Paul. 2004. *After Empire: Multiculture or Postcolonial Melancholia*. Abingdon: Routledge.
Gilroy, Paul. 2011. *Black Britain: A Photographic History*. London: Saqi in Association with Getty Images.
Glissant, Édouard. 1997. "Errantry, Exile." In *Édouard Glissant: Poetics of Relation*. Ann Arbor: University of Michigan Press. 11–22.
Goffman, Erving. 1974. *Frame Analysis: An Essay on the Organization of Experience*. New York: Harper & Row.
Goldblatt, Cullen. 2021. *Beyond Collective Memory: Structural Complicity and Future Freedoms in Senegalese and South African Narratives*. New York: Routledge.
Gollac, Sibylle, and Alexandra Oeser. 2011. "Comparing Family Memories in France and Germany: The Production of History(ies) within and through Kin Relations." *Journal of Comparative Family Studies* 42 (3): 385–397. https://doi.org/10.3138/jcfs.42.3.385.
Göller, Karl Heinz. 1987. "Sir Hugh of Lincoln: From History to Nursery Rhyme." In *Jewish Life and Jewish Suffering as Mirrored in English and American Literature*, edited by Bernd Engler and Kurt Müller. Paderborn: Schöningh. 17–31.
Graf, Peter, and Daniel L. Schacter. 1985. "Implicit and Explicit Memory for New Associations in Normal and Amnesic Subjects." *Journal of Experimental Psychology: Learning, Memory, and Cognition* 11 (3): 501–518. https://doi.org/10.1037/0278-7393.11.3.501.
Graumann, Carl F. 1986. "Memorabilia, Mementos, Memoranda: Toward an Ecology of Memory." In *Human Memory and Cognition*, edited by Friedhart Klix and Herbert Hagendorf. Amsterdam: North Holland. 63–69.
Graziosi, Barbara. 2016. *Homer*. Oxford: Oxford University Press.
Graziosi, Barbara, and Emily Greenwood, eds. 2010. *Homer in the Twentieth Century: Between World Literature and the Western Canon*. Oxford: Oxford University Press.
Greenwood, Emily. 2010. *Afro-Greeks: Dialogues between Anglophone Caribbean Literature and Classics in the Twentieth Century*. Oxford: Oxford University Press.
Grillo, Ralph D. 2008. *The Family in Question: Immigrant and Ethnic Minorities in Multicultural Europe*. Amsterdam: Amsterdam University Press.
Grønning, Anette. 2021. "Micro-Memories: Digital Modes of Communication across Three Generations." *Memory Studies* 14 (4): 733–746. https://doi.org/10.1177/1750698020959810.
Grusin, Richard A. 2004. "Premediation." *Criticism* 46 (1): 17–39. https://doi.org/10.1353/crt.2004.0030.
Grusin, Richard A. 2010. *Premediation: Affect and Mediality after 9/11*. New York: Palgrave Macmillan.
Guha, Ranajit. 1983. *Elementary Aspects of Peasant Insurgency in Colonial India*. Delhi: Oxford University Press.
Guldi, Jo, and David Armitage. 2014. *The History Manifesto*. Cambridge: Cambridge University Press.

Gülüm, Erol. 2024. "Remembering a Disastrous Past to Imagine Catastrophic Future(s) on Social Media: The Expected Istanbul Earthquake." *Media, Culture & Society* 46(5), 959–974. https://doi.org/10.1177/01634437241228724.

Gülüm, Erol, Paul Leworthy, Justyna Tabaszewska, and Hanna Teichler, eds. 2024. *Memory and Environment*. Special Issue, *Memory Studies Review* 1 (1).

Gutman, Yifat, Jenny Wüstenberg, Irit Dekel, Kaitlin M. Murphy, Benjamin Nienass, Joanna Wawrzyniak, and Kerry Whigham, eds. 2023. *The Routledge Handbook of Memory Activism*. Abingdon: Routledge. https://doi.org/10.4324/9781003127550.

Habermas, Tilmann. 2019. *Emotion and Narrative: Perspectives in Autobiographical Storytelling*. Cambridge: Cambridge University Press.

Hajek, Andrea. 2013. "Challenging Dominant Discourses of the Past: 1968 and the Value of Oral History." *Memory Studies* 6 (1): 3–6. https://doi.org/10.1177/1750698012463887.

Halbwachs, Maurice. 1941. *La topographie légendaire des Évangiles en Terre Sainte: Étude de mémoire collective*. Paris: Presses Universitaires de France.

Halbwachs, Maurice. 1980 [1950]. *The Collective Memory*. Translated by Francis J. Ditter and Vida Yazdi Ditter. New York: Harper & Row.

Halbwachs, Maurice. 1992. *On Collective Memory*. Edited and translated by Lewis Coser. Chicago: Chicago University Press.

Halbwachs, Maurice. 1994 [1925]. *Les cadres sociaux de la mémoire*, edited by Gérard Namer. Paris: Albin Michel.

Halbwachs, Maurice. 1997 [1950]. *La mémoire collective*, edited by Gérard Namer. Paris: Albin Michel.

Hall, Catherine, Nicholas Draper, Keith McClelland, Katie Donington, and Rachel Lang. 2014. *Legacies of British Slave-Ownership: Colonial Slavery and the Formation of Victorian Britain*. Cambridge: Cambridge University Press.

Hall, Edith. 2008. *The Return of Ulysses: A Cultural History of Homer's Odyssey*. Baltimore, MD: Johns Hopkins University Press.

Hall, Stuart. 1988. "New Ethnicities." In *Black Film, British Cinema*, edited by Kobena Mercer. London: Institute of Contemporary Arts. 27–31.

Hanink, Johanna. 2017. *The Classical Debt: Greek Antiquity in an Era of Austerity*. Cambridge, MA: Harvard University Press.

Hannerz, Ulf. 1996. *Transnational Connections: Culture, People, Places*. London: Routledge.

Haraway, Donna J. 1988. "Situated Knowledges: The Science Question in Feminism and the Privilege of Partial Perspective." *Feminist Studies* 14 (3): 575–599.

Haraway, Donna J. 2016. *Staying with the Trouble: Making Kin in the Chthulucene*. Durham, NC: Duke University Press.

Hardwick, Lorna. 2009. "Editorial." *Classical Receptions Journal* 1 (1): 1–3.

Hart, Anne. 2003. *The Beginner's Guide to Interpreting Ethnic DNA Origins for Family History: How Ashkenazi, Sephardi, Mizrahi and Europeans Are Related to Everyone Else*. New York: Universe.

Hartman, Saidiya V. 2008. *Lose Your Mother: A Journey along the Atlantic Slave Route*. New York: Farrar, Straus & Giroux.

Hartnell, Anna. 2011. *Rewriting Exodus: American Futures from Du Bois to Obama*. London: Pluto Press.

Hartog, François. 2017. *Regimes of Historicity: Presentism and Experiences of Time*. New York: Columbia University Press.

Haslam, Nick. 2016. "Concept Creep: Psychology's Expanding Concepts of Harm and Pathology." *Psychological Inquiry* 27 (1): 1–17. https://doi.org/10.1080/1047840X.2016.1082418.

Hassin, Ran R., James S. Uleman, and John A. Bargh, eds. 2005. *The New Unconscious*. New York: Oxford University Press.

Hastings, Chris, and Beth Jones. 2005. "Lottery-Funded Film under Fire for Anti-British Bias." *The Telegraph*. https://www.telegraph.co.uk/news/uknews/1496148/Lottery-funded-film-under-fire-for-anti-British-bias.html.

Haubold, Johannes. 2013. *Greece and Mesopotamia: Dialogues in Literature*. New York: Cambridge University Press.

Hayles, Katherine. 2017. *Unthought: The Power of the Cognitive Nonconscious*. Chicago: University of Chicago Press.

Hemmings, Claire. 2022. "'We Thought She Was a Witch': Gender, Class and Whiteness in the Familial Memory Archive." *Memory Studies* 16 (2): 185–197. https://doi.org/10.1177/17506980211066578.

Henig, Lital, and Tobias Ebbrecht-Hartmann. 2022. "Witnessing Eva Stories: Media Witnessing and Self-Inscription in Social Media Memory." *New Media & Society* 24 (1): 202–226. doi:10.1177/1461444820963805.

Henke, Daniela, and Tom Vanassche, eds. 2019. *Ko-Erinnerung/Co-Memoration: Grenzen, Herausforderungen und Perspektiven des Neueren Shoah-Gedenkens/Limits, Challenges, and Possibilities in Contemporary Shoah Remembrance*. Berlin: De Gruyter.

Henty, George Alfred. 1881. *In Times of Peril: A Tale of India*. London: Griffith & Farran.

Herbert, Christopher. 2008. *War of No Pity: The Indian Mutiny and Victorian Trauma*. Princeton, NJ: Princeton University Press.

Herman, David. 2008. *Basic Elements of Narrative*. Oxford: Blackwell.

Herman, David. 2013. *Storytelling and the Sciences of Mind*. Cambridge, MA: MIT Press.

Hibbert, Christopher. 1980. *The Great Mutiny, India 1857*. London: Penguin Books.

Hirsch, Marianne. 1997. *Family Frames: Photography, Narrative, and Postmemory*. Cambridge, MA: Harvard University Press.

Hirsch, Marianne. 2012. *The Generation of Postmemory: Writing and Visual Culture after the Holocaust*. New York: Columbia University Press.

Hirsch, Marianne, and Nancy K. Miller, eds. 2011. *Rites of Return Diaspora Poetics and the Politics of Memory*. New York: Columbia University Press.

Hirsch, Matthew. 2024. "Cape Town 'Pilgrims' Walk the Length of the Gaza Strip to Raise Awareness." *Ground Up News*. https://groundup.org.za/article/cape-town-pilgrims-walk-length-gaza-strip-to-raise-awareness/.

Hirst, William. 2020. "Remembering COVID-19." *Social Research: An International Quarterly* 87 (2): 251–252. https://doi.org/10.1353/sor.2020.0028.

Hirst, William, ed. 2020. "Cultural Trauma." *Social Research: An International Quarterly* 87 (3).

Hirst, William, and Alin Coman. 2018. "Building a Collective Memory: The Case for Collective Forgetting." *Current Opinion in Psychology* 23: 88–92.

Hirst, William, Travis G. Cyr, and Clinton Merck. 2020. "Witnessing and Cultural Trauma: The Role of Flashbulb Memories in the Trauma Process." *Social Research: An International Quarterly* 87 (3): 591–613. https://doi.org/10.1353/sor.2020.0055.

Hirst, William, and Gerald Echterhoff. 2012. "Remembering in Conversations: The Social Sharing and Reshaping of Memories." *Annual Review of Psychology* 63: 55–79. https://doi.org/10.1146/annurev-psych-120710-100340.

Hirst, William, and Robert Meksin. 2018. "Aligning Flashbulb and Collective Memories." In *Flashbulb Memories: New Challenges and Future Perspectives*, edited by Olivier Luminet and Antonietta Curci. Abingdon: Routledge. 201–218.

Hirst, William, and Clinton Merck. 2024. "Memory for Salient Shared Events: A Top-Down Approach to Collective Memory." In *The Oxford Handbook of Human Memory*, edited by Michael J. Kahana and Anthony D. Wagner. Oxford: Oxford University Press. 2139–2168.

Hirst, William, and Elizabeth A. Phelps. 2016. "Flashbulb Memories." *Current Directions in Psychological Science* 25 (1): 36–41. https://doi.org/10.1177/0963721415622487.

Hirst, William, Elizabeth A. Phelps, Randy L. Buckner, Andrew E. Budson, Alexandru Cuc, John D. E. Gabrieli, Marcia K. Johnson, Cindy Lustig, Keith B. Lyle, Mara Mather, Robert Meksin, Karen J. Mitchell, Kevin N. Ochsner, Daniel L. Schacter, Jon S. Simons, and Chandan J. Vaidya. 2009. "Long-Term Memory for the Terrorist Attack of September 11: Flashbulb Memories, Event Memories, and the Factors That Influence Their Retention." *Journal of Experimental Psychology: General* 138 (2): 161–176. https://doi.org/10.1037/a0015527.

Hirst, William, Elizabeth A. Phelps, Robert Meksin, Chandan J. Vaidya, Marcia K. Johnson, Karen J. Mitchell, Randy L. Buckner, Andrew E. Budson, John D. E. Gabrieli, Cindy Lustig, Mara Mather, Kevin N. Ochsner, Daniel Schacter, Jon S. Simons, Keith B. Lyle, Alexandru Cuc, and Andreas Olsson. 2015. "A Ten-Year Follow-Up of a Study of Memory for the Attack of September 11, 2001: Flashbulb Memories and Memories for Flashbulb Events." *Journal of Experimental Psychology: General* 144 (3): 604–623. https://doi.org/10.1037/xge0000055.

Hirst, William, and Charles B. Stone. 2015. "A Unified Approach to Collective Memory: Sociology, Psychology, and the Extended Mind." In *The Ashgate Research Companion to Memory Studies*, edited by Siobhan Kattago. London: Ashgate. 103–116.

Hirst, William, Jeremy K. Yamashiro, and Alin Coman. 2018. "Collective Memory from a Psychological Perspective." *Trends in Cognitive Sciences* 22 (5): 438–451. https://doi.org/10.1016/j.tics.2018.02.010.

Hoffman, Eva. 2004. *After Such Knowledge: Memory, History, and the Legacy of the Holocaust*. New York: Public Affairs.

Hogan, Patrick C. 2014. *Ulysses and the Poetics of Cognition*. New York: Routledge.

Homer. 2017. *The Odyssey*. Translated by Emily Wilson. New York: Norton.

Honigsbaum, Mark. 2023. "Walking the Wall: COVID-19 and the Politics of Memory." In *When This Is Over: Reflections on an Unequal Pandemic*, edited by Amy Cortvriend, Lucy Easthope, Jenny Edkins, and Kandida Purnell. Bristol: Bristol University Press. 232–250.

Hoskins, Andrew. 2001. "New Memory: Mediating History." *Historical Journal of Film, Radio and Television* 21 (4): 333–346.

Hoskins, Andrew. 2009. "Flashbulb Memories, Psychology, and Media Studies: Fertile Ground for Interdisciplinarity?" *Memory Studies* 2 (2): 147–150. https://doi.org/10.1177/1750698008102049.

Hoskins, Andrew. 2011. "Media, Memory, Metaphor: Remembering and the Connective Turn." *Parallax* 17 (4): 19–31. https://doi.org/10.1080/13534645.2011.605573.

Hoskins, Andrew. 2016. "Memory Ecologies." *Memory Studies* 9 (3): 348–357. doi:10.1177/1750698016645274.

Hoskins, Andrew, ed. 2017. *Digital Memory Studies: Media Pasts in Transition*. New York: Routledge.

Hoskins, Andrew, and Huw Halstead. 2021. "The New Grey of Memory: Andrew Hoskins in Conversation with Huw Halstead." *Memory Studies* 14 (3): 675–685.

Hou, Song. 2023. "A Critical Review of Research on Translation and Memory. Theories, Themes, and Prospects." FORUM. *Revue internationale d'interprétation et de traduction/International Journal of Interpretation and Translation* 21 (2): 213–235. https://doi.org/10.1075/forum.22019.hou.

Hutcheon, Linda. 1988. *A Poetics of Postmodernism: History, Theory, Fiction.* New York; London: Routledge.

Hutcheon, Linda. 2006. *A Theory of Adaptation.* New York: Routledge.

Hutton, Patrick. 1993. *History as an Art of Memory.* Hanover, NH: University Press of New England.

Huyssen, Andreas. 1995. *Twilight Memories: Marking Time in a Culture of Amnesia.* New York: Routledge.

Huyssen, Andreas. 2003. *Present Pasts: Urban Palimpsests and the Politics of Memory.* Stanford, CA: Stanford University Press.

Hynes, Samuel. 1990. *A War Imagined: The First World War and English Culture.* London: The Bodley Head.

Hynes, Samuel. 1997. *The Soldiers' Tale: Bearing Witness to Modern War.* New York: Allen Lane.

Innis, Harold A. 1951. *The Bias of Communication.* Toronto: University of Toronto Press.

Iraqi, Amjad. 2013. "Echoes of South Africa's 'District Six' in the Negev." *+972 magazine.* https://www.972mag.com/echoes-of-south-africas-district-six-in-the-negev/.

Isnenghi, Mario, ed. 1987. *I Luoghi Della Memoria.* Vol. 3. Rome: Laterza.

Jacobsen, Ben, and David Beer. 2021. *Social Media and the Automated Production of Memory: Classification, Ranking and the Sorting of the Past.* Bristol: Bristol University Press.

Jameson, Fredric. 2019. *Allegory and Ideology.* New York: Verso.

Jeftic, Alma, Thomas Van de Putte, Johana Wyss, eds. 2023. *Memory and Narrative.* Special Issue of *Narrative Inquiry* 33 (2).

Jenkins, Henry. 2006. *Convergence Culture: Where Old and New Media Collide.* New York: New York University Press.

Jeppie, Shamil, and Soudien Crain, eds. 1990. *The Struggle for District Six: Past and Present.* Cape Town: Buchu Books.

Jirgal, Ernst. 1931. *Die Wiederkehr des Weltkrieges in der Literatur.* Wien: Reinhold.

Johnson, Niall P.A.S, and Jürgen Müller. 2002. "Updating the Accounts: Global Mortality of the 1918-1920 'Spanish' Influenza Pandemic." *Bulletin of the History of Medicine* 76 (1): 105–115.

Johnston, Andrew James, and Kai Wiegandt, eds. 2017. *The Return of the Historical Novel? Thinking about Fiction and History after Historiographic Metafiction.* Heidelberg: Universitätsverlag Winter.

Jordan, Christina. 2019. "From Private to Public: Royal Family Memory as Prospective Collective Memory in a Jubilee Tribute to the Queen by the Prince of Wales (2012)." *Journal of Aesthetics & Culture* 11 (Suppl 1): 48–55. https://doi.org/10.1080/20004214.2019.1635426

Joyce, James. 1959 [1907]. "Ireland, Island of Saints and Sages." In *The Critical Writings of James Joyce*, edited by Richard Ellmann and Mason Ellsworth. Ithaca, NY: Cornell University Press. 154–174.

Joyce, James. 1986. *Ulysses: The Corrected Text*. Edited by Hans Walter Gabler. London: Penguin.
Judt, Tony. 1998. "A la Recherche du Temps Perdu. Review of Pierre Nora, *The Realms of Memory: The Construction of the French Past*." *New York Review of Books*, December 3. 51–58.
Juneja, Monica. 2015. "Circulation and Beyond: The Trajectories of Vision in Early Modern Eurasia." In *Circulations in the Global History of Art*, edited by Thomas D.C. Kaufmann, Catherine Dossin, and Béatrice Joyeux-Prunel. London: Routledge. 59–78.
Jung, Carl Gustav. 2014. *The Archetypes and the Collective Unconscious*. London: Routledge.
Jünke, Claudia. 2023. "Transcultural Memory and Literary Translation: Mapping the Field (with a Case Study on Lydie Salvayre's Pas Pleurer and Its Spanish Translation)." *Memory Studies* 16 (5): 1280–1297.
Jünke, Claudia, and Désirée Schyns, eds. 2024. *Translating Memories of Violent Pasts: Memory Studies and Translation Studies in Dialogue*. London: Routledge.
Kahneman, Daniel. 2011. *Thinking, Fast and Slow*. Toronto: Anchor Canada.
Kampourakis, Kostas. 2023. *Ancestry Reimagined: Dismantling the Myth of Genetic Ethnicities*. New York: Oxford University Press.
Kansteiner, Wulf, and Morina, Christina, eds. 2025. *The Oxford Handbook of History and Memory*. New York: Oxford University Press (in preparation).
Kansteiner, Wulf. 2004. "Genealogy of a Category Mistake: A Critical Intellectual History of the Cultural Trauma Metaphor." *Rethinking History* 8: 193–221.
Kansteiner, Wulf. 2006. *In Pursuit of German Memory: History, Television, and Politics after Auschwitz*. Athens: Ohio University Press.
Kansteiner, Wulf. 2018. "History, Memory, and Film: A Love/Hate Triangle." *Memory Studies* 11 (2): 131–136. https://doi.org/10.1177/1750698017754167.
Kaplan, E. Ann. 2016. *Climate Trauma: Foreseeing the Future in Dystopian Film and Fiction*. New Brunswick:, NJ Rutgers University Press.
Kattago, Siobhan, ed. 2015. *The Ashgate Research Companion to Memory Studies*. London: Ashgate.
Kattago, Siobhan. 2021. "Ghostly Pasts and Postponed Futures: The Disorder of Time during the Corona Pandemic." *Memory Studies* 14 (6): 1401–1413. https://doi.org/10.1177/17506980211054015.
Kaushik, Roy, ed. 2008. *1857 Uprising: A Tale of an Indian Warrior*. Kolkata: Anthem Press.
Kavoori, Anandam P., and Aswin Punathambekar, eds. 2008. *Global Bollywood*. New York: New York University Press.
Kaye, Sir John William, and George Bruce Malleson. 1897. *History of the Indian Mutiny of 1857–8*. Vol. 6. London: Longmans, Green & Co.
Keenan, Thomas, and Eyal Weizman. 2012. *Mengele's Skull: The Advent of a Forensic Aesthetics*. Berlin: Sternberg Press.
Keightley, Emily. 2022. "Rethinking Technologies of Remembering for a Postcolonial World." *Memory, Mind & Media* 1 (e17):1–15. doi:10.1017/mem.2022.9.
Kellermann, Natan P. 2013. "Epigenetic Transmission of Holocaust Trauma: Can Nightmares Be Inherited?" *The Israel Journal of Psychiatry and Related Sciences* 50 (1): 33–39.

Kelly, Andrew. 2002. *"All Quiet on the Western Front": The Story of a Film*. London: I. B. Tauris.

Kennedy, Rosanne. 2013. "Soul Music Dreaming: The Sapphires, the 1960s, and Transnational Memory." *Memory Studies* 6 (3): 331–344. https://doi.org/10.1177/1750698013485506.

Kennedy, Rosanne, and Maria Nugent, eds. 2016. "Scales of Memory: Reflections on an Emerging Concept." *Australian Humanities Review* 59: 61–259.

Kenner, Hugh. 1987. *Ulysses: Revised Edition*. Baltimore, MD: Johns Hopkins University Press.

Keppler, Angela. 1994. *Tischgespräche: Über Formen kommunikativer Vergemeinschaftung in Familien*. Frankfurt am Main: Suhrkamp.

Kershner, R. Brandon. 1998. "'Ulysses' and the Orient." In *ReOrienting Joyce*, edited by R. Brandon Kershner and Carol Loeb Shloss. *James Joyce Quarterly* 35 (2–3): 273–296.

Kilbourn, Russell J. A., and Eleanor Ty, eds. 2013. *The Memory Efffect: The Remediation of Memory in Literature and Film*. Waterloo, ON: Wilfrid Laurier University Press.

King, Jason. 2014. "Commemorating *Ulysses*, the Bloomsday Centenary, and the Irish Citizenship Referendum." In *Memory Ireland*. Vol 4, *James Joyce and Cultural Memory*, edited by Katherine O'Callaghan and Oona Frawley. New York: Syracuse University Press. 172–186.

Kingsley, Patrick. 2016. *The New Odyssey: The Story of Europe's Refugee Crisis*. London: Guardian Faber.

Kırpıklı, Deniz. 2022. "New Ways of Identification: Black Diaspora and Memory in Caryl Phillips's *In the Falling Snow*." *Neophilologus* 107 (2): 329–344. https://doi.org/10.1007/s11061-022-09753-6.

Klemperer, Victor. 2013 [1947]. *Language of the Third Reich. LTI: Lingua Tertii Imperii*. New York: Bloomsbury Academic.

Knittel, Susanne C. 2023. "Ecologies of Violence: Cultural Memory (Studies) and the Genocide–Ecocide Nexus." *Memory Studies* 16 (6): 1563–1578. https://doi.org/10.1177/17506980231202747.

Knudsen, Britta Timm. 2016. "The Besieged City in the Heart of Europe: Sniper Alley in Sarajevo as Memorial Site on YouTube." In *Mediating and Remediating Death*, edited by Dorthe Refslund Christensen and Kjetil Sandvik. London: Routledge. 111–132.

Korte, Barbara, and Eva U. Pirker. 2011. *Black History, White History: Britain's Historical Programme between Windrush and Wilberforce*. Bielefeld: Transcript.

Korte, Barbara, and Claudia Sternberg. 2004. *Bidding for the Mainstream? Black and Asian British Film since the 1990s*. Amsterdam: Rodopi.

Koselleck, Reinhart. 2004 [1979]. *Futures Past: On the Semantics of Historical Time*. Translated byKeith Tribe. Cambridge, MA: MIT Press.

Kristeva, Julia. 1969. *Semeiotikè: Recherches pour une Sémanalyse*. Paris: Éditions du Seuil.

Kroon, Richard W. 2010. *A/V A to Z: An Encyclopedic Dictionary of Media, Entertainment and Other Audiovisual Terms*. Jefferson, NC: McFarland.

Kuhn, Annette. 1995. *Family Secrets: Acts of Memory and Imagination*. London: Verso.

Kuiper, N. A., and T. B Rogers. 1979. "Encoding of Personal Information: Self–Other Differences." *Journal of Personality and Social Psychology* 37 (4): 499–514. https://doi.org/10.1037/0022-3514.37.4.499.

Kvavilashvili, Lia, and George Mandler. 2004. "Out of One's Mind: A Study of Involuntary Semantic Memories." *Cognitive Psychology* 48 (1): 47–94.

Kvavilashvili, Lia, Jennifer Mirani, Simone Schlagman, and Diana E. Kornbrot. 2003. "Comparing Flashbulb Memories of September 11 and the Death of Princess Diana: Effects of Time Delays and Nationality." *Applied Cognitive Psychology* 17 (9): 1017–1031. https://doi.org/10.1002/acp.983.

La Guma, A. 2006 [1962]. *A Walk in the Night and Other Stories*. Edited by Nahem Yousaf. Nottingham: Trent Editions.

Laanes, Eneken. 2021. "Born Translated Memories: Transcultural Memorial Forms, Domestication and Foreignisation." *Memory Studies* 14 (1): 41–57. https://doi.org/10.1177/1750698020976459.

Laanes, Eneken, Jessica Ortner, and Tea Sindbæk Andersen, eds. 2025. *Literature and Mnemonic Migration: Remediation, Translation, Reception*. Berlin: De Gruyter.

Lakoff, George, and Mark Johnson. 1980. *Metaphors We Live By*. Chicago: University of Chicago Press.

Landsberg, Alison. 2004. *Prosthetic Memory: The Transformation of American Remembrance in the Age of Mass Culture*. New York: Columbia University Press.

Lanser, Susan Sniader. 1992. *Fictions of Authority: Women Writers and Narrative Voice*. Ithaca, NY: Cornell University Press.

Larbaud, Valéry. 1922. "The 'Ulysses' of James Joyce." *The Criterion* 1 (1): 94–103.

Latacz, Joachim. 1989. *Homer: Der erste Dichter des Abendlands*. München: Artemis.

Latour, Bruno. 2005. *Reassembling the Social: An Introduction to Actor-Network-Theory*. New York: Oxford University Press.

Lawrence, Karen. 1981. *The Odyssey of Style in Ulysses*. Princeton, NJ: Princeton University Press.

Lecheler, Sophie, and Claes H. de Vreese. 2019. *News Framing Effects*. London: Routledge.

Leckey, Edward. 1859. *Fictions Connected with the Indian Outbreak of 1857 Exposed*. Bombay: Chesson & Woodhall.

Ledent, Bénédicte. 2009. "Black British Literature." In *The Oxford Companion to English Literature*, edited by Dinah Birch and Margaret Drabble. Oxford: Oxford University Press. 6–22.

Ledent, Bénédicte, and Daria Tunca, eds. 2012. *Caryl Phillips: Writing in the Key of Life*. Amsterdam: Rodopi.

Lefebvre, Henri. 2017. *Rhythmanalysis: Space, Time and Everyday Life*. London: Bloomsbury Academic.

Lefkowitz, Mary R., and Guy MacLean Rogers, eds. 1996. *Black Athena Revisited*. Chapel Hill: University of North Carolina Press.

Leggewie, Claus. 2009. "Von der Visualisierung zur Virtualisierung des Erinnerns." In *Erinnerungskultur 2.0. Kommemorative Kommunikation in digitalen Medien*, edited by Erik Meyer. Frankfurt am Main: Campus. 9–28.

Leggewie, Claus, and Anne Lang. 2011. *Der Kampf um die europäische Erinnerung: Ein Schlachtfeld wird besichtigt*. München: C. H. Beck.

Lennon, J. J., and Malcolm Foley, eds. 2000. *Dark Tourism*. London: Continuum.

Lentz, Carola, and Isidore Lobnibe. 2022. *Imagining Futures: Memory and Belonging in an African Family*. Bloomington: Indiana University Press.

Lenz, Claudia. 2006. "Mind the Gap! Sprechen über den Holocaust zwischen nationalen und universellen Narrativen." *Zeitschrift für Genozidforschung* 7 (2): 45–66. https://doi.org/10.5771/1438-8332-2006-2-45.

Lenz, Claudia, and Harald Welzer. 2007. "Opa in Europa. Erste Befunde einer Vergleichenden Tradierungsforschung." In *Der Krieg der Erinnerung: Holocaust, Kollaboration und Widerstand im Europäischen Gedächtnis*, edited by Harald Welzer. Frankfurt am Main: Fischer. 7–40.

Levin, Irene, Nicole Hennum, Claudia Lenz, and Tone Schou Wetlesen, eds. 2011. Special Issue, *Families and Memories: Continuities and Social Change. Journal of Comparative Family Studies* 42 (3).

Levy, Andrea. *Small Island*. London: Headline Review, 2004.

Levy, Daniel, and Natan Sznaider. 2006 [2001]. *The Holocaust and Memory in the Global Age. Politics, History, and Social Change*. Translated by Assenka Oksiloff. Philadelphia: Temple University Press.

Leys, Ruth. 2000. *Trauma: A Genealogy*. Chicago: University of Chicago Press.

Lin, Jian, and Jeroen de Kloet. 2023. "TikTok and the Platformisation from China: Geopolitical Anxieties, Repetitive Creativities, and Future Imaginaries." *Media, Culture & Society* 45 (8): 1525–1533. https://doi.org/10.1177/01634437231209203.

Lindsey, McEwen, Joanne Garde-Hansen, and Andrew Holmes. 2016. "Sustainable Flood Memories, Lay Knowledges and the Development of Community Resilience to Future Flood Risk." *E3s Web of Conferences* 7: 1–6.

Lizardo, Omar. 2022. "What Is Implicit Culture?" *Journal for the Theory of Social Behaviour* 1 (26): 412–437. https://doi.org/10.1111/jtsb.12333.

Lloyd, Katrina, Dirk Schubotz, Rosellen Roche, Joel Manzi, and Martina McKnight. 2023. "A Mental Health Pandemic? Assessing the Impact of COVID-19 on Young People's Mental Health." *International Journal of Environmental Research and Public Health* 20 (16): 6550. doi:10.3390/ijerph20166550.

Loftus, Elizabeth F., and Katherine Ketcham. 1994. *The Myth of Repressed Memory: False Memories and Allegations of Sexual Abuse*. New York: St. Martin's Press.

Lohmeier, Christine, and Rieke Böhling. 2017. "Communicating Family Memory: Remembering in a Changing Media Environment." *Communications* 42 (3): 277–292. https://doi.org/10.1515/commun-2017-0031.

Lorenz, Chris, and Berber Bevernage, eds. 2013. *Breaking Up Time: Negotiating the Borders between Present, Past, and Future*. Göttingen: Vandenhoeck & Ruprecht.

Loshitzky, Yosefa. 2010. *Screening Strangers: Migration and Diaspora in Contemporary European Cinema*. Bloomington: Indiana University Press.

Lothe, Jakob, and Jeremy Hawthorn, eds. 2013. *Narrative Ethics*. Amsterdam: Rodopi.

Lothspeich, Pamela. 2007. "Unspeakable Outrages and Unbearable Defilements: Rape Narratives in the Literature of Colonial India." *Postcolonial Text* 3 (1): 1–19.

Lowe, Hannah. 2018. "'Remember the Ship': Narrating the Empire Windrush." *Journal of Postcolonial Writing* 54 (4): 542–555. https://doi.org/10.1080/17449855.2017.1411416.

Luckhurst, Roger. 2008. *The Trauma Question*. London: Routledge.

Luhmann, Niklas. 2000 [1997]. *Art as a Social System*. Transl. Eva M. Knodt. Stanford, CA: Stanford University Press.

Luminet, Olivier, and Antonietta Curci, eds. 2018 [2009]. *Flashbulb Memories: New Issues and New Perspectives*. Hove: Psychology Press.

Luminet, Olivier, and Rose Spijkerman. 2017. "'11 November 1918 an Exceptional Day!': Flashbulb Memories of the World War I Armistice in Belgium from a Psychological and a Historical Perspective." *Memory Studies* 10 (3): 347–362. https://doi.org/10.1177/1750698017701617.

Lustiger Thaler, Henri, and Habbo Knoch, eds. 2017. *Witnessing Unbound: Holocaust Representation and the Origins of Memory*. Detroit: Wayne State University Press.
Maart, Rozena. 2004. *Rosa's District 6*. Toronto: TSAR.
Macdonald, Sharon. 2013. *Memorylands: Heritage and Identity in Europe Today*. London: Routledge.
Mahaffey, Vicki. 1999. "Sidereal Writing: Male Refractions and Malefactions in 'Ithaca.'" In *Ulysses: En-Gendered Perspectives: Eighteen New Essays on the Episodes*, edited by Kimberly J. Devlin and Marilyn Reizbaum. Columbia: University of South Carolina Press. 254–266.
Mahr, Johannes B., Penny van Bergen, John Sutton, Daniel L. Schacter, and Cecilia Heyes. 2023. "Mnemicity: A Cognitive Gadget?" *Perspectives on Psycholological Science*. 18 (5):1160–1177. doi:10.1177/17456916221141352.
Majerus, Benoît, Sonja Kmec, Pit Péporté, and Michel Margue, eds. 2008. *Lieux de mémoire au Luxembourg: Usages du passé et construction nationale. Erinnerungsorte in Luxembourg. Umgang mit der Vergangenheit und Konstruktion der Nation*. Luxembourg: Éditions Saint-Paul.
Makhortykh, Mykola. 2020. "Remediating the Past: YouTube and Second World War Memory in Ukraine and Russia." *Memory Studies* 13 (2): 146–161. https://doi.org/10.1177/1750698017730867.
Makhortykh, Mykola. 2023. "The User Is Dead, Long Live the Platform? Problematising the User-Centric Focus of (Digital) Memory Studies." *Memory Studies* 16 (6): 1500–1512. https://doi.org/10.1177/17506980231202849.
Malik, Salahuddin. 2008. *1857 War of Independence or Clash of Civilization?: British Public Reactions*. Oxford: Oxford University Press.
Mandelstam, Osip. 1997. *The Complete Critical Prose*. Edited and translated by Jane G. Harris and Constance Link. Ann Arbor: Ardis.
Mandolessi, Silvana. 2023. "The Digital Turn in Memory Studies." *Memory Studies* 16 (6): 1513–1528. https://doi.org/10.1177/17506980231204201.
Manier, David, and William Hirst. 2010. "A Cognitive Taxonomy of Collective Memories." In *A Companion to Cultural Memory Studies*, edited by Astrid Erll and Ansgar Nünning. Berlin: De Gruyter. 253–262. https://doi.org/10.1515/9783110207262
Mannheim, Karl. 1952 [1928]. "The Problem of Generations." In *Karl Mannheim: Essays on the Sociology of Knowledge*, edited by Paul Kecskemeti. London: Routledge. 276–322.
Marks, Laura U. 2000. *The Skin of the Film: Intercultural Cinema, Embodiment, and the Senses*. Durham, NC: Duke University Press.
Marx, Karl, and Friedrich Engels. 1960. *The First Indian War of Independence, 1857–1859*. Moscow: Foreign Languages Publishing House.
May, Jon, and Nigel J. Thrift, eds. 2001. *Timespace: Geographies of Temporality*. London: Routledge.
Mazierska, Ewa, and Laura Rascaroli. 2006. *Crossing New Europe: Postmodern Travel and the European Road Movie*. London: Wallflower Press.
Mazzucchelli, Francesco, and Mario Panico. 2021. "Pre-Emptive Memories: Anticipating Narratives of Covid-19 in Practices of Commemoration." *Memory Studies* 14 (6): 1414–1430. https://doi.org/10.1177/17506980211053984.
Mbembe, Achille. 2017. *Critique of Black Reason*. Translated by Laurent Dubois. Durham, NC: Duke University Press.

McAdams, Dan P. 2008. "Personal Narratives and the Life Story." In *Handbook of Personality: Theory and Research*, edited by Oliver P. John, Richard W. Robins, and Lawrence A. Pervin. New York: Guilford Press. 242–262.

McConnell, Taylor. 2019. "Memory Abuse, Violence and the Dissolution of Yugoslavia: A Theoretical Framework for Understanding Memory in Conflict." *Innovation: The European Journal of Social Science Research* 32 (3): 331–343.

McCormick, Kay. 2002. *Language in Cape Town's District Six*. Oxford: Oxford University Press.

McEachern, Charmaine. 2002. *Narratives of Nation: Media, Memory and Representation in the Making of the New South Africa*. New York: Nova Science Publishers.

McGlothlin, Erin Heather. 2006. *Second-Generation Holocaust Literature: Legacies of Survival and Perpetration*. Rochester: Camden House.

McIvor, Charlotte, and Emilie Pine. 2017. "Roundtable 'Moving Memory.'" Participants: Stef Craps, Astrid Erll, Paula McFetridge, Ann Rigney, and Dominic Thorpe. *Irish University Review: A Journal of Irish Studies* 47 (1): 165–196.

McLean, Kate C., Monisha Pasupathi, and Jennifer L. Pals. 2007. "Selves Creating Stories Creating Selves: A Process Model of Self-Development." *Personality and Social Psychology Review* 11 (3): 262–278. https://doi.org/10.1177/1088868307301034.

McLeod, John. 2010."Extra Dimensions, New Routines." *Wasafiri* 25 (4): 45–52. https://doi.org/10.1080/02690055.2010.510652.

McLeod, John. 2019. "When Memories Fade: Remembering Anti-Racism in Contemporary Black British Writing." *Wasafiri* 34 (4): 18–23. https://doi.org/10.1080/02690055.2019.1635748.

McLuhan, Marshall. 1964. *Understanding Media: The Extensions of Man*. London: Routledge & Kegan Paul.

Mead, Matthew. 2009. "Empire Windrush: The Cultural Memory of an Imaginary Arrival." *Journal of Postcolonial Writing* 45 (2): 137–149. https://doi.org/10.1080/17449850902819920.

Meade, Michelle L., and Henry L. Roediger. 2002. "Explorations in the Social Contagion of Memory." *Memory & Cognition* 30: 995–1009.

Meineck, Peter, and David Konstan, eds. 2014. *Combat Trauma and the Ancient Greeks*. Basingstoke, UK: Palgrave Macmillan.

Melas, Natalie. 2007. *All the Difference in the World: Postcoloniality and the Ends of Comparison*. Stanford, CA: Stanford University Press.

Merck, Cyr, and William Hirst. 2022. "Distinguishing Collective Memory and History: A Community's Identity and History Are Derived from Distinct Sources." *Journal of Applied Research in Memory and Cognition* 11(4): 598–609. https://doi.org/10.1037/mac0000029.

Meredith, G. B. 2021. "'Dominant' First World War Memory: Race, Nation and the Occlusion of Empire." *First World War Studies* 12 (2): 89–109. https://doi.org/10.1080/19475020.2022.2034511.

Merry, Sally Engle. 2006. "Transnational Human Rights and Local Activism: Mapping the Middle." *American Anthropologist* 108 (1): 38–51.

Metcalf, Thomas R. 1989. *An Imperial Vision: Indian Architecture and the British Raj*. London: Faber.

Metcalf, Thomas R. 1995. *Ideologies of the Raj*. Cambridge: Cambridge University Press.

Meyer, Christine, and Anna Gvelesiani, eds. 2024. *Postmemory und die Pluralisierung der deutschen Erinnerungskultur*. Berlin: De Gruyter.

Meyler, Shanique Y., Charles. B. Stone, Olivier Luminet, Robert Meksin, and William Hirst. 2022. *The Intergenerational Transmission of Flashbulb Memories and Event Memories Surrounding the Attack of September 11, 2001*. Unpublished.

Michaelian, Kourken, and John Sutton. 2019. "Collective Mental Time Travel: Remembering the Past and Imagining the Future Together." *Synthese* 196: 4933–4960. https://doi.org/10.1007/s11229-017-1449-1.

Milevski, Urania, and Wetenkamp, Lena. 2022. "Introduction: Relations between Literary Theory and Memory Studies." *Journal of Literary Theory* 16 (2): 197–212. https://doi.org/10.1515/jlt-2022-2022.

Misra, Amaresh. 2005. *Mangal Pandey: The True Story of an Indian Revolutionary*. New Delhi: Rupa.

Misra, Amaresh. 2008. *War of Civilizations: India AD 1857*. New Delhi: Rupa.

Mitchell, David B. 2006. "Nonconscious Priming after 17 Years: Invulnerable Implicit Memory?" *Psychological Science* 17 (11): 925–929. https://doi.org/10.1111/j.1467-9280.2006.01805.x.

Mitchell, Stephen A. 2000. *Relationality: From Attachment to Intersubjectivity*. Hillsdale, NJ: Analytic Press.

Mol, Annemarie. 2010. "Actor-Network Theory: Sensitive Terms and Enduring Tensions." *Kölner Zeitschrift für Soziologie und Sozialpsychologie* 50: 253–269.

Monk, John. 1998. "The Digital Unconscious." In *Virtual/Embodied Presence/Practice/Technology*, edited by John Wood. London: Routledge. 30–44.

Moses, A. Dirk. 2011. "Genocide and the Terror of History." *Parallax* 17 (4): 90–108. https://doi.org/10.1080/13534645.2011.605583.

Moses, Michael Valdez, Lucy Valerie Graham, John Marx, Gerald Gaylard, Ralph Goodman, and Stefan Helgesson. 2010. "District 9: A Roundtable." *Safundi: The Journal of South African and American Studies* 11 (1–2): 155–175.

Mosse, George L. 1990. *Fallen Soldiers: Reshaping the Memory of the World Wars*. New York: Oxford University Press.

Mottolese, William C. 2008. "Traveling Ulysses." In *Joyce, Imperialism and Postcolonialism*, edited by Leonard Orr. Syracuse, NY: Syracuse University Press. 91–111.

Mukherjee, Meenakshi. 2000. *The Perishable Empire: Essays on Indian Writing in English*. New Delhi: Oxford University Press.

Mukherjee, Meenakshi. 2003. "The Beginnings of the Indian Novel." In *A History of Indian Literature in English*, edited by Krishna Arvind Mehrotra. London: Hurst & Company. 92–102.

Mukherjee, Rudrangshu. 1984. *Awadh in Revolt, 1857–1858: A Study of Popular Resistance*. Delhi: Oxford University Press.

Mukherjee, Rudrangshu. 1998. *Spectre of Violence: The 1857 Kanpur Massacres*. London: Viking.

Munteán, László, Liedeke Plate, and Anneke Smelik, eds. 2016. *Materializing Memory in Art and Popular Culture*. New York: Routledge.

Murray, Noléen, Nick Shepherd, and Martin Hall, eds. 2007. *Desire Lines: Space, Memory and Identity in the Post-Apartheid City*. London: Routledge.

Mututa, Addamms. 2023. "Theorizing Afrophobia beyond Apartheid: Conflict Cultures in Neill Blomkamp's District 9." *Critical Arts* 37 (3): 17–31. 10.1080/02560046.2023.2268196.

Mwambari, David. 2023. *Navigating Cultural Memory: Commemoration and Narrative in Postgenocide Rwanda*. Oxford: Oxford University Press.
Naficy, Hamid. 2011. *An Accented Cinema: Exilic and Diasporic Filmmaking*. Princeton, NJ: Princeton University Press.
Namer, Gérard. 2000. *Halbwachs et la mémoire sociale*. Paris: L'Harmattan.
Nasta, Susheila. 2002. *Home Truths: Fictions about the South Asian Diaspora in Britain*. Basingstoke: Palgrave.
Nasta, Susheila, and Mark Stein, eds. 2019a. *The Cambridge History of Black and Asian British Writing*. Cambridge: Cambridge University Press.
Nasta, Susheila, and Mark Stein. 2019b. "Introduction." In Nayar, Pramod K, ed. 2007. *The Penguin 1857 Reader*. New Delhi: Penguin.
Neiger, Mordechai, Oren Meyers, and Eyal Zandberg. 2011. *On Media Memory: Collective Memory in a New Media Age*. Houndmills: Palgrave Macmillan.
Neisser, Ulric. 1982. "Snapshots or Benchmarks?" In *Memory Observed: Remembering in Natural Contexts*, edited by Ulric Neisser. San Francisco: W. H. Freeman. 43–48.
Neisser, Ulric, ed. 1982. *Memory Observed: Remembering in Natural Contexts*. New York: Freeman.
Neisser, Ulric, and Nina Harsh. 1992. "Phantom Flashbulbs: False Recollections of Hearing the News about Challenger." In *Affect and Accuracy in Recall: Studies of "Flashbulb" Memories*, edited by Eugene Winograd and Ulric Neisser. Cambridge: Cambridge University Press. 9–31.
Newell, William Wells. 1884. *Games and Songs of American Children*. New York: Harper & Brothers.
Nichols, Bill. 2010. *Introduction to Documentary*. Bloomington: Indiana University Press.
Niethammer, Lutz. 2000. *Kollektive Identität: Heimliche Quellen einer Unheimlichen Konjunktur*. Reinbek: Rowohlt.
Nixon, Rob. 2011. *Slow Violence and the Environmentalism of the Poor*. Cambridge, MA: Harvard University Press.
Nora, Pierre, ed. 1984–1992. *Les lieux de mémoire*. 3 Vols. Paris: Gallimard.
Nora, Pierre, ed. 1984. *Les lieux de mémoire I: La république*. Paris: Gallimard.
Nora, Pierre, ed. 1986. *Les lieux de mémoire II: La nation*. Paris: Gallimard.
Nora, Pierre. 1989. "Between Memory and History: Les Lieux de Mémoire." *Representations* 26 (Spring): 7–26.
Nora, Pierre. 1990. "Vorwort." In Pierre Nora: *Zwischen Geschichte und Gedächtnis*. Translated by Wolfgang Kaiser. Frankfurt am Main: Fischer. 7–10.
Nora, Pierre, ed. 1992. *Les lieux de mémoire III: Les France*. Paris: Gallimard.
Norris, Margot. 2009. "Stephen Dedalus's Anti-Semitic Ballad: A Sabotaged Climax in Joyce's *Ulysses*." In *De-Familiarizing Readings: Essays from the Austin Joyce Conference*, edited by Alan W. Friedman and Charles Rossman. Amsterdam: Rodopi. 54–75.
Norton Cru, Jean. 1929. *Témoins: Essai d'analyse et de critique des souvenirs des combattants édits en France de 1915 à 1928*. Paris: Les Étincelles.
Nudelman, Craig. 2022. "Memory, Reconciliation, and the Jewish History of District Six." *Cape Jewish Chronicle* 39 (3): 40.
Nünning, Ansgar. 1997. "Crossing Borders and Blurring Genres: Towards a Typology and Poetics of Postmodernist Historical Fiction in England since the 1960s." *European Journal of English Studies* 1 (2): 217–238.

Nünning, Ansgar. 2003. "Fictions of Memory." *Journal for the Study of British Cultures* 10 (1): 49–75.
Nuttall, Sarah. 2009. *Entanglement: Literary and Cultural Reflections on Post-Apartheid.* Johannesburg: Wits University Press.
Nuttall, Sarah, and Carli Coetzee, eds. 1998. *Negotiating the Past: The Making of Memory in South Africa.* Cape Town: Oxford University Press.
O'Dea, Meghan. 2013. "Reflecting on the Present Burdened by the Past: German-Polish Relations in Robert Thalheim's Film Am Ende kommen Touristen (2007)." *German Politics & Society* 31 (4): 40–58.
Olick, Jeffrey K. 1999. "Collective Memory: The Two Cultures." *Sociological Theory* 17 (3): 333–348. https://doi.org/10.1111/0735-2751.00083.
Olick, Jeffrey K. 2007. *The Politics of Regret: On Collective Memory and Historical Responsibility.* New York: Routledge.
Olick, Jeffrey K. 2008. "The Ciphered Transits of Collective Memory: Neo-Freudian Impressions." *Social Research: An International Quarterly* 75 (1): 1–22. https://doi.org/10.1353/sor.2008.0058.
Olick, Jeffrey K. 2010. "From Collective Memory to the Sociology of Mnemonic Practices and Products." In *A Companion to Cultural Memory Studies*, edited by Astrid Erll and Ansgar Nünning. Berlin: De Gruyter. 151–162.
Olick, Jeffrey K. 2016. *The Sins of the Fathers: Germany, Memory, Method.* Chicago: University of Chicago Press.
Olick, Jeffrey K. 2025. "Who Is Afraid of Collective Memory." In Jeffrey K. Olick: *In the Grip of the Past.* New York: Oxford University Press (in press).
Olick, Jeffrey K., and Joyce Robbins. 1998. "Social Memory Studies: From 'Collective Memory' to the Historical Sociology of Mnemonic Practices." *Annual Review of Sociology* 24: 105–140. http://www.jstor.org/stable/223476.
Olick, Jeffrey K. and Christina Simko. 2021. "What We Talk about When We Talk about Culture: A Multi-Facet Approach." *American Journal of Cultural Sociology* 9 (4): 431–459.
Olick, Jeffrey K., Vered Vinitzky-Seroussi, and Daniel Levy, eds. 2010. *The Collective Memory Reader.* Oxford: Oxford University Press.
Öner, Sezin, Lynn Ann Watson, Zeynep Adıgüzel, İrem Ergen, Ezgil Bilgin, Antonietta Curci, Scott Cole, Manuel L. de la Mata, Steve M. J. Janssen, Tiziana Lanciano, Ioanna Markostamou, Veronika Nourkova, Andrés Santamaría, Andrea Taylor, Krystian Barzykowski, Miguel Bascón, Christina Bermeitinger, Rosario Cubero-Pérez, Steven Dessenberger, Maryanne Garry, Sami Gülgöz, Ryan Hackländer, Lucrèce Heux, Zheng Jin, María Lojo, José Antonio Matías-García, Henry L. Roediger III, Karl Szpunar, Eylul Tekin, and Oyku Uner. 2022. "Collective Remembering and Forecasting during the COVID-19 Pandemic: How the Impact of COVID-19 Affected the Themes and Phenomenology of Global and National Memories across 15 Countries." *Memory & Cognition* 51 (3): 729–751.
Ong, Walter J. 1982. *Orality and Literacy: The Technologizing of the Word.* London: Methuen.
Orrells, Daniel, Gurminder K. Bhambra, and Tessa Roynon, eds. 2011. *African Athena: New Agendas.* Oxford: Oxford University Press.
Ortner, Jessica, Tea Sindbæk Andersen, and Fedja Wierød Borčak. 2022. "'Fiction Keeps Memory about the War Alive': Mnemonic Migration and Literary Representations of the War in Bosnia." *Memory Studies* 15 (4): 918–934.

Osborne, Deirdre, ed. 2016. *The Cambridge Companion to British Black and Asian Literature (1945–2010)*. Cambridge: Cambridge University Press.
Otele, Olivette. 2022. *African Europeans: An Untold History*. London: Basic Books.
Otele, Olivette, Luisa Gandolfo, and Yoav Galai, eds. 2021. *Post-Conflict Memorialization: Missing Memorials, Absent Bodies*. Basingstoke: Palgrave Macmillan.
Outka, Elizabeth. 2019. *Viral Modernism: The Influenza Pandemic and Interwar Literature*. New York: Columbia University Press.
Parnes, Ohad, Ulrike Vedder, and Stefan Willer. 2008. *Das Konzept der Generation: Eine Wissenschafts- und Kulturgeschichte*. Frankfurt am Main: Suhrkamp.
Parui, Avishek, and Merin Simi Raj, eds. 2025. *Memory Studies in India. Texts and Contexts*. Amsterdam: Brill.
Parui, Avishek, and Merin Simi Raj. 2021. "The COVID-19 Crisis Chronotope: The Pandemic as Matter, Metaphor and Memory." *Memory Studies* 14 (6): 1431–1444. https://doi.org/10.1177/17506980211054346.
Passerini, Luisa. 1992. *Memory and Totalitarianism*. Oxford: Oxford University Press.
Passerini, Luisa. 1999. *Europe in Love, Love in Europe*. New York: New York University Press.
Pati, Biswamoy, ed. 2007. *The 1857 Rebellion: Debates in Indian History and Society*. Delhi: Oxford University Press India.
Patterson, Orlando. 1982. *Slavery and Social Death: A Comparative Study*. Cambridge, MA: Harvard University Press.
Pender, Sebastian Raj. 2022. *The 1857 Indian Uprising and the Politics of Commemoration*. Cambridge: Cambridge University Press.
Pennebaker, James W, Darío Páez, and Bernard Rimé, eds. 1997. *Collective Memory of Political Events: Social Psychological Perspectives*. Mahwah, NJ: Erlbaum.
Pentzold, Christian, and Christine Lohmeier, eds. 2023. *Handbuch kommunikationswissenschaftliche Erinnerungsforschung*. Berlin: De Gruyter.
Pentzold, Christian, Christine Lohmeier, and Thomas Birkner. 2023. "Communicative Remembering: Revisiting a Basic Mnemonic Concept." *Memory, Mind & Media* 2 (e9): 1–15. doi:10.1017/mem.2023.7.
Petrarch, Francesco. 1985. *Letters on Familiar Matters: Rerum Familiarium Libri XVII–XXIV*. Translated by S. Bernardo. Baltimore, MD: Johns Hopkins University Press.
Phillips, Caryl. 1999. "Following On: The Legacy of Lamming and Selvon." *Wasafiri* 14 (29): 34–36. https://doi.org/10.1080/02690059908589629.
Phillips, Caryl. 2010. *In the Falling Snow*. London: Vintage.
Phillips, Howard, and David Killingray. 2001. *The Spanish Flu Pandemic of 1918: New Perspectives*. London: Routledge.
Phillips, Trevor, and Mike Phillips, eds. 1998. *Windrush: The Irresistible Rise of Multi-Racial Britain*. London: Harper Collins.
Pieterse, Jan Nederveen. 2003. *Globalization and Culture: Global Mélange*. Lanham, MD: Rowman & Littlefield.
Pillemer, David B. 2001. "Momentous Events and the Life Story." *Review of General Psychology* 5 (2): 123–134. https://doi.org/10.1037/1089-2680.5.2.123.
Pillemer, David B. 2009. "'Hearing the News' versus 'Being There': Comparing Flashbulb Memories and the Recall of First-Hand Experiences." In *Flashbulb Memories: New Issues and New Perspectives*, edited by Olivier Luminet and Antonietta Curci. Hove: Psychology Press. 125–140.

Pirker, Eva Ulrike. 2011. *Narrative Projections of a Black British History*. New York: Routledge.
Pistorius, Penny, Marco Bezzoli, Rafael Marks, and Martin Kruger. 2002. *Texture and Memory: The Urbanism of District Six*, 2nd ed. Cape Town: Sustainable Urban and Housing Development Research Unit, Dept. of Architectural Technology, Cape Technikon.
Plate, Liedeke. 2010. *Transforming Memories in Contemporary Women's Rewriting*. Basingstoke: Palgrave Macmillan.
Polletta, Francesca, and Alex Maresca. 2021. "Claiming Martin Luther King, Jr. for the Right: The Martin Luther King Day Holiday in the Reagan Era." *Memory Studies* 16 (2): 386–402. https://doi.org/10.1177/1750698021995932.
Pound, Ezra. 1935. *Make It New: Essays*. New Haven, CT: Yale University Press.
Pound, Ezra. 1954 [1922]. *Literary Essays of Ezra Pound*. Edited by T. S. Eliot. London: Faber and Faber.
Pound, Ezra. 1977 [1975]. *Selected Poems. 1908–1969*. London: Faber and Faber.
Powell, Christopher. 2013. "Radical Relationism: A Proposal." In *Conceptualizing Relational Sociology: Ontological and Theoretical Issues*, edited by Christopher Powell and François Dépelteau. New York: Palgrave Macmillan. 187–208.
Price, Vincent, and David Tewksbury. 1997. "News Values and Public Opinion: A Theoretical Account of Media Priming and Framing." In *Progress in the Communication Sciences*, Vol. 13, edited by George A. Barnett and Franklin J. Boster. New York: Ablex. 173–212.
Prior, Markus. 2010. *Post-Broadcast Democracy: How Media Choice Increases Inequality in Political Involvement and Polarizes Elections*. Cambridge: Cambridge University Press. https://doi.org/10.1017/CBO9781139878425.
Proctor, Robert N., and Londa L. Schiebinger, eds. 2008. *Agnotology: The Making and Unmaking of Ignorance*. Stanford, CA: Stanford University Press.
Prosalendis, Linda. 1999. "District Six—Kanaladorp." *Nordisk Museologi* 1: 135–146.
Prümm, Karl. 1974. *Die Literatur des Soldatischen Nationalismus der 20er Jahre (1918–1933)*. Kronberg im Taunus: Scriptor Verlag.
Puran Chandra, Joshi, ed. 1994. *1857 in Folk Songs*. New Delhi: People's Publishing House.
Rabinow, Paul, ed. 1984. *The Foucault Reader*. New York: Pantheon Books.
Race, William H. 2014. "Phaeacian Therapy in Homer's *Odyssey*." In *Combat Trauma and the Ancient Greeks*, edited by Peter Meineck and David Konstan. Basingstoke: Palgrave Macmillan. 47–66.
Racine, Nicole, Brae Anne McArthur, Jessica E. Cooke, Rachel Eirich, Jenney Zhu, and Sheri Madigan. 2021. "Global Prevalence of Depressive and Anxiety Symptoms in Children and Adolescents During COVID-19: A Meta-Analysis." *JAMA Pediatrics* 175 (11): 1142–1150. doi:10.1001/jamapediatrics.2021.2482.
Radstone, Susannah. 2011. "What Place Is This? Transcultural Memory and the Locations of Memory Studies." *Parallax* 17 (4): 109–123. https://doi.org/10.1080/13534645.2011.605585.
Radstone, Susannah, and Katharine Hodgkin, eds. 2003. *Memory Cultures: Memory, Subjectivity, and Recognition*. New Brunswick, NJ: Transaction.
Rakoff, Vivian, John J. Sigal, and Nathan V. Epstein. 1966. "Children and Families of Concentration Camp Survivors." *Canada's Mental Health* 14: 24–25.

Ramey, James. 2007. "Intertextual Metempsychosis in *Ulysses*: Murphy, Sinbad, and the 'U.P.: up' Postcard." *James Joyce Quarterly* 45 (1): 97–114.

Ramsden-Karelse, Ruth. 2023. "A Precarious Archive: Using Photography to Enable Liveable Lives in District Six, Cape Town." *Gender, Place & Culture*: 1–21. doi:10.1080/0966369X.2023.2179024.

Rassool, Ciraj. 2006. "Making the District Six Museum in Cape Town." *Museum International* 58: 9–18.

Rassool, Ciraj and Sandra Prosalendis, eds. 2001. *Recalling Community in Cape Town: Creating and Curating the District Six Museum*. Cape Town, South Africa: District Six Museum.

Rastogi, Pallavi, and Jocelyn Fenton Stitt, eds. 2008. *Before Windrush: Recovering an Asian and Black Literary Heritage within Britain*. Newcastle-upon-Tyne: Cambridge Scholars.

Raugh, Harold E. 2017. "The Battle of the Books: An Indian Mutiny Historiography, Part Two." *Journal of the Society for Army Historical Research* 95 (381): 34–51. http://www.jstor.org/stable/44233171.

Ray, Rajat Kanta. 2003. *The Felt Community: Commonality and Mentality before the Emergence of Indian Nationalism*. Delhi: Oxford University Press.

Reading, Anna. 2016. *Gender and Memory in the Global Age*. London: Palgrave Macmillan.

Reizbaum, Marilyn. 1999. *James Joyce's Judaic Other*. Stanford, CA: Stanford University Press.

Remarque, Erich Maria. 1929. *All Quiet on the Western Front*. Translated by A. W. Wheen. Boston: Little, Brown.

Renner, Hackett C. 2017. "Validity Effect." In *Cognitive Illusions: Intriguing Phenomena in Thinking, Judgment and Memory*, edited by Rüdiger F. Pohl. London: Routledge. 201–213.

Reulecke, Jürgen. 2010. "Generation/Generationality, Generativity, and Memory." In *A Companion to Cultural Memory Studies*, edited by Astrid Erll and Ansgar Nünning. Berlin: De Gruyter. 119–126.

Rich, Adrienne. 1972. "When We Dead Awaken: Writing as ReVision." *College English* 34 (1): 18–30. https://doi.org/10.2307/375215.

Richards, Jeffrey. 1973. *Visions of Yesterday*. London: Routledge and Kegan Paul.

Rickard, John S. 1999. *Joyce's Book of Memory: The Mnemotechnic of Ulysses*. Durham, NC: Duke University Press.

Ricœur, Paul. 1984 [1983]. *Time and Narrative*, Vol 1. Chicago: University of Chicago Press.

Rigney, Ann. 1990. *The Rhetoric of Historical Representation: Three Narrative Histories of the French Revolution*. Cambridge: Cambridge University Press.

Rigney, Ann. 2004. "Portable Monuments: Literature, Cultural Memory, and the Case of Jeanie Deans." *Poetics Today* 25 (2): 361–396. doi:10.1215/03335372-25-2-361.

Rigney, Ann. 2005. "Plenitude, Scarcity and the Circulation of Cultural Memory." *Journal of European Studies* 35 (1–2): 209–226. https://doi.org/10.1177/0047244105051158.

Rigney, Ann. 2010. "The Dynamics of Remembrance: Texts between Monumentality and Morphing." In *A Companion to Cultural Memory Studies*, edited by Astrid Erll and Ansgar Nünning. Berlin: De Gruyter. 345–353.

Rigney, Ann. 2012a. *The Afterlives of Walter Scott: Memory on the Move*. Oxford: Oxford University Press.

Rigney, Ann. 2012b. "Transforming Memory and the European Project." *New Literary History* 43 (4): 607–628.

Rigney, Ann. 2016. "Differential Memorability and Transnational Activism: Bloody Sunday, 1887–2016." *Australian Humanities Review* 59: 77–95.

Rigney, Ann. 2018. "Remembering Hope: Transnational Activism Beyond the Traumatic." *Memory Studies* 11 (3): 368–380.

Rigney, Ann. 2020. "Mediations of Outrage: How the Killing of Demonstrators Is Remembered." *Social Research* 87 (3): 707–733.

Rigney, Ann. 2021. "Remaking Memory and the Agency of the Aesthetic." *Memory Studies* 14 (1): 10–23.

Rigney, Ann. 2023. "Decommissioning Monuments, Mobilizing Materialities." In *The Routledge Handbook of Memory Activism*, edited by Yifat Gutman and Jenny Wüstenberg. London: Taylor & Francis. 21–27.

Rive, Richard. 1986. *Buckingham Palace, District Six*. Berlin: Cornelsen.

Rive, Richard. 1990. "District Six: Fact and Fiction." In *The Struggle for District Six: Past and Present*, edited by Shamil Jeppie and Soudien Crain. Cape Town: Buchu Books. 110–116.

Roediger, Henry L. 1990. "Implicit Memory: Retention Without Remembering." *American Psychologist* 45 (9): 1043–1056.

Roediger, Henry L., III, and James V. Wertsch, eds. 2021. *National Memories. Constructing Identity in Populist Times*. New York: Oxford University Press.

Roediger, Henry L., III, and James V. Wertsch, eds. 2022. *Constructing National Identity: Conflicting Memories and Narratives*. New York: Oxford University Press.

Roediger, Henry L., III, and Christopher L. Zerr. 2022. "Who Won World War II? Conflicting Narratives among the Allies." *Progress in Brain Research* 274 (1): 129–147.

Rosa, Hartmut. 2017. *Social Acceleration: A New Theory of Modernity*. New York: Columbia University Press.

Rosenfeld, Gavriel D. 2009. "A Looming Crash or a Soft Landing? Forecasting the Future of the Memory 'Industry.'" *Journal of Modern History* 81 (1): 122–158.

Rosenstone, Robert A., ed. 1995. *Visions of the Past: The Challenge of Film to Our Idea of History*. Cambridge, MA: Harvard University Press.

Roskos-Ewoldsen, David R., Beverly Roskos, and Francesca R. Dillman Carpentier. 2009. "Media Priming: A Synthesis." In *Media Effects: Advances in Theory and Research*, 3rd ed., edited by Jennings Bryant and Mary Beth Olivier. New York: Routledge. 97–120.

Røssaak, Eivind, ed. 2010. *The Archive in Motion: New Conceptions of the Archive in Contemporary Thought and New Media Practices*. Oslo: Novus Press.

Rothberg, Michael. 2009. *Multidirectional Memory: Remembering the Holocaust in the Age of Decolonization*. Stanford, CA: Stanford University Press.

Rothberg, Michael. 2013. "Remembering Back: Cultural Memory, Colonial Legacies, and Postcolonial Studies." In *The Oxford Handbook of Postcolonial Studies*, edited by Graham Huggan. Oxford: Oxford University Press. 359–379.

Rothberg, Michael. 2019. *The Implicated Subject: Beyond Victims and Perpetrators*. Stanford, CA: Stanford University Press.

Rothberg, Michael. 2022a. "Cultural Memory Studies and the *Beloved* Paradigm: From Rememory to Abolition in the Afterlives of Slavery." In *The Oxford Handbook of Twentieth-Century American Literature*, edited by Leslie Bow and Russ Castronovo. Oxford: Oxford University Press. 398–416.

Rothberg, Michael. 2022b. "Lived Multidirectionality: 'Historikerstreit 2.0' and the Politics of Holocaust Memory." *Memory Studies* 15 (6): 1316–1329.
Rothberg, Michael, and Yasemin Yildiz. 2011. "Memory Citizenship: Migrant Archives of Holocaust Remembrance in Contemporary Germany." *Parallax* 17 (4): 32–48. https://doi.org/10.1080/13534645.2011.605576.
Rothermund, Dietmar, ed. 2015. *Memories of Post-Imperial Nations: The Aftermath of Decolonization, 1945–2013*. Delhi: Cambridge University Press.
Rubin, David C. 1995. *Memory in Oral Traditions: The Cognitive Psychology of Epic Ballads and Counting-Out Rhymes*. New York: Oxford University Press.
Rubin, David C., and Marc Kozin. 1984. "Vivid Memories." *Cognition* 16 (1): 81–95. https://doi.org/10.1016/0010-0277(84)90037-4.
Rubin, David C., and Matthew D. Schulkind. 1997. "The Distribution of Autobiographical Memories Across the Lifespan." *Memory & Cognition* 25 (6): 859–866.
Ruchatz, Jens. 2010. "The Photograph as Externalization and Trace." In *A Companion to Cultural Memory Studies*, edited by Astrid Erll and Ansgar Nünning. Berlin: De Gruyter. 367–378.
Ruin, Hans. 2018. *Being with the Dead: Burial, Ancestral Politics, and the Roots of Historical Consciousness*. Stanford, CA: Stanford University Press.
Rupp, Jan. 2010. *Genre and Cultural Memory in Black British Literature*. Trier: WVT.
Rüsen, Jörn. 2017. *Evidence and Meaning: A Theory of Historical Studies*. Translated by Diane Kerns and Katie Digan. New York: Berghahn.
Ryan, Marie-Laure, ed. 2004. *Narrative across Media: The Languages of Storytelling*. Lincoln: Nebraska University Press.
Ryan, Marie-Lauren. 2006. *Avatars of Story*. Minneapolis: Minnesota University Press.
Ryan, Marie-Laure. 2015. "Transmedia Storytelling: Industry Buzzword or New Narrative Experience?" *Storyworlds: A Journal of Narrative Studies* 7 (2): 1–19.
Sabin, Margery. 2002. *Dissenters and Mavericks: Writings about India in English, 1765–2000*. Oxford: Oxford University Press.
Sabyasachi, Bhattacharya, ed. 2007. *Rethinking 1857*. New Delhi: Orient Longman.
Said, Edward. 1978. "Orientalism". *Western Conceptions of the Orient*. New York: Pantheon Books.
Said, Edward W. 1983. *The World, the Text, and the Critic*. Cambridge, MA: Harvard University Press.
Sambo, Kouthar. February 20, 2024. "The District Six Museum Welcomes the New Appointment of Ms Zeenat Parker-Kasker as the Executive Director." *The Voice of the Cape*. https://www.vocfm.co.za/the-district-six-museum-welcomes-the-new-appointment-of-ms-zeenat-parker-kasker-as-the-executive-director/.
Sambumbu, Sipokazi. 2010. "Reading Visual Representations of 'Ndabeni' in the Public Realms." *Kronos* 36: 184–206.
Sardar, Ziauddin, and Sean Cubitt. 2002. *Aliens R Us: The Other in Science Fiction Cinema*. London: Pluto Press.
Sauerberg, Lars Ole. 2009. "The Gutenberg Parenthesis—Print, Book, and Cognition." *Orbis Litterarum* 64 (2): 79–80. https://doi.org/10.1111/j.1600-0730.2009.00962.x
Saunders, Max. 2010. "Life-Writing, Cultural Memory, and Literary Studies." In *A Companion to Cultural Memory Studies*, edited by Astrid Erll and Ansgar Nünning. Berlin: De Gruyter. 321–332.
Savarkar, Vinayak Damodar. 1970 [1909]. *The Indian War of Independence, 1857*. Delhi: Rajdhani Granthagar.

Savelsberg, Joachim J. 2021. *Knowing about Genocide: Armenian Suffering and Epistemic Struggles*. Oakland: University of California Press.
Savolainen, Ulla. 2017. "Tellability, Frame and Silence: The Emergence of Internment Memory." *Narrative Inquiry* 27 (1): 24–46. https://doi.org/10.1075/ni.27.1.02sav.
Schacter, Daniel L. 1987. "Implicit Memory: History and Current Status." *Journal of Experimental Psychology: Learning, Memory and Cognition* 13 (3): 501–518. doi:10.1037/0278-7393.13.3.501.
Schacter, Daniel L. 1996. *Searching for Memory: The Brain, the Mind, and the Past*. New York: Basic Books.
Schacter, Daniel L. 2002. *The Seven Sins of Memory: How the Mind Forgets and Remembers*. Boston: Houghton Mifflin Harcourt.
Schacter Daniel L., and Donna Rose Addis. 2007. "The Cognitive Neuroscience of Constructive Memory: Remembering the Past and Imagining the Future." *Philosophical Transactions of the Royal Society B: Biological Sciences* 362: 773–786.
Schacter, Daniel L., and Michael Welker. 2016. "Memory and Connection: Remembering the Past and Imagining the Future in Individuals, Groups, and Cultures." *Memory Studies* 9 (3): 241–244.
Schank, Roger. C., and Robert Abelson. 1977. *Scripts, Plans, Goals, and Understanding*. Hillsdale, NJ: Erlbaum.
Schankweiler, Kerstin, Verena Straub, and Tobias Wendl. 2018. *Image Testimonies: Witnessing in Times of Social Media*. London: Routledge. https://doi.org/10.4324/9780429434853.
Schemer, Christian. 2013. "Priming, Framing, Stereotype." In *Handbuch Medienwirkungsforschung*, edited by Wolfgang Schweiger and Andreas Fahr. Wiesbaden: Springer VS. 153–169.
Scherer, Madeleine. 2021. *Memories of the Classical Underworld in Irish and Caribbean Literature*. Berlin: De Gruyter.
Scheufele, Dietram A. 1999. "Framing as a Theory of Media Effects." *Journal of Communication* 49 (1): 103–122.
Schiff, Brian. 2017. *A New Narrative for Psychology*. Oxford: Oxford University Press. https://doi.org/10.1093/oso/9780199332182.001.0001.
Schneider, Thomas F. 2007. *Erich Maria Remarques Roman "Im Westen Nichts Neues" Text, Edition, Entstehung, Distribution und Rezeption (1928–1930)*. Tübingen: Niemeyer.
Scholberg, Henry. 1993. *The Indian Literature of the Great Rebellion*. New Delhi: South Asia Books.
Schrire, Gwynne. 2021. "District Six Removals: The Ignored Community." *Jewish Affairs* 76 (3): 28–38.
Schudson, Michael. 1997. "Lives, Law, and Language: Commemorative Versus Non-Commemorative Forms of Effective Public Memory." *The Communication Review* 2 (1): 3–17.
Schudson, Michael. 2014. "Journalism as a Vehicle of Non-Commemorative Cultural Memory." In *Journalism and Memory*, edited by Barbie Zelizer, and Keren Tenenboim-Weinblatt. Basingstoke: Palgrave Macmillan. 85–96.
Schulze-Engler, Frank. 2013. "Irritating Europe." In *The Oxford Handbook of Postcolonial Studies*, edited by Graham Huggan. Oxford: Oxford University Press. 669–691.

Schuman, Howard, and Amy Corning. 2012. "Generational Memory and the Critical Period: Evidence for National and World Events." *Public Opinion Quarterly* 76 (1): 1–31. https://doi.org/10.1093/poq/nfr037.
Schuman, Howard, and Jacqueline Scott. 1989. "Generations and Collective Memories." *American Sociological Review* 54 (3): 359–381. https://doi.org/10.2307/2095611.
Schwab, Gabriele. 2010. *Haunting Legacies: Violent Histories and Transgenerational Trauma*. New York: Columbia University Press.
Schwartz, Barry. 2009. "Collective Forgetting and the Symbolic Power of Oneness: The Strange Apotheosis of Rosa Parks." *Social Psychology Quarterly* 72 (2): 123–142.
Schwarz, Bill. 2011. *Memories of Empire*. Oxford: Oxford University Press.
Sebald, W. G. 2003. "Hitlers Pyromanische Phantasien: Interview mit Volker Hage." In *Zeugen der Zerstörung: Die Literaten und der Luftkrieg*, edited by Volker Hage. Frankfurt am Main: Fischer. 259–279.
Seet, Seth, and Edson C. Tandoc. 2024. "Re-meme-bering Tiananmen? From Collective Memory to Meta-memory on TikTok." *Media, Culture & Society* 46 (2): 272–291. https://doi.org/10.1177/01634437231191413.
Selvon, Samuel. 1956. *The Lonely Londoners*. London: Allan Wingate.
Sen, Amartya Kumar. 2006. *Identity and Violence: The Illusion of Destiny*. New York: Norton.
Sengupta Frey, Indra, ed. 2009. *Memory, History, and Colonialism: Engaging with Pierre Nora in Colonial and Postcolonial Contexts*. London: German Historical Institute.
Sharot, Tali, Elizabeth A. Martorella, Mauricio R. Delgado, and Elizabeth A. Phelps. 2007. "How Personal Experience Modulates the Neural Circuitry of Memories of September 11." *Proceedings of the National Academy of Sciences of the United States of America* 104 (1): 389–394. https://doi.org/10.1073/pnas.0609230103.
Sharpe, Jenny. 1993. *Allegories of Empire: The Figure of Woman in the Colonial Text*. Minneapolis: Minnesota University Press.
Shay, Jonathan. 1995. *Achilles in Vietnam: Combat Trauma and the Undoing of Character*. New York: Scribner.
Shay, Jonathan. 2002. *Odysseus in America: Combat Trauma and the Trials of Homecoming*. New York: Scribner.
Shepherd, W. J. 1879. *A Personal Narrative of the Outbreak and Massacre at Cawnpore during the Sepoy Revolt of 1857*. London: Lucknow.
Siddique, Soofia. 2012. " Remembering the Revolt of 1857: Contrapuntal Formations in Indian Literature and History." PhD dissertation, Department of South Asia, School of Oriental and African Studies, University of London.
Silverman, Maxim. 2013. *Palimpsestic Memory: The Holocaust and Colonialism in French and Francophone Fiction and Film*. New York: Berghahn.
Simko, Christina. 2021. "Mourning and Memory in the Age of COVID-19." *Sociologica*, 26: 109–124.
Simko, Christina, and Jeffrey K. Olick. 2020. "Between Trauma and Tragedy." *Social Research: An International Quarterly* 87 (3): 651–676.
Sindbæk Andersen, Tea, and Barbara Törnquist-Plewa, eds. 2016. *Disputed Memory: Emotions and Memory Politics in Central, Eastern and South-Eastern Europe*. Berlin: De Gruyter.
Sindbæk Andersen, Tea, and Barbara Törnquist-Plewa, eds. 2017. *The Twentieth Century in European Memory: Transcultural Mediation and Reception*. Leiden: Brill.

Smaoui, Sélim. 2023. "The Construction of Family Memory through Activist Engagement: The Case of Relatives of the Disappeared in Spain." *Memory Studies* 17 (4), 813–832. https://doi.org/10.1177/17506980231155575.
Smelser, Neil J. 2004. "Psychological Trauma and Cultural Trauma." In *Cultural Trauma and Collective Identity*, edited by Jeffrey Alexander, Ron Eyerman, Bernhard Giesen, Neil J. Smelser, and Piotr Sztompka. Berkeley: University of California Press. 31–59.
Smit, Rik. 2024. "The Platformization of Memory." In *Dynamics, Mediation, and Mobilization: Doing Memory Studies with Ann Rigney*, edited by Astrid Erll, Susanne Knittel, and Jenny Wüstenberg. Berlin: De Gruyter. 123-127.
Smit, Rik, Benjamin Jacobsen, and Taylor Annabell. 2024. "The Multiplicities of Platformed Remembering." *Memory, Mind & Media* 3 (e3): 1–6. https://doi.org/10.1017/mem.2024.3.
Smith, Helen Zenna. 1989 [1930]. *Not So Quiet . . . Stepdaughters of War*. New York: The Feminist Press.
Smith, Tina, and Jenny Marsden. 2019. *KEWPIE: Daughter of District Six*. Cape Town: District SIX Museum /GALA.
Smith, Tina, and Jenny Marsden. 2020. "Photographs and Memory Making: Curating Kewpie: Daughter of District Six." In *Women and Photography in Africa: Creative Practices and Feminist Challenges*, edited by Darren Newbury, Lorena Rizzo, and Kylie Thomas. Abingdon: Routledge. 163–189.
Smith, Zadie. 2001 [2000]. *White Teeth*. London: Penguin Books.
Sollors, Werner. 1986. "First Generation, Second Generation, Third Generation: The Cultural Construction of Descent." In *Beyond Ethnicity: Consent and Descent in American Culture* by Werner Sollors. New York: Oxford University Press. 208–236.
Sonnett, John. 2019. "Priming and Framing: Dimensions of Communication and Cognition." In *The Oxford Handbook of Cognitive Sociology*, edited by Wayne H. Brekhus and Gabe Ignatow. Oxford: Oxford University Press. 226–240.
Sontag, Susan. 2003. *Regarding the Pain of Others*. London: Penguin.
Sooryamoorthy, Radhamany, and Mzwandile Makhoba. 2016. "The Family in Modern South Africa: Insights from Recent Research." *Journal of Comparative Family Studies* 47 (3): 309–321. https://doi.org/10.3138/jcfs.47.3.309.
Soudien, Amie. 2019. "Memory, Multiplicity, and Participatory Curation at the District Six Museum, Cape Town." *Critical Arts* 33 (6): 67–82.
Southall, Roger. 2023. "The Middle Class and Suburbia: Desegregation Towards Non-Racialism in South Africa?" *Journal of Contemporary African Studies* 41 (1): 60–74. doi:10.1080/02589001.2022.2083589
Souza Sutter, Luana de. 2019. "Remembering Slavery: Intergenerational Memory and Trauma in Toni Morrison's *Beloved* (1987) and Conceição Evaristo's *Ponciá Vicêncio* (2003)." *Contemporary Women's Writing* 13 (3): 321–338. https://doi.org/10.1093/cww/vpaa002.
Sowerby, Robin. 1997. "Early Humanist Failure with Homer (I)." *International Journal of the Classical Tradition* 4 (1): 37–63.
Spinney, Laura. 2018. *Pale Rider: The Spanish Flu of 1918 and How It Changed the World*. London: Vintage.
Squire, Larry R. 1987. *Memory and Brain*. Oxford: Oxford University Press.
Stanford, William B. 1954. *The Ulysses Theme: A Study in the Adaptability of a Traditional Hero*. Oxford: Blackwell.

Stein, Mark. 2004. *Black British Literature: Novels of Transformation*. Columbus: Ohio State University Press.
Stokes, Eric. 1986. *The Peasant Armed: The Indian Revolt of 1857*. Oxford: Clarendon.
Stoler, Ann Laura. 2008. *Along the Archival Grain: Thinking through Colonial Ontologies*. Princeton, NJ: Princeton University Press.
Stoler, Ann Laura. 2016. *Duress: Colonial Durabilities in Our Times*. Durham, NC: Duke University Press.
Stone, Charles B., and Alexander C. V. Jay. 2018. "A Comparison of Flashbulb Memories for Positive and Negative Events and Their Biopsychosocial Functions." In *Flashbulb Memories: New Issues and New Perspectives*, edited by Olivier Luminet and Antonnietta Curci. Hove: Psychology Press. 161–181.
Straub, Jürgen, and Jörn Rüsen, eds. 2011 [1998]. *Dark Traces of the Past: Psychoanalysis and Historical Thinking*. New York: Berghahn Books.
Sturken, Marita. 1997. *Tangled Memories the Vietnam War, the AIDS Epidemic, and the Politics of Remembering*. Berkeley: University of California Press.
Suleiman, Susan R. 2002. "The 1.5 Generation: Thinking about Child Survivors and the Holocaust." *American Imago* 59 (3): 277–295. https://doi.org/10.1353/aim.2002.0021.
Sutton, John, Celia B. Harris, Paul G. Keil, and Amanda J. Barnier. 2010. "The Psychology of Memory, Extended Cognition, and Socially Distributed Remembering." *Phenomenology and the Cognitive Sciences* 9 (4): 521–560.
Švaříčková Slabáková, Radmila, ed. 2020. *Family Memory: Practices, Transmissions, and Uses in a Global Perspective*. New York: Routledge.
Svob, Connie, and Norman R. Brown. 2012. "Intergenerational Transmission of the Reminiscence Bump and Biographical Conflict Knowledge." *Psychological Science* 23 (11): 1404–1409. https://doi.org/10.1177/0956797612445316.
Szpunar, Piotr M., and Karl K. Szpunar. 2016. "Collective Future Thought: Concept, Function, and Implications for Collective Memory Studies." *Memory Studies* 9 (4): 376–389.
Tabaszewska, J. 2023. "Future in Memory Studies and Functions of Alternative Histories." In *Voicing Memories, Unearthing Identities: Studies in the Twenty-First-Century Literatures of Eastern and East-Central Europe*, edited by Aleksandra Konarzewska and Anna Nakai. Wilmington, Delaware: Vernon Press. 3–24.
Tai, Hue-Tam Ho. 2001. "Remembered Realms: Pierre Nora and French National Memory." *American Historical Review* 106 (3): 906–922. https://doi.org/10.2307/2692331.
Tajfel, Henri, and John C. Turner. 2004. "Social Identity Theory of Intergroup Behavior." In *Political Psychology: Key Readings*, edited by John T. Jost and Jim Sidanius. Hove: Psychology Press. 276–293. https://doi.org/10.4324/9780203505984-16.
Talarico, Jennifer M., Amanda Kraha, Heather Self, and Adriel Boals. 2019. "How Did You Hear the News? The Role of Traditional Media, Social Media, and Personal Communication in Flashbulb Memory." *Memory Studies* 12 (4): 359–376. https://doi.org/10.1177/1750698017714835.
Talarico, Jennifer M., and David C. Rubin. 2003. "Confidence, Not Consistency, Characterizes Flashbulb Memories." *Psychological Science* 14 (5): 455–461. https://doi.org/10.1111/1467-9280.02453.
Tamm, Marek, ed. 2015. *Afterlife of Events: Perspectives on Mnemohistory*. Basingstoke: Palgrave.
Tappert, Wilhelm. 1889. *Wandernde Melodien. Eine Musikalische Studie*, 2nd ed. Berlin: Brachvogel & Ranft.

Taylor, Diana. 2003. *The Archive and the Repertoire: Performing Cultural Memory in the Americas*. Durham, NC: Duke University Press.
Taylor, P. J., ed. 1996. *A Companion to the "Indian Mutiny" of 1857*. Delhi: Oxford University Press.
Taylor, Shelley E. 2006. "Tend and Befriend: Biobehavioral Bases of Affiliation under Stress." *Current Directions in Psychological Science* 15 (6): 273–277. https://doi.org/10.1111/j.1467-8721.2006.00451.x.
Tchen, John Kuo Wei, and Dylan Yeats. 2014. *Yellow Peril! An Archive of Anti-Asian Fear*. London: Verso.
Teichler, Hanna. 2021. *Carnivalizing Reconciliation: Contemporary Australian and Canadian Literature beyond the Victim Paradigm*. New York: Berghahn.
Tenenboim-Weinblatt, Keren. 2013. "Bridging Collective Memories and Public Agendas: Toward a Theory of Mediated Prospective Memory." *Communication Theory* 23 (2): 91–111. https://doi.org/10.1111/comt.12006.
Tewksbury, David, and Dietram A. Scheufele. 2009. "News Framing Theory and Research." In *Media Effects: Advances in Theory and Research*, 3rd ed., edited by Mary Beth, Arthur A. Raney, and Jennings Bryant. New York: Routledge. 17–33.
Thakkar, Sonali. 2011. "Foreign Correspondence." In *Rites of Return: Diaspora Poetics and the Politics of Memory*, edited by Marianne Hirsch and Nancy K. Miller. New York: Columbia University Press. 200–215
Thiele, Martina, and Tanja Thomas. 2023. "Really?! Sophie Scholl on Instagram: An Analysis of the Journalistic Discourse." *Journalistik* 6 (1): 6–31. doi:10.1453/2569-152X-23021-11525-en.
Thomas, Adam. 2018. "The Windrush Crisis and Britain's Memory Problem." *AAIHS Black Perspectives*. Available at: https://www.aaihs.org/the-windrush-crisis-and-britains-memory-problem/.
Thompson, Edward. 1925. *The Other Side of the Medal*. London: Hogarth Press.
Thompson, Frederick Diodati. 1893. *In the Track of the Sun: Diary of a Globetrotter*. New York: D. Appleton.
Thompson, Paul. 1978. *The Voice of the Past: Oral History*. Oxford: Oxford University Press.
Thomson, Mowbray. 1859. *The Story of Cawnpore*. London: Bentley.
Tickell, Alex. 2005. "Introduction." In *Shoshee Chunder Dutt: Selections from Bengaliana*, edited by Alex Tickell. Nottingham: Trent Editions. 7–22.
Tinti, Carla, Susanna Schmidt, Igor Sotgiu, Silvia Testa, and Antonietta Curci. 2009. "The Role of Importance/Consequentiality Appraisal in Flashbulb Memory Formation: The Case of the Death of Pope John Paul II." *Applied Cognitive Psychology* 23 (2): 236–253. https://doi.org/10.1002/acp.1452.
Todman, Daniel. 2005. *The Great War: Myth and Memory*. London: Hambledon Continuum.
Tollebeek, Johan, and Geert Buelens, eds. 2008. *België, Een Parcours van Herinnering: Plaatsen van Geschiedenis en Expansie*. Amsterdam: Bakker.
Topcu, Meymune N., and William Hirst. 2022. "Collective Mental Time Travel: Current Research and Future Directions." *Progress in Brain Research*. 274 (1): 71–97. doi:10.1016/bs.pbr.2022.06.002.
Tota, Anna Lisa, and Trever Hagen, eds. 2016. *Routledge International Handbook of Memory Studies*. London: Routledge.

Tucking, Roy. 1975. "Images of Empire: G. A. Henty and John Buchan." *Journal of Popular Culture* 9 (3): 734–740.
Tulving, Endel. 1983. *Elements of Episodic Memory.* Oxford: Oxford University Press.
Tulving, Endel. 1985. "Memory and Consciousness." *Canadian Psychol.* 26: 1–12.
Tulving, Endel, and Fergus I. M. Craik. 2000. *The Oxford Handbook of Memory.* New York: Oxford University Press.
Tumpey, Terence M., et al. 2005. "Characterization of the Reconstructed 1918 Spanish Influenza Pandemic Virus." *Science* 310 (5745): 77–80. doi: 10.1126/science.1119392.
Turnbaugh, Roy. 1975. "Images of Empire. G.A. Henty and John Buchan." Journal of Popular Culture 9: 734–740.
Turner, Mark. 1996. *The Literary Mind.* New York: Oxford University Press.
Van Dijck, José. 2007. *Mediated Memories in the Digital Age.* Stanford, CA: Stanford University Press.
Van Dijck, José. 2010. "Flickr and the Culture of Connectivity: Sharing Views, Experiences, Memories." *Memory Studies* 4 (4): 401–415.
Van Dijck, José, Thomas Poell, and Martijn de Waal. 2018. *The Platform Society.* New York: Oxford University Press.
van Heyningen Elizabeth, Nigel Worden, and Vivian Bickford-Smith. 1999. *Cape Town in the Twentieth Century: An Illustrated Social History.* Claremont: D. Philip.
van Prooijen, Jan-Willem, and Karen M. Douglas. 2017. "Conspiracy Theories as Part of History: The Role of Societal Crisis Situations." *Memory Studies* 10 (3): 323–333. doi:10.1177/1750698017701615.
Vansina, Jan. 1985. *Oral Tradition as History.* Madison: Wisconsin University Press.
Veena, R. 1999. "The Literature of the Events of 1857: A Postcolonial Reading." In *Writing in a Postcolonial Space*, edited by Surya Nath Pandey. New Delhi: Atlantic Publishers. 1–9.
Vinitzky-Seroussi, Vered. 2011. "'Round Up the Unusual Suspects': Banal Commemoration and the Role of the Media." In *On Media Memory: Collective Memory in a New Media Age*, edited by Motti Neiger, Eyal Zandberg, and Oren Meyers. Basingstoke: Palgrave Macmillan. 48–61.
Vinitzy-Seroussi, Vered, and Mathias Jalfim Maraschin. 2021. "Between Remembrance and Knowledge: The Spanish Flu, COVID-19, and the Two Poles of Collective Memory." *Memory Studies* 14 (6): 1475–1488. https://doi.org/10.1177/175069802110543.
Vondung, Klaus. 1980. *Kriegserlebnis: Der Erste Weltkrieg in der literarischen Gestaltung und symbolischen Deutung der Nationen.* Göttingen: Vandenhoeck und Ruprecht.
Vromen, Suzanne. 1975. " The Sociology of Maurice Halbwachs." PhD dissertation, New York University.
Vygotskij, Lev S. 1978 [1930–1934]. *Mind in Society.* Edited by Mike Cole, V. John-Steiner, S. Scribner, and E. Soubermann. Cambridge, MA: Harvard University Press.
Wagner, Kim A. 2010. *The Great Fear of 1857: Rumours, Conspiracies and the Making of the Indian Uprising.* Oxford: Peter Lang.
Wagner, Kim A. 2011. "The Marginal Mutiny: The New Historiography of the Indian Uprising of 1857." *History Compass* 9 (10): 760–766.
Wagner, Kim A. 2018. *The Skull of Alum Bheg.* New York: Oxford University Press.
Wagner-Pacifici, Robin. 2017. *What Is an Event?* Chicago: University of Chicago Press.
Wagoner, Brady. 2017. *The Constructive Mind: Bartlett's Psychology in Reconstruction.* Cambridge: Cambridge University Press.

Wagoner, Brady, ed. 2018. *Handbook of Culture and Memory*. Oxford: Oxford University Press.
Walcott, Derek. 2008 [1990]. *Omeros*. New York: Paw Prints.
Wang, Qi, and Cağla Aydin. 2018. "Culture in Flashbulb Memory." In *Flashbulb Memories: New Challenges and Future Perspectives*, edited by Olivier Luminet and Antonietta Curci. New York: Routledge. 240–262.
Warburg, Aby. 2000 [1924]. *Der Bilderatlas Mnemosyne*, edited by Martin Warnke and Claudia Brink. Berlin: Akademie-Verlag.
Ward, Abigail. 2007. "An Outstretched Hand: Connection and Affiliation in Crossing the River." *Moving Worlds* 7 (1): 20–32.
Ward, Abigail. 2011. "'Looking across the Atlantic' in Caryl Phillips's *In the Falling Snow*." *Journal of Postcolonial Writing* 47 (3): 296–308. https://doi.org/10.1080/17449855.2011.560013.
Ward, Andrew. 1996. *Our Bones Are Scattered: The Cawnpore Massacres and the Indian Mutiny of 1857*. London: John Murray.
Ward, Stuart, and Astrid Rasch, eds. 2019. *Embers of Empire in Brexit Britain*. London: Bloomsbury.
Weigel, Sigrid. 2002a. "'Generation' as a Symbolic Form: On the Genealogical Discourse of Memory since 1945." *The Germanic Review: Literature, Culture, Theory* 77 (4): 264–277. https://doi.org/10.1080/00168890209597872.
Weigel, Sigrid. 2002b. "Generation, Genealogie, Geschlecht. Zur Geschichte des Generationenkonzepts und seiner wissenschaftlichen Konzeptualisierung seit dem Ende des 18. Jahrhunderts." In *Kulturwissenschaften. Forschung – Praxis – Positionen*, edited by Lutz Musner and Gotthart Wunberg. Wien: WUV. 161–190.
Weigel, Sigrid. 2006. *Genea-Logik: Generation, Tradition und Evolution zwischen Kultur und Naturwissenschaften*. Paderborn: Wilhelm Fink Verlag.
Weingarten, Jutta Karen. 2012. " Narrating Generations: Representations of Generationality and Genealogy in Contemporary British Asian Narratives." PhD dissertation, Justus-Liebig-Universität Gießen.
Weitzman, Mark, Robert J. Williams, and James Wald, eds. 2023. *The Routledge History of Antisemitism*. Abington: Routledge
Welsch, Wolfgang. 1999. "Transculturality—the Puzzling Form of Cultures Today." In *Spaces of Culture: City, Nation, World*, edited by Mike Featherstone and Scott Lash. London: Sage. 194–213.
Welzer, Harald, ed. 2001. *Das Soziale Gedächtnis: Geschichte, Erinnerung, Tradierung*. Hamburg: Hamburger Edition.
Welzer, Harald. 2002. *Das kommunikative Gedächtnis: Eine Theorie der Erinnerung*. Munich: C. H. Beck.
Welzer, Harald, ed. 2007. *Der Krieg der Erinnerung: Holocaust, Kollaboration und Widerstand im Europäischen Gedächtnis*. Frankfurt am Main: Fischer.
Welzer, Harald. 2010a. "Communicative Memory." In *A Companion to Cultural Memory Studies*, edited by Astrid Erll and Ansgar Nünning. Berlin: De Gruyter. 285–298.
Welzer, Harald. 2010b. "Re-Narrations: How Pasts Change in Conversational Remembering." *Memory Studies* 3 (1): 5–17. https://doi.org/10.1177/1750698009348279.
Welzer, Harald, Sabine Moller, and Karoline Tschuggnall. 2002." *Opa War Kein Nazi"*: *Nationalsozialismus und Holocaust im Familiengedächtnis*. Frankfurt am Main: Fischer.

Wertsch, James V. 2002. *Voices of Collective Remembering*. Cambridge: Cambridge University Press.
Wertsch, James V. 2019. "National Narratives as Habits of Thought." In *Our American Story: The Search for a Shared National Narrative*, edited by Joshua A. Claybourn. Lincoln, NE: Potomac Books. 19–27. https://doi.org/10.2307/j.ctvfjd02q.5
Wertsch, James V. 2021. *How Nations Remember: A Narrative Approach*. New York: Oxford University Press.
Wesseling, Elisabeth. 1991. *Writing History as a Prophet: Postmodernist Innovations of the Historical Novel*. Amsterdam: John Benjamins.
West, Martin L. 1997. *The East Face of Helicon: West Asiatic Elements in Greek Poetry and Myth*. Oxford: Clarendon Press.
Westwell, Guy. 2006. *War Cinema: Hollywood on the Front Line*. London: Wallflower.
White, Hayden. 1973. *Metahistory: The Historical Imagination in Nineteenth-Century Europe*. Baltimore, MD: Johns Hopkins University Press.
Whitman, Walt. 1882. *Specimen Days*. Philadelphia: Rees Welsh & Company.
Whittlesea, Bruce W. A., Lisa D. Jacoby, and Krista Girard. 1990. "Illusions of Immediate Memory: Evidence of an Attributional Basis for Feelings of Familiarity and Perceptual Quality." *Journal of Memory and Language* 29 (6): 716–732. https://doi.org/10.1016/0749-596X(90)90045-2.
Wievorka, Annette. 2017. "Witnesses and Witnessing. Some Reflections." In *Witnessing Unbound: Holocaust Representation and the Origins of Memory*, edited by Habbo Knoch and Paul Thaler Lustiger. Detroit: Wayne State University Press. 31–53.
Wilson, Robert A. 2005. "Collective Memory, Group Minds, and the Extended Mind Thesis." *Cognitive Processing* 6 (4): 227–236.
Winter, Jay. 1995. *Sites of Memory, Sites of Mourning: The Great War in European Cultural History*. Cambridge: Cambridge University Press.
Winter, Jay. 2007. "The 'Moral Witness?' And the Two World Wars." *Ethnologie Française* 37 (3): 467–474. https://doi.org/10.3917/ethn.073.0467.
Winter, Jay. 2010. "Sites of Memory and the Shadow of War." In *A Companion to Cultural Memory Studies*, edited by Astrid Erll and Ansgar Nünning. Berlin: De Gruyter. 61–76.
Winter, Jay. 2011. "Filming War." *Daedalus* 140 (3): 100–111.
Winter, Jay, and Emmanuel Sivan, eds. 1999. *War and Remembrance in the Twentieth Century*. Cambridge: Cambridge University Press.
Wohl, Robert. 1979. *The Generation of 1914*. Cambridge, MA: Harvard University Press.
Wolf, Werner. 2003. "Narrative and Narrativity: A Narratological Reconceptualization and its Applicability to the Visual Arts." *Word & Image* 19 (3): 180–197. https://doi.org/10.1080/02666286.2003.10406232.
Wright, Richard. 1961. "In the Falling Snow." *Ebony* 16: 92.
Wüstenberg, Jenny. 2023. "Towards Slow Memory Studies." In *Critical Memory Studies: New Approaches*, edited by Brett Ashley Kaplan. London: Bloomsbury Academic. 59–67.
Yamashiro, Jeremy, Abram Van Engen, and Henry L. Roediger III. 2022. "American Origins: Political and Religious Divides in U.S. Collective Memory." *Memory Studies* 15 (1): 1–18.
Young, Philip H. 2003. *The Printed Homer: A 3000 Year Publishing and Translation History of the Iliad and the Odyssey*. Jefferson, NC: McFarland.
Zamponi, Lorenzo. 2018. *Social Movements, Memory and Media: Narrative in Action in the Italian and Spanish Student Movements*. Basingstoke: Palgrave Macmillan.

Zelizer, Barbie. 2022. "What Journalism Tells Us about Memory, Mind, and Media." *Memory, Mind & Media* 1 (1–11). doi:10.1017/mem.2021.9.

Zerubavel, Eviatar. 2008. *The Elephant in the Room: Silence and Denial in Everyday Life.* New York: Oxford University Press.

Zerubavel, Eviatar. 2015. *Hidden in Plain Sight: The Social Structure of Irrelevance.* Oxford: Oxford University Press.

Filmography

Am Ende kommen Touristen [And Along Come Tourists]. 2007. DVD. Directed by Robert Thalheim. Germany: 23/5 Filmproduktion.

Calais: The Last Border. 2003. Directed by Marc Isaacs. Great Britain: Diverse Productions.

The Charge of the Light Brigade. 1936. VHS. Directed by Michael Curtiz. United States: Warner Home Video.

Chia e tazi pesen? [Whose is this Song?]. 2003. Directed by Adela Peeva. Sofia, Bulgaria: Adela Media Film and TV Productions.

District 9. 2009. DVD. Directed by Neill Blomkamp. United States: TriStar Pictures.

Gandhi. 1982. DVD. Directed by Richard Attenborough. India and United Kingdom: Columbia Pictures.

The Rising: Ballad of Mangal Pandey. 2005. DVD. Directed by Ketan Mehta. India: Yash Raj Films.

Index

For the benefit of digital users, indexed terms that span two pages (e.g., 52–53) may, on occasion, appear on only one of those pages.

9/11. *See* September 11

Actor-Network Theory (ANT), 288–289
Adorno, Theodor W. and Max Horkheimer
　Dialectic of Enlightenment (1948), 57
agency of the aesthetic, 321
Akomfrah, John, 39
allegory, 295–297
All Quiet on the Western Front (1929). *See*
　Remarque, Erich Maria
Amritsar massacre, 198–199, 277–278
analogical fallacy, 2–3, 285, 287, 323–324
analytical and normative memory
　research, 325
Anthropocene, 32–33, 83, 110–112
anti-Semitism, 247–255
apartheid, 205, 207–209, 230–232
Appadurai, Arjun, 26
Appiah, Anthony Kwame, 300–302
archive, 77, 179, 228
　precarious archive, 228–229
　and repertoire, 187
assemblage, 171, 288
Assmann, Aleida, 42–43, 87, 102–104
Assmann, Jan, 4–5, 102–104, 287, 301–302, 304
atrocity stories, 176–178
autobiographical memory, 83–84, 94, 118, 160, 170, 306, 312

Ball, Charles
　History of the Indian Mutiny (1858), 181–182
ballads, 250–252
Barad, Karen, 85
Bartlett, Frederic
　Remembering (1932), 259
Bernal, Martin
　Black Athena (1987), 63–64
Black British writing, 134–138, 140–142
Black Lives Matter, 86, 267–268

Boccaccio, 61
Bollywood, 196–199
Bond, Lucy, 291–292, 296–297
Breytenbach, Cloete, 213–215
　The Spirit of District Six (1970), 213–221
British Empire, 172–196
British imperialism, 183–186
British Press, 176–178
Brown, Roger, and James Kulik, 307, 310
Butler, Judith, 298

cadres sociaux de la mémoire. *See* social
　frameworks of memory
carriers of memory, 26
censorship, 195–196
classical reception studies. 57, 292–293
Clifford, James, 25
cognitive psychology
collected and collective memory, 93, 286–287
collective memory, 1–3, 23–24, 95–97, 266, 306
collective texts, 158
colonialism, memories of, 79, 135, 141, 172, 275–279
commemorative memory, 87–88, 263–264
communication studies, 272–274
communicative memory, 102–104, 142–143, 316
connectivity of memory, 35–36n5, 230–232
contents of memory, 27
coronavirus pandemic, 70
cosmopolitan memory, 21–22, 27–28, 108–109, 231, 254
counter-memories, 187
COVID-19, 70
Craps, Stef, 230, 291–292, 296–297
Crimean War, 194
crosscutting, 47–49
cross-fading, 199
culture, 17–18

cultural globalization, 32
cultural memory, 102–104, 142–143, 316
cultural memory studies, 17
cultural trauma, 283–286, 309
curiosity in memory research, 30–31

de-commemoration, 86–87
dialogue in memory research, 323
diasporic memory, 213, 293–297
digital media. *See mediation of memory*
Dilthey, Wilhelm, 117
distributed agency, 288–289
distributed memory, 324–325
District Six (South Africa), 207–209
District Six Museum, 209–210
dynamics and stability of memory, 29, 233–234
Dutt, Shoshee Chunder, 188
  Shunkur (1877/1878), 186–192

ecologies of memory, 289n12
  digital memory ecology, 169–170
  ecologies of trauma, 284–285
Egoyan, Atom, 38–39
environmental memory studies, 32–33. *See also* ecologies of memory
episodic memory, 151–152, 264
Europe and memory
  European film, 34. *See also* film and memory
  European heritage, 57–58
Evaristo, Bernadine
  Girl, Woman, Other (2019), 142
event, 307
extended mind, 286–287
Exodus, 294
eyewitness account, 179–180

family memory, 91
  family as a social framework of memory, 93–95
  family studies, 91, 110
fast thinking, 265–266
fiction
  fictions of generational memory, 153–154
  fictions of memory, 157–158
figures of memory, 28. *See also* schemata
film and memory, 34, 167–169, 197–198, 203–207
films
  11'09''01 September 11 (2002, dir. Samira Makhmalbaf), 320–321

All Quiet on the Western Front (1930, dir. Lewis Milestone)
All Quiet on the Western Front (2022, Netflix, dir. Edward Berger)
Am Ende kommen Touristen (2007, dir. Robert Thalheim), 40–43
Calais: The Last Border (2003, dir. Marc Isaacs), 46–50
Chia e tazi pesen? [*Whose is This Song?*] (2003, dir. Adela Peeva), 43–45
District 9 (2009, dir. Neill Blomkamp), 203–207, 232–234
The Charge of the Light Brigade (1936, dir. Michael Curtiz), 192–196
The Rising (2005, dir. Ketan Mehta), 196–199
First World War, 114–116
  centenary (2014–2018), 158
Fivush, Robyn, 94
flat ontology of collective memory, 290
flashbulb memories, 307–308
forced removals, 208, 230
folksongs, 186
forgetting, collective, 29, 266–267
formative period, 117
future, 88, 218–221. *See also* temporalities
future thinking, 279
frame/framing, 271–273
Freud, Sigmund, 281

Gay and Lesbian Memory in Action (GALA) archive (Johannesburg), 225
gender and memory, 125–126
generation, 113
genealogy, 126–128
  genea-logic, 55–58
  genealogies of Black Britain, 146–150
  genetics, 136–137
generationality, 115
  "generation of 1914," 114–126
  "lost generation," 114–126
  "the generation of postmemory," 128–133
generational memory, 83–84, 87
  intergenerational memory, 96, 317–318
  intergenerational transmission of memory, 128–130
  transgenerational memory, 316–318
  See also fictions of generational memory
generativity, 268–269
Gilroy, Paul, 25
Goffmann, Erving, 271

Halbwachs, Maurice, 1–2, 23–24, 91–93, 272. *See also* collective memory
Hamid, Mohsin
  The Reluctant Fundamentalist (2007), 313–314
heritage, 56–57
  relational heritage, 68
  musical heritage, 43–45
Haraway, Donna, 112, 288–289
Harry Hughes of Lincoln, story of, 250–251
Hartman, Saidiya, 111
Henty, G. A.
  In Times of Peril (1881), 183–186
Hirsch, Marianne, 105–106, 130–131
Hirst, William, 286–287, 305
historical analogy, 78–79, 86
history and memory, 4
historiography, 4, 180
Hollywood, 166–167, 192–196, 270
Holocaust memory, 40–43, 108–109, 128–133, 170, 230–232
  in film, 40–43, 232
Homer, 55–56, 62–65, 259–260. *See also Odyssey*
Hoskins, Andrew, 318–319
Hynes, Samuel, 119

iconization, 213–221
identity, collective, 300–304
imagination and memory, 246
implicated subject, 268–269, 300–301
implicit collective memory, 253, 266–269
implicit memory, 265
India and memory, 200–202
  Indian English Literature, 186–192
  Indian independence, 173–174, 198–199
  See also Bollywood, Indian Rebellion
Indian Rebellion of 1857–1858, 173, 276
  as a shared site of memory, 173
  myth of the "Indian Mutiny," 174, 176, 276
interdisciplinarity, 6–7, 282, 305–306, 323
intermediality, 163–164, 184–185
Israel-Hamas war, 232

Joyce, James, 67–68, 235–236
  memory in *Ulysses*, 235–236
  Ulysses (1922), 67–68, 235

Kewpie (1941–2012), 225
Kewpie collection (South Africa), 223–230
Kingsley, Patrick
  The New Odyssey (2016), 52, 69, 299–300

knowledge-pole of collective memory, 78. *See also* semantic memory

Levy, Andrea
  Small Island (2004), 135
Levy, Daniel, 21–22, 108–109
lieux de mémoire. *See* sites of memory
literature and memory, 52, 80, 88, 113, 183–186
localization of memory, 30
longue durée, 8, 26, 53–54, 257–258, 273–275

Maart, Rozena
  Rosa's District 6 (2004), 213, 215, 221
Mannheim, Karl, 83–84, 114–119
mediation of memory, 5–6, 157–159
  digital media, 169–171
  mass media, 73
  media of memory, 26–27, 157–159
  media culture, 5–6, 174–175
  media event, 318
  media history, 318–319
  platformization of memory, 170–171
  social media, 170, 319
  See also intermediality, plurimedial constellations of memory, premediation, remediation
mémoire collective. *See* collective memory
memorability, 76
memory abuse, 82
memory activism, 267–268, 325
memory in culture, 18
memory *before* violence, 107–108
memory-making novel (and film), 158
memory studies, three phases of, 16
mental time travel, 1, 310
methodological nationalism, in memory research, 21
migration and memory, 26, 52–54, 148–149
  and generation, 133–138
  and literary memory, 140–142
  in film, 46–50
  in South Africa, 233
  See also diasporic memory, refugees and memory
mnemohistory, 4–5, 54–55, 58–60, 172, 275–279, 287n8
mnemonic actor, 288–289
mnemonic forms, 28
mnemonic potential, 159–160, 167–168
mnemonic premediation. *See* premediation

mnemonic relationality, 36–37, 65–68
modern memory
  modernism and memory, 235–236, 255–260
  modernity and ancient memory, 257–260
modes of remembering, 159–163
  agonistic, 163
  antagonistic, 161–162
  experiential, 160
  historicizing, 161
  mythicizing, 160–161
  reflexive, 162–163, 259
  relational, 163
multiculturality, loss of, 221, 225
multidirectional memory, 246–247. 254, 320–321
multidirectional montage, 47–50
multiperspectivity, 303

Nakba, 230–232
national memory, 18–19
narrative
  narrative alignment, 308–310
  narrative ethics, 237–238
  narrative psychology, 270–271
  narratives, as mnemonic actors, 290–291
  narrativity, 76–77, 311
  narrativization, 82, 221–223
  national narratives, 269–271
Neisser, Ulric, 308
neuroscience, 104–105, 281–282, 324–325
news and memory, 176–178
non-conscious memory, 264
Nora, Pierre, 18–19, 100–102, 174

Odyssey, 7–9, 52–54, 255–260, 290–300. *See also* Homer
  Odyssean travels of memory, 9
Olick, Jeffrey K., 1–2, 93, 282, 286–287
opposition, 302–303
orientalism, 238–246
OvaHerero and Nama genocide, 232n41, 275–276

past potentiality, 201, 213–221, 223, 229. *See also* temporalities
Petrarch, 60–62
Phillips, Caryl, 148
  In the Falling Snow (2009), 140
photography and memory, 213–221, 223–230

photography as externalization and trace, 228–229
photography and narrative, 311
planetariness, 73
plurimedial constellations of memory, 167–169, 211–213
Post-Traumatic Stress Disorder (PTSD). *See* trauma, combat trauma
postcolonial studies, 36–37, 65–66
posthumanism, 70–71, 112
postmemory, 105–106; 128–133
  affiliative postmemory, 131–133
  See also queer postmemory
practices of memory, 27–28
premediation, 76, 164–165, 176–178, 235, 277, 321
  by the "Indian Mutiny", 277–278
  by the *Mahabharata*, 191
  by orientalist schemata, 239–240, 245
  by anti-Semitic schemata, 250–254
  ethics of, 255
  self-reflexive, 245
  See also mediation of memory
priming, 264–266, 271–273
prosthetic memory, 315
psychoanalysis, 291–292
psychology, 264–266

queer memory, 223–230
queer postmemory, 111–112, 230

racism, 63, 140–142, 205, 207–209
rape-revenge plot, 190
reception, 122
reconstructivity of memory, 96
refugees and memory, 46–50, 52–54
  refugees in film, 46–50
relationality, 36, 59–60, 288–289, 301
  human-nonhuman, 83
  relational remembering, 62, 68
  relationality of the remembered, 62–65, 68
  See also mnemonic relationality
remembering, collective, 266–267
Remarque, Erich Maria
  All Quiet on the Western Front (1929), 119–126, 157–158
  film adaptation (1930), 123
  Netflix adaptation (2022), 158
  rewriting (*Not So Quiet... Stepdaughters of War*, 1930), 125–126
  translation, 123

remediation, 164–166, 170, 178–183, 188–189, 249–250, 277
remembering-pole of collective memory, 78. *See also* episodic memory
reminiscence bump, 83–84
rhetoric of collective memory, 159–163. *See also* modes of remembering
Rigney, Ann, 174, 321
Rive, Richard, 222–223
  Buckingham Palace, District Six (1986), 215, 230–231
rhythmanalysis, 71
Rothberg, Michael, 315–316

scales of memory, 309
Schacter, Daniel, 266, 281–282
schemata, 28, 207, 256–257, 268
Second World War
  in film, 166–167
  memories of, 78–79
Selvon, Sam
  The Lonely Londoners (1956), 148–149
semantic memory, 264
September 11, 16, 165–166, 313–314, 317–318, 320–321
Shay, Jonathan, 291–293
silofication of memory research, 324
sites of memory, 18–19, 100–102, 174
  in colonial contexts, 172–175
slavery, 111, 295
Smith, Zadie
  White Teeth (2000), 135–137
social frameworks of memory, 93–95, 272
social identity, 312–314
social media. *See* mediation of memory
source amnesia, 265
Spanish flu, 74–78
Spiegelman, Art
  In the Shadows of No Towers (2004), 320
Spinney, Laura
  Pale Rider (2018), 74–75, 77–78
Sznaider, Natan, 21–22, 108–109

tellability, 64–65, 76–77, 311–312
temporalities, 103, 223. *See also* future, urban futures past, past potentialities
  temporal regime, 255–260
  transtemporality, 55, 292
temporalization, of phenomena, 323
terminology, 6–7
Thompson, Frederick Diodati
  In the Track of the Sun (1893), 239–240
time, 3–4. *See also* temporalities
topization, 221–223
tradition, 97–98
transcultural memory, 22–25, 60–62
  as actors' category, 24, 35
  as observers' category, 24, 35
  unreflexive, 46
transcultural memory studies, 20–22
transculturality, 20, 35–36
translation and memory, 33, 61
  in memory research, 278–279
transnational memory, 212–213, 309, 314
trauma, 283–286
  combat trauma, 291–293
  and flashbulb memories, 310
  transcultural trauma, 297–300
  transgenerational trauma, 129
travel writing
traveling memory, 3, 25–30, 35, 314–316
traveling memory film, the, 37–40
traveling schema, 209, 230
Trojan Women (in the *Odyssey*), 297–299
Tulving, Endel, 1, 264, 310
turns, in memory studies, 32–33

Ukraine, Russian invasion of (2022), 270
unconscious, the, 281
urban futures past, 221–223. *See also* temporalities

Vergleichende Tradierungsforschung (comparative research on transmission), 104
vicarious memory, 309, 315
Victorian novels, 183–186
violence and memory, 7

Walcott, Derek, 66
  Omeros (1990), 67, 295–297
Warburg, Aby, 24, 280–281
we-narratives, 121, 312
Weigel, Sigrid, 126–127
Welsch, Wolfgang, 20
Welzer, Harald, 104–107
Wertsch, James, 269–270
Whitman, Walt, 316–317
Windrush generation, 135, 142–143, 149
Winter, Jay, 101–102
witnessing, 309
world risk society (U. Beck), 70, 74
Wright, Richard, 150